Brain-to-Computer Interfaces Using Machine Learning and Deep Learning

Scrivener Publishing
100 Cummings Center, Suite 541J
Beverly, MA 01915-6106

Publishers at Scrivener
Martin Scrivener (martin@scrivenerpublishing.com)
Phillip Carmical (pcarmical@scrivenerpublishing.com)

Brain-to-Computer Interfaces Using Machine Learning and Deep Learning

Edited by

Tawseef Ahmed Teli

Syed Immamul Ansarullah

Arun Kumar Rana

Suman Lata Tripathi

and

Kashif Nisar

Scrivener Publishing

WILEY

This edition first published 2026 by John Wiley & Sons, Inc., 111 River Street, Hoboken, NJ 07030, USA and Scrivener Publishing LLC, 100 Cummings Center, Suite 541J, Beverly, MA 01915, USA

For more information about Scrivener publications please visit www.scrivenerpublishing.com.

Wiley Global Headquarters
111 River Street, Hoboken, NJ 07030, USA

For details of our global editorial offices, customer services, and more information about Wiley products visit us at www.wiley.com.

The manufacturer's authorized representative according to the EU General Product Safety Regulation is Wiley-VCH GmbH, Boschstr. 12, 69469 Weinheim, Germany, e-mail: Product_Safety@wiley.com.

Library of Congress Cataloging-in-Publication Data

ISBN 978-1-394-38950-6

Cover image: Generated with AI using Adobe Firefly
Cover design by Russell Richardson

Set in size of 11pt and Minion Pro by Manila Typesetting Company, Makati, Philippines

Printed in the USA

10 9 8 7 6 5 4 3 2 1

Contents

Preface

The rapid advancement of Brain–Computer Interfaces (BCIs) has created exciting opportunities at the intersection of neuroscience, artificial intelligence, machine learning, and deep learning. What was once considered a futuristic concept is now emerging as a powerful technology capable of transforming healthcare, rehabilitation, communication, assistive systems, and human-machine interaction.

This book, *Brain-to-Computer Interfaces Using Machine Learning and Deep Learning*, aims to provide a comprehensive understanding of the principles, techniques, and recent developments in brain signal processing and neural decoding. The chapters included in this volume explore important areas such as neural signal acquisition, preprocessing methods, feature extraction, machine learning approaches, deep learning architectures, motor imagery decoding, speech and thought interpretation, neurorehabilitation, and ethical concerns related to AI-driven BCIs.

A major strength of this book is its interdisciplinary approach. It combines concepts from neuroscience and computational intelligence to help readers understand how intelligent systems can learn from and interpret neural activity. The contributors have presented both foundational knowledge and emerging research directions in a way that is informative and accessible to students, researchers, academicians, and professionals working in related fields.

Along with discussing current technologies and applications, this book also highlights several important challenges faced in BCI research, including signal variability, real-time processing, model interpretability, privacy, adaptability, and long-term usability. At the same time, it points toward promising future directions such as explainable AI, adaptive learning systems, multimodal neural interfaces, and intelligent assistive technologies.

We hope this book serves as a useful reference for readers interested in understanding and advancing the field of brain signal decoding. More importantly, it inspires further research and innovation toward building intelligent, ethical, and human-centered neurotechnologies that can improve lives and expand the possibilities of human-computer interaction.

We sincerely express our gratitude to all authors, reviewers, and contributors whose efforts and expertise made this book possible.

Editors

1

Topography of Brain-Machine Interfaces: Mapping Neural Signals for Advanced Interaction

Sheikh Umar Mushtaq[1]*, Bazila Farooq[1], Umar Bashir[2] and Sophiya Sheikh[1]

[1]School of Computer Application, Lovely Professional University, Phagwara, Punjab, India
[2]Department of Computer Science and IT, University of Jammu, Jammu, J&K, India

Abstract
Brain-machine interfaces (BMIs) have appeared as a transformative technology, linking the gap between neural movement and peripheral devices to allow direct individual communication paths for individuals with motor disabilities, neurorehabilitation, and cognitive augmentation. The topography of BMIs, referring to the spatial and efficient mapping of neural signals, plays a significant role in improving signal processing and analysis. This chapter discovers the elementary principles of neuronic topography in BMI systems, with a focus on electrophysiological signal sources and adaptive machine learning techniques for translating brain activity. We delve into different signal acquisition methods, highlighting their depths, limitations, and applications in actual and real scenarios. In order to enhance the functionality of brain-machine interactions, this chapter examines how the brain's innate capacity for adaptation, or neuroplasticity, and its signal processing mechanisms are crucial. Researchers are figuring out how to map and better comprehend brain activity by merging knowledge from signal processing methods, sophisticated algorithms, and brain imaging. The development of brain-machine systems that are not only quicker and more precise but also more trustworthy, flexible, and easy to use is made possible by this better knowledge.

Keywords: Neuronic topography, electrophysiological signals, adaptive machine learning, neural flexibility

**Corresponding author*: Shiekhumar12@gmail.com

Tawseef Ahmed Teli, Syed Immamul Ansarullah, Arun Kumar Rana, Suman Lata Tripathi and Kashif Nisar (eds.) Brain-to-Computer Interfaces Using Machine Learning and Deep Learning, (1–16)

of the brain. The technique, known as ECoG, is widely used in hospitals, particularly for patients with epilepsy, where the doctors need to identify the exact spot in the brain that is causing seizures. It has other applications in high-end BMIs, which control robotic limbs or assist people with profound movement impairments. But because ECoG requires surgery, LFP is predominantly applied in clinical but non-daily contexts [10]. Another one is referred to as Local Field Potentials (LFPs). These recorded signals of specific areas help the brain experts to understand the mechanism of how the brain cells work together. These record signals from specific areas of the brain and help scientists understand how groups of brain cells work together. LFPs are also helpful in treating patients with such diseases as Parkinson's *via* deep-brain stimulation. LFPs also find use in the development of smart BMIs that learn in real-time how to respond to the way the brain is behaving [11]. However, this method is also invasive, meaning it is mainly deployed in hospitals and research labs. For the most precise readings of the brain, scientists implement an approach known as single-neuron recording. This can involve inserting small wires directly into the brain to detect signals from single brain cells. It provides very high-resolution data, which is crucial for creating high-tech tools such as brain-controlled limbs or, potentially, systems that enable people to communicate from brain to brain. But this has associated risks such as brain damage or infection, so it is largely restricted to research [12]. All these techniques contribute to the advancement of BMI technology. Non-invasive methods such as EEG are user-friendly and can be applied to non-professionals [13]. More invasive approaches, such as ECoG, LFPs, and single-neuron recording, enable more precise and powerful systems but are confined to hospitals or experiments [14]. Intensive research focused on developing accurate and practical devices also indicates a promising future for BMIs. The objective is to develop a portable, smart, and non-invasive BMI for daily life and health.

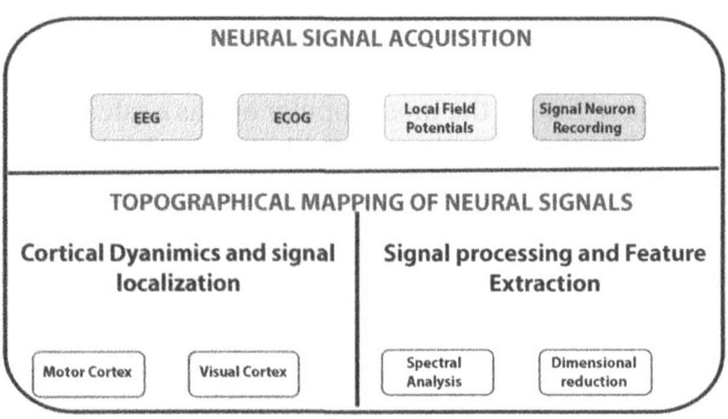

1.3 Topographical Mapping of Neural Signals

1.3.1 Cortical Dynamics and Signal Localization

Brain-machine interfaces (BMIs) are most effective when they accurately locate and organize the brain regions responsible for movement, tactile sensation, and cognition. This mechanism, termed cerebral dynamism and message localization, is crucial for ensuring the system operates seamlessly and can precisely control devices such as robotic arms or speaking equipment. The brain has several regions, each designated for certain functions. The main nervous system regulates free motion, whereas the cortex of somatosensory function facilitates tactile perception and spatial awareness of body components [15]. Researchers use sophisticated brain imaging technologies such as fMRI and MEG to precisely identify the locations and functions of these regions. fMRI (functional magnetic resonance imaging) assesses cerebral activity by quantifying variations in blood oxygenation levels. It provides a definitive representation of the brain regions engaged during activities such as cognition, locomotion, or verbalization. This assists researchers in developing improved brain-machine interfaces, particularly for those who are paralyzed and need assistance with communication or control of devices. MEG (magnetoencephalography) monitors the brain's magnetic impulses in real-time. It has a very fast update time, and this makes it suitable for studying quick cognitive processes like decision-making or tactile responses [16]. By using both MRI and MEG, researchers gain more information on how the brain works during different tasks. This improves BMIs' capacity to decode what a user wants to do in real-time with more fidelity and respond more accurately. Integration of artificial intelligence (AI) allows enormous amounts of neural data to be processed; it also makes these devices smarter and more personal for the user concerned.

1.3.2 Signal Processing and Feature Extraction

Brain signals need to be processed when they are used to control equipment, such as wheelchairs or robotic arms, and the raw signals have to be dried, and different frequencies reveal different methods are invoked to extract the pivotal information from this raw data, which includes a lot of noise from adjacent objects as well as useful information. Spectrum analysis is one of the approaches that explores the various wavelengths of brain waves. More than one frequency equates to different kinds of brain activity. Spatial filtering is another helpful approach that improves the signal-to-noise ratio by focusing on the active regions of our brain. For example, action is correlated with specific rhythms like mu (8–13 Hz) and beta (13–30 Hz) [17].

Researchers can determine when a person is considering moving by examining these radio signals, which enables the BMI to respond instantly. An additional beneficial method that enhances signal efficiency by emphasizing primarily the active areas of the brain is spatial filtering. Common spatial patterns (CSP) is a strategy that is often used here. It identifies the most helpful aspects of brain signals, particularly when a person is visualizing doing something. As a result, the system becomes more dependent and precise. To make the brain data even more useful, scientists also use dimensionality reduction techniques like principal component analysis (PCA) and independent component analysis (ICA). These tools simplify the data by keeping only the most important parts. PCA focuses on patterns that show the biggest changes, while ICA separates different sources of brain activity, helping filter out noise [18]. Together, these techniques make BMIs smarter, faster, and easier to use. By combining brain mapping, signal processing, and artificial intelligence, BMIs are becoming more accurate and adaptable. In the future, this will allow people, especially those with disabilities, to control devices naturally with their thoughts, giving them more freedom and independence in daily life.

1.4 Machine Learning in BMI Signal Translation

The field of BMIs has been revolutionized by machine learning (ML), which has allowed BMIs to become more accurate, adaptive, and easy to use. BMIs in the past based their interpretation of brain signals on fixed algorithms with simple signal processing. Yet, these older methods generally struggled with noisy data, fluctuations in the signal, and individual differences. Now, ML, in general, but especially guided and autonomous learning, improves BMIs in understanding unique brains. These algorithms, which learn from the massive data in the brain, train on individual activity patterns and evolve. As a result, the technology is more intelligent and personalized, therefore more effective and engaging.

1.4.1 Supervised Learning Approaches

Supervised learning algorithm is widely utilized techniques in BMIs in which brain signals are decoded into commands. The prominent method is support vector machines (SVMs), which also perform particularly well on tasks like "motor imagery," where people are imagining themselves moving something to control devices. They are very good at discerning multiple mental activities: thoughts about right or left-hand movements, for example. Their ability to handle mixed signals, such as possibly redundant and noisy data, makes them appropriate for EEG data analysis as well [19].

Researchers employ DL techniques for increasingly complex tasks, such as assessing a person's mental state or interpreting brain signals to determine speech. RNNs and CNNs are two popular types. CNNs excel in identifying patterns in brain signals from various brain regions, but RNNs, particularly the LSTM type, are made to comprehend how these signals evolve. Even when used by varying people or in various scenarios, these models allow BMIs to grasp what the user is thinking in real time, increasing system precision and dependability [20].

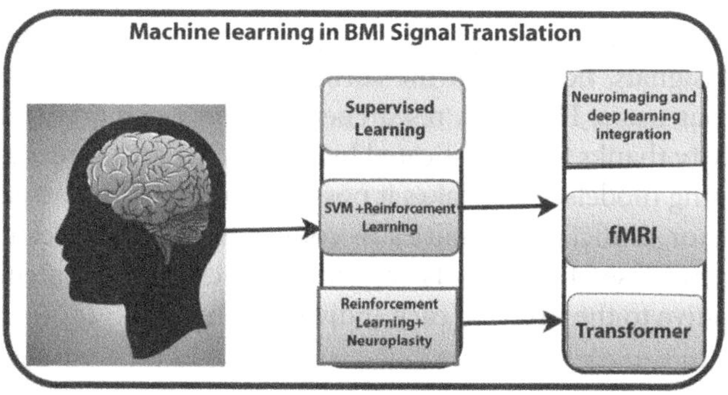

1.4.2 Adaptive Learning and Neural Plasticity

Due to cutting-edge learning techniques like adaptive learning, brain-machine interfaces (BMIs) are becoming more intelligent and customized. Reinforcement learning (RL) is one fascinating method. With this approach, the machine, like humans, learns by making mistakes. For instance, the system recognizes that it made a mistake and learns from it if someone attempts to move a robotic arm and it doesn't move correctly. The whole experience seems more seamless and natural as it improves over time at deciphering the user's brain signals and reacting more precisely [21]. Neurofeedback training is another useful technique. This takes advantage of neuroplasticity, the brain's innate capacity for adaptation. Here, an individual receives real-time input that demonstrates how their brain is functioning, such as noises or images. They become better at managing their brain impulses with experience. This training may improve the accuracy and dependability of BMI devices. Patients who have had strokes or who

Case study	Institution/ researchers	BMI type	Key findings	Applications
Neuralink's brain implant [27]	Neuralink (Elon Musk)	Invasive	Achieved high-resolution brain signal mapping with real-time translation into commands	Neuroprosthetics, brain-controlled devices
Braingate [7]	Brown University, Stanford	Invasive	Enabled paralyzed patients to control robotic arms *via* cortical signal mapping	Assistive robotics, neurorehabilitation
Hybrid EEG-fMRI BMI [28]	University of Tübingen	Hybrid	Combined EEG and fMRI for improved spatial and temporal resolution	Brain mapping, cognitive research
Motor imagery-based BMI [29]	Graz University of Technology	Non-Invasive	Used EEG to decode motor imagery signals for hands-free device control	Rehabilitation, assistive communication
ECoG-based speech synthesis [30]	University of California, San Francisco	Invasive	Converted brain signals into synthetic speech with high accuracy	Speech restoration for ALS patients
Closed-loop BMI for stroke recovery [31]	Johns Hopkins University	Non-Invasive	Used an EEG-based BMI to assist motor recovery in stroke patients	Neurorehabilitation, physiotherapy
Deep learning in BMI [32]	MIT & Harvard	Non-Invasive	Applied CNNs and RNNs to improve BMI accuracy	AI-enhanced brain-computer interaction

BCI for locked-in syndrome [33]	Wyss Center, Switzerland	Non-Invasive	Enabled communication in locked-in patients through EEG-based decoding	Assistive communication
Optical imaging for BMI [34]	Stanford University	Non-Invasive	Used near-infrared optical imaging for neural signal mapping	Cognitive monitoring, brain mapping

1.7 Challenges and Future Directions

There has been some progress, but still, there are some challenges, including biocompatibility, real-time processing, and ethical aspects, for BMIs [35]. Dealing with these matters is crucial for their long-term reliability and accessibility.

1.7.1 Biocompatibility and Longevity of Implants

Invasive BMIs experience electrode deterioration, and the corresponding immune response can lead to deterioration in signal quality [36]. Advancements in biocompatible materials such as graphene and flexible bio-electronics aim to enhance implant retention, reduce inflammation, and prolong the lifetime of implants.

1.7.2 Real-Time Processing and Latency Reduction

Latency minimization is crucial for real-time BMI applications [37]. Edge computing and (ultra) energy-efficient neuromorphic chip design could speed up the signal transformation and hence shorten the latency in neuroprosthetics and assistive devices quickly.

1.7.3 Ethical and Privacy Concerns

Security of neural data is an important issue, and it needs to have strong encryption and a transparent consent policy providing protection to the end-users [38]. Additionally, there is a desire for fair provision of BMI technology so that there is no socioeconomic pattern to the uptake of neurotechnology.

1.8 Conclusion

The neural signal spatial distribution mapping is an important factor to enhance the accuracy and practical applicability of the BMI. By localizing and mapping brain areas responsible for movement, cognitive, and sensory function, BMI systems can better interpret neural activity into actionable commands. This is more precise and fine-grained control over external equipment, meaning it's becoming more and more valuable for those with paralysis and neurodegenerative diseases (or for those who just want to boost their cognitive performance). The advancement of neuroimaging, adaptive ML, and signal processing has also contributed significantly to BMI technology. fMRI and MEG are effective tools to identify activated brain areas, while EEG and ECoG signal neuroelectric responses in real time for BMI research. ML-based approaches, such as DL and RL, will be better off as they learn the user's neural pattern and, hence, are likely to improve in better accuracy and usability. Even drug BMIs can be increasingly faster, more reliable, and more comfortable. However, multiple challenges still exist. One is the need to ensure technical challenges, such as the signal-to-noise ratio and the delay of the signal, are solved and optimized in real-time. Another is the numerous ethical issues that arise, especially regarding privacy. After all, we are directly obtaining neural data from BMIs. The third area is the need to make them more widespread and affordable to make them available to more people who need these technologies. In the future, BMIs will need to deal with these factors while advancing non-invasive, adaptive, and precise BMIs even more. With the rapid progress, the future of BMIs may change healthcare, neurorehabilitation, and human cognition, and finally bridge the gap between the human brain and technology in ways that were never considered possible before.

AI disclosure statement: The author confirms that no artificial intelligence (AI)-generated content or AI-assisted writing tools were used in the preparation of this chapter (including summaries and the abstract). All text, analysis, and conclusions are the result of the author's original work.

References

1. Dehghani, S.M.M. and Moradi, M.H., Deep Learning Models for Brain Machine Interfaces. *Ann. Math. Artif. Intell.*, 88, 11–12, 1223–1245, Dec. 2020.
2. Lebedev, M.A. and Nicolelis, M.A., Brain–Machine Interfaces: From Basic Science to Neuroprostheses. *Physiol. Rev.*, 97, 2, 767–837, Apr. 2017.
3. Chang, E.F., Ostrem, J.R., Starr, P.N., Invasive Brain–Computer Interfaces. *Neurotherapeutics*, 16, 1, 168–179, Jan. 2019.
4. Bastos, A.M. and Schoffelen, J.M., A Tutorial Review of Functional Connectivity Analysis Methods and Their Interpretational Pitfalls. *Front. Syst. Neurosci.*, 9, 175, Jan. 2016.
5. Schalk, G., A General Framework for Dynamic Cortical Function: The Function–Structure Cycle. *Front. Hum. Neurosci.*, 14, 571, Nov. 2020.
6. Karim, A.A., Hinterberger, M., Richter, J., Birbaumer, N., Neurofeedback-Based Brain Computer Interface: A New Paradigm for Controlling Brain Activity. *J. Neural Eng.*, 3, 4, R56–R63, Dec. 2006.
7. Hochberg, L.R., *et al.*, Reach and Grasp by People with Tetraplegia Using a Neurally Controlled Robotic Arm. *Nature*, 485, 7398, 372–375, May 2012.
8. Lopes, A.M., *et al.*, A Review of Electrocorticography-Based Brain-Computer Interfaces and Their Applications. *IEEE Trans. Neural Syst. Rehabil. Eng.*, 29, 1367–1378, Jul. 2021.
9. Wolpaw, J.R. and Wolpaw, E.W., Brain-Computer Interfaces: Something New Under the Sun. *IEEE Trans. Neural Syst. Rehabil. Eng.*, 25, 10, 1421–1422, Oct. 2017.
10. Schalk, G. and Leuthardt, E.C., Brain-Computer Interfaces Using Electrocorticographic Signals. *IEEE Rev. Biomed. Eng.*, 4, 140–154, 2011.
11. McFarland, D.J. and Wolpaw, J.R., Brain-Computer Interfaces for Communication and Control. *Commun. ACM*, 54, 5, 60–66, May 2011.
12. Simeral, J.D., *et al.*, Home Use of a Percutaneous Wireless Intracortical Brain-Computer Interface by Individuals With Tetraplegia. *IEEE Trans. Biomed. Eng.*, 68, 7, 2313–2325, Jul. 2021.
13. Buzsáki, G., Large-Scale Recording of Neuronal Ensembles. *Nat. Neurosci.*, 7, 5, 446–451, May 2004.
14. Yanagisawa, T., *et al.*, Electrocorticographic Control of a Prosthetic Arm in Paralyzed Patients. *Ann. Neurol.*, 71, 3, 353–361, Mar. 2012.
15. Gencer, N.G. and Malmivuo, J.A., Comparison of the Properties of EEG and MEG in Detecting the Electric Activity of the Brain. *Brain Topogr.*, 25, 3, 235–249, Jul. 2012, doi: 10.1007/s10548-012-0225-0.
16. Wendel, K., *et al.*, EEG/MEG Source Imaging: Methods, Challenges, and Open Issues. *Comput. Intell. Neurosci.*, 2009, Article ID 656092, 12, 2009, doi: 10.1155/2009/656092.
17. Malmivuo, A., Sensitivity Distribution of Multichannel MEG-Detectors. *Med. Biol. Eng. Comput.*, 25, 4, 413–419, Jul. 1987, doi: 10.1007/BF02441656.

18. Gencer, N.G. and Malmivuo, J.A., Distribution of M.E.G. Detector Sensitivity: An Application of Reciprocity. *Med. Biol. Eng. Comput.*, 18, 5, 569–577, Sep. 1980, doi: 10.1007/BF02442453.
19. Tyagi, A. and Nehra, Classification of motor imagery EEG signals using SVM, k-NN and ANN. *CSI Trans. ICT*, 4, 135–139, Dec. 2016.
20. DiGiovanna, J., Mahmoudi, B., Fortes, J., Principe, J.C., Sanchez, J.C., Coadaptive brain-machine interface *via* reinforcement learning. *IEEE Trans. Biomed. Eng.*, 56, 1, 54–64, Jan. 2009.
21. Hou, Y., Jia, S., Lun, X., Zhang, S., Chen, T., Wang, F., Lv, J., Deep Feature Mining *via* the Attention-Based Bidirectional Long Short Term Memory Graph Convolutional Neural Network for Human Motor Imagery Recognition. *Front. Bioeng. Biotechnol.*, 10, 2022.
22. Sakhavi, S., Guan, C., Yan, S., Parallel Convolutional-LSTM Neural Networks for Feature Extraction and Classification of EEG Signals. *Front. Neurosci.*, 12, 2018.
23. Jaipriya, D. and Sriharipriya, K.C., Brain–machine interfaces using functional near-infrared spectroscopy: a review. *Artif. Life Rob.*, 25, 2, 204–212, 2020.
24. Ehsan, N., Jawad, M., Khalil, K., Hong, K.-S., EEG-fNIRS-based hybrid image construction and classification using CNN-LSTM. *J. Neural Eng.*, 19, 4, 0460d9, 2022.
25. Zhang, D., Li, H., Xie, J., MI-CAT: A transformer-based domain adaptation network for motor imagery classification. *Neural Networks*, 165, 451–462, 2023.
26. Luo, J., Wang, Y., Xia, S., Lu, N., Ren, X., Shi, Z., A shallow mirror transformer for subject-independent motor imagery BCI. *Comput. Biol. Med.*, 164, 107254, 2023.
27. Neuralink, Neuralink — Pioneering Brain Computer Interfaces, [Online]. Available:https://neuralink.com/. [Accessed: Apr. 3, 2025].
28. López-Larraz, E., Birbaumer, N., Ramos-Murguialday, A., A hybrid EEG-EMG BMI improves the detection of movement intention in cortical stroke patients with complete hand paralysis, in: *Proc. Annu. Int. Conf. IEEE Eng. Med. Biol. Soc.*, Honolulu, HI, USA, Jul. 2018, pp. 2000–2003, doi: 10.1109/EMBC.2018.8512711.
29. Pfurtscheller, G. and Neuper, C., Motor imagery and direct brain-computer communication. *Proc. IEEE*, 89, 7, 1123–1134, Jul. 2001, doi: 10.1109/5.939829.
30. Chang, E.F., *et al.*, High-resolution spatiotemporal mapping of speech articulation networks in humans. *Neuron*, 77, 2, 277–289, Jan. 2013, doi: 10.1016/j.neuron.2012.11.016.
31. Lin, D., Clinically Relevant Biomarkers and Outcomes for Motor Recovery after Stroke, Johns Hopkins Department of PM&R's Grand Rounds, Sep. 2020.

32. Yu, K.K., *Deep Learning for Biomedical Data*, Harvard Medical School, Semester Spring, 2025. https://khyu.scholars.harvard.edu/class/deep-learning-biomedical-data.
33. Birbaumer, N., *et al.*, A spelling device for the paralysed. *Nature*, 398, 6725, 297–298, Mar. 1999, doi: 10.1038/18581.
34. Stanford University NIRS Lab, NIRS Lab – Stanford University. https://cibsrnirs.sites.stanford.edu/about/mobile-neuroimaging.
35. Burwell, S., Ethical aspects of brain computer interfaces: a scoping review. *BMC Med. Ethics*, 18, 1, 60, Nov. 2017.
36. Synchron's Brain-Computer Interface Now Has Nvidia's AI, Wired, Mar. 2025.
37. Glannon, W., Ethical issues with brain-computer interfaces. *Front. Syst. Neurosci.*, 8, 136, Jul. 2014.
38. Wu, D., Privacy-Preserving Brain-Computer Interfaces: A Systematic Review, arXiv preprint arXiv:2412.11394, Dec. 2024.

2

Understanding Nerve Signal and the Nervous System

Irtiqa Amin[1]*, Quraazah Akeemu Amin[2], Sheikh Ikhlaq[3] and Obaid Ahmad Bhat[4]

[1]*School of Computer Application Lovely Professional University, Phagwara, Punjab, India*
[2]*Division of Food Science and Technology, SKUAST-Kashmir, Srinagar, Jammu and Kashmir, India*
[3]*Cyber, Enterprise Security, Deloitte, Hyderabad, Telangana, India*
[4]*School of Renewable Energy, Maejo University, Chiang Mai, Thailand*

Abstract

The nervous system processes sensory information, coordinates responses, and regulates the physiological functions of the human body. This chapter discusses the structure, function, and mechanisms underlying neural communication. It begins with an introduction of neuroanatomy, the role of neurons, the elementary building blocks of the nervous system, its neuroanatomy, types, and their vital support provided by neuroglial cells. Furthermore, the chapter focuses on nerve signal transmission, highlighting action potentials, ion channels, neurotransmitters, and synapses in neural communication. It covers synaptic transmission, neurotransmitter types, and neurodegenerative diseases like Parkinson's, Alzheimer's, and epilepsy. The chapter also discusses the fundamental concepts like reflexes, motor control, learning, memory, and emotions. Finally, it reviews neural study methods, brain imaging, and advances like brain-computer interfaces, neuroprosthetics, and new treatments for nervous system disorders.

***Keywords*:** Nervous system, neurotransmission, synapse, neurological command center, peripheral nerve structure, autonomic nervous system (ANS), neurodegenerative diseases

**Corresponding author*: irtiqa.amin7100@gmail.com

Tawseef Ahmed Teli, Syed Immamul Ansarullah, Arun Kumar Rana, Suman Lata Tripathi and Kashif Nisar (eds.) Brain-to-Computer Interfaces Using Machine Learning and Deep Learning, (17–34) © 2026 Scrivener Publishing LLC

2.1 Introduction

The NS is a complex biological system formed by neurons and auxiliary cellular units that relay impulses throughout the body. It acts as a vital component in handling and interpreting external and internal stimuli, combining data, and initiating appropriate responses. This system consists of specialized structures such as the brain, SC, and PN that collectively control bodily activities and interactions with the environment. The human nerve structure (as described in Figure 2.1) is broadly classified into two key units: CNS and PNS. The CNS consists of the brain, and the SC serves as the central processor and interpreter of sensory content. It helps coordinate thoughts, emotions, recall, and reasoning. Whereas, the PNS has a set of nerves and ganglia external to the CNS *via* different organs, limbs, and skin.

The PNS is further subdivided into two major categories: SNS and ANS. The SNS checks voluntary movement and perceptual information, and the ANS normalizes reflex processes such as heartbeat and digestion. The ANS is sectioned into two types: "sympathetic division" and "parasympathetic division." The SD handles the anxiety of the human body, whereas the parasympathetic division endorses tranquillity and energy conservation.

Figure 2.2 below illustrates the ANS, highlighting its two major divisions, SD and PD, thus outlining their structure and functions.

The human brain and nerve structure are fundamental parts of human physiology, essential for controlling nearly all physiological processes. By transmitting electrical and chemical signals, it empowers the body to

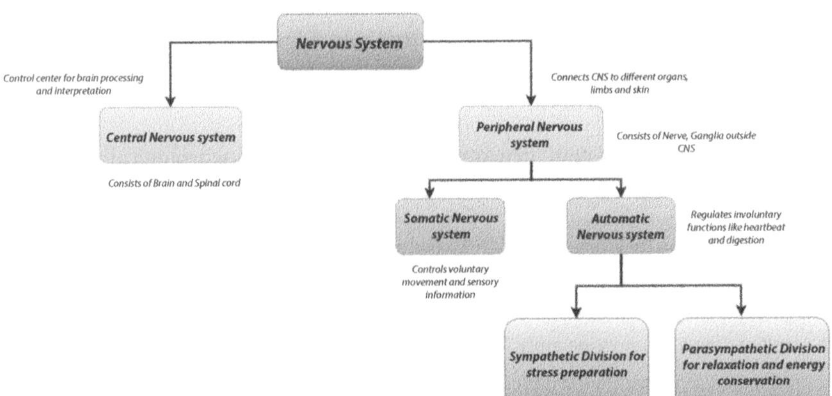

Figure 2.1 Structural and functional overview of the human nervous system.

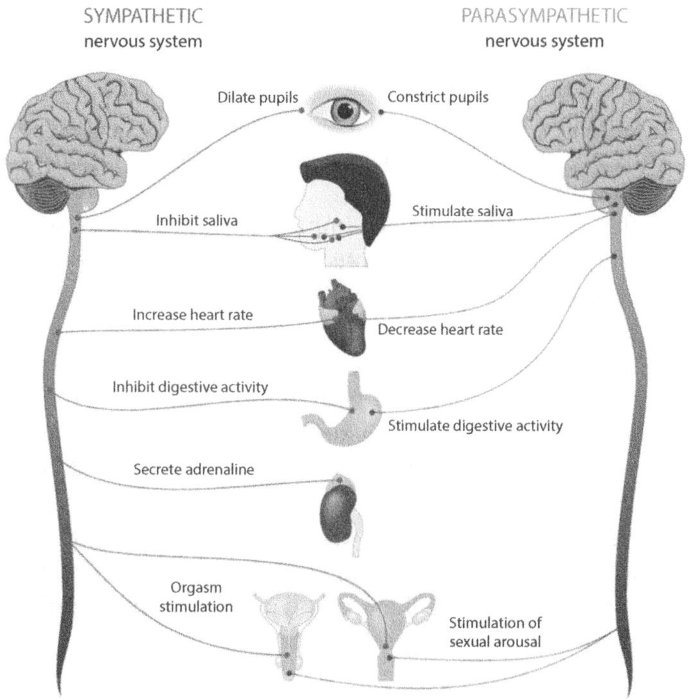

Figure 2.2 Functioning of ANS.

perceive stimuli, react to changes, and maintain internal stability. Its intricate mechanisms not only support basic survival but also enable higher cognitive abilities, making it one of the key systems in the human body. The human nervous system performs a variety of necessary functions for persistence and adaptation, including

- Sensory function: The sensory function detects external and internal stimuli through sensory receptors, conveys indications from sensory body parts like eyes, ears, skin, tongue, and nose to the CNS, and allows perception of touch, temperature, pain, sound, and vision.
- Integrative function: It processes sensory information in the brain and spinal cord, interprets stimuli, makes decisions for appropriate responses, and involves cognitive processes such as intellectual growth, recall ability, reasoning skills, and complex thinking.

- Motor function: It harmonizes complex motor activities like walking, writing, and speaking.
- Homeostasis and autonomic regulation: It maintains internal stability and controls hormone secretion in coordination with the endocrine system and adjusts body responses to environmental changes.
- Reflex action: It facilitates immediate responses to stimuli through reflex arcs. It protects the body from harm and operates without conscious thought, ensuring rapid protective actions.
- Communication and coordination: It ensures seamless contact between different body parts and synchronizes the activities of organs and tissues. It enables interaction with the environment through sensory perception and motor responses.
- Increased executive skills: It supports thinking, language, emotions, and decision-making, and also acts as a vital function in creativity, intelligence, and problem-solving and governs consciousness and self-awareness.

2.1.1 Structure and Components of the HNS

The HNS is a complex network that integrates and coordinates all bodily functions. It is structurally divided as follows:

a) CNS

The CNS is the headquarters of the human body, which integrates the sensory input, coordinates the responses, and regulates the vital functions. The human brain controls thoughts, memory, emotions, and voluntary actions, while the spinal cord transmits information and manages reflexes. Together, these structures ensure the body's ability to respond to stimuli, adapt to changes, and maintain homeostasis, making the CNS essential for survival and daily functioning.

Figure 2.3 below shows the basic components of the HNS. The following subsections provide a detailed explanation of each part and its specific functions.

i. HB

"It is the most complex organ in the human body that contains billions of neurons and glial cells, which work together to process information,

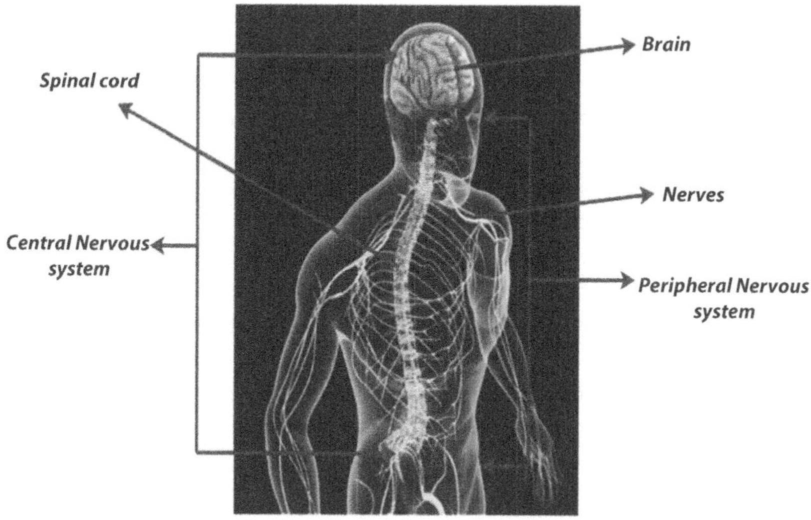

Figure 2.3 Basic components of the human nervous system.

regulate bodily functions, and control behavior." It can be categorized into three major regions, such as FB, MB, and HB, which are depicted in Figure 2.4.

- **FB:** The prosencephalon is responsible for cognition, emotion, memory, sensory processing, and voluntary movement. The main parts of the forebrain include the cerebrum, diencephalon (TH, HTH, and ETH), and LS. The cerebrum

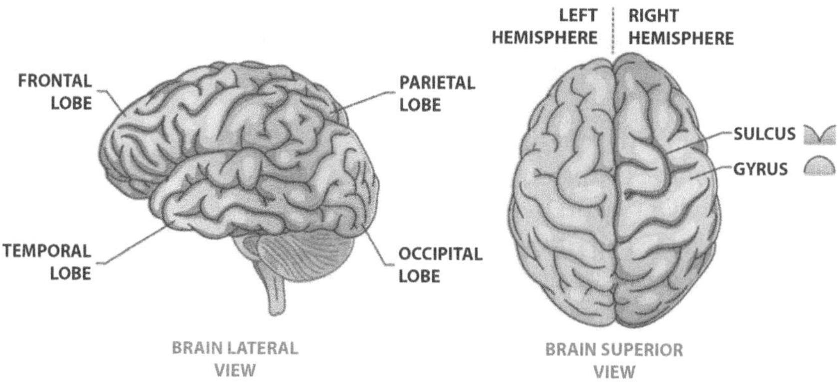

Figure 2.4 Components of HB.

is divided into left and right hemispheres, each regulating the body's contralateral half. Each hemisphere is further divided into lobes, such as FL, PL, TL, and OL, each with specific functions. The TH is a relay station that is used to deliver sensory information to the cerebral cortex. It aims for proper sleep, alertness, and consciousness. The HTH regulates homeostasis by controlling body heat, starvation, thirst, and hormone secretion, and connects the NS with the endocrine system *via* the pituitary gland. Finally, the LS governs emotional responses, motivation, and learning.

- **MB:** The mesencephalon functions as a relay center for auditory and visual signals. It contains the substantia nigra, for locomotive coordination, which is associated with Parkinson's disease and regulates eye movement, motor control, and alertness.
- **HB:** The rhombencephalon controls vital automatic functions such as breathing, heart rate, and motor coordination. The main parts of the hindbrain are the cerebellum, pons, and medulla oblongata.

ii. Spinal Cord

The SC is a perilous element of the CNS, spreading from the brainstem down to the lower backbone, enclosed within the vertebral column. It serves as the main communication highway between the brain and the rest of the body. The structure of the spinal cord includes gray matter, located at its center, which contains neurons responsible for processing and relaying information. Surrounding it is white matter, composed of myelinated nerve fibers that transmit signals between the brain and peripheral nerves (Figure 2.5). The structure of the spinal cord is as follows. It is enclosed within the vertebral column and is divided into 31 segments, each giving rise to a pair of spinal nerves.

- Cervical (8 pairs)
- Thoracic (12 pairs)
- Lumbar (5 pairs)
- Sacral (5 pairs)
- Coccygeal (1 pair)

b) PNS

PNS refers to the section of the NS beyond the HB and SC. It connects the CNS to the limbs, organs, and skin, enabling the body to respond to

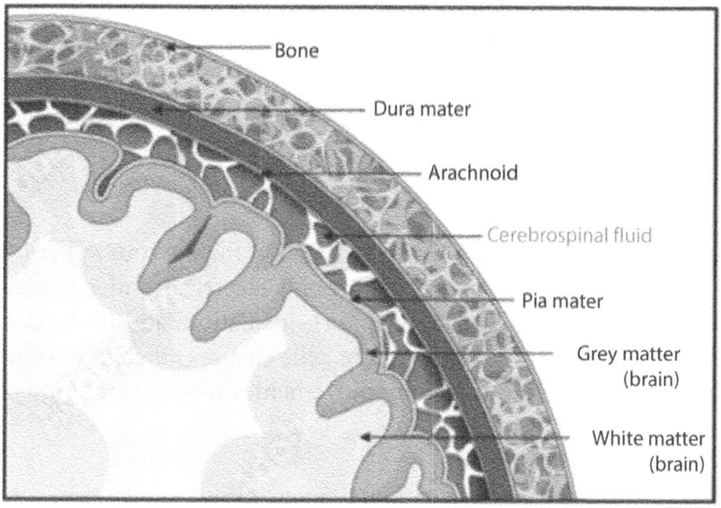

Figure 2.5 The components of the spinal cord.

internal and external stimuli. The main components of the PNS are cranial nerves (these are 12 pairs) and spinal nerves (these are 31 pairs). The PNS is divided into the SNS and ANS.

- **SNS:** It governs intentional SM actions and allows bodily motion and reflex actions. It also includes sensory nerves that carry information from skin, muscles, and joints to the CNS. The functions of the SNS include voluntary movement control, which sends commands from the brain to the SM for movement and allows actions such as walking, grasping, and speaking. Similarly, sensory perception transmits external stimuli (touch, pain, heat, and cold) to the brain and assists the body in interacting with and responding to the environment. The reflex actions involve spinal reflexes, where sensory input bypasses the brain and directly triggers motor responses.
- **ANS:** It regulates involuntary bodily functions essential for survival, like heartbeat, digestion, and breathing. ANS is further divided into SNS (fight or flight), PNS (rest and digest), and ENS (controlling gastric functions).

Comparison between SNS and ANS

The human PNS is divided into two key branches, somatic and autonomic, each playing a distinct yet complementary role in controlling the body's functions. The comparison of the somatic and autonomic NS is shown in Table 2.1.

c) Neurons and Neuroglia

Neurons and neuroglia form the foundation of the nervous system. While neurons facilitate communication through electrical and chemical signals, neuroglia provide essential support, insulation, and protection. The interaction between these two types of cells ensures efficient nervous system function, enabling perception, movement, thought, and homeostasis.

Table 2.1 Comparison of the somatic and autonomic nervous systems.

Feature	SNS	ANS
Regulation type	Intentional	Unintentional
Effectors	Somatic muscles	Visceral muscles, myocardium, endocrine
Function	Movement and sensory response	Regulates internal processes
Neurotransmitters	Acetylcholine	Acetylcholine and norepinephrine
Example action	Moving your arm	Adjusting heart rate or digestion

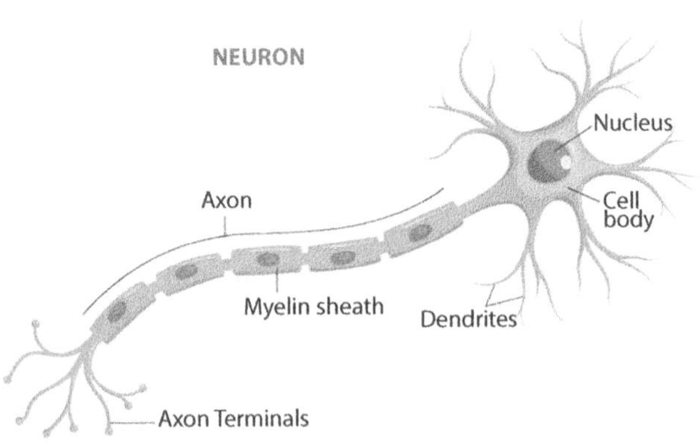

Figure 2.6 Basic structure and components of a neuron.

Understanding their structure and roles is crucial for comprehending neurological health and disorders (shown in Figure 2.6 above).

The human neurological network is formed of two principal neural classifications: nerve cells and glial cells.

A typical human neuron consists of the following major parts:

- **Cell Body (Soma):** It contains the nucleus and most organelles and produces neurotransmitters and proteins necessary for neuron function.
- **Dendrites:** These are the short, branched extensions that receive signals from other neurons or sensory receptors and conduct electrical impulses toward the cell body.
- **Axon:** An axon is a long, single projection that transmits impulses away from the cell body to other neurons, muscles, or glands.
- **Axon Hillock:** It is a cone-shaped region where the axon originates from the cell body and acts as the trigger zone for generating action potentials.
- **Myelin Sheath:** It is a fatty insulating layer that increases the speed of electrical impulse conduction.
- **Nodes of Ranvier:** These are the gaps between segments of the myelin sheath, which allow for saltatory conduction, speeding up impulse transmission.
- **Axon Terminals (Synaptic Boutons):** These are the end branches of the axon that form synapses with other neurons or effector cells. It releases neurotransmitters to transmit signals across the synaptic cleft.

Table 2.2 Comparison of neurons and neuroglia.

Feature	Neurons	Neuroglia
Function	Transmit electrical signals	Support, protect, and nourish neurons
Ability to divide	No (cannot regenerate easily)	Yes (can multiply and repair tissues)
Types	Sensory, motor, interneuron	Astrocytes, oligodendrocytes, microglia, Schwann cells, etc.
Example role	Conducting nerve impulses	Forming myelin, removing debris

of life. Advances in brain imaging, electrophysiology, and neuroscience models help scientists understand and treat these conditions. Additionally, the role of neurotransmitters and brain plasticity highlights how the nervous system adapts to learning and emotional experiences. Understanding these mechanisms can lead to better treatments for ND and MHD.

- ND involves the gradual loss of neurons and their functions. These conditions typically worsen over time and currently have no cure, such as Alzheimer's disease (AD), which is an advancing brain disorder causing memory loss, perceptual failure, and interactive deviations. It primarily affects the hippocampus and disrupts neural function with genetic and environmental factors. The symptoms are short-term memory loss, confusion, mood swings, and difficulty speaking. Neurodegenerative diseases also cause Parkinson's disease (PD, which results from genetic mutations, environmental toxins, and aging. The symptoms include tremors, MR, slowed movement (bradykinesia), and balance issues. Furthermore, ND also causes MS, where the immune system attacks the myelin sheath, disrupting nerve signal transmission. It causes genetic predisposition, viral infections, and environmental triggers. It also results in neuropathy and nerve damage, which results in pain, weakness, numbness, and tingling. It causes neuropathic diabetes, infections, autoimmune diseases, and toxic exposure. The types consist of peripheral neuropathy affecting hands, feet, and arms and autonomic neuropathy affecting involuntary functions (heart rate, digestion). Neuropathy and nerve damage can cause ischemic stroke blocking, which results in the loss of strength or inability to move either side of the body, slurred speech, and vision loss and damages the brain regions controlling movement, speech, memory, and coordination.
- Methods of Studying the NS: Understanding the NS requires advanced tools and techniques to observe brain structure and function. Brain imaging techniques use strong magnetic fields and radio waves to perceive tumors, brain damage, and multiple sclerosis. Similarly, CT scans are helpful to detect strokes, tumors, and brain injuries. Furthermore, EEG is used to diagnose epilepsy, sleep disorders, and brain function changes. Electrophysiology and nerve conduction studies measure the electrical activity of neurons and

Table 2.4 Role of neurotransmitters in emotions and mood regulation.

Neurotransmitter	Function	Related disorders
Dopamine	Reward, motivation, pleasure	Parkinson's, addiction
Serotonin	Mood, sleep, emotional stability	Depression, anxiety
GABA	Reduces neuron excitability (inhibition)	Epilepsy, anxiety
Glutamate	Learning, memory (excitatory)	Stroke damage, neurotoxicity
Norepinephrine	Alertness, stress response	PTSD, ADHD

muscles to assess nerve function and are used for diagnosing neuropathy, multiple sclerosis, and muscle disorders.

- Experimental Models in Neuroscience: Scientists use animal models, brain organoids, and AI simulations to study neural functions and diseases. Genetically modified mice help researchers understand Alzheimer's and Parkinson's disease mechanisms. The role of neurotransmitters in emotions and mood regulation is shown in Table 2.4.

2.4 Advances in Neuroscience and Future Advancements

Neuroscience has seen rapid advancements in recent years, transforming our understanding of the HB and NS. Breakthroughs in neuroimaging, artificial intelligence, brain-machine interfaces, and neurogenetics are revolutionizing diagnostics, treatment, and brain function enhancement. Below is a detailed discussion of recent advancements and future directions in neuroscience.

- Brain Imaging and Mapping Technologies: Modern imaging techniques allow scientists to visualize the brain with unprecedented detail. fMRI measures brain activity by detecting changes in blood flow and helps identify brain regions involved in cognition, emotion, and motor functions. Similarly, PET uses radioactive tracers to study neurotransmitter activity. It is used for Alzheimer's and Parkinson's disease research. High-resolution brain mapping consists of the Human Connectome Project (HCP), which maps neural connections to understand brain function, and light sheet microscopy, which enables 3D imaging of entire neural networks.

- Artificial Intelligence (AI) and Neuroscience are transforming neuroscience by analyzing large datasets and simulating brain functions. Deep learning helps detect Alzheimer's, stroke, and brain tumors from MRI scans. AI models mimic neural networks, advancing our understanding of cognition and consciousness. Neuro-inspired computing neuromorphic chips replicate brain-like processing, improving machine learning efficiency.
- BCIs and neuroprosthetics enable direct communication between the brain and external devices, offering solutions for paralysis and neurodegenerative diseases. Neural implants for paralysis treatment, such as Elon Musk's Neuralink and similar technologies, use brain implants to control devices with thoughts and help patients with spinal cord injuries regain movement. Neuroprosthetics are the mind-controlled robotic limbs that help amputees regain functionality.
- Neurogenetics and Gene Therapy: Advances in genetics and molecular biology have opened new treatment avenues for neurological disorders. CRISPR gene editing in neuroscience, such as CRISPR-Cas9, allows precise editing of genes involved in neurological disorders. The potential treatments for Huntington's disease, ALS, and genetic epilepsy. For stem cell therapy for brain repair, scientists use stem cells to regenerate damaged brain tissue. Potential treatment for Parkinson's, stroke, and spinal cord injuries. Personalized medicine in neurology, such as genetic testing, helps tailor treatments for Alzheimer's, schizophrenia, and depression based on individual DNA.
- Optogenetics and neuromodulation use light-sensitive proteins (opsins) inserted into neurons, which can be activated or inhibited using laser pulses. It is used for treating Parkinson's disease by controlling dopamine-producing neurons, researching memory formation, and regulating emotions.

- Neuroscience of Consciousness and Cognitive Enhancement: Understanding consciousness and cognition is a major goal of modern neuroscience. Researchers use EEG, fMRI, and AI models to map brain activity during consciousness and sleep. Investigating near-death experiences and altered states of consciousness. Cognitive enhancement and brain stimulation, such as transcranial magnetic stimulation (TMS), enhance memory and problem-solving skills. Nootropics (smart drugs) are being explored to boost cognition.

Future Directions in Neuroscience:

- Curing Neurodegenerative Diseases: Advances in gene therapy, stem cells, and neuroprotection could provide cures for Alzheimer's, Parkinson's, and ALS. Early detection and intervention through AI-based diagnostics.
- As brain technologies continue to grow, people are becoming more concerned about the ethical issues related to brain implants, AI-based consciousness, and mind-reading tools. In the future, researchers need to carefully think about privacy, personal identity, independence, and free will to make sure these technologies are developed in a safe and responsible way.
- Merging Humans with AI (Transhumanism): The concept of brain-cloud interfaces, where human cognition is augmented with AI. Memory implants could allow humans to store and retrieve knowledge instantly.
- Full Brain Simulation and Digital Consciousness: Scientists are working on simulating the entire human brain on a computer. This could lead to digital immortality and advanced AI with human-like intelligence [5].

2.5 Conclusion

This chapter has explored the intricate processes that enable neurons to communicate, emphasizing the role of action potentials, ion channels, and synapses in facilitating electrical and chemical signaling. These mechanisms are fundamental to everything from basic reflex actions to complex cognitive processes like learning, memory, and emotional regulation.

A key aspect of this discussion is the ANS, which is responsible for maintaining homeostasis by regulating involuntary physiological responses. By distinguishing between the sympathetic and parasympathetic divisions, this chapter has illustrated how the body adapts to different internal and external conditions, ensuring survival and optimal function. The delicate balance between these systems underscores the importance of neural control in everyday bodily operations.

Furthermore, the chapter examined the implications of disruptions in neural signaling, which can lead to neurological disorders. Gaining a deeper understanding of the underlying causes of these conditions presents valuable knowledge into potential treatment approaches and highlights the significance of maintaining neural health. Advances in neuroscience, such as brain-computer interfaces and neuroprosthetics, offer promising solutions for individuals with nervous system disorders. Furthermore, the study of neural activity through techniques like brain imaging and electrophysiology has deepened our understanding of brain function and dysfunction. These technological advancements not only enhance diagnostic capabilities but also pave the way for innovative therapeutic interventions. As research continues to evolve, new discoveries will further enhance our ability to diagnose, treat, and potentially prevent neurological disorders.

Abbreviations	Definition
NS	Nervous system
SC	Spinal cord
PNS	Peripheral nervous system
CNS	Central nervous system
SNS	Somatic nervous system
ANS	Autonomic nervous system
ENS	Enteric nervous system
SD	Sympathetic division
PD	Parasympathetic division
HNS	Human nervous system
HB	Human brain
FB	Fore brain
MB	Mid brain
HIB	Hind brain

ND	Neurodegenerative diseases
MHD	Mental health disorder
MR	Muscle rigidity
MS	Muscle sclerosis
CB	Cerebrum
TH	Thalamus
HTH	Hypothalamus
ETH	Epithalamus
LS	Limbic system
FL	Frontal lobe
PL	Parietal lobe
TL	Temporal lobe
OL	Occipital lobe
VC	Vetebral column
SM	Skeletal muscles

AI disclosure statement: The author acknowledges the use of AI-based tools for minor language editing or grammatical correction. However, all intellectual contributions, analyses, and conclusions presented in this chapter are entirely the author's own.

Bibliography

1. Strominger, N.L., Demarest, R.J., Laemle, L.B., *Noback's Human Nervous System, Seventh Edition: Structure and Function*, 7, Humana Totowa, NJ, 2012, ISBN: 978-1-61779-778-1, https://doi.org/10.1007/978-1-61779-779-8.
2. Kandel, E.R., Schwartz, J.H., Jessell, T.M., *Principles of Neural Science*, Sixth Edition, McGraw-Hill Education, New York, NY, USA, 2021.
3. Brown, A.G., *Nerve Cells and Nervous Systems: An Introduction to Neuroscience*, 2nd Edition, Springer, London, UK (Springer-Verlag London), 2001, ISBN: 978-3540760900.
4. Mitchell, T., The Nervous System (Wonders of the Human Body), Master Books, 2017, ISBN: 978-1683440277.
5. Marcus, G. and Freeman, J., *The Future of the Brain: Essays by the World's Leading Neuroscientists*, Princeton Science Library, Princeton, NJ, USA (Princeton University Press), 2024.

3

Acquisition of Brain Signals and Preprocessing for Machine Learning

Viveka S.

Department of Computing Technologies, School of Computing, College of Engineering and Technology, SRM Institute of Science and Technology, SRM University, Kattankulathur, Chennai, Tamil Nadu, India

Abstract

Brain signals are critical to the functioning of the body. They help to perform all day-to-day activities and provide important insights into brain function. They are pivotal for health care applications, especially in neuroscience and Brain–Computer Interface (BCI) technologies. Machine learning (ML) is being used as a transformative tool to recognize the signals from the brain. Many applications, like cognitive signals and state monitoring, use brain signals. Electrical and magnetic signals and hemodynamic activity of the brain are gathered using brain signal acquisition technologies like electroencephalography (EEG). These dedicated devices and protocols help confirm the accuracy and reliability of the collected signals, though these signals may have artifacts. These raw signals are preprocessed and analyzed using machine learning to identify the meaningful patterns and insights. As this is related to human life, highly powerful and capable preprocessing techniques must be employed, such as filtering, artifact removal, and normalization. ML models are fed with these complex brain signals to extract the hidden features and unseen patterns to perform classification, prediction, and anomaly detection. Incorporation of ML into brain signal analysis enhances the development of intelligent diagnostic systems. This integration accelerates human life by boosting the accuracy, speed, and efficiency of neurophysiological interpretations, paving the way for more adaptive and personalized neurological applications.

Keywords: Brain-computer interface, signal acquisition, signal preprocessing, machine learning

Email: vivekas@srmist.edu.in

Tawseef Ahmed Teli, Syed Immamul Ansarullah, Arun Kumar Rana, Suman Lata Tripathi and Kashif Nisar (eds.) Brain-to-Computer Interfaces Using Machine Learning and Deep Learning, (35–60) © 2026 Scrivener Publishing LLC

3.1 Introduction

The brain is the source of control for all living beings. The brain acts like a music director conducting an orchestra, controlling all the activities. We can say the human brain orchestrates a harmonious interplay of physiological and cognitive functions. The brain is the master of all the activities and ensures that every part of the body performs its role. The brain helps the body to have all kinds of senses, like touch and taste, and to perform activities like walking, dancing, and even complex problem-solving. These activities are done accurately by the body parts by processing the signals received from the brain. The signals come from the traditional neuromuscular pathway and act as a communication medium, enabling coordination and response to both internal and external events. Brain diseases like neuropathies, myopathies, or some head injuries may affect the brain and impair the sending of signals to some parts of the body. This causes trouble in the partial or complete functionality of the body, like movement or other essential abilities. Understanding and handling these brain signals is vital, not only for identifying neurological conditions but also for creating new applications in healthcare. For example, advanced technologies such as brain-computer interfaces are used in decoding the brain signals to bridge the gap triggered by neurological losses. By analyzing brain activity, these systems facilitate individuals with severe disabilities in regaining control over the environment, increasing their quality of life. In addition, processing the signals that come from the brain leads to an enhancement in rehabilitation therapies, designing prosthetic devices, etc., and aids in developing applications for healthcare [1].

3.2 Brain Signal Acquisition

The collection of brain signals is the crucial part of the BCI research to provide improvements in the field of health care.

3.2.1 Brain–Computer Interface (BCI)

This system helps to create an interaction between the human brain and other external devices like computers or prostheses. BCI bypasses the normal neuromuscular pathways, which helps people affected by the brain disease lead their normal lives. BCI attracts research, and there are many designs for BCI systems presented by researchers.

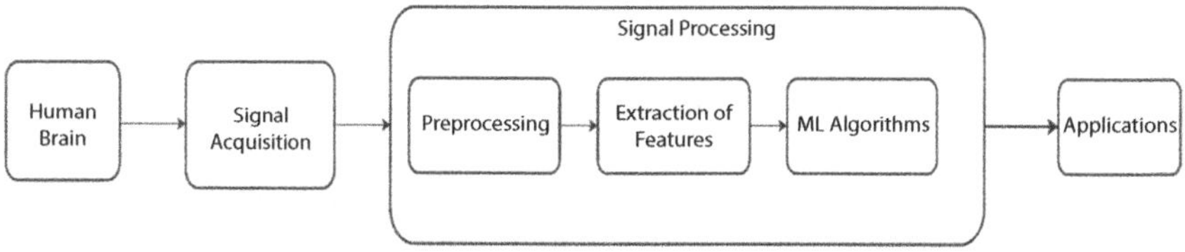

Figure 3.1 Brain computer interface.

3.2.2 Working of BCI

This system collects and records brain signals in two stages. The signal acquisition and signal processing are the major stages of BCI systems. During the first stage (signal acquisition), the electrodes are positioned on the scalp of the test subject. In the second stage, the brain activity is collected and recorded as electrical signals. BCI systems then translate the electrical signal received from the brain into commands that may be understood by external devices like computers, robotic arms, or wheelchairs. This is shown in Figure 3.1. This kind of interaction allows one to bypass the neurological pathway. This aids the people who are affected with neurological disorders or with affected or missing body parts [2].

3.3 Types of Brain Signals and Acquisition Methods

- Electrical signals (e.g., EEG and ECoG)
- Magnetic signals (e.g., MEG)
- Hemodynamic activity (e.g., fMRI and fNIRS)

In physiology, there are many methods available to acquire the brain signals. Early systems primarily use electroencephalography (EEG) to collect brain signals. Nowadays, electrocorticography (ECoG) is used to acquire the signals accurately.

3.3.1 Electroencephalography (EEG)

EEG is employed to collect the electrical activity of the human brain. During this process, electrodes are fixed on the scalp. Simple, cost-effective, and the ability to record real-time neural oscillations are the significant features of this method. These signals are prone to low spatial resolution and are vulnerable to environmental conditions such as muscle movements or surrounding noise [3].

3.3.2 Electrocorticography (ECoG)

Here, electrodes are directly positioned on the brain's surface, beneath the skull and scalp, to acquire the signals. This approach provides better quality signals compared to EEG, making it highly useful in operating theatre arrangements for brain surgery and BCI applications. Despite its many advantages, the aggressive nature of this method reduces the wide range of adoption [4].

3.3.3 Functional Magnetic Resonance Imaging (fMRI)

It is a widely recognized minimally invasive approach to measure and map brain activity. fMRI acquires hemodynamic activity, detects variations in oxygen levels in the blood, and offers excellent spatial resolution. This spatial resolution enables the precise localization of the brain regions that are involved in various cognitive and physiological processes. However, the method has limited temporal resolution, as neural activity is indirectly measured through changes in blood flow, which is relatively slow, and thus makes it less suitable for real-time applications.

3.3.4 Magnetoencephalography (MEG)

Magnetoencephalography (MEG) provides superior spatial and temporal resolution for detecting the presence of magnetic fields generated by brain activity. This also makes it ideal for investigating rapid and localized neural processes. Its ability to provide accurate measurements of both the timing and location of supposed brain activity makes it suitable for clinical diagnostics and cognitive neuroscience research. However, the requirement for highly specialized equipment, such as magnetically shielded rooms and superconducting sensors, is a significant drawback [5].

3.3.5 Functional Near-Infrared Spectroscopy (fNIRS)

This is employed to measure blood oxygenation level changes and hemodynamic activity of the brain using near-infrared light. This light, penetrating the scalp and through the skull, reaches cortical regions of the human brain to monitor neural activity. This method is suitable for cognitive and emotional studies, stroke rehabilitation applications, and monitoring neurodegenerative diseases. It is lightweight compared to fMRI. It facilitates BCI to create neurofeedback and motor control. Despite these limitations, fNIRS is a vital tool for understanding brain activity where other imaging techniques are infeasible. Recent research has focused on wireless fNIRS systems, providing an expanded view of their utility in monitoring cognitive activities in real-world environments.

Current research developments in brain signal acquisition have concentrated on hybrid systems, as the combination of multiple modalities helps to reduce the limitations of individual methods. For example, integrating EEG and fMRI enables researchers to attain both good temporal and spatial resolution, thereby providing a complete view of brain activity. Developing non-invasive methodologies, such as near-infrared spectroscopy (NIRS), is gathering attention due to their capability to measure brain hemodynamic increases. These methods are helpful in portable and wearable applications. This method ramps up the real-time monitoring of brain-computer interface systems [6].

The selection of the brain signal acquisition method varies based on different needs and applications, the degree of tolerable invasiveness, and the required resolution. Each method has its pros and cons, which must be carefully selected during the design and implementation of BCI systems.

3.4 Preprocessing Methods

Preprocessing is an initial step in brain signal analysis, as raw signals habitually contain noise, artifacts, and variability that can hide the meaningful patterns. Noise may come from many internal and external sources, likely internal muscle movements or eye blinks, and other external environmental factors like electrical interference. These events reduce the signal strength, so preprocessing is needed to ensure the quality and reliability for future use. Machine learning models will not give better results if preprocessing is not done properly. This section discusses preprocessing methods suitable for brain signal analysis.

3.4.1 Independent Component Analysis (ICA)

ICA is used as a preprocessing technique when we want to remove noise or artifacts in signals like EEG or in image data (fMRI). ICA is employed to analyze a complex and highly correlated data set. ICA is a predominant method in the realm of data science, and it can separate and identify the fundamental independent sources in a multivariate data set. This approach offers insights into the hidden structure of the brain signal data and has many applications, like signal processing. As the raw signal contains noise that affects the outcome of the analysis, the next step is to perform preprocessing. This approach is employed to maximize the signal-to-noise ratio [7].

3.4.2 Filters in Signal Processing

Filters play an important role in brain signal preprocessing. They are assigned to extract vital information from raw brain signals. Filters remove noise, interference, or irrelevant frequencies from the brain signal. Filters do play a vital part in improving the quality of the brain signals.

While processing EEG or MEG signals of the brain, filters are used to separate the neural activity of interest by suppressing artifacts created *via* environmental noise, muscle movements, or baseline drifts. By employing suitable filters, researchers can focus on the required frequency bands associated with cognitive or physiological processes.

Filters are classified based on their functionality:

- **Low-Pass Filters**: Hold low-frequency signals and remove high-frequency noise.
- **High-Pass Filters**: Preserve high-frequency signals by eliminating low-frequency drifts.
- **Band-Pass Filters**: Retain signals within a specific frequency range.
- **Notch Filters**: Remove narrowband interference.
- **Adaptive Filters**: Work for real-time noise cancellation and can dynamically change the signal condition.

High-quality, precise signals are needed for health care applications for accurate diagnosis [8].

3.4.3 Surface Laplacian (SL)

Surface Laplacian (SL), also referred to as Current Source Density (CSD), is one of the predominant spatial filtering methodologies, and it improves the precision of neural activity localization. The main objective of the technique is to record the activity directly below each electrode that gets placed on the scalp. SL is at the top of the preprocessing workflow, as it eliminates the problem of spatial artifacts and enhances the quality of spatial resolution. The placement of the electrode, the methodology used to remove the artifacts, and the parameters used for computation help improve the effectiveness of this technique [9].

3.4.4 Common Spatial Pattern (CSP)

This algorithm is also used to preprocess the EEG and ECoG signals; the CSP algorithm is also used. The algorithm provides the difference between two states, i.e., it can effectively separate the signals connected with left- and right-hand movement. This process is done by finding the best spatial filters that show the highest and lowest variance. CSP gives importance to class-based neural activity of the brain, making CSP crucial for BCI applications. However, CSP is less commonly applied in fMRI signals due to their slower, hemodynamic, and high-dimensional nature. CSP produces better results with EEG and ECoG but is limited to artifacts and outliers. CSP can be enhanced by including the methodology to remove artifacts and covariance estimation. This makes CSP work with multi-modalities and machine learning–based neuroimaging [10].

3.4.5 Normalization and Standardization

Normalization and standardization are the basic preprocessing techniques applied across all kinds of signals like EEG, ECoG, and fMRI. This method ensures that the signals are at the correct frequency for analysis. These methods minimize the difference caused by environmental conditions, physiological factors, and equipment.

Normalization

This method changes the amplitude of signals that are in the range of 0–1 or −1 to 1. This kind of scaling provides the chance for all parameters to participate equally during the analysis and eliminates the domination of a feature with a large-scale value. This method is applied to signals like EEG and ECoG to address inter-subject variability and improve comparability. Normalization regulates voxel strengths to account for baseline differences in fMRI, enabling cross-subject comparisons in brain activity studies.

Standardization

Z-score transformation is used to perform standardization among a variety of modalities. This method converts the data such that its mean is zero and standard deviation is one. In EEG and ECoG, Z-score standardization reduces inter-subject variability, helping identify the abnormalities from normal patterns, for example, those associated with neurological conditions. In fMRI, Z-score standardization is applied to normalize brain activation patterns from different participants by improving the group-level analyses [11].

These preprocessing steps are very important to extract the features and enhance the performance of ML models. They play a vital role in confirming robust and meaningful analyses of brain signals, enabling advancements in neuroscience research and clinical applications.

3.4.6 Baseline Correction

This method is a vital preprocessing method aimed at eliminating or decreasing the unwanted background signals, including spectral data, EEG signals, and earthquake accelerograms. It separates the required signals for analysis by modifying or subtracting the baseline and ensuring the difference in signal value represents the fluctuations in the true signal, not from the artifacts or noise. This is vital in the fields of neuroscience, seismology, and spectroscopy. Implementation of a proper baseline correction method enhances the signal quality and pattern recognition.

Baseline correction is one of the preprocessing techniques for analyzing brain signals. All kinds of brain signals, like EEG, ECoG, and fMRI, are correctly isolated by employing this method, which works by removing baseline variability or isolating task- or stimulus-related activity. This method generally involves selecting a pre-stimulus window, identifying the mean or median signal value during that period, and eliminating it from the entire signal. By regularizing the data, baseline correction decreases noise, reduces inter-trial variability, and augments the clarity of stimulus-induced changes.

In EEG studies, baseline correction is used to ensure that event-related potentials (ERPs), like the P300, accurately represent neural responses to stimuli instead of being influenced by baseline noise. Similarly, in fMRI, baseline correction normalizes the Blood Oxygen Level Dependent (BOLD) signal, relative to a pre-task resting phase, allowing for a more accurate assessment of percent signal changes. However, the effectiveness of this approach relies heavily on selecting an appropriate baseline to prevent the introduction of artifacts or distortions [12].

3.4.7 Temporal Preprocessing

Temporal preprocessing involves techniques applied to brain signal data to refine and organize it based on its temporal (time-related) characteristics. These methods ensure that modalities are properly aligned, noise is reduced, and critical information is accurately represented. Temporal preprocessing is essential because brain signals are recorded as a continuous stream of time series data, which can be affected by noise, artifacts, and extraneous information.

Segmentation

Segmentation, also known as epoching, is achieved by dividing continuous brain signal recordings into many small segments that are time-locked to some specific events or stimuli. This process splits the signal into smaller chunks for accurate analysis based on events or stimuli. These smaller segments of the signals are called epochs. This approach helps the researchers to separate the brain signals easily based on a specific task or a specific condition by eliminating the unwanted signals from the record. In an example situation, while collecting the EEG, epochs are often obtained relative to the event onset (-100 ms to 900 ms) to examine event-related potentials (ERPs). Accurate epoching is important for precise analysis to identify the neural responses to cognitive or sensory stimuli [13].

Downsampling

This is another notable temporal preprocessing technique, used to reduce the sampling rate of the brain signal by minimizing data size while preserving important information. This is employed to preprocess the high-resolution signal, like ECoG or fMRI. For example, by minimizing the sampling frequency of the signal from 2000 Hz to 250 Hz in EEG, this approach increases the computational efficiency without losing essential temporal features [14].

3.4.8 Spatial Preprocessing

Re-Referencing

Re-referencing is the basic spatial preprocessing method applied to analyze EEG and ECoG signals. The quality of the signal is improved by redefining the orientations of each electrode. The average reference is calculated by subtracting the mean voltage of all electrodes from every channel's signal. This is a simple and powerful method to identify a single reference electrode that influences analysis, also improving the detection of brain activity based on the location. Current research suggests that the average reference method can efficiently minimize the noise and enhance event-related potentials (ERPs). Along with this approach, the reference electrode standardization technique (REST) method is also employed to enhance the accuracy of EEG connectivity. These advanced techniques, like REST, are used to provide an efficient neutral reference framework [15].

Source Localization

Source localization is an important spatial preprocessing technique. The origin of neural activity of the brain is identified by employing this approach. This technique is used to detect the places in the scalp that generate the electrical signals with the help of computational methods. eLORETA (exact Low Resolution Electromagnetic Tomography) is the approach employed for this purpose. Neurophysiologically plausible activation patterns can be generated with the integration of sLORETA and standardized head models, even in the absence of individual MRI data. Precise source localization is achieved by combining EEG with fMRI. These new research improvements show the necessity of spatial preprocessing to accurately understand the brain signal [16].

3.4.9 Denoising

Denoising is a preprocessing technique that aims to reduce noise and artifacts to enhance the clarity and reliability of brain signals.

Wavelet Denoising

This is a powerful technique that uses time-based localization properties of wavelets. This approach isolates the needed brain signal by suppressing the noise. Wavelet denoising segments brain signals into multiple frequency bands across various scales. This segmentation enables the removal of noise without affecting the transient or non-stationary features, and this is completely different from other traditional filtering methods. This approach is very suitable for EEG and fMRI brain signals; they have non-stationary characteristics. By enhancing the quality of the signal by removing artifacts in complex and noisy environments, wavelet denoising methods give a better solution [17].

3.5 Feature Extraction and Selection

Feature extraction and selection are the next steps in analyzing brain signals like EEG, ECoG, and fMRI. This is used to ensure the machine learning models are fed with important data that gives meaningful insights from these complex datasets. During the preprocessing, the noise in the brain signals is filtered, and artifacts are removed, resulting in clean data for further analysis [18].

For example, ICA (independent component analysis) finds its application in brain signals, removing the artifacts caused by the surrounding environments, like eye blinks and muscle movements. Once the preprocessing is over, the next step in feature extraction identifies the crucial patterns from the signals to understand the brain activity, for instance, the selection of frequency bands in EEG or voxel activation in fMRI. The next step is the systematic elimination of redundant or irrelevant features while preserving critical features for further analysis, and is called feature selection. This feature selection method minimizes the dimensionality and improves the efficiency and machine learning accuracy [19].

Norman *et al.* [20] state that for fMRI analysis, alignment and smoothing of the brain signals are completed during preprocessing, and regions of interest (ROIs) are identified during feature extraction, then feature selection narrows down the ROIs critical for the target behaviour or condition. This systematic methodology guarantees that high-quality inputs are given to the ML models, and the accuracy of the result is more robust and interpretable predictions in neuroscience applications.

Like other signals, the sequence of steps in data analysis is also applied to brain signals. During this process, the only essential feature from the raw signal is collected and refined. The selection of feature extraction methodology is dependent on the application type and based on the signal needed for the application. The brain signals are broadly classified into temporal, spectral, and spatial domains.

3.5.1 Temporal Feature Extraction

This refers to the extraction of brain signals based on the time domain. These signals' amplitude or shape depends on time, and these signals tell the crucial neural dynamics. The brain signal contains peak amplitude, mean value, variance, skewness, kurtosis, and zero-crossing rate, and these are some of the common temporal features. EEG signals show different temporal patterns during different cognitive or motor tasks, so this time-based analysis helps in BCI implementation. Signal power (activity), mean frequency (mobility), and frequency (complexity) changes are the notable Hjorth parameters that describe the signal in the time domain. The Hjorth parameters, coined by Bo Hjorth in 1970, were commonly applied in the processing of biomedical signals and time series analysis. Temporal features play a vital role in the effective implementation of BCI systems.

Preprocessing is done to remove the noise and artifacts. Events like epileptic spikes, motor imagery, or event-related potentials (ERPs) are easily identified using temporal features. Integrating temporal features with spatial and spectral features gives better accuracy in classification [21].

3.5.2 Spatial Feature Extraction

Focusing on the location-based aspects of brain signals, spatial feature extractions help modalities such as fMRI and ECoG that offer high spatial resolution. These features represent the way brain activity varies across different regions or electrodes. Dominant spatial patterns are identified by techniques like principal component analysis (PCA), as it helps reduce dimensionality. Independent sources like neural networks or artifacts can be separated using independent component analysis (ICA). Features like voxel-based statistical measures or activation maps of specific regions of interest (ROIs) may be included in fMRI that indicate task-related changes. Common spatial patterns and other spatial filtering methods are used to optimize spatial features, aiding in efficient classification of motor imagery or cognitive tasks involving EEG and ECoG data. Localized brain responses, functional connectivity, or pathological zones like epileptogenic foci can be efficiently identified by extracting spatial features. Classification and interpretability can be improved greatly by using special features to capture interactions between brain regions, as brain signals are fundamentally spatially correlated. A comprehensive representation of brain dynamics can be obtained by combining spatial with temporal or spectral features [22].

3.5.3 Time-Frequency Feature Extraction

Temporal and spectral analysis are combined in time-frequency feature extraction and are used to capture stationary brain signal characteristics that differ over time and frequency. Wavelet Transform (WT) is the widely used method to detect transient events like epileptic spikes or cognitive responses by decomposing the signals into time- and frequency-localized components. WT enables multi-resolution analysis, unlike FFT, which makes it ideal for the rapidly changing frequency content of EEG and ECoG signals. The features like wavelet coefficients, instantaneous power, or energy in specific time-frequency windows are included in time-frequency. These features are helpful in detecting seizures, recognizing emotions, and instantaneous power or energy in specific time-frequency windows, which heavily depend on the timing of oscillatory events. The short-time Fourier transform (STFT) is another time-frequency technique with fixed resolution limitations. The information about the evolution of neural oscillations is obtained by analyzing time-frequency, providing rich information about brain function and anomalies. Connectivity features by analyzing synchrony between time-frequency representations of different brain structures are efficiently extracted by this method [23].

3.5.4 Connectivity Feature Extraction

The aim of the connectivity feature is to quantify the interaction and communication between different brain regions that reflect functional or effective brain networks. Synchronized activity patterns during cognitive tasks or rest can be revealed by measuring the statistical dependencies between signals, such as coherence, correlation, or phase locking value. On the other hand, methods like Granger causality or dynamic causal modelling (DCM) are used by effective connectivity to infer causal influences and directionality. These features are used in fMRI and ECoG studies to understand the orientation of neural networks, brain disorders like epilepsy, and the design of brain-computer interfaces. Connectivity features can distinguish between normal and pathological states of cognitive conditions by capturing large-scale brain dynamics. Computing pairwise relationships across multiple channels or voxels is required to extract connectivity, and as a result, it produces high-dimensional data that needs dimensionality reduction. Due to advancements in graph theory, the connectivity of networks can be characterized using measures such as node degree, clustering coefficient, and path length. Connectivity-based features complement the traditional time- or frequency-domain features and offer a network-level perspective on brain function [24].

3.5.5 Entropy-Based Feature Extraction

Complexity, randomness, or regularity of brain signals from EEG or psychological data can be quantified by the entropy-based feature extraction method. Measures like Shannon entropy, sample entropy, approximate entropy, and spectral entropy are used in the transformation of raw time-series data to efficiently capture the underlying dynamics of the signal by transforming raw time-series data into meaningful numerical features. As an instance, chaotic complexes may indicate high entropy or repetitive activity. These features provide valuable insights in applications like emotion recognition, stress detection, and cognitive state assessments, helping to learn about brain and psychological processes. Datasets like DEAP use entropy-based extraction to capture subtle variations in signals that are critical for accurate analysis [25].

Advanced Feature Extraction Techniques

- Deep Learning-based Feature Extraction: Neural network algorithms, such as convolutional neural networks and recurrent neural networks, are used to extract features.
- Hybrid Approaches: Combining manual and deep learning-based features.
- Transfer Learning: Utilizing pre-trained models to extract features.

3.5.6 Feature Selection Techniques for Brain Signals

1. Principal Component Analysis (PCA)

It is used to eliminate redundant and highly correlated features in the dataset. It simplifies the dataset by performing a transformation on the original features into a new set of orthogonal components, depending on the amount of variance present in the data. For high-dimensional data with intercorrelated features used by the brain signal DEAP, PCA is particularly useful. Redundancy is reduced, targeting the vital informative parts of the signal, while at the same time maintaining the variability of the dataset. As an instance, PCA can improve computational efficiency by compressing information from multiple EEG channels and time-series data into a smaller feature set, without significant loss of signal quality [12].

2. Recursive Feature Elimination (RFE)

Some methods used for feature selection, like RFE, are wrapper-based and are used to iteratively remove the most unimportant features. Datasets like DEAP, involving the recognition of emotions using EEG signals, use RFE as it identifies the highest predictive of the target labels. When the goal is to prioritize features like frequency bands or temporal characteristics, RFE is preferred, as it focuses on the top-ranked features, enhancing the interpretability and reducing computational complexity while ensuring high predictive accuracy [25].

3. Mutual Information (MI)

Dependency between individual features and the target variable is measured by mutual information, making it an effective filter-based method for datasets like WESAD and DEAP. Non-linear relationships make the best use of MI, which is often used in psychological signals like ECG, EDA, and EEG. For example, MI can be used to highlight features from frequency bands or statistical measures strongly correlating with stress levels in psychological signals like ECG, EDA, and EEG. ML can be used in the identification of EEG features critical for emotion classification in DEAP. This is a computationally efficient method and enhances model performance, as only the most relevant features are retained [26].

3.6 Machine Learning in Brain Signal Analysis

ML is a set of computational techniques that allows the machine to learn and make informed decisions on its own without explicit human intervention. In brain signal analysis, ML plays a significant role in decoding complex and high-dimensional neural data that are noisy and exhibiting high variability, especially data collected from EEG, ECoG, and fMRI signals. Since they make traditional analysis of the data very difficult, ML models can be effectively used to detect meaningful patterns from the highly complex data, allowing them to be used in applications like brain-computer interfaces (BCI), neurological disorder diagnosis, and cognitive state monitoring [21].

3.6.1 Categories of Machine Learning Models

ML models are classified into three categories, depending on their learning approach [27].

1. Supervised Learning: This involves training the model with previously available labeled brain signals. Each input signal is paired with its corresponding output or outcome. Linear Regression, logistic regression, decision trees (DT), support vector machines (SVM), K-nearest neighbors (KNN), and random forest (RF) are the best examples of supervised learning algorithms. These supervised algorithms are used to perform classification or regression tasks like motor imagery classification and seizure detection.
2. Unsupervised Learning: This learning algorithm is used to find the hidden patterns or structures in the unlabeled data. These methods are used to group similar signals or features. Clustering, association, and dimensionality reduction algorithms come under unsupervised algorithms.

3. Deep Learning: This is the subset of ML, employed with multilayered neural networks, that helps to automatically learn hierarchical representations from raw brain signals or from the minimally processed data. Researchers have effectively used neural networks to decode brain signals, showcasing the potential of deep learning in neuroscience.

3.6.2 Importance of Machine Learning in Brain Signal Interpretation

Brain signals are complex, non-stationary, and susceptible to noise and artifacts by nature. ML offers powerful tools to handle these issues by automating processes like extraction and classification. ML is adaptable in nature, allowing its generalization across different subjects and experimental conditions, and as a result, it has enabled personalized brain-computer interfaces and applications in the clinical industry. Moreover, ML can detect unseen patterns linked to the cognitive or pathological states that traditional signal processing may overlook. This capability paves the way for real-time brain signal interpretation and improved patient care by accelerating research and development in neuroscience and clinical diagnostics [28].

3.7 Application of Machine Learning on Brain Signals: DEAP Dataset Case Study

The DEAP dataset is a collection of EEG signals and their relationship with emotional states. This dataset is a valuable resource for brain signal analysis. This section demonstrates the practical workflow for preprocessing EEG data, extracting and selecting features, and classifying emotions using machine learning [29].

3.7.1 EEG Channels and Their Significance

The DEAP dataset is a collection of EEG signals from 32 channels, with 32 electrodes placed in the frontal, central, temporal, parietal, and occipital areas on the scalp and following the 10-20 International System. A detailed spatial map of the brain is collected by the electrodes, and each electrode maps to a specific channel. For example, emotional and cognitive processing of the brain are associated with the frontal channels Fp1 and Fp2.

Visual activity of the brain is associated with the O1 and O2 channels of the occipital region of the brain. This experimental setup, collecting brain signals using 32 channels, ensures comprehensive brain coverage, and this helps to conduct research in emotion recognition and brain-computer interfaces (BCI).

Description of EEG Signals Before Preprocessing

The raw brain signal contains impurities that are irrelevant for analysis. Irrelevant or noisy components create issues in accuracy and reliability. The following section shows the EEG signal in the DEAP dataset before preprocessing.

Figure 3.2 illustrates the raw time-series EEG signals recorded from a subset of 20 channels of the DEAP dataset during a 10-second interval. Each line represents the electrical activity recorded from a specific scalp electrode (e.g., Fp1, AF3, F7). The x-axis shows time (seconds), while the y-axis displays the signal amplitude in microvolts (μV), offset for clarity. Observations from this visualization include:

> **Channel Subset**: Although the dataset contains recordings from 32 EEG channels and additional peripheral signals, this graph focuses on 20 channels for better clarity.
> **Signal Variations**: Variations in amplitude reflect neural activity, while some channels may exhibit noise or artifacts, like low-frequency drifts or high-frequency spikes.

This representation provides an overview of neural activity captured by EEG electrodes, highlighting the importance of preprocessing to enhance signal quality and remove artifacts.

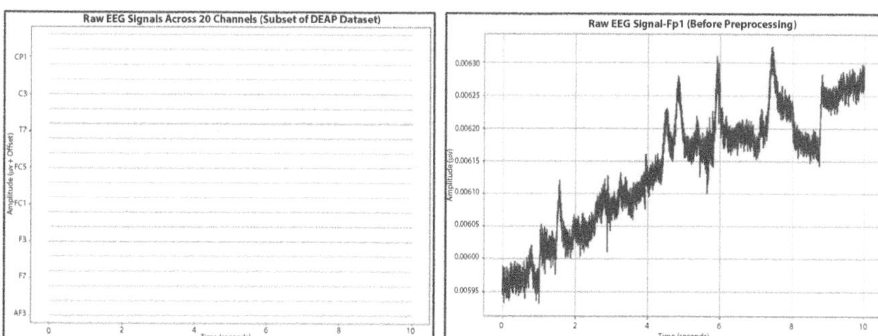

Figure 3.2 Visual representation of all the signals and channel Fp1 of sample 1.

1. Before Bandpass Filtering

- **Characteristics of the EEG Signals**:
    - Raw EEG signals include neural oscillations encompassing a wide range of frequencies (0 Hz to over 100 Hz).
    - Low-frequency noise (below 4 Hz) can result from baseline drifts caused by movement, respiration, or electrode impedance issues.
    - High-frequency noise (above 45 Hz) is often due to electrical interference (e.g., power line noise at 50/60 Hz) or muscle artifacts.
- **Challenges**:
    - Neural activity of the brain is hidden due to the irrelevant components of the EEG signal frequency, such as the alpha (8–13 Hz), beta (13–30 Hz), and theta (4–8 Hz) bands.
    - Insights of the signal are reduced due to the noise and other artifacts.

2. Before Downsampling

- **Signal Characteristics**:
    - To record the temporal activity of the brain, the raw EEG recordings are often sampled at high rates, such as 256 Hz or higher.
    - The high sampling rates give elaborate details, but they suffer from computational costs.
- **Challenges**:
    - Delays in real-time applications and increased computational costs for ML algorithms due to large data size.
    - Temporal data redundancy can be witnessed, as most EEG dynamics can be captured at lower sampling rates (e.g., 128 Hz).

3. Before Artifact Removal

- **Signal Characteristics**:
  - Eye blinks and movements: Large amplitude noise in frontal channels.
  - Muscle movements: High-frequency noise superimposed on the EEG.
  - Electrode pops or shifts: Sudden spikes in the signal due to poor electrode contact.
- **Challenges**:
  - There is a chance for misinterpretation during analysis, as genuine neural activities can be masked or mimicked by artifacts.
  - For instance, oscillations like delta and theta waves can be masked by eye blinks that dominate the low-frequency range.

3.7.2 Significance of Preprocessing

- **Bandpass Filtering**: Separates the important neural frequency bands, eliminates the changed signal that deviates from the correct frequency due to electrode instability, baseline shifts, etc., and the noise.
- **Downsampling**: Reduces data redundancy while preserving essential temporal features, making the dataset more manageable.
- **Artifact Removal (ICA)**: Cleans the signal of external influences, ensuring the extracted features reflect genuine brain activity. Figure 3.3 shows the visual representation of Sample 1 before and after preprocessing; here, all 32 channels are used for processing to give a clear representation.

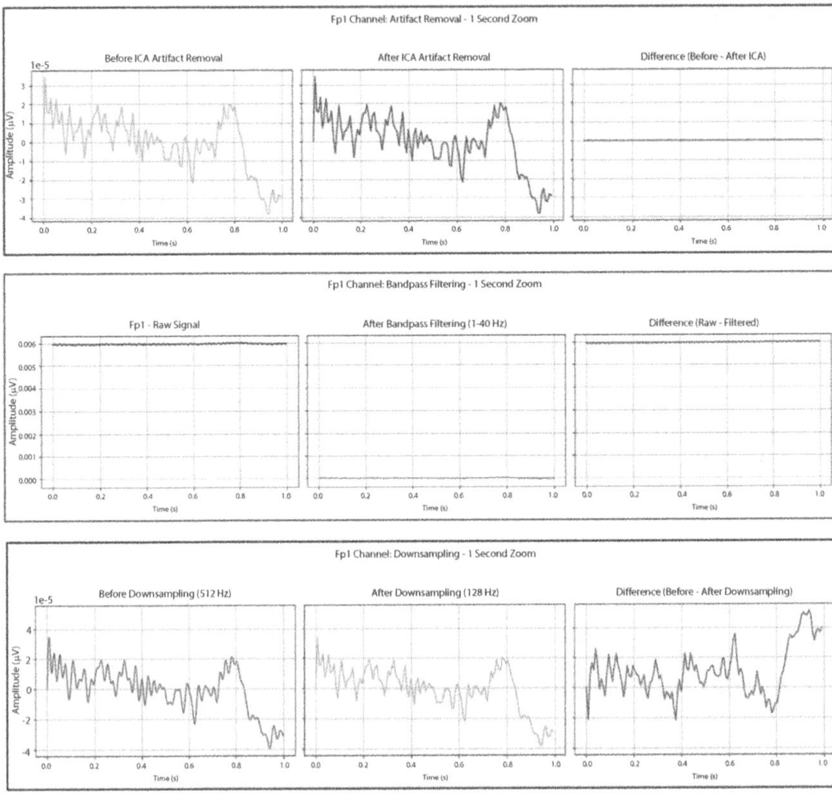

Figure 3.3 Visual representation of sample 1 before and after preprocessing.

3.7.3 Feature Extraction

Feature extraction is the process of converting the preprocessed EEG signal in the DEAP dataset into a proper numerical representation for machine learning models. With the sampling rate of 128 Hz, all the 256 samples are segmented into 2-second windows that don't overlap to preserve the temporal information. From each segment, spectral features are calculated to encapsulate different aspects of brain activity. The Welch method is employed to calculate power within specific EEG frequency ranges, categorized as theta (4–8 Hz), alpha (8–13 Hz), beta (13–30 Hz), and gamma (30–40 Hz). These frequency bands capture distinct spectral characteristics of the brain's electrical activity. It is a vital method in

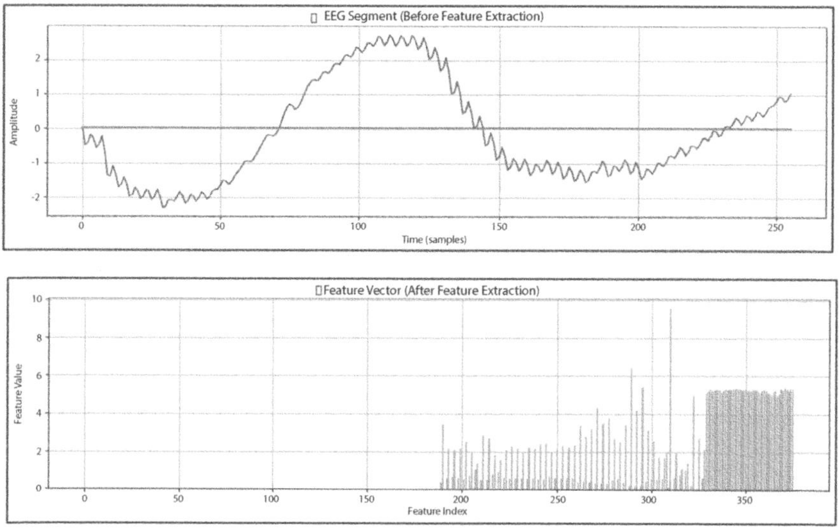

Figure 3.4 Visual representation of sample 1 before and after feature extraction.

spectral feature extraction. This is used in understanding the distribution of power across these spectral bands connected with cognitive and physiological states. Along with spectral features, temporal features (Hjorth parameters—activity, mobility, and complexity) are also extracted. Finally, Shannon entropy is identified for all the segments, quantifying the randomness or disorder in the EEG signal, which reflects neural complexity. Figure 3.4 shows the visual representation of signals from sample 1 before and after feature extraction.

3.7.4 Feature Selection

In the example application, PCA is employed to minimize the high-dimensional feature matrix collected from EEG signal segments. PCA selects the principal feature by analyzing the calculated covariance matrix, eigenvalues, and eigenvectors of the feature space, which captures the maximum variance. Here, the variance threshold is set as 95%; PCA identifies and selects the most important components that hold the significant information. This is shown in Figure 3.5.

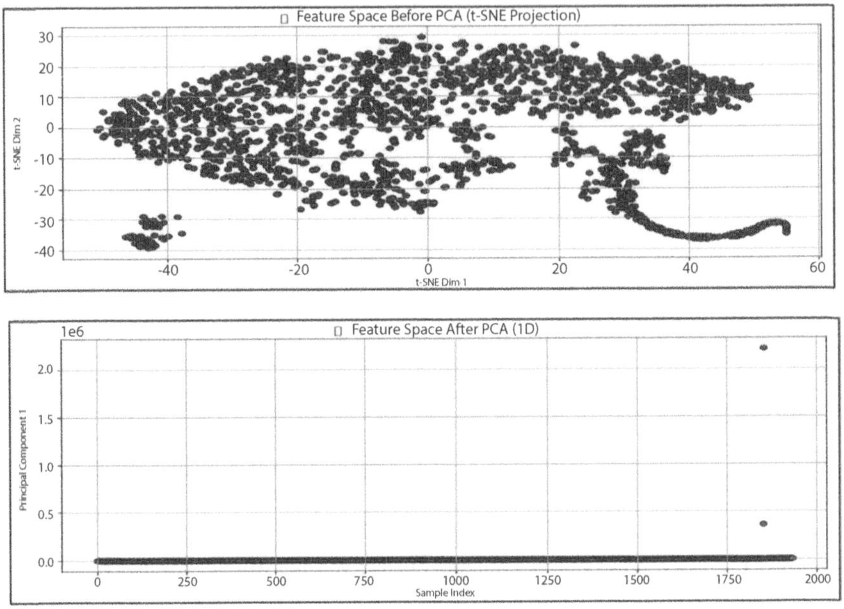

Figure 3.5 Visual representation of sample 1 before and after feature selection.

3.7.5 Support Vector Machines (SVM) in Brain Signal Analysis

Regression and classification can be performed using the SVM algorithm. SVM intends to find a hyperplane separating the data points from different classes optimally so that the margin between them is maximum. This makes SVM highly effective at handling the high-dimensional data produced by EEG and fMRI signals, where the number of features can be very large relative to sample size.

In brain signal analysis, SVMs are highly popular, as they can generalize well in noisy environments and avoid overfitting, which is important given the variability and artifacts in the neural recordings. As an example, in motor imagery-based BCI systems, SVM classifiers distinguish different imagined movements by learning patterns in EEG features that Common Spatial Patterns (CSP) or wavelet transforms extract.

The kernel trick allows SVM to be flexible and operate in transformed feature spaces and model nonlinear relationships without explicit computation of the transformation. Linear, polynomial, and radial basis function (RBF) kernels are the common kernels used. This adaptability is better than linear models in effectively capturing the complex dynamics of brain signals.

Despite the advantages, careful parameter tuning, such as the choice of kernel and regularization parameters, is required by SVM to achieve optimal performance. Model robustness is validated by cross-validation techniques. Brain signal classification tasks still use SVM because of its efficiency and reliability in classification tasks. Some tasks, like the detection of seizures and the monitoring of cognitive states, use SVM.

Figure 3.6 illustrates the binary classification of EEG segments from the DEAP dataset using SVM, along with a radial basis function (RBF) kernel. The high-dimensional EEG features, including bandpower, Hjorth parameters, and Shannon entropy, were reduced to two dimensions, theta dominance and complexity axis, using principal component analysis (PCA) for visualization.

Each point in the graph represents an EEG segment, color-coded to indicate the binary labels, such as low and high valence. The SVM decision boundary is depicted by the contour in the plot, maximizing the margin between classes and separating the data points. This visualization demonstrates the distinctive power of the extracted EEG features and highlights the effectiveness of combining PCA and SVM for emotion recognition and cognitive state monitoring, providing insights for applications like BCIs and assessing mental health.

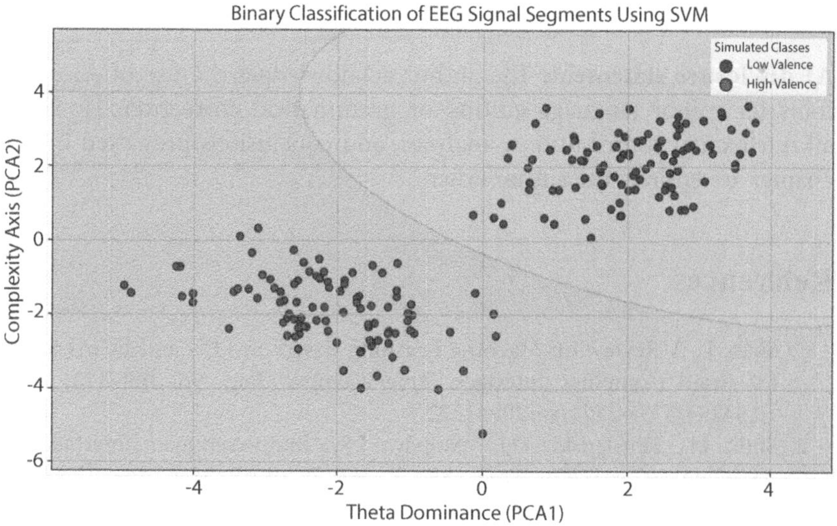

Figure 3.6 Result of binary classification using SVM.

3.8 Conclusion

The acquisition and preprocessing of brain signals are the first step for a brain-computer interface (BCI) or neurological system. Brain signals offer insights into neural function and facilitate the creation of applications in healthcare, rehabilitation, and assistive technology for people suffering from brain disorders or diseases. Raw brain signals contain noise and complex artifacts, and are very complex to understand and find the insights directly. Preprocessing methodologies like filtering, artifact removal, and normalization are essential to ensure signal quality before applying machine learning techniques.

With machine learning, it is easier to uncover complex hidden patterns and make precise predictions or classifications from brain signals. The predominant SVM algorithm is demonstrated to show the result of brain signal classification. This paves the way for intelligent and interactive systems that have the power to assist patients with motor disabilities. This can also apply to enhance the mental health monitoring and support for cognitive research. While integrating with neurotechnology, the synergy between advanced brain signal acquisition methods and machine learning will create the next generation of human-computer interaction. Ultimately, this integration will not only enhance the diagnostics and clinical trials but also help individuals interact with their environment in novel and life-changing ways.

AI disclosure statement: The author acknowledges the use of AI-based tools for minor language editing or grammatical correction. However, all intellectual contributions, analyses, and conclusions presented in this chapter are entirely the author's own.

References

1. Shao, J., A Review on Machine Learning Based on EEG and ECoG Signal for Brain Computer Interface. *Appl. Comput. Eng.*, 96, 169–174, 2024, 10.54254/2755-2721/96/20241272.
2. Shih, J.J., Krusienski, D.J., Wolpaw, J.R., Brain-computer interfaces in medicine. *Mayo Clin. Proc.*, 87, 3, 268–79, 2012 Mar, doi: 10.1016/j.mayocp.2011.12.008. Epub 2012 Feb 10. PMID: 22325364; PMCID: PMC3497935.

3. Kumar, S. and Sharma, A., Advances in non-invasive EEG-based brain-computer interfaces: Signal acquisition, processing, emerging approaches, and applications, in: *Signal Processing Strategies*, A.S. El-Baz and J.S. Suri (Eds.), pp. 281–310, Academic Press, London, UK, 2025, doi: https://doi.org/10.1016/B978-0-323-95437-2.00014-8.
4. https://en.wikipedia.org/wiki/Brain%E2%80%93computer_interface.
5. Bom, M.S., Brak, A.M.A., Raemaekers, M., *et al.*, Large-scale fMRI dataset for the design of motor-based Brain-Computer Interfaces. *Sci. Data*, 12, 804, 2025, https://doi.org/10.1038/s41597-025-05134-1.
6. Victorio, M., Dieffenderfer, J., Songkakul, T., Willeke, J., Bozkurt, A., Pozdin, V.A., Wearable Wireless Functional Near-Infrared Spectroscopy System for Cognitive Activity Monitoring. *Biosensors*, *15*, 2, 92, 2025, https://doi.org/10.3390/bios15020092.
7. https://medium.com/data-science/introduction-to-ica-independent-component-analysis-b2c3c4720cd9.
8. https://faculty.washington.edu/seattle/brain-physics/textbooks/sanei.pdf
9. Carvalhaes, C. and de Barros, J.A., The surface Laplacian technique in EEG: Theory and methods. *Int. J. Psychophysiol.*, 97, 3, 174–188, 2015, https://doi.org/10.1016/j.ijpsycho.2015.04.023.
10. Ramoser, H., Müller-Gerking, J., Pfurtscheller, G., Optimal spatial filtering of single trial EEG during imagined hand movement. *IEEE Trans. Rehabil. Eng.*, 8, 4, 441–446, 2000, https://doi.org/10.1109/86.895946.
11. Apicella, A., Isgrò, F., Pollastro, A., Prevete, R., On the effects of data normalization for domain adaptation on EEG data. *Eng. Appl. Artif. Intell.*, 118, 106205, 2023, https://doi.org/10.1016/j.engappai.2023.106205.
12. Sanei, S. and Chambers, J.A., *EEG Signal Processing*, Wiley, Hoboken, NJ, USA, 2007.
13. Michel, C.M. and Koenig, M., EEG microstates as a tool for studying the temporal dynamics of whole-brain neuronal networks: A review. *NeuroImage*, 180, 577–593, 2018, doi: 10.1016/j.neuroimage.2017.11.062.
14. Cohen, M.X., *Analyzing Neural Time Series Data: Theory and Practice*, MIT Press, Cambridge, MA, USA, 2014.
15. McKeown, M.J., *et al.*, Spatially independent activity patterns in functional MRI data during the Stroop color-naming task. *Proc. Natl. Acad. Sci. U.S.A.*, 95, 3, 803–810, 1998, doi: 10.1073/pnas.95.3.803.
16. Pascual-Marqui, R.D., Standardized low-resolution brain electromagnetic tomography (sLORETA): Technical details. *Methods Find. Exp. Clin. Pharmacol.*, 24, Suppl D, 5–12, 2002.
17. Nagarajan, R. and Casanova, J.E., Wavelet denoising of EEG signals: A comparative study. *Biomed. Signal Process. Control*, 18, 48–58, 2015, doi: 10.1016/j.bspc.2015.03.007.
18. Guyon, I. and Elisseeff, A., An Introduction to Variable and Feature Selection. *J. Mach. Learn. Res.*, 3, 1157–1182, 2003.

19. Makeig, S., Bell, A.J., Jung, T.P., Sejnowski, T.J., Independent Component Analysis of Electroencephalographic Data. *Adv. Neural Inf. Process. Syst.*, 8, 145–151, 1996.
20. Norman, K.A., Polyn, S.M., Detre, G.J., Haxby, J.V., Beyond Mind-Reading: Multi-Voxel Pattern Analysis of fMRI Data. *Trends Cognit. Sci.*, 10, 9, 424–430, 2006.
21. Subasi, A., *EEG Signal Processing and Machine Learning*, Academic Press, London, UK, 2021, https://doi.org/10.1016/B978-0-12-820326-2.00001-5.
22. Blankertz, B., Lemm, S., Treder, M., Haufe, S., Müller, K.R., Single-trial analysis and classification of ERP components—a tutorial. *NeuroImage*, 56, 2, 814–825, 2011, https://doi.org/10.1016/j.neuroimage.2010.06.048.
23. Addison, P.S., *The Illustrated Wavelet Transform Handbook: Introductory Theory and Applications in Science, Engineering, Medicine and Finance*, 2nd ed., CRC Press, Boca Raton, FL, USA, 2017.
24. Friston, K.J., Functional and effective connectivity: A review. *Brain Connect.*, 1, 1, 13–36, 2011, https://doi.org/10.1089/brain.2011.0008.
25. bdelAal, M.A., Alsawy, A.A., Hefny, H.A., EEG-Based Emotion Recognition Using a Wrapper-Based Feature Selection Method, in: *Proceedings of the International Conference on Advanced Intelligent Systems and Informatics 2017 (AISI 2017)*, vol. 639, A. Hassanien, K. Shaalan, T. Gaber, M. Tolba (Eds.), pp. 263–273, Springer, Cham, Switzerland, 2018, doi: 10.1007/978-3-319-64861-3_23.
26. Li, J., Feng, G., Ling, C., Ren, X., Liu, X., Zhang, S., Wang, L., Chen, Y., Zeng, X., Chen, R., A Resource-Efficient Multi-Entropy Fusion Method and Its Application for EEG-Based Emotion Recognition. *Entropy (Basel)*, 27, 1, 96, 2025 Jan 20, doi: 10.3390/e27010096. PMID: 39851716; PMCID: PMC11764894.
27. https://www.geeksforgeeks.org/machine-learning/.
28. Roy, Y., Banville, H., Albuquerque, I., Gramfort, A., Falk, T.H., Faubert, J., Deep learning-based electroencephalography analysis: a systematic review. *J. Neural Eng.*, 17, 4, 041001, 2020, https://doi.org/10.1088/1741-2552/ab279a.
29. Koelstra, S., Muhl, C., Soleymani, M., Lee, J., Yazdani, A., Ebrahimi, T., Pun, T., Nijholt, A., Patras, I., DEAP: A Database for Emotion Analysis Using Physiological Signals. *IEEE Trans. Affective Comput.*, 3, 1, 18–31, Jan.–Mar. 2012, doi: 10.1109/T-AFFC.2011.15.

4

Basics of Machine Learning for Brain Signal Decoding

Richa* **and Sakshi Mittal**

Department of ECE, Galgotias College of Engineering & Technology, Greater Noida, U.P, India

Abstract

This chapter covers the basic concepts of machine learning (ML) related to brain signal decoding, pointing out its significance in understanding neural activity and for applications such as BCI, neurofeedback, and cognitive monitoring. It describes different modalities for brain signals, including EEG, fMRI, and MEG, and discusses vital stages in the decoding process, from signal acquisition and preprocessing, to feature extraction and model training. This emphasizes how the role of ML deals with the high-dimensional nature of the data, contending with noise, and achieving real-time decoding through dimensionality reduction, pattern recognition, and time-series analysis. This chapter also explores the challenges regarding variability, noise, and computational delays in the decoding process and discusses how advanced techniques, including deep learning, are increasingly being implemented. Finally, the chapter points to promising future developments while acknowledging ML's tremendous potential to revolutionize neurotechnology and the improvement of healthcare delivery.

Keywords**:** Brain signal decoding, machine learning, feature extraction, neural signal processing (EEG/fMRI/MEG), real-time pattern recognition

4.1 Introduction to Brain Signal Decoding

Brain signal decoding is a technical term to define the processes of interpreting neural signals to ascertain, in one way or another, the brain activity

**Corresponding author*: richa.sharma70@gmail.com

Tawseef Ahmed Teli, Syed Immamul Ansarullah, Arun Kumar Rana, Suman Lata Tripathi and Kashif Nisar (eds.) Brain-to-Computer Interfaces Using Machine Learning and Deep Learning, (61–82) © 2026 Scrivener Publishing LLC

pattern, intention, or even emotion. Technological advancements have ensured that machine learning (ML) stands as one of the important tools for analyzing complex brain data and unveiling the underlying mechanisms of brain activities. In this chapter, we discuss the fundamentals of brain signal decoding, the challenges, and the applications of ML.

Brain signal decoding involves extracting some useful bits of information out of neural signals to interpret the activity of the brain. The neural signals, per se, can be electrical, magnetic, or metabolic signals that arise as a result of an interplay of large ensembles of neurons in the brain. These signals mirror real-time brain activity, such as cognition, motor functions, or any emotional state. The whole spectrum of brain signal decoding demands the development of sophisticated techniques and tools to interpret the very complex high-dimensional data emanating from the brain.

4.1.1 Types of Brain Signals

The brain produces a variety of signals that can be measured and decoded, as shown in Figure 4.1.

Common techniques to capture these signals include:

- **Electroencephalography (EEG):** is a non-invasive technique that measures brain electrical activity, where electrodes are placed on the scalp. It is applied extensively in the study of brain waves related to states such as those of sleep, attentiveness, and mental fatigue, among others.
- **Functional Magnetic Resonance Imaging (fMRI):** is a method of measuring blood flow to various parts of the brain indirectly reflecting neural activity. With great spatial resolution, the technique is mostly applied to map brain activity during tasks like those involving thinking, problem-solving, or emotional processing.
- **Electrocorticography (ECoG):** involves the placement of electrodes directly on the surface of the brain to register its electrical activity. This technique gives high temporal and spatial resolution and is primarily used for patients being treated for epilepsy or those undergoing brain surgery.
- **Magnetoencephalography (MEG):** detects the magnetic fields induced by neuronal activity and provides information on brain dynamics with temporal resolution. This method is useful for examining the timing and localization of brain responses.

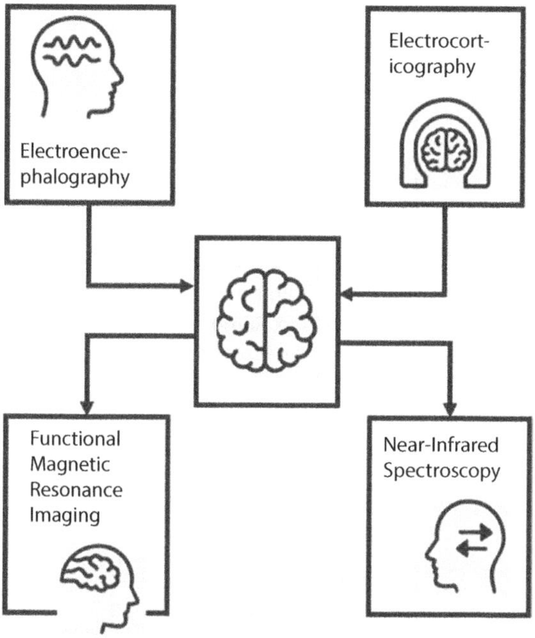

Figure 4.1 Type of brain signals.

- **Near-Infrared Spectroscopy (NIRS):** measures variations in blood oxygenation levels in the brain, giving an indirect estimate of their neural activity.

4.2 What Does Brain Signal Decoding Involve

Mainly, brain signal decoding works to interpret the neural signals into useful information indicating some underlying cognitive, emotional, or physiological state. In all such processes, various stages are involved, as presented in Figure 4.2.

1. **Signal Acquisition:** The capturing of signals from the brain is performed by different techniques, like EEG, fMRI, or ECoG. Brain activity during simple motor tasks or even advanced cognitive processes will reflect very well through these signals.
2. **Preprocessing:** The acquired signals generally contain noise or artifacts (e.g., eye blinks, muscle movements,

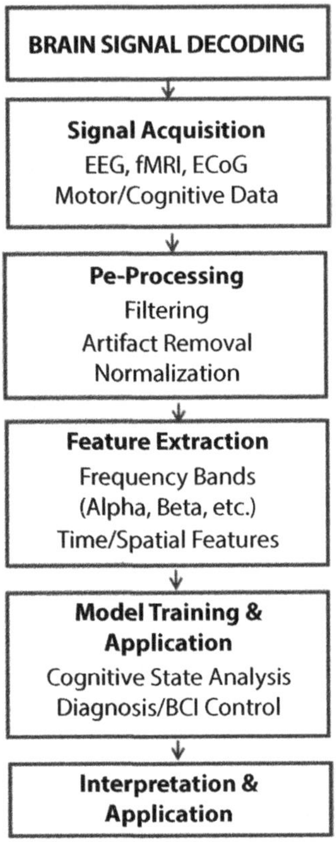

Figure 4.2 Key stages of brain signal decoding.

electrical interference). Preprocessing methods are methods used to clean the data before performing further analysis, including filtering, artifact removal, and normalization.

3. **Feature Extraction:** This stage consists of the identification of relevant characteristics of the brain signals representing the cognitive states. Examples could include the extraction of features such as power in specific frequency bands (α, β, θ) in EEG analysis pertaining to attention, relaxation, or cognitive workload.
4. **Model Training and Decoding:** After feature extraction, the trained machine learning models find data patterns related to specific brain states. Then, these models can be used to decode new brain signals for the prediction of the state or intention of the individual.

5. **Interpretation and Application:** The final decoded results can be interpreted to understand brain activity, diagnose medical conditions, or control external devices in brain-computer interface (BCI) systems.

4.3 Machine Learning's Role in Brain Signal Decoding

Neural activity signal decoding with ML is crucial because of its capability to analyze vast amounts of data arising from high-dimensional neural sources across the space and time domains to find the hidden truth behind this signal. In contrast to the usual methods, which more or less rely on well-structured and instructed means or statistical analyses, ML is all about letting the system learn the patterns in the data to provide greater insight into the types of brain signals that we work with. Signal decoding can be considered to be the deciphering and coding of neural signals into meaningful data or meaningful commands, particularly for applications dealing with brain-computer interfaces (BCIs), neuroprosthetics, and monitoring cognitive states. Because of the complexity, variability, and high-dimensional nature of EEG, MEG, or fMRI brain signals, ML has become an indispensable tool. These ML algorithms automate the recognition of complex patterns, handle large datasets, and provide adaptive systems to learn and improve over time [1, 2].

The following are the primary ways in which ML is used in brain signal decoding:

4.3.1 Pattern Recognition

ML is indeed very essential in brain signal decoding applications like brain-computer interface (BCI), neurorehabilitation, and cognitive monitoring. It discovers much sophistication in the analysis of brain data relevant to emotional, cognitive, or motor states by pattern identification. The heart of the brain signal decoding goes in the direction of translating the raw signals of the brain into meaning or interpretation of their initial thoughts, emotions, and intentions. Most of these neurological signals are collected by noninvasive means such as EEG, which is an electroencephalographic method of recording brain waves from one's scalp. Brain signal decoding employs two bases, yielding the crucial pattern recognition from identifying the difference in neural signatures attached to specific mental states, activities, or stimuli.

Brain signals are highly complex and often noisy. However, they contain hidden patterns that correspond to various **cognitive** (thinking-related), **emotional**, or **motor** (movement-related) states. For example:

- **Cognitive states** might include attention, memory recall, or decision-making.
- **Emotional states** can manifest as feelings, such as happiness, stress, or anxiety.
- **A motor state** is the conscious action of doing any of the physical movements or behaving with the thought of that movement, such as raising an arm or walking.

Machine learning algorithms excel at identifying and learning these **underlying patterns** from the data, even when they are subtle or nonlinear. This ability makes ML particularly well-suited for brain signal decoding tasks.

Pattern recognition refers to the process of detecting regularities, trends, or structures in data. In brain signal decoding, this means identifying unique "neural signatures"—that is, signal patterns that consistently appear when a person performs or imagines a particular task.

For instance, during **motor imagery** (where a person imagines moving a body part without physically doing so), EEG signals show specific spatial and temporal patterns. These patterns vary depending on whether the person imagines moving their left & right hand or foot. ML algorithms can be trained to identify and distinguish these patterns.

Machine learning algorithms in Use for pattern recognitions

Several ML models have been successfully applied to pattern recognition in brain signal decoding:

a) **Support Vector Machines:** SVMs are a learning technique used in differentiation problems. It works by finding the ideal hyperplane that distinguishes different classes (e.g., left- vs. right-hand motor imagery) in a high-dimensional space. SVMs are robust to small datasets and are particularly effective when the data is well-separated [5].
b) **Convolutional Neural Networks:** These deep learning techniques are used to identify spatial features in data. In brain signal decoding, CNNs can process raw or minimally

preprocessed EEG signals to learn features such as the strength and location of brain activity across electrodes. CNNs are often used when spatial structure in the signal is important [6].

c) **Recurrent Neural Networks (RNN):** These models are built to manage sequential information, making them ideal for analyzing signals that vary over time, such as EEG. They have internal memory that allows them to learn temporal relationships between data points. Long Short-Term Memory (LSTM) networks, a variant of RNNs, are especially well-suited for capturing long-term relationships in neural data [1, 7].

These algorithms are **trained on labeled datasets**, where each EEG recording is associated with a known mental task. Over time, the models learn to map patterns in the signal to specific tasks and mental states, such as differentiating between imagined left- and right-hand movements, a common benchmark in BCI research [2].

4.3.2 Dimensionality Reduction

Brain signals are typically high-dimensional, especially when recorded from multiple EEG electrodes or fMRI voxels. When working with brain signals—particularly data collected through techniques like **EEG** and **fMRI**—one encounters a significant challenge: **high dimensionality**. This means that the datasets often contain a large number of variables, such as signal readings from multiple EEG electrodes or thousands of spatial points (voxels) in an fMRI scan. Machine learning on swarm datasets comprises challenges unique to the arbitrary distributions of volume, hence the principal workhorse identifications and parallel algorithms specific to SGD networks. While more data might seem beneficial, it can actually **hinder performance** in machine learning tasks due to issues like increased computational cost, redundancy, and the **"curse of dimensionality"**—as the feature space grows, data becomes increasingly sparse, making it difficult for models to learn effectively. To tackle these issues, **dimensionality reduction techniques** are employed to compress the data into fewer variables while preserving the most important features. Dimensionality reduction is needed because of the following reasons:

- **Computational Efficiency:** Reducing the number of variables decreases the time and resources needed to train machine learning models.
- **Noise Reduction:** Many raw signals include irrelevant or noisy features, such as signals from muscle activity or eye movements.
- **Better Generalization:** Fewer variables reduce the risk of overfitting, where a model performs well on training data but poorly on new data.
- **Visualization:** Lower-dimensional data can be visualized more easily, helping researchers to interpret results or detect patterns.

Dimensionality reduction techniques like Principal Component Analysis (PCA), Independent Component Analysis (ICA), and t-SNE are frequently used to simplify the input space while preserving the most critical information [6]. The details of different techniques are given below:

a. **Principal Component Analysis (PCA):** A method used to minimize dimensionality by reorienting the database along new axes that successively capture the largest possible variance in the data.
   Use in brain signals: PCA can identify the most influential components in EEG data, filtering out noise and redundancy.
   Advantage: It simplifies data while retaining trends and patterns that are critical for classification or pattern recognition.
b. **Independent Component Analysis (ICA):** ICA goes a step further by not just finding uncorrelated components (like PCA), but statistically independent components.
   Use in EEG/fMRI: ICA is particularly powerful in separating brain sources from artifacts, e.g., eye blinks, muscle movements, and line noise. For instance, when analyzing EEG data, ICA can isolate a component that corresponds to eye movement, allowing it to be removed without affecting the true brain signal.
   Advantage: Enhances signal clarity and improves the performance of machine learning models by feeding them cleaner input data [6].
c. **t-distributed Stochastic Neighbor Embedding (t-SNE):** t-SNE is a nonlinear dimensionality reduction technique primarily used for visualization of high-dimensional data.

Working principle: It maps similar data points closer together in a low-dimensional space (usually 2D or 3D), making patterns and clusters in the data easier to observe.
Application in neuroscience: t-SNE is often used to visualize how brain signal patterns change with different tasks or mental states, helping researchers understand the structure of the data.
Limitation: t-SNE is computationally intensive and not ideal for real-time systems, but it is very useful for offline analysis and exploration.

An EEG system recording from 64 electrodes at 512 Hz can generate thousands of values from just a few seconds of data. Training a classifier on all these variables is inefficient and might include irrelevant or noisy signals. Using PCA or ICA helps reduce the dataset to the most meaningful signals, leading to better performance and faster processing in applications like emotion detection, motor imagery decoding, or sleep stage classification.

4.3.3 Time Series Analysis

Brain signals—such as those recorded by EEG (Electroencephalography), MEG (Magnetoencephalography), or even fMRI (Functional Magnetic Resonance Imaging)—are **not static**; they unfold continuously over time. This makes them **time-dependent** or **sequential**, meaning that the current value of a brain signal is often influenced by its previous values. Such data is best analyzed using **time series analysis**, a set of methods designed to study temporal sequences of data points [1, 5]. In the context of **brain signal decoding**, time series analysis helps in understanding how brain activity evolves moment by moment. This is essential for applications like **seizure prediction**, **motor intention decoding**, and **cognitive workload estimation**, where the brain's response is dynamic and changes in real time. Time series data is any dataset where the values are recorded at consistent time intervals, and the order of the data points is meaningful. For example, EEG signals sampled at 512 Hz provide 512 data points per second for each electrode—this forms a time series. In brain signals:

- Each point in the signal depends on the past, which means **temporal patterns** and trends must be considered.
- Analyzing these signals without accounting for time dependencies may ignore critical information.

Why Time Series Analysis is Important in Neuroscience

- **Capturing Temporal Dependencies:** Neural processes like attention shifts, emotional changes, or epileptic seizures unfold over time. Understanding **how** and **when** certain brain states emerge requires a model that can learn from the sequence itself, not just isolated data points.
- **Pattern Evolution:** Unlike images (which are static), brain signal patterns change and evolve. A model trained to capture temporal evolution can identify the **onset** of cognitive states or predict **transitions** (e.g., from normal to seizure state).
- **Predictive Modeling:** By recognizing patterns in how brain signals change, it becomes possible to **predict future events,** like an impending seizure or the next movement a person intends to make.

Machine Learning Models Used in Time Series Analysis

a. **Long Short-Term Memory (LSTM) Networks: LSTM** networks are a type of **Recurrent Neural Network (RNN)** specially designed to overcome the limitations of traditional RNNs, such as the **vanishing gradient problem**, which makes it difficult to learn long-term dependencies. LSTMs have memory cells that can selectively remember or forget information over long time periods. They use three gates:

    - **Input gate:** Decides how much new information to write.
    - **Forget gate:** Decides what old information to discard.
    - **Output gate:** Decides what part of the memory to send forward.

- **Use in brain decoding:** LSTMs are particularly effective in:

    - **Seizure prediction**, where they learn the pre-ictal (before seizure) patterns in the EEG.
    - **Intention decoding**, such as predicting whether a person intends to move a hand or speak, is based on temporal neural cues. Table 4.1 shows the real word applications of different models in brain signal decoding.

Table 4.1 Real-world applications of time series models in brain signal decoding.

Application	Description
Seizure prediction	LSTM models can detect patterns in EEG that typically occur before a seizure.
Motor intention	Predicting when and how a user intends to move using EEG and time-series models.
Sleep stage analysis	HMMs can model transitions between sleep stages (REM, NREM, etc.) over time.
Cognitive load monitoring	Tracking changes in brain activity to assess fatigue or mental effort.

- **Advantage:** They are capable of learning **both short-term and long-term** temporal dependencies in the signal [1].

b. **Hidden Markov Models (HMMs): HMMs** are statistical models where the system is assumed to follow a **Markov process** with hidden (unobservable) states. In simple terms, an HMM assumes that the signal we observe is the outcome of an underlying process that transitions between states over time.

- **Use in neuroscience:** HMMs are commonly used for:
  - Modeling **brain state transitions** (e.g., sleep stages or attention levels).
  - **Speech and movement decoding**, where a sequence of observations (EEG signals) is used to infer the most likely hidden state (spoken word or motion).

- **How it works:** Each time point has:
  - A hidden state (e.g., "planning to move" or "resting")
  - An observed signal (e.g., EEG amplitude). The model determines the sequence of hidden states to best explain the given data [5].

- **Advantage:** HMMs are interpretable and effective when there are **discrete** transitions between brain states. Applications of real time decoding is given in Table 4.2.

Table 4.2 Applications of real-time decoding.

Application	Real-time output
BCI-controlled prosthetics	Controlling robotic limbs based on motor imagery
Speller systems for locked-in patients	Selecting letters on a screen using brain activity
Gaming and entertainment	Interacting with virtual environments using thoughts
Neurofeedback therapy	Providing instant feedback to users to regulate emotions
Seizure monitoring	Predicting or detecting seizure onset in real-time

4.3.4 Real-Time Decoding

Real-time decoding refers to the immediate or near-instantaneous processing of brain signals to extract meaningful information and generate responses without perceptible delay. This is particularly crucial in applications like **BCIs**, **neuroprosthetics**, and **assistive communication devices**, where the objective is to convert neural signals into meaningful outputs (e.g., cursor movement, robotic arm control) as events are happening [2]. Unlike offline decoding, where data is analyzed after collection, real-time decoding must **acquire, preprocess, analyze, and act upon** brain signals in a continuous and low-latency manner. In practical scenarios, such as a **paralyzed individual using a BCI to control a wheelchair** or a **person with a speech disorder using brain signals to communicate**, the system must work without significant delay. Any lag between the user's intention and the system's response can render the device frustrating or even unusable. Key reasons for needing real-time decoding:

- **Timely user interaction**
- **Safety and reliability** (especially in prosthetic or assistive tech)
- **Natural user experience** that mimics regular movement or speech
- **Clinical relevance**, especially in seizure detection or neurofeedback

4.3.5 Unsupervised Learning and Clustering

In brain signal analysis, particularly in fields like cognitive neuroscience or clinical neurophysiology, acquiring labeled data is often time-consuming, expensive, or infeasible. Many brain signal datasets—such as EEG, MEG, or fMRI—are collected without associated labels indicating cognitive states, mental tasks, or neurological conditions. This is where unsupervised learning becomes essential [7]. Unsupervised learning is a branch of ML that identifies patterns in signals without requiring labeled examples. It aims to group or reduce data based on inherent similarities, helping researchers uncover latent variables, unknown states, or hidden features within brain signals. Practical application of unsupervised learning in neuroscience is given in Table 4.3. Unsupervised learning is crucial in neuroscience because of the following reasons:

- **Lack of labeled data:** Labeling brain states manually is subjective and often requires expert annotation.
- **Discovery of novel patterns:** Unsupervised methods can reveal previously unknown mental states or neural processes.
- **Data exploration:** These techniques help understand the structure of large, complex, and high-dimensional brain signal datasets.

Table 4.3 Practical applications in neuroscience.

Application	Unsupervised method used	Description
Sleep stage classification	K-means, hierarchical clustering	Identifying REM, NREM, and awake stages from EEG without labeled data [7].
Mental workload detection	Autoencoders, K-means	Grouping brain patterns under low/high workload during tasks.
Cognitive state discovery	Autoencoders + clustering	Detecting patterns related to memory, attention, or fatigue.
Neurological disorder subtyping	Hierarchical clustering	Uncovering patient subgroups in epilepsy, ADHD, or Alzheimer's.

- **Preprocessing:** They are often used as a first step before applying supervised models, such as in feature extraction **or** data segmentation.

Key Techniques in Unsupervised Learning and Their Application in Brain Signals

a. **K-Means Clustering: K-means** is a widely used algorithm that partitions data into k distinct groups (clusters) based on feature similarity.
    - o Each data point is assigned to the cluster whose centroid is closest.
    - o The algorithm iteratively updates the centroids to minimize the distance of the data points to their respective centroids.

- **Use in brain decoding:**

    - o Classifying **sleep stages** based on EEG signal patterns.
    - o Separating different **cognitive load levels** during task performance.
    - o Grouping participants based on **mental workload** or **emotional states**.

- **Advantage:** Simple and computationally efficient for large datasets.

b. **Hierarchical Clustering:** It builds a dendrogram of nested clusters. It eliminates the need to predefine the number of clusters.

- **Types:**

    - o **Agglomerative:** Bottom-up approach (starts with individual data points and merges them).
    - o **Divisive:** Top-down approach (starts with one large cluster and splits it).

- **Use in brain decoding:**

    - o Studying **functional connectivity** across brain regions.

- Identifying **temporal states** in continuous EEG data.
- Analyzing **brain disorder subtypes** (e.g., grouping patients with different depression profiles).

- **Advantage**: Allows exploration of different levels of data grouping.

c. **Autoencoders:** It is a type of neural network used for non-linear dimensionality reduction and feature learning.

- Composed of an **encoder** that compresses the data and a **decoder** that reconstructs it.
- The compressed representation captures the most relevant features.

- **Use in brain decoding:**

- Discovering **latent variables** in neural recordings.
- **Noise reduction** in EEG or fMRI data.
- Pretraining for more complex models.

- **Advantage:** Capable of capturing complex, nonlinear relationships in the data.

4.4 Signal Preprocessing and Feature Extraction

Preprocessing is a vital step in the pipeline of brain signal decoding, ensuring that raw neural data becomes usable for machine learning algorithms. The raw signals captured from the brain (e.g., EEG, fMRI) often contain noise and artifacts that can confuse meaningful patterns. Preprocessing helps reduce these confounding elements, isolate significant features, and prepare the data for robust machine learning analysis. This step typically involves:

Filtering: Filtering is the process of removing unwanted components from brain signals to enhance data quality. Neural signals are prone to contamination by different types of noise, like high-frequency noise (which includes electronic interference or random fluctuations not related to brain activity) and physiological artifacts (signals from eye movements, i.e., electrooculographic artifacts; muscle contraction, i.e., electromyographic artifacts, and heartbeats can interfere with neural data). In the filtering process, two types of filters are used: bandpass filters and notch filters.

a) **Bandpass Filters:** These are commonly used to retain frequencies of interest while removing irrelevant high-frequency or low-frequency noise. For example, in EEG data, a typical bandpass filter might retain frequencies between 0.5 and 50 Hz, as this range encompasses most neural activity.
b) **Notch Filters:** These are utilized to eliminate certain frequencies, e.g., 50/60 Hz powerline noise.

High-frequency noise and artifact removal, therefore, constitute the filtering process (e.g., eye movement, muscle contraction) [11].

Segmentation: Segmentation pertains to the act of partitioning continuous neural signals into short and manageable segments or epochs. It is a crucial step in analyzing brain signals for event-related studies at discrete time intervals. Segmentation is used to simplify data analysis, as the signal can be cut into uniform time windows. It aligns the brain signals with a specific stimulus or event (e.g., task onset or button press). There are two approaches for segmentation:

a) **Fixed-length segmentation:** Dividing the signal into equal-length windows, such as 1-second intervals.
b) **Event-related segmentation:** Extracting segments around specific events or triggers, such as stimulus presentation or motor actions.
    - **Feature Extraction:** The most crucial step in brain signal decoding. Features are extracted from raw signals to represent essential information. Common features include:
        - **Time-domain features:** Obtained from the raw signal in the time domain to capture basic statistical properties. For example, mean, variance, skewness, kurtosis, etc. Time-domain features are often used in tasks like emotion recognition, where overall trends in brain activity are meaningful.
        - **Frequency-domain features:** These features are derived by converting the signal into the frequency domain using methods, like fast Fourier transform (FFT).

These features reflect how energy is distributed across different frequency bands. Common frequency bands are shown in Table 4.4. Key features of the frequency domain are the power spectral density and the band. Frequency-domain features are widely used in EEG-based studies for tasks such as stress detection and mental workload assessment.

- **Time-frequency features:** Time-frequency features combine information from both the time and frequency domains to capture how the frequency content of a signal evolves over time. Wavelet transform and STFT techniques are used for extracting features. Time-frequency features are particularly useful in detecting transient brain events, such as epileptic seizures or event-related potentials as given in Table 4.4.
- **Connectivity features:** Connectivity features measure the functional relationships of various brain regions. These features play a critical role in understanding brain network dynamics. Two types of connectivity are used: functional connectivity and effective connectivity. Connectivity features are often used in fMRI or MEG studies to explore brain networks related to tasks like memory, attention, and decision-making

Feature extraction is the most critical step in preprocessing because it transforms raw signals into meaningful representations that machine learning models can analyze. Features are quantitative metrics that summarize specific aspects of brain activity. Different types of features provide insights into various dimensions of neural signals.

Table 4.4 EEG bands and associated brain activities.

Band	Frequency range	Application
δ	0.5–4 Hz	deep sleep and relaxation
θ	4–8 Hz	memory and learning processes
α	8–13 Hz	relaxation and idle states
β	13–30 Hz	active thinking and motor activity

4.5 Challenges in Brain Signal Decoding

Brain signal decoding is a challenging task due to several factors:

1. **Noise and Artifacts:** Brain signals are often contaminated by noise from various sources (e.g., muscle activity, eye blinks, electrical interference). Effective preprocessing techniques are necessary to mitigate these [8].
2. **Inter-individual Variability:** Different individuals' brain signals vary greatly, and models trained on any person's data may not generalize well to others. Personalized approaches and transfer learning are often required [8].
3. **High Dimensionality:** Brain signal data is usually high-dimensional, meaning there are many features per sample, which can lead to overfitting in machine learning models. Dimensionality reduction techniques and regularization methods can help tackle this issue [11].
4. **Real-time Decoding:** For applications like BCIs, decoding brain signals in real time poses computational and latency challenges [14].

4.6 Applications of Machine Learning in Brain Signal Decoding

ML has found numerous applications in brain signal decoding, ranging from medical diagnosis to advanced neurotechnology. Some key applications include:

1. **Brain-Computer Interfaces:** BCIs let the brain communicate directly with machines. Machine learning algorithms decode brain signals to control robotic limbs, computers, or even assistive devices for individuals with disabilities [14].
2. **Neurofeedback:** Neurofeedback techniques use real-time brain signal decoding to help individuals control their brain activity. Machine learning algorithms interpret the brain's signals and provide feedback to optimize brain states for improved cognitive performance or mental health [3].
3. **Disease Diagnosis:** ML-based brain signal analysis can be used to detect neurological conditions like epilepsy,

Parkinson's disease, and schizophrenia. Through classification of brain signal patterns, these models help in early detection & monitoring of disease progression [9].

4. **Cognitive State Monitoring:** Machine learning helps monitor cognitive states, such as attention, stress, or fatigue, through real-time decoding of brain signals. These applications are particularly useful in fields like education, aviation, and healthcare [10].

4.7 Future Trends in Brain Signal Decoding

The field of brain signal decoding is rapidly evolving with the advancement of machine learning techniques and neuroimaging technologies. Some exciting trends are:

- **Deep Learning:** The techniques like CNNs and RNNs are gaining traction for brain signal analysis, particularly in handling complex, sequential data [17].
- **Real-Time Decoding Systems:** With improvements in computational power and algorithms, real-time brain signal decoding will become more reliable, enabling more practical applications in BCIs and neurofeedback.
- **Interfacing with Artificial Intelligence (AI):** Integrating AI systems with brain decoding technology can open new frontiers in understanding brain functions and creating advanced neurotechnological tools for medical and cognitive enhancement purposes.

4.8 Conclusion

Machine learning is revolutionizing the way we interpret brain signals and decode the activity of the brain. By utilizing algorithms that can handle high-dimensional, noisy data, we can unlock new possibilities in neurotechnology, healthcare, and cognitive research. However, the challenges of noise, inter-individual variability, and real-time performance need to be addressed to make brain signal decoding more effective and widespread.

This chapter serves as an introduction to the fundamental concepts of ML in brain signal decoding. As technology advances and new methods emerge, the possibilities for a better understanding of the brain and creating assistive devices become more promising.

AI disclosure statement: The author acknowledges the use of AI-based tools for minor language editing or grammatical correction. However, all intellectual contributions, analyses, and conclusions presented in this chapter are entirely the author's own.

Bibliography

1. Bashivan, P., Rish, I., Yeasin, M., Codella, N., Learning representations from EEG with deep recurrent-convolutional neural networks, arXiv preprint arXiv:1511.06448, 2016.
2. Lotte, F., Congedo, M., Lécuyer, A., Lamarche, F., Arnaldi, B., A review of classification algorithms for EEG-based brain–computer interfaces. *J. Neural Eng.*, 4, 2, R1–R13, 2007.
3. Breiman, L., Random forests. *Mach. Learn.*, *45*, 1, 5–32, 2001.
4. Cortes, C. and Vapnik, V., Support-vector networks. *Mach. Learn.*, *20*, 3, 273–297, 1995.
5. Schirrmeister, R.T., *et al.*, Deep learning with convolutional neural networks for EEG decoding and visualization. *Hum. Brain Mapp.*, 38, 11, 5391–5420, 2017.
6. Makeig, S., Bell, A.J., Jung, T.P., Sejnowski, T.J., Independent component analysis of electroencephalographic data. *Adv. Neural Inf. Process. Syst.*, 8, 1996.
7. Roy, Y., *et al.*, Deep learning-based electroencephalography analysis: a systematic review. *J. Neural Eng.*, 16, 5, 051001, 2019.
8. Hammond, D.C., Neurofeedback treatment of depression and anxiety. *J. Neurother.*, *15*, 4, 35–42, 2011.
9. Hedrich, M., *et al.*, Brain signal artifacts in EEG and ECoG: Challenges for signal decoding. *NeuroImage*, *199*, 105–114, 2019.
10. He, H., *et al.*, Transfer learning for brain-computer interfaces: A Euclidean space data alignment approach. *IEEE Trans. Biomed. Eng.*, *66*, 2, 462–470, 2019.
11. Jung, T.P., *et al.*, Removing electroencephalographic artifacts: Comparison between ICA and PCA. *IEEE Trans. Biomed. Eng.*, *47*, 1, 1–11, 2000.
12. Lal, T.N., *et al.*, Support vector machines for brain-computer interfaces. *IEEE Trans. Biomed. Eng.*, *51*, 6, 1003–1010, 2004.
13. LeCun, Y., *et al.*, Deep learning. *Nature*, *521*, 7553, 436–444, 2015.
14. Lega, B.C., *et al.*, Brain-computer interfaces in neurodegenerative diseases. *Neurobiol. Aging*, *78*, 111–121, 2019.

15. Lebedev, M.A. and Nicolelis, M.A., Brain–machine interfaces: Past, present and future. *Trends Neurosci.*, *29*, 9, 536–546, 2006.
16. Ramoser, H., *et al.*, Independent component analysis (ICA) for brain-computer interfaces. *IEEE Trans. Biomed. Eng.*, *47*, 3, 293–298, 2000.
17. Schirrmeister, R.T., *et al.*, Deep learning with convolutional neural networks for brain mapping and decoding of brain activity. *NeuroImage*, *146*, 1–9, 2017.

5

Deep Learning Architectures for Brain Signal Processing

Goldwyn Sudhakar Jebaraj, Vidhya S. and Konguvel Elango*

School of Electronics Engineering, Vellore Institute of Technology, Vellore, Tamil Nadu, India

Abstract

This chapter provides an overview of deep learning systems and their application in complex brain signal processing. It illustrates how modern neural network models are built upon decades of scientific inquiry, tracing the evolution of neuroscience and brain signal monitoring. Core deep learning architectures, including convolutional neural networks (CNNs), recurrent neural networks (RNNs), graph neural networks (GNNs), autoencoders (AEs), and variational autoencoders (VAEs), are thoroughly examined. The chapter clarifies how their distinct design principles address challenges posed by highly structured, time-varying, and network-based neural data. To enhance conceptual comprehension and demonstrate real-world applicability, this chapter incorporates practical examples and exercises alongside technical explanations. Additionally, it meticulously analyzes the utility of these architectures across diverse brain imaging modalities, such as functional magnetic resonance imaging (fMRI), intracranial EEG/electrocorticography (ECoG), neuronal spike recordings, structural MRI, diffusion tensor imaging (DTI), and positron emission tomography/single-photon emission computed tomography (PET/SPECT) imaging. The final section of the chapter explores potential directions for future research and emerging trends, emphasizing promising opportunities for both foundational brain studies and advanced clinical applications. This chapter serves as a vital resource and guide for experts, students, and professionals in brain signal processing.

**Corresponding author*: konguvel.e@vit.ac.in

Tawseef Ahmed Teli, Syed Immamul Ansarullah, Arun Kumar Rana, Suman Lata Tripathi and Kashif Nisar (eds.) Brain-to-Computer Interfaces Using Machine Learning and Deep Learning, (83–138) © 2026 Scrivener Publishing LLC

***Keywords*:** Deep learning, brain signal processing, electroencephalography (EEG), functional magnetic resonance imaging (FMRI), convolutional neural networks (CNNs), recurrent neural networks (RNNs), graph neural networks (GNNs), autoencoders (AEs)

5.1 Introduction to Deep Learning in Neuroscience

Neuroscience is the study of the brain, which contains millions of interconnected neurons. By leveraging deep learning techniques, researchers are now able to map brain structure and function with remarkable accuracy, producing vast amounts of data ranging from continuous time-series signals to complex volumetric scans. So, modern neuroimaging is one of the most important parts of brain study today. It connects hundreds of years of research that started with philosophical questions and ended with complex scientific investigations. Chemical and electrical messages dance in the brain, which is an amazingly complex biological system that controls our thoughts, feelings, and actions. Thoughts have been drawn to its secrets for thousands of years. From the first logical thoughts in ancient Greece, by people like Alcmaeon of Croton, who dared to say that the brain is where intelligence really lives, to Galen's in-depth studies of anatomy all over the Roman Empire, people have been trying to figure out how things work. Even though the first ideas, like Galen's "ventricular hypothesis," were very simple, they were very important because they set the stage for a scientific journey that would last hundreds of years.

The important finding of bioelectricity was the start of our empirical journey into the brain's dynamic core. In the late 1700s, Luigi Galvani did important research on frog muscles that showed how electrical impulses are essential to all living things. This important realization made it possible for Richard Caton to do the amazing thing that he did in 1875: he recorded the first direct electrical activity from animal brains. Yet, the most important event in human history may have happened in 1924, when Hans Berger did what seemed impossible: he recorded the first non-invasive activity of the human brain. This was the first step toward electroencephalography (EEG). Scientists could now look directly into the brain's life, changing states by measuring its brainwaves from the scalp. At the same time, great neuroanatomists like Santiago Ramón y Cajal were carefully drawing the neuron itself, proving that it is the basic building block of the nervous system and, by extension, the cell that makes all brain functions possible.

Then, in the middle of the 20th century, structural imaging became a huge deal. Computed tomography (CT) scans came out in the 1970s, and magnetic resonance imaging (MRI) scans came out right after in the 1980s. Not only did these technologies make visualization better, but they also changed the way we saw brain anatomy by giving us unprecedented levels of detail that let us find problems, tumors, and lesions exactly. But it wasn't until the 1990s that functional neuroimaging really took off. Here, positron emission tomography (PET) and functional magnetic resonance imaging (fMRI) came into being. Indirect measurement techniques such as magnetoencephalography (MEG), which records the brain's magnetic fields to provide real-time information, and electrocorticography (ECoG), an advanced invasive method, have revolutionized the field of neuroscience.

5.2 Foundational Deep Learning Architectures

Deep learning models represent some of the most advanced computational architectures capable of interpreting brain signals. These models employ various core neural network algorithms to address a wide range of research problems in neuroscience.

5.2.1 Convolutional Neural Networks (CNNs)

Convolutional neural networks (CNNs) are designed to handle the complexity and high dimensionality of neuroscience data through their grid-like structure. They can process various input types, such as 2D images, 3D volumes, extended video sequences, and long-term EEG recordings.

The main idea: How Convolution Works:
Convolution is a mathematical process that uses a sliding filter to detect patterns in brain signals. It's a very advanced way to find patterns in data that is fed into it. A filter or kernel (K), which is a small, learnable matrix or tensor at the heart of this process, works as a compact, trainable pattern to find specific local features in the data. This could be anything from a line in a picture to a peak in a time series or even a small pattern of activity in a group of brain regions. Importantly, the numbers in this kernel are not set in stone; instead, they are learnt by the network as it is trained to find the best features for the job at hand, like telling the difference between brain states that are healthy and those that aren't.

The kernel systematically "slides" (or "convolves") across the entire input data (I). At each position, it performs an **element-wise multiplication** between its own values and the corresponding values of the small local region of the input it currently covers. All these products are then **summed up** to produce a single output value. This value quantifies the degree to which the specific feature represented by the kernel was detected at that location in the input. As the kernel traverses the entire input and repeats this multiplication-and-summation process, it generates a new matrix, or tensor, termed a **feature map** (F). Each value in this feature map indicates the presence and strength of the feature detected by that specific kernel at the corresponding location in the original input. A high value signifies a strong match for the feature, while a low or negative value indicates a weak or inverse match. It is common for a convolutional layer to employ *multiple* distinct kernels, each learning to detect a different feature, thereby generating multiple feature maps.

The mathematical representation of a 2D convolution for an input image I and a filter (kernel) K, yielding the output feature map F, is calculated as:

$$F(i,j) = \sum_m \sum_n I(i-m, j-n) \cdot K(m,n) \tag{5.1}$$

In Equation (5.1), $I(i-m, j-n)$ represents the value of the input image at coordinates $(i-m, j-n)$, and $K(m,n)$ represents the value of the filter at coordinates (m,n). The summations are performed over all dimensions of the filter. This equation formally encapsulates the sliding and multiplying process, demonstrating how each point (i,j) in the output feature map is derived from a weighted sum of a local neighborhood in the input, with the weights precisely defined by the filter.

Illustrative Example: 2D Convolution

To clarify the convolution operation, consider a simple 2D input matrix (e.g., a small segment of a brain image) and a 2x2 filter:

Input Matrix (I):

$$\begin{pmatrix} 1 & 0 & 1 & 0 \\ 0 & 1 & 0 & 1 \\ 1 & 0 & 1 & 0 \\ 0 & 1 & 0 & 1 \end{pmatrix}$$

Filter (K):

$$\begin{pmatrix} 1 & 0 \\ 0 & 1 \end{pmatrix}$$

Let's compute the first element of the output feature map F(0,0) by placing the filter at the top-left corner of the input. Equation (5.2) demonstrates the resulting multiplication and summation:

$$F(0,0) = (1\cdot 1) + (0\cdot 0) + (0\cdot 0) + (1\cdot 1) = 1 + 0 + 0 + 1 = 2 \tag{5.2}$$

Next, slide the filter one step to the right to compute F(0,1). Equation (5.3) shows that the output for this position is:

$$F(0,1) = (0\cdot 1) + (1\cdot 0) + (1\cdot 0) + (0\cdot 1) = 0 + 0 + 0 + 0 = 0 \tag{5.3}$$

By continuing this process across the entire input, the full feature map is generated. This step-by-step multiplication and summation process allows the filter to detect specific patterns (in this case, a diagonal line pattern) within the input data.

Key Characteristics and Components within a CNN Workflow

Some of the most important features and parts of a CNN workflow CNNs include more than just the basic convolution action. They have many extra layers and mechanisms that make them better at processing complex data. CNNs share parameters, which means that a single filter (or kernel) is applied repeatedly to all of the input. This makes it possible to learn a lot fewer parameters than with a fully connected network. This not only speeds up computations but also keeps them from fitting too well, which is especially helpful when working with high-dimensional data like medical pictures.

The main aim of finding even a small change in the data (neuroscience images, videos, etc.) is found as a feature by moving the CNN's small filter again. In neuroscience, this is more important. This creates translational invariance, which lets the network find a feature no matter where it is in the data. In neuroscience, where brain patterns may show small changes in space between people or over time, this trait is especially important. This CNN is also built in layers, helping to learn these features in a hierarchical way. The lower layers find simple, low-level features, like basic oscillatory patterns in brain signals, and the higher layers combine these to find more complex and abstract features like specific cognitive states or pathological signatures.

A common CNN workflow also includes "activation layers are used to understand the complex, non-linear relationship in brain signals." A rectified linear unit (ReLU) is what the ReLU function does. It comes after each neural step to make the model less linear. This non-linearity is essential for enabling the network to capture the complex, non-linear relationships present in brain signals that purely linear models cannot represent. The ReLU function is defined as in Equation (5.4):

$$f(x) = \max(0, x) \tag{5.4}$$

Following activation, **pooling layers** (e.g., max pooling, average pooling) systematically reduce the spatial dimensions (width, height, or depth) of the feature maps. This downsampling serves a dual purpose: it decreases the computational cost for subsequent layers and increases the model's robustness by rendering detected features less sensitive to small shifts or distortions in the input, such as minor head movements in an fMRI scan. Max pooling, for example, selects the maximum value within a predefined window, effectively retaining the most prominent feature response. After several convolutional and pooling stages, the high-level, abstract features learnt by the network are typically flattened into a one-dimensional vector and fed into one or more standard **fully connected layers**. These layers globally combine the extracted features to make the final prediction, such as classifying a disease or decoding a specific brain state. The network culminates in an **output layer**, which produces the ultimate prediction, tailored to the specific task (e.g., probabilities for different classes in a classification problem, or a continuous value in a regression problem).

Figure 5.1 illustrates a typical sequence of operations within a convolutional neural network. Input data, such as a 2D EEG topo-map or an fMRI slice, undergoes successive transformations through convolutional, activation, and pooling layers to extract hierarchical features. These features are then flattened and fed into fully connected layers for the final prediction.

Subtypes of CNNs for Brain Signal Processing

The dimensionality of a CNN typically refers to the number of dimensions over which the convolutional kernel slides, making different subtypes suitable for distinct brain signal data structures. **1D convolutional neural networks (1D CNNs)** employ a kernel that slides along a single dimension.

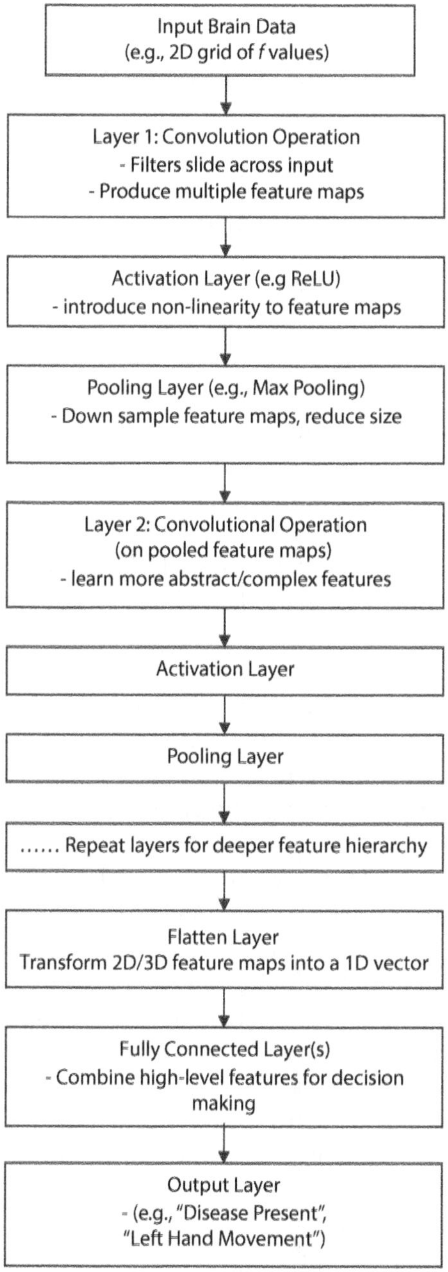

Figure 5.1 Generic CNN workflow.

1D CNNs are primarily used for sequential data, where patterns evolve over time. This includes data such as raw EEG/MEG time series from a single channel or spike train data, which are processed by a sliding 1D CNN kernel. Their applications include the detection of specific transient events (e.g., spikes, K-complexes) in EEG, the classification of short segments of brain activity, and the processing of individual neuronal firing patterns.

In contrast, **2D convolutional neural networks (2D CNNs)** utilize a kernel that slides across two dimensions, typically height and width. The images from fMRI, structural MRI, or PET scans, as well as 2D topographic maps of EEG/MEG activity across the scalp, are ideal representations for this type of CNN. These applications can include analyzing single slices from fMRI, structural MRI, or PET scans, or examining 2D topographic maps of EEG/MEG activity across the scalp at a given time point. Their applications span image classification (e.g., classifying brain tumor presence from an MRI slice), pattern recognition on EEG topo-plots, and segmenting brain regions in 2D.

For truly volumetric data, **3D convolutional neural networks (3D CNNs)** are employed, where the kernel slides across three dimensions (height, width, and depth/slices). These are well-suited for processing entire 3D structural MRI scans, PET scans, or full 4D fMRI datasets, where the fourth dimension (time) can be treated as additional "depth" or channels in the initial layers. Their utility extends to end-to-end classification of brain diseases from whole brain volumes, segmenting intricate brain structures in 3D, and analyzing spatiotemporal patterns in fMRI by treating time as the third "spatial" dimension.

A specialized and efficient variant is the **depthwise separable convolutional neural network**. This architecture decomposes the standard convolution into two distinct steps: a depthwise convolution, where a single filter is applied to *each input channel independently*, followed by a pointwise convolution (a 1x1 convolution) that combines the outputs from the depthwise convolution across channels. This decomposition significantly reduces the number of learnable parameters and computational cost compared to standard convolutions, often without a substantial loss in accuracy. Consequently, these models are more efficient, faster to train, and particularly suitable for deployment on resource-constrained devices, making them common in lightweight EEG models (e.g., EEGNet) for mobile brain-computer interfaces (BCIs) and other applications where computational efficiency is paramount.

Practice Exercises: Convolutional Neural Networks

These exercises are designed to test your understanding of the core concepts and applications of convolutional neural networks.

Q1: Convolution Operation: Given the following 3x3 input matrix I and a 2x2 filter K:

Input Matrix (I):

$$\begin{pmatrix} 2 & 1 & 3 \\ 0 & 4 & 1 \\ 5 & 2 & 0 \end{pmatrix}$$

Filter (K):

$$\begin{pmatrix} -1 & 1 \\ 0 & 2 \end{pmatrix}$$

Calculate the output feature map F, assuming a stride of 1 and no padding. Show your step-by-step calculations for each element of the output feature map.

Q2: ReLU Activation: Apply the ReLU activation function to the following feature map:

$$\begin{pmatrix} -0.5 & 1.2 & 0 \\ 2.1 & -0.1 & 0.8 \\ -1.0 & 3.0 & -0.2 \end{pmatrix}$$

What is the resulting output?

Q3: Max Pooling: Given the following 4x4 feature map, apply a 2x2 max pooling operation with a stride of 2:

$$\begin{pmatrix} 1 & 5 & 2 & 8 \\ 3 & 2 & 7 & 1 \\ 4 & 0 & 6 & 9 \\ 1 & 3 & 0 & 5 \end{pmatrix}$$

What is the resulting pooled feature map?

Q4: Parameter Sharing: Explain the concept of "parameter sharing" on CNNs. How does it benefit the processing of brain imaging data (e.g., MRI scans)?

Q5: CNN Subtypes: For each of the following brain signal data types, suggest the most appropriate CNN subtype (1D, 2D, 3D, or depthwise separable) and briefly explain why:

1. Raw, continuous EEG data from a single electrode channel.
2. A single slice of a structural MRI scan.
3. A full 3D fMRI volume captured at one time point.
4. A lightweight CNN model for real-time EEG classification on a mobile device.

Q6: CNN Design for Brain Disease Classification: You are tasked with designing a preliminary CNN architecture to classify whether a patient has Alzheimer's disease based on their 3D structural MRI brain scan.

1. What type of CNN (e.g., 1D, 2D, or 3D) would be most suitable for this task, and why?
2. Describe the typical sequence of layers you would include in your CNN architecture, explaining the purpose of each type of layer (e.g., convolutional, activation, pooling, flattening, fully connected, output).
3. Briefly explain how "hierarchical feature learning" would apply in this context, from raw pixel data to a final diagnosis.

Q7: Understanding CNN Advantages in Brain Signal Analysis: Consider the challenges of analyzing large brain signal datasets (e.g., fMRI or multi-channel EEG). Discuss how the key characteristics of CNNs, specifically *parameter sharing* and *translational invariance*, are advantageous in this domain. Provide a specific example for each characteristic related to brain signal processing.

5.2.2 Recurrent Neural Networks (RNNs)

The comprehension of sequential data, where the order of elements is paramount, and the interpretation of a current element depends on preceding elements, necessitates specialized processing architectures. This characteristic is particularly relevant for many types of brain signals, which are inherently time series in nature. **Recurrent neural networks (RNNs)** are specifically designed to address this requirement. Unlike traditional neural networks or even convolutional neural networks (CNNs), which typically process inputs as independent units or fixed-size grids, RNNs are perfect for jobs that need to capture dependencies between times. In an RNN, the output at each step relies on both the current input and the information that has been built up from the inputs that came before it.

Core Principle: The "Memory Loop"
An RNN is defined by its repeated link, which is often called a "memory loop." This structure lets the network keep an internal, or hidden, state (h_t) that sends information about the parts that came before it. The RNN gets two inputs at each time step t: the current input (x_t) and the previous hidden state $((h_{t-1})$. These two inputs together show the sequence's past background. The network then takes these inputs and puts them together to make an output (y_t). It also changes its hidden state (h_t) to and sends this to the next step. The RNN can describe temporal patterns and contextual dependencies over time thanks to its chain-like structure.

Figure 5.2 illustrates the general pipeline for processing EEG data with deep learning, from raw time series to actionable insights.

In this general pipeline, x_t represents the input at time step t, h_t represents the hidden state (memory) at time step t, and y_t represents the output at time step t.

The mathematical representation of a simple RNN's hidden state h_t at time step t is typically calculated as:

$$h_t = \tanh(W_{hh}h_{t-1} + W_{xh}x_t + b_h) \tag{5.5}$$

And the output y_t at time step t is:

$$y_t = W_{hy}h_t + b_y \tag{5.6}$$

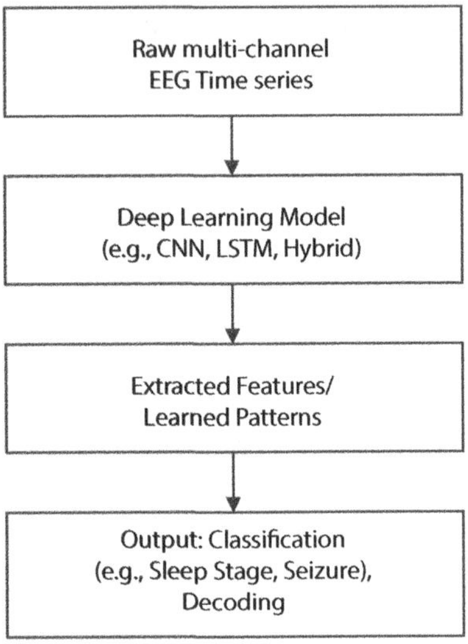

Figure 5.2 Conceptual flow for EEG data processing.

In these Equations (5.5) and (5.6), x_t is the input vector at time step t, h_t is the hidden state vector at time step t, and h_{t-1} is the hidden state vector from the previous time step. $W_{hh}, W_{xh},$ and W_{hy} are learnable weight matrices for the recurrent, input-to-hidden, and hidden-to-output connections, respectively, while b_h and b_y are bias vectors. The tanh function is a common choice for the activation function. The following example demonstrates how the current hidden state h_t is a function of both the current input x_t and the previous hidden state h_{t-1}, enabling the network to retain and process information from past inputs.

Illustrative Example: Simple RNN Step-by-Step Calculation

To illustrate the operation of a simple RNN, let's consider a scenario with a single input feature and a single hidden unit.

Assume the following initial values and learnt weights:

- Initial hidden state $h_0 = 0$
- Input-to-hidden weight $W_{xh} = 0.5$
- Hidden-to-hidden weight $W_{hh} = 0.8$
- Hidden bias $b_h = 0.1$
- Hidden-to-output weight $W_{hy} = 1.0$
- Output bias $b_y = 0$

Consider an input sequence $X = [x_1, x_2, x_3] = [1.0, 2.0, 0.5]$. We will use the tanh activation function.

Time Step 1 ($t = 1$):
Input $x_1 = 1.0$, previous hidden state $h_0 = 0$.
Calculate h_1:

$$h_1 = \tanh(W_{hh}h_0 + W_{xh}x_1 + b_h)$$
$$h_1 = \tanh\big((0.8 \cdot 0) + (0.5 \cdot 1.0) + 0.1\big)$$
$$h_1 = \tanh(0 + 0.5 + 0.1)$$
$$= \tanh(0.6) \approx 0.537$$

Calculate y_1:

$$y_1 = W_{hy}h_1 + b_y$$
$$y_1 = (1.0 \cdot 0.537) + 0 = 0.537$$

Time Step 2 ($t = 2$):
Input $x_2 = 2.0$, previous hidden state $h_1 = 0.537$.
Calculate h_2:

$$h_2 = \tanh(W_{hh}h_1 + W_{xh}x_2 + b_h)$$
$$h_2 = \tanh\big((0.8 \cdot 0.537) + (0.5 \cdot 2.0) + 0.1\big)$$
$$h_2 = \tanh(0.4296 + 1.0 + 0.1)$$
$$= \tanh(1.5296) \approx 0.910$$

Calculate y_2:

$$y_2 = W_{hy}h_2 + b_y$$
$$y_2 = (1.0 \cdot 0.910) + 0 = 0.910$$

Time Step 3 ($t = 3$):
Input $x_3 = 0.5$, previous hidden state $h_2 = 0.910$.

Calculate h_3:

$$\begin{aligned} h_3 &= \tanh(W_{hh}h_2 + W_{xh}x_3 + b_h) \\ h_3 &= \tanh\big((0.8\cdot 0.910) + (0.5\cdot 0.5) + 0.1\big) \\ h_3 &= \tanh(0.728 + 0.25 + 0.1) \\ &= \tanh(1.078) \approx 0.792 \end{aligned}$$

Calculate y_3:

$$y_3 = (1.0\cdot 0.792) + 0 = 0.792$$

This example demonstrates how the hidden state at each step incorporates information from the current input and the context from previous steps, showcasing the RNN's ability to process sequential data.

Key Challenge: Vanishing/Exploding Gradients

Here's the corrected and integrated version of your text, addressing the grammar and flow issues while retaining your intended points:

Despite their capabilities in processing sequential data, a simple RNN encounters a significant challenge during training known as the vanishing and exploding gradients problems. Since RNN use repeated multiplication of gradients through the recurrent connection over many steps of time, challenges arise. In the case of vanishing gradients, as information propagates backward through time during backpropagation, the gradients (signals that guide learning) can become extremely small. This phenomenon makes it exceedingly difficult for the network to learn long-range dependencies, effectively causing it to "forget" information from the distant past within the sequence. Conversely, exploding gradients lead to unstable training with the gradient becoming excessively large. This also leads to erratic weight updates and potential divergence of the learning process. These problems severely limit the practical ability of simple RNNs to learn from very long sequences, which are common in many brain signal applications, such as analyzing hours of continuous EEG data or long fMRI time courses. This fundamental limitation inspired the development of more sophisticated RNN architectures designed to mitigate these gradient issues.

Subtypes of RNNs for Brain Signal Processing (Addressing the Memory Problem)

To address the memory constraints of basic RNNs, two major variants emerged as the foundation for modern sequence learning: long short-term memory (LSTM) networks and gated recurrent units (GRUs).

The long short-term memory (LSTM) and gated recurrent unit are proposed to overcome the limitations of simple RNNs. This modification makes the RNN address the memory constraints while handling long sequential data.

Long Short-Term Memory (LSTM) Networks: LSTM (long short-term memory) introduces gates that control the information that comes in, stays, or leaves the memory of each unit. Therefore, three gates, input, forget, and output gates, are used to perform the respective tasks. This sophisticated design allows LSTMs to selectively remember or forget information, enabling them to capture long-range dependencies effectively. Since the data is handled wisely, the memory is managed efficiently by keeping only the relevant data and leaving the unwanted data without any loss, and it is able to capture the patterns from seconds to minutes. This is a key skill for figuring out patterns in continuous brain signals like slow changes in neural rhythms or cognitive states. Because of this, LSTMs are used for many things, like finding seizures, figuring out the stage of sleep using long EEG records, figuring out what movements people are trying to make from ECoG signals, and looking at how functional connectivity changes over time in fMRI time series.

Gated Recurrent Units (GRUs): In GRUs, the gates of LSTM are combined into one cell to make it easier to interpret the operation. These alternatives to LSTMs are simpler and can work similarly in many situations. This smaller design makes it easier to use less computing power and speeds up training. This makes GRUs a good choice when resources are limited or when testing needs to happen quickly. Even though GRUs have a simpler structure, they still have the important ability to record long-range dependencies. This makes them perfect for similar tasks to LSTMs, such as classifying long EEG sequences and modelling changing brain states when working with time-series neuroimaging data.

Practice Exercises: Convolutional Neural Networks

These exercises are designed to test your understanding of the core concepts and applications of recurrent neural networks.

Q1: Simple RNN Step Calculation: Consider a simple RNN with the following parameters:

- Initial hidden state $h_0 = 0.2$
- Input-to-hidden weight $W_{xh} = 0.7$
- Hidden-to-hidden weight $W_{hh} = 0.6$
- Hidden bias $b_h = 0.05$
- Hidden-to-output weight $W_{hy} = 0.9$
- Output bias $b_y = 0.1$

Assume the activation function is ReLU $f(x) = \max(0, x))$ for both the hidden state and output. Given an input sequence $X = [x_1, x_2] = [1.0, 0.5]$:

4. Calculate the hidden state h_1 and output y_1 for time step 1.
5. Calculate the hidden state h_2 and output y_2 for time step 2.

Show your step-by-step calculations.

Q2: Vanishing Gradient Problem: Explain the "vanishing gradient problem" in simple RNNs. Why is this a significant issue for analyzing long brain signal recordings (e.g., hours of EEG data)?

Q3: LSTM Gates: Conceptually, how do the "gates" in an LSTM network help to overcome the vanishing gradient problem encountered in simple RNNs? Briefly describe the role of at least two different types of gates.

Q4: RNN vs. CNN for Time Series: You have a dataset of single-channel EEG time series, each representing a 5-second segment of brain activity. You want to classify these segments into one of three cognitive states (e.g., relaxed, focused, or drowsy).

6. Would an RNN (e.g., LSTM) or a 1D CNN typically be more suitable for this task? Justify your answer based on their core strengths.
7. Can a hybrid model combine the strengths of both? If so, how?

Q5: Designing an RNN for Sleep Stage Classification: You are tasked with designing a deep learning model to automatically classify sleep stages (Wake, N1, N2, N3, REM) from continuous, multi-channel EEG recordings collected over an entire night (several hours).

1. What specific type of RNN architecture (e.g., simple RNN, LSTM, or GRU) would you choose for this task, and why?

2. Explain how this chosen architecture would process the continuous EEG data to make predictions for each 30-second epoch of sleep.
3. Discuss the advantages of using an RNN-based approach over a traditional, epoch-by-epoch classification method that treats each 30-second segment independently.

Q6: Temporal Dependencies in Brain Signals: Discuss the importance of capturing "long-term temporal dependencies" in the context of analyzing brain signals for neurological disorders. Provide an example of a neurological disorder where understanding these dependencies using RNNs (or their variants) would be particularly beneficial.

5.2.3 Graph Neural Networks (GNNs)

The analysis of complex relational data, such as social networks, where understanding community structures and information flow is crucial, requires specialized methodologies. Similarly, the brain functions as an intricate network, with neurons forming complex circuits and distinct brain regions interconnected by white matter tracts or exhibiting correlated activity. These structures are best represented as graphs, where individual neurons or brain regions are nodes, and their connections (physical or functional) are edges.

There is a new type of deep learning model called graph neural networks (GNNs) that is intended to work directly on graph-structured data. CNNs work best with grids, and RNNs work best with sequences. GNNs, on the other hand, can learn complex patterns and relationships within freely structured graphs. This makes them very useful for studying brain connectivity and how information moves and is processed across neural networks.

Core Principle: Information Aggregation and Update over a Graph
Basically, GNNs learn a representation (an "embedding") for each node in a graph by collecting information from its peers repeatedly and then updating the node's own representation based on this new information. This process goes back and forth, so each node can learn about its immediate surroundings and, after a few rounds, even parts of the graph that are far away. When talking about a graph, **nodes** (v_i) stand for separate parts of the network, like a single cell or a different part of the brain, like the hippocampus.

Each node might have its own set of information, like the average fMRI signal intensity, the thickness of the cortex, or measurements that are special to a certain area. When two nodes are next to each other, they are connected by **edges** (e_{ij}). In neuroscience, these links could be white matter tracts that connect different areas, functional relationships between fMRI time series, or synaptic links between neurons. Edges can also have attributes, which can be measures like how strong a link is or which way it points. It is basic for graph neural networks (GNNs) to do two things: **message passing** (also called aggregation) and **node update**. During the passing phase, each node gets "messages" from the nodes that are close to it. Using an aggregation function like a sum, mean, or maximum, these new features are put together to make a short summary of the neighborhood's features. After aggregation, each node changes its own picture of features by adding this neighborhood's summary to the ones it already has. In this step of updating, a learnable neural network part, like a small multi-layer perceptron, is often used.

Messages are sent, and nodes are updated repeatedly in this cycle, which is called a network layer. Each time through the process, a node's representation gets better by adding data from peers that are farther away in the graph. In this way GNNs learn representations that consider not only a node's local traits but also its position and impact on the overall network structure through an iterative process. In neuroscientific terms, this lets the model guess how a brain area or cell works in relation to the whole system, which gives us useful information about how the brain is organized at the network level.

Visualizing the Message Passing

Consider a brain network where each circle represents a region and lines denote connections. The process of passing messsages allows information to propagate through this network:

The core mechanism of node feature aggregation and update in a graph neural network is mathematically depicted in Figure 5.3, which shows how each node's representation is iteratively refined by combining information from its neighbors.

For a node v_i, its feature vector $h_i^{(l+1)}$ at layer $(l+1)$ is calculated by aggregating and transforming features from its neighbors $(N(v_i))$ from the previous layer (l):

$$h_i^{(l+1)} = \sigma\left(\sum_{j \in N(v_i) \cup i} \frac{1}{\sqrt{\deg(v_i)\deg(v_j)}} W^{(l)} h_j^{(l)}\right) \tag{5.7}$$

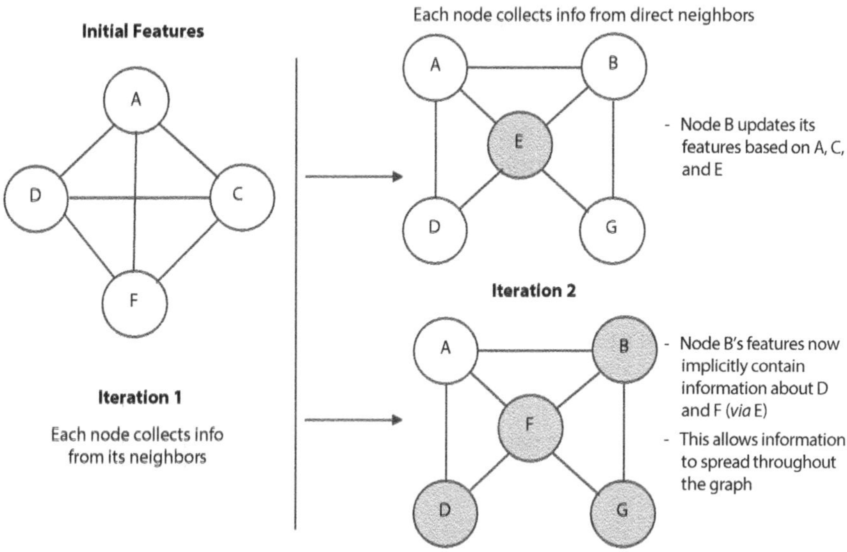

Figure 5.3 Mathematical representation of a simple GNN layer (graph convolutional network - GCN).

In Equation (5.7), $h_i^{(l)}$ is the feature vector of node i at layer $l, N(v_i)$ is the set of neighbors of node v_i, and $W^{(l)}$ is the learnable weight matrix for layer l. $\deg(v_i)$ represents the degree (number of connections) of node v_i, and σ is a non-linear activation function (e.g., ReLU). The term $\frac{1}{\sqrt{\deg(v_i)\deg(v_j)}}$ serves as a normalization constant (derived from symmetric normalization), which helps prevent features from becoming excessively large and accounts for node degrees. This formula illustrates that each node's new representation is a weighted sum of its own and its neighbors' previous representations, transformed by a learnable weight matrix, and subsequently passed through an activation function.

Illustrative Example: Graph Convolutional Network (GCN) Layer Calculation (Simplified)

To provide a clear, step-by-step understanding of the GNN's core mechanism, we will use a simplified aggregation and update rule that captures the essence of message passing.

Consider a graph with three nodes and their initial features:

- Node 1: $h_1^{(0)} = [1.0, 0.0]$

- Node 2: $h_2^{(0)} = [0.0, 1.0]$
- Node 3: $h_3^{(0)} = [1.0, 1.0]$

Connections: Node 1 is connected to Node 2. Node 2 is connected to Node 1 and Node 3. Node 3 is connected to Node 2. This forms a linear graph structure: 1–2–3.

Let's assume a simple aggregation rule: a node's aggregated feature is the average of its own feature and the features of its direct neighbors from the previous layer. After aggregation, a linear transformation (using a weight matrix $W^{(0)}$) is applied, followed by a ReLU activation function.

Step 1: Aggregation: For each node, we compute an aggregated feature vector (Agg_i) by averaging its own feature and its neighbors' features from layer 0:

- **Node 1's aggregated feature (Agg_1):** Neighbors are Node 2 (and itself).

$$\begin{aligned} Agg_1 &= \left(h_1^{(0)} + h_2^{(0)}\right)/2 \\ &= ([1.0, 0.0] + [0.0, 1.0])/2 \\ &= [0.5, 0.5] \end{aligned}$$

- **Node 2's aggregated feature (Agg_2):** Neighbors are Node 1, Node 3 (and itself).

$$\begin{aligned} Agg_2 &= \left(h_1^{(0)} + h_2^{(0)} + h_3^{(0)}\right)/3 \\ &= ([1.0, 0.0] + [0.0, 1.0] + [1.0, 1.0])/3 \\ &= [2.0/3, 2.0/3] \approx [0.667, 0.667] \end{aligned}$$

- **Node 3's aggregated feature (Agg_3):** Neighbors are Node 2 (and itself).

$$\begin{aligned} Agg_3 &= \left(h_2^{(0)} + h_3^{(0)}\right)/2 \\ &= ([0.0, 1.0] + [1.0, 1.0])/2 \\ &= [0.5, 1.0] \end{aligned}$$

Step 2: Update (Linear Transformation and Activation): Now, we apply a learnable weight matrix $W^{(0)}$ to these aggregated features, followed by the ReLU activation function to compute the new node features for layer 1 $(h_i^{(1)})$. Let's use the following Equation (5.8) $W^{(0)}$:

$$W^{(0)} = \begin{pmatrix} 0.5 & -0.5 \\ 0.5 & 0.5 \end{pmatrix} \tag{5.8}$$

- **Node 1's new feature $(h_1^{(1)})$:**

$$h_1^{(1)} = \text{ReLU}(Agg_1 \cdot W^{(0)})$$

$$\begin{aligned} Agg_1 \cdot W^{(0)} &= [0.5, 0.5]\begin{pmatrix} 0.5 & -0.5 \\ 0.5 & 0.5 \end{pmatrix} \\ &= [(0.5 \cdot 0.5 + 0.5 \cdot 0.5), (0.5 \cdot -0.5 + 0.5 \cdot 0.5)] \\ &= [0.25 + 0.25, -0.25 + 0.25] = [0.5, 0] \end{aligned}$$

$$h_1^{(1)} = \text{ReLU}([0.5, 0]) = [0.5, 0]$$

- **Node 2's new feature $(h_2^{(1)})$:**

$$h_2^{(1)} = \text{ReLU}(Agg_2 \cdot W^{(0)})$$

$$\begin{aligned} Agg_2 \cdot W^{(0)} &= [0.667, 0.667]\begin{pmatrix} 0.5 & -0.5 \\ 0.5 & 0.5 \end{pmatrix} \\ &= [(0.667 \cdot 0.5 + 0.667 \cdot 0.5), (0.667 \cdot -0.5 + 0.667 \cdot 0.5)] \\ &= [0.3335 + 0.3335, -0.3335 + 0.3335] = [0.667, 0] \end{aligned}$$

$$h_2^{(1)} = \text{ReLU}([0.667, 0]) = [0.667, 0]$$

- **Node 3's new feature** ($h_3^{(1)}$):

$$h_3^{(1)} = \text{ReLU}(Agg_3 \cdot W^{(0)})$$

$$Agg_3 \cdot W^{(0)} = [0.5, 1.0]\begin{pmatrix} 0.5 & -0.5 \\ 0.5 & 0.5 \end{pmatrix}$$

$$= [(0.5 \cdot 0.5 + 1.0 \cdot 0.5), (0.5 \cdot -0.5 + 1.0 \cdot 0.5)]$$

$$= [0.25 + 0.5, -0.25 + 0.5] = [0.75, 0.25]$$

$$h_3^{(1)} = \text{ReLU}([0.75, 0.25]) = [0.75, 0.25]$$

This simplified example demonstrates how each node's feature representation is updated by aggregating information from its neighbors and applying a learnable transformation, allowing information to propagate across the graph. In a real GCN, this aggregation is implicitly handled by the normalized adjacency matrix multiplication as shown in the mathematical representation.

Key Advantages of GNNs for Brain Signals

When it comes to analyzing brain signals, graph neural networks (GNNs) are the best because they work well with the brain's natural network design. One of their main strengths is that they can handle graphs directly **(direct graph processing)**. When you use convolutional or recurrent neural networks, the underlying network must be reshaped into grids or sequences, which always loses important topological features. GNNs work directly with graph-structured data, which keeps the detailed knowledge about connections that is essential for understanding how the brain is organized. One more big benefit is that they are good at learning through relationships **(relationship learning)**. GNNs are specially made to understand and describe the complicated connections and dependencies between nodes, which in this case are brain regions or individual neurons. This focus on relationships is important for understanding the brain, since patterns of connectivity and coordinated activity can tell us more than just looking at separate parts. GNNs are also naturally flexible, as they can handle jobs at both the **node and graph levels**. This means they can answer both specific questions, like finding out if a certain part of the brain shows signs of disease based on its local network context, and more general questions, like putting whole brain networks into groups based on their global connectivity patterns, like telling the difference between healthy and diseased brain states. These features make GNNs a strong tool for studying brain networks in the modern world.

Subtypes of GNNs for Brain Signal Processing

Though there are many types of designs in the field of graph neural networks, in analyzing brain signals, graph convolutional networks (GCNs) and graph attention networks (GATs) perform better and are discussed briefly.

Graph Convolutional Networks (GCNs): In the graph-structured data, the convolution principle is directly adapted to form the Graph Convolutional Networks (GCN). They learn node features by aggregating information from a node's immediate neighbors in a "convolutional" manner, typically employing aggregation functions such as weighted sums or means. The mathematical formulation presented earlier (Equation 5.4) is a common GCN variant. As in CNN, the GCN also learns local patterns of neuroscience data effectively and propagates information across the graph. They are generally simpler to implement than more complex GNN architectures, making them a foundational choice. Their application in neuroscience is widespread, including classifying brain states based on functional connectivity networks (e.g., fMRI functional connectomes), identifying altered structural connectivity in neurological disorders (from diffusion tensor imaging (DTI) data), and predicting disease progression from brain networks.

Graph Attention Networks (GATs): To further improve the performance of the graph neural networks, the attention mechanism is introduced in the GCN. Instead of treating all neighbors equally (or with weights based solely on node degrees), GATs learn to assign differential "attention weights" to each neighbor's message. This implies that information from certain neighbors might be considered more significant than others for a given node's update. This mechanism allows the network to focus on more relevant neighbors, potentially improving performance in complex graphs, where some connections are more salient for a specific task. Furthermore, this enhances the interpretability of the model and also improves the performance of the complex graphs where some connections are more salient for a specific task. This makes the GATs useful for tasks where specific brain connections may be more critical for a particular function or pathology, such as identifying key dysfunctional pathways in psychiatric disorders or pinpointing critical nodes within a brain network.

Practice Exercises: Graph Neural Networks

These exercises are designed to test your understanding of the core concepts and applications of graph neural networks.

Q1: Node Aggregation (Simplified GNN) Consider a graph with 4 nodes and their initial features:

- Node A: $h_A^{(0)} = [1,2]$
- Node B: $h_B^{(0)} = [3,0]$
- Node C: $h_C^{(0)} = [0,4]$
- Node D: $h_D^{(0)} = [2,1]$

Connections: A-B, B-C, and C-D (node A is connected to B, B to C, and C to D). Assume a simplified aggregation rule where a node's aggregated feature is the *sum* of its own feature and its direct neighbors' features from the previous layer.

Calculate the aggregated feature vector for each node $(Agg_A, Agg_B, Agg_C, Agg_D)$ after one aggregation step.

Q2: Node Update (Simplified GNN): Using the aggregated features from question G1 and a learnable weight matrix $W^{(0)}$:

$$W^{(0)} = \begin{pmatrix} 0.5 & 0.5 \\ -0.5 & 0.5 \end{pmatrix}$$

Apply this weight matrix and a ReLU activation function to calculate the new feature vector for Node B $(h_B^{(1)})$.

Q3: Direct Graph Processing: Explain what "direct graph processing" means in the context of GNNs for brain signals. Why is this a significant advantage compared to using CNNs or RNNs for analyzing brain networks?

Q4: GNN Subtypes: Distinguish between Graph Convolutional Networks (GCNs) and Graph Attention Networks (GATs). When might you prefer to use a GAT over a GCN for analyzing brain connectivity?

Q5: Relational Learning: How do GNNs facilitate "relational learning" in brain networks? Provide an example of a type of relationship they might learn.

Q6: GNN for Functional Brain Connectivity Analysis: You are developing a deep learning model to classify patients with a specific neurological disorder based on their fMRI functional connectivity data. You have already preprocessed the fMRI data to derive functional connectivity matrices, where nodes represent brain regions and edges represent the strength of functional correlation between them.

4. Explain why a graph neural network (GNN) is a suitable choice for this task, detailing how the fMRI functional connectivity data maps to a graph structure for GNN input.
5. Describe the overall workflow of a GNN for this classification task, from input graph to final prediction.
6. Discuss how the "message passing" mechanism in the GNN would help in identifying disorder-specific patterns in the functional brain network.

Q7: GNNs vs. Traditional Network Analysis: Traditional network analysis methods (e.g., graph theory metrics like centrality and clustering coefficient) are often used to study brain networks. Discuss the advantages of using GNNs for brain network analysis compared to these traditional methods. Consider aspects like feature learning and scalability.

5.2.4 Autoencoders and Variational Autoencoders (VAEs)

Beyond classification and regression, deep learning offers powerful tools for unsupervised learning, representation learning, and generative modeling. **Autoencoders (AEs)** and their probabilistic variant, **variational autoencoders (VAEs)**, are particularly relevant for brain signal analysis, where high-dimensional, unlabeled data is abundant, and understanding underlying data structures or generating realistic synthetic data can provide profound insights.

Core Principle: Learning Efficient Data Representations
At its core, an autoencoder is a type of neural network designed to learn an efficient, low-dimensional **representation** (or "encoding") of input data in an unsupervised manner. It achieves this by attempting to reconstruct its own input. The architecture consists of two main parts:

Encoder: This part maps the high-dimensional input data (x) into a lower-dimensional latent space representation (z). It acts as a dimensionality reduction component.
Decoder: This part takes the latent space representation (z) and maps it back to the original input data space, attempting to reconstruct the input $(\hat{x})$.

The network is trained by minimizing the **reconstruction loss** (e.g., mean squared error) between the original input x and its reconstructed output $\hat{x}$. By forcing the network to compress information into a bottleneck (the latent space z) and then reconstruct it, the autoencoder is compelled to learn the most salient and informative features of the data, effectively performing unsupervised feature learning or dimensionality reduction. The learnt latent representations (z) are often more compact, less noisy, and more interpretable than the raw input data.

A typical autoencoder structure can be visualized as:

Figure 5.4 illustrates the typical architecture of an autoencoder, showing how the encoder compresses the input into a latent space and the decoder reconstructs the original data.

Training objective: $\min||x-\hat{x}||^2$ (L2 norm) or $\min \text{BCE}(x-\hat{x})$ (binary cross-entropy for binary data).

Illustrative Example: Simple Autoencoder for MNIST-like Data

Let's consider a very simple autoencoder for dimensionality reduction, mapping a 4-dimensional input to a 2-dimensional latent space.

Input $x=[x_1,x_2,x_3,x_4]$, latent space $z=[z_1,z_2]$ and reconstruction $\hat{x}=[\hat{x}_1,\hat{x}_2,\hat{x}_3,\hat{x}_4]$

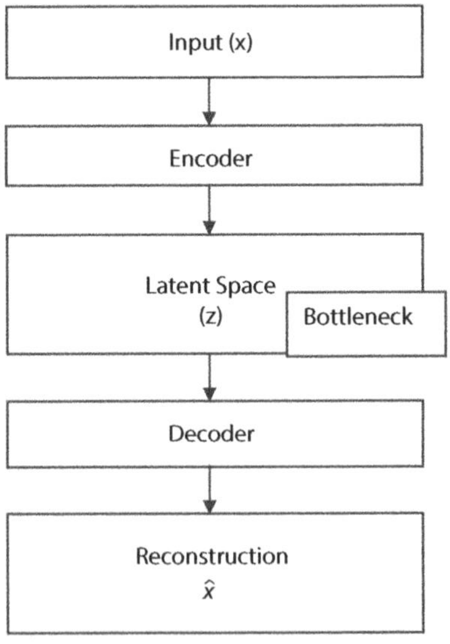

Figure 5.4 Autoencoder visualization.

Encoder Weights and Biases:

$$W_{enc} = \begin{pmatrix} 0.8 & 0.2 \\ 0.1 & 0.7 \\ 0.3 & 0.9 \\ 0.6 & 0.4 \end{pmatrix} (\text{4 input features,2 latent features})$$

$$b_{enc} = [0.1, 0.2] \text{ Activation: ReLU}$$

Decoder Weights and Biases:

$$W_{dec} = \begin{pmatrix} 0.7 & 0.3 & 0.1 & 0.9 \\ 0.2 & 0.8 & 0.5 & 0.4 \end{pmatrix} (\text{2 latent features, 4 output features})$$

$$b_{dec} = [0.05, 0.1, 0.05, 0.1] \text{ Activation: Linear (for reconstruction values)}$$

Let's trace an input $x = [1.0, 0.5, 0.8, 0.2]$.

1. Encoder Step: Calculate Latent Representation z:

$$z = \text{ReLU}(x \cdot W_{enc} + b_{enc})$$

First,

$$x \cdot W_{enc} : [1.0, 0.5, 0.8, 0.2] \begin{pmatrix} 0.8 & 0.2 \\ 0.1 & 0.7 \\ 0.3 & 0.9 \\ 0.6 & 0.4 \end{pmatrix}$$

$$= [(1 \cdot 0.8 + 0.5 \cdot 0.1 + 0.8 \cdot 0.3 + 0.2 \cdot 0.6), (1 \cdot 0.2 + 0.5 \cdot 0.7$$
$$+ 0.8 \cdot 0.9 + 0.2 \cdot 0.4)]$$
$$= [(0.8 + 0.05 + 0.24 + 0.12), (0.2 + 0.35 + 0.72 + 0.08)]$$
$$= [1.21, 1.35]$$

Now, add bias

$$b_{enc}: [1.21, 1.35] + [0.1, 0.2] = [1.31, 1.55]$$

Apply ReLU:

$$z = \text{ReLU}([1.31, 1.55]) = [1.31, 1.55] \text{ (since both are positive)}$$

So, the latent representation is

$$z = [1.31, 1.55].$$

2. Decoder Step: Calculate Reconstruction $\hat{x}$:

$$\hat{x} = z \cdot W_{dec} + b_{dec} \text{ (linear activation)}$$

First,

$$z \cdot W_{dec} : [1.31, 1.55] \begin{pmatrix} 0.7 & 0.3 & 0.1 & 0.9 \\ 0.2 & 0.8 & 0.5 & 0.4 \end{pmatrix}$$

$$= [(1.31 \cdot 0.7 + 1.55 \cdot 0.2), (1.31 \cdot 0.3 + 1.55 \cdot 0.8), (1.31 \cdot 0.1 + 1.55 \cdot 0.5), (1.31 \cdot 0.9 + 1.55 \cdot 0.4)]$$

$$= [(0.917 + 0.31), (0.393 + 1.24), (0.131 + 0.775), (1.179 + 0.62)]$$

$$= [1.227, 1.633, 0.906, 1.799]$$

Now, add bias

$$b_{dec}: [1.227, 1.633, 0.906, 1.799] + [0.05, 0.1, 0.05, 0.1]$$

$$\hat{x} = [1.277, 1.733, 0.956, 1.899]$$

The reconstructed output $\hat{x}$ is then compared to the original input x to calculate the reconstruction loss, which drives the learning process. This simple example shows how data is compressed into a latent space and then decoded.

Variational Autoencoders (VAEs): Beyond Simple Reconstruction

While standard autoencoders learn a deterministic mapping to the latent space, **variational autoencoders (VAEs)** take a probabilistic approach. Instead of mapping an input to a single point z in the latent space, the encoder of a VAE maps it to parameters of a probability distribution (typically a multivariate Gaussian distribution) in the latent space, specifically a mean (μ) and a log-variance $(\log\sigma^2)$.

The VAE then samples a latent vector z from this learnt distribution. The decoder then reconstructs the input from this sampled z. This probabilistic formulation enforces a continuous, well-structured latent space, enabling VAEs to perform powerful **generative modeling**.

The VAE's objective function is a combination of two terms:

Reconstruction Loss: Measures how well the decoder reconstructs the input (same as AE).

KL Divergence Loss: Measures how much the learnt latent distribution deviates from a prior distribution (typically a standard normal distribution). This term acts as a regularizer, forcing the latent space to be structured and continuous, preventing "holes" in the latent space, and making it suitable for generating new, realistic samples by sampling from the prior.

By optimizing this combined loss, VAEs learn a robust and interpretable latent space where similar inputs are mapped to similar distributions, and new samples can be generated by simply sampling from the prior and passing them through the decoder.

Key Advantages of Brain Signals

Autoencoders and VAEs offer several unique advantages for brain signal analysis:

Unsupervised Feature Learning/Dimensionality Reduction: Brain signals are high-dimensional and often unlabeled. AEs/VAEs can learn compact, meaningful low-dimensional representations (latent features) of complex EEG, MEG, or fMRI data without requiring explicit labels. These learnt features can then be used for downstream supervised tasks (e.g., classification, regression) or for visualizing data structure.

Noise Reduction and Denoising: By learning to reconstruct the original input, AEs can implicitly learn to filter out noise, acting as a powerful denoising tool, which is critical for inherently noisy brain signals.

Anomaly Detection: Anomalous brain signals (e.g., seizure onset, artifactual activity) might be poorly reconstructed by an AE trained on normal

data, leading to a high reconstruction error. This property can be leveraged for anomaly detection.
Generative Modeling (VAEs): VAEs can generate synthetic, realistic brain signals (e.g., synthetic EEG waveforms, fMRI connectivity patterns). This is valuable for data augmentation (especially for rare neurological events), understanding the manifold of normal/abnormal brain activity, or simulating brain states.
Latent Space Exploration and Interpretation: The continuous latent space learnt by VAEs allows for interpolation between different brain states or subject groups. Researchers can explore how traversing the latent space corresponds to changes in reconstructed brain signals, potentially revealing underlying biological gradients or disease trajectories.

Applications in Brain Signal Processing
EEG/MEG Denoising and Artifact Removal: Training AEs to reconstruct clean signals from noisy inputs, effectively removing common artifacts (e.g., eye blinks, muscle activity) without explicit feature engineering.
Feature Extraction for Classification: Using the latent representations learnt by AEs as features for classifying cognitive states, sleep stages, or neurological disorders from raw or minimally preprocessed EEG/fMRI.
Generative Modeling of Brain Rhythms: VAEs can learn the distribution of normal EEG rhythms (e.g., alpha and theta waves) and then generate novel, physiologically plausible EEG segments for data augmentation or to study the range of normal variability.
Identifying Biomarkers from fMRI Connectivity: Applying AEs to fMRI functional connectivity matrices to discover low-dimensional network biomarkers for psychiatric conditions or neurodegenerative diseases. VAEs can also be used to generate synthetic connectivity matrices representing different conditions.
Brain State Manifold Learning: Using VAEs to map complex, high-dimensional brain states (e.g., from continuous EEG) into a low-dimensional, interpretable manifold, allowing visualization and analysis of state transitions.

Autoencoders and VAEs provide powerful unsupervised learning capabilities that are essential for uncovering hidden structures and generating insights from the complex, often unlabeled, landscape of brain signal data.

Practice Exercises: Autoencoders

These exercises are designed to test your understanding of autoencoders and variational autoencoders.

Q1: Autoencoder Reconstruction: Consider a simple autoencoder with the following specifications:

Input $x = [2.0, 5.0, 1.0]$ (3 features)
Latent space z (2 features)

Encoder weights: $W_{enc} = \begin{pmatrix} 0.6 & 0.3 \\ 0.2 & 0.7 \\ 0.5 & 0.1 \end{pmatrix}$

Encoder bias: $b_{enc} = [0.1, 0.1]$
Encoder activation: ReLU

Decoder weights: $W_{dec} = \begin{pmatrix} 0.8 & 0.2 & 0.5 \\ 0.3 & 0.7 & 0.1 \end{pmatrix}$

Decoder bias: $b_{dec} = [0.05, 0.05, 0.05]$
Decoder activation: Linear

Calculate the reconstructed output $\hat{x}$. Show all intermediate steps.

Q2: Purpose of Latent Space: What is the primary purpose of the "latent space" (bottleneck) in an autoencoder? How does its dimensionality (e.g., smaller than input) contribute to this purpose?

Q3: VAE vs. Standard AE - Key Difference: Explain the fundamental difference between a standard autoencoder and a variational autoencoder (VAE) in terms of how they map input to the latent space. What is the significance of this difference for generative modeling?

Q4: KL Divergence Loss in VAE: Beyond reconstruction loss, variational autoencoders incorporate a KL divergence loss term. What is the purpose of this term, and how does it regularize the latent space?

Q5: Anomaly Detection with Autoencoders: Briefly explain how an autoencoder can be used for anomaly detection in brain signals (e.g., detecting unusual EEG patterns).

Q6: VAE for Synthetic EEG Data Generation: You are working on a project to develop a machine learning model for detecting a rare neurological event from EEG. The scarcity of real data for this event makes training challenging.

1. Explain how a variational autoencoder (VAE) could be used to generate synthetic EEG data for this rare event.
2. Describe the typical VAE architecture and training objective in this context (assume input is short, multi-channel EEG segments).

3. Discuss the benefits and potential limitations of using VAE-generated synthetic data for data augmentation in this scenario.

Q7: Autoencoders for Brain Signal Feature Learning: Discuss how autoencoders can facilitate unsupervised feature learning from raw, high-dimensional brain signals (e.g., continuous EEG or fMRI time series). Provide an example of how these learnt features could then be used in a downstream task.

5.3 Deep Learning Applications and Advanced Topics in Brain Signal Processing

After going over the basic concepts of deep learning architectures, this part goes into more depth about how they can be used in real life and some more advanced ideas related to brain signal processing. We will first group these apps by the specific type of neuroimaging or neurophysiological modality they use, focusing on the architectural choices that were made for each one. Next, we look at the different ways of learning and jobs that deep learning can be used for, such as generative modeling, unsupervised discovery, and supervised classification. Last, we'll explore multimodal data fusion, an important area that brings together various brain signal sources for a fuller understanding.

5.3.1 Classification by Brain Signal Modality & Specific Adaptation

After discussing the basics of deep learning, this part explains how these models can be changed and used with different kinds of brain data. Since various neuroimaging and neurophysiological techniques have different data structures, noise levels, and records of different neural events, we need custom architectural choices and processing strategies for effective analysis and useful insights in both research and clinical settings.

Deep Learning for Electroencephalography (EEG)
Electroencephalography (EEG) records the brain's electrical activity using electrodes placed on the scalp. This method offers high temporal resolution, capturing brain events in milliseconds. However, its low spatial resolution makes it difficult to pinpoint exact sources deep within the brain. EEG data

is naturally time-series and multi-channel, often showing oscillatory patterns across various frequency bands. Much effort has gone into adapting deep learning models to use these traits for different analysis tasks [5].

Common Architectures and Rationale for EEG Processing

Convolutional neural networks (CNNs) are often used for EEG research because they are good at finding local patterns in both time and space. In particular, 1D convolutions are very good at finding specific patterns or short-lived events (like spikes and K-complexes) in the raw EEG time series. For multi-channel EEG, 2D convolutions can be used on electrode topographies or time-frequency representations (spectrograms) to find patterns in space and time across the head. Structures like EEGNet, DeepConvNet, and ShallowConvNet are well-known examples. For example, EEGNet uses depthwise and separable convolutions to make small and efficient models. This makes it ideal for processing EEG signals in environments with limited resources. This is something that has been emphasized in recent reviews on CNN architectures for EEG feature extraction [16].

These models can learn frequency-specific features straight from raw or spectrally transformed EEG data, which helps make feature learning more reliable. Recurrent neural networks (RNNs), especially long short-term memory (LSTM) networks and gated recurrent units (GRUs), are very good at modeling long-term temporal relationships and sequences of events because the EEG is a continuous time series. This feature is very important for knowing how brain states change over time or guessing brain states from raw EEG data [7]. LSTMs, with their gating mechanisms, are adept at capturing patterns that change over seconds or minutes, making them suitable for tasks like seizure prediction from long EEG recordings [1].

The coming up of hybrid CNN-RNN models lets the best parts of both CNNs and RNNs work together. In these designs, CNNs are used to pull out specific spatial and temporal features (like waveform shapes or frequency bursts) from short EEG segments. Then, RNNs are used to predict how these features change over time and in different situations. In the field of brain-computer interfaces (BCIs) [11] and the diagnosis of psychiatric diseases [21], these hybrid models have shown a lot of promise.

EEG can only show a small amount of space, but it can estimate how functionally connected electrodes are to each other. This means that the brain can be shown as a graph, with electrodes as nodes and connection strength as edges.

Graph neural networks (GNNs) can work directly on these graph representations to learn biomarkers at the network level, revealing hidden topological relationships. Song *et al.* [13] stress the rising importance of detecting emotions, seizures in people with epilepsy, and neurological diseases. Graph neural network models have been used for disease and brain-state classification by leveraging graph-structured brain connectivity [13].

Noise and artifacts, like eye blinks and muscle activity, can really mess up EEG readings. Autoencoders (AEs) offer a way to solve this problem without supervision. They can learn to put together clean EEG patterns from noisy inputs, which is the same thing as unsupervised denoising but better for future analyses. They can also learn meaningful, compressed features from raw EEG, which is very important for getting rid of unnecessary dimensions in large amounts of data [10]. For example, a convolutional autoencoder could be taught to get rid of eye-blink artifacts from EEG by putting together clean EEG from sources that have artifacts. This would help make neurological diagnoses more accurate.

The long EEGs that could last hours or days are analyzed better by Transformer models. They capture very long-range temporal relationships and global context with their architecture. Gao *et al.* [20] say that their ability to model complex relationships between space and time has led to new ways of tracking mental health. A transformer could look at an entire night's worth of EEG data to find small sleep problems or predict unusual neural events that last for a long time. This would give them a full picture of brain activity over long periods of time.

Typical Applications of Deep Learning in EEG

After using deep learning models on EEG data, progress has been made in many different areas. In classification tasks, they are used for decoding motor imagery in brain-computer interfaces (BCIs) [11], recognizing emotions [21], figuring out cognitive load, and finding alertness. Deep learning has also enabled advances in neural decoding and reconstruction from population activity recordings [14]. Models can find epileptic events or guess when they will happen from continuous EEG, which makes patient care much better [1] when it comes to seizure detection and prediction. One more important area is sleep stage classification, which involves automatically putting sleep into different states (wake, N1, N2, N3, REM) to help find sleep disorders. Furthermore, deep learning facilitates anomaly detection, identifying unusual brain activity patterns indicative of pathology or acute events, and contributes to the identification of neurological disorders like depression, ADHD, or autism based on EEG biomarkers, including applications in mental health monitoring [6, 21].

Deep Learning for Magnetoencephalography (MEG)

Magnetoencephalography (MEG) directly measures the tiny magnetic fields produced by electrical currents in the brain. Similar to EEG, it offers **very high temporal resolution** (milliseconds) but provides **superior spatial localization** compared to EEG, especially for activity originating from deeper cortical sources. MEG data is also inherently **time series** and **multi-channel**, often with hundreds of sensors.

Figure 5.5 illustrates the general pipeline for processing MEG data with deep learning, emphasizing its high temporal and improved spatial resolution.

Common Architectures and Rationale for MEG Processing

CNN-based models are frequently used for MEG analysis. 1D CNNs are effective for extracting temporal features from raw MEG time series, similar to their application in EEG. 2D CNNs can be applied to sensor layout maps or time-frequency representations (spectrograms) to capture spatio-temporal patterns across the sensor array. For source-localized MEG data, which represent estimated current distributions within the brain volume, 3D CNNs can be employed to process these volumetric representations. For instance, a 1D CNN could analyze the raw MEG signal from

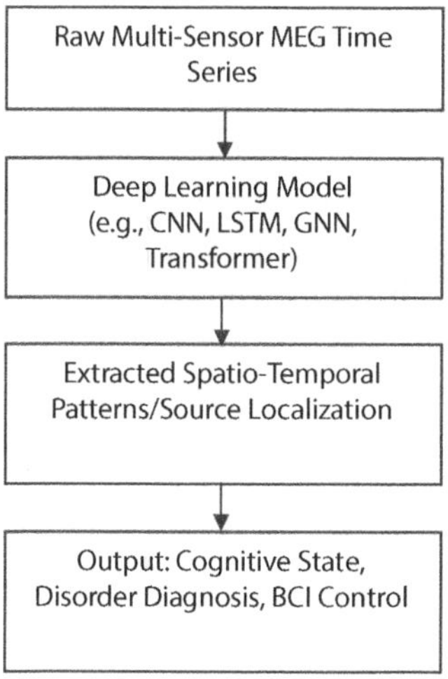

Figure 5.5 Conceptual flow for MEG data processing.

individual sensors to detect specific evoked responses, while a 2D CNN might process a topographical map of MEG activity across sensors to classify cognitive states [17].

The high temporal resolution of MEG makes RNN/LSTM/GRU-based models highly suitable for modeling the dynamic evolution of brain states, tracking cognitive processes, and predicting future neural events from continuous MEG streams. An LSTM, for example, could track changes in MEG power spectra over time to decode complex cognitive processes like attention or memory recall, leveraging its ability to learn long-term on MEG's superior spatial resolution for network construction [7].

Autoencoders (AEs) are valuable for MEG data, which is susceptible to various noise sources such as environmental magnetic interference and physiological artifacts. AEs can be used for unsupervised denoising and for learning compact representations of complex MEG patterns. A sparse autoencoder, for example, could learn to extract underlying neural components from noisy MEG data, effectively separating true brain activity from confounding signals [10].

Given MEG's ability to capture long-range interactions and its high dimensionality (many sensors, long time series), transformers are increasingly being explored. Their attention mechanism allows them to model complex spatio-temporal dependencies and global brain dynamics more comprehensively than traditional recurrent or convolutional approaches. A transformer could analyze the entire multi-channel MEG recording to identify subtle patterns indicative of early-stage neurodegenerative diseases, leveraging its ability to attend to relevant information across the entire dataset [20].

Typical Applications of Deep Learning in MEG

MEG's deep learning covers a wide range of important areas. A lot of people use them to decode cognitive states, which means using MEG patterns to figure out states like focus, memory, or decision-making. Deep learning also improves source localization, which makes it easier to figure out exactly which parts of the brain are making the magnetic fields. Furthermore, these models make a big difference in finding neurological disorders. By looking at changes in brain dynamics and connectivity, they help doctors diagnose conditions like epilepsy, Alzheimer's disease, Parkinson's disease, and many mental disorders. Deep learning models are used in brain-computer interfaces (BCIs) to figure out motor plans or other commands from MEG signals for assistive technologies [17].

Deep Learning for Functional Magnetic Resonance Imaging (fMRI)

Functional magnetic resonance imaging (fMRI) indirectly measures brain activity by detecting changes in blood flow (Blood-Oxygen-Level Dependent, BOLD signal). This modality provides **high spatial resolution** (down to millimeters) but **relatively low temporal resolution** (seconds). fMRI data is typically **volumetric** (3D images) collected over time, resulting in **4D data** (3D space + time).

Figure 5.6 illustrates the general pipeline for processing fMRI data with deep learning, highlighting its volumetric and temporal dimensions.

Common Architectures and Rationale for fMRI Processing

3D CNNs are ideally suited for processing the volumetric nature of fMRI data. They can learn hierarchical spatial features directly from the raw 3D brain volumes, capturing complex anatomical and functional patterns across the entire brain. For example, a 3D CNN can be trained end-to-end to classify Alzheimer's disease by learning subtle atrophy patterns or altered functional activation directly from raw or minimally preprocessed fMRI volumes [15].

While fMRI has lower temporal resolution compared to EEG/MEG, the BOLD signal still evolves over time. **RNN/LSTM/GRU**-based models can effectively model the temporal dynamics of regional brain activity or connectivity patterns, capturing how brain states transition over the course of an experiment or during a resting state. An LSTM, for instance, could process the time series of BOLD signals from a set of regions of interest (ROIs) to decode a sequence of cognitive states during a task [7].

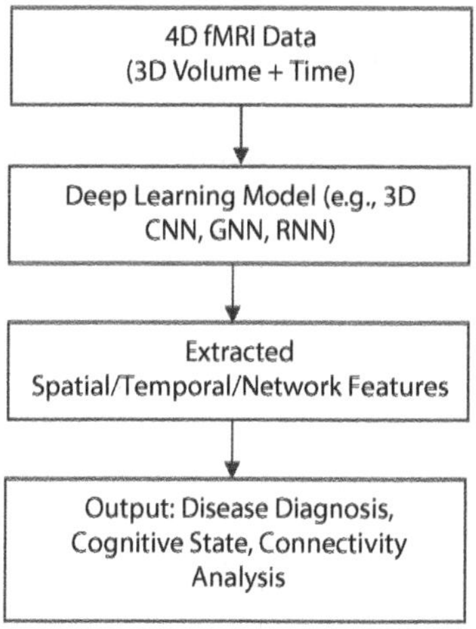

Figure 5.6 Conceptual flow for fMRI data processing.

fMRI is extensively used to derive functional connectivity networks (where nodes are brain regions and edges represent statistical dependencies between their BOLD time series). **Graph neural networks (GNNs)** are perfectly suited to analyze these graph-structured representations, identifying altered network topology or information flow in various conditions. A GCN, for example, could classify individuals with autism spectrum disorder by identifying unique patterns of functional hypoconnectivity or hyperconnectivity in their fMRI-derived brain networks [13].

Autoencoders (AEs) and variational autoencoders (VAEs) are valuable for unsupervised feature learning and dimensionality reduction in fMRI data, which is typically very high-dimensional. AEs can learn compact, meaningful latent representations of fMRI scans and reduce dimensionality while preserving critical information. VAEs can also generate synthetic fMRI data for data augmentation or to explore the latent space of brain variability. A 3D VAE, for instance, could learn a latent space representing different healthy brain activity patterns, allowing for the detection of anomalous fMRI scans from patients with neurological conditions [10].

Transformers are increasingly explored for fMRI, given their ability to model long-range spatial dependencies across the entire brain volume (e.g., by treating fMRI patches as tokens, similar to Vision Transformers) or long-range temporal dependencies in fMRI time series. This can potentially capture global brain dynamics more comprehensively. A Transformer could analyze the entire sequence of fMRI volumes to predict treatment response in psychiatric disorders, attending to relevant brain regions and time points across the entire scan [20].

Typical Applications of Deep Learning in fMRI

Deep learning models are widely applied to fMRI data for various purposes. These include **disease classification** and aiding in the diagnosis of neurological (e.g., Alzheimer's, Parkinson's, stroke) and psychiatric (e.g., depression, schizophrenia) disorders based on functional fMRI patterns [21]. They are also used for **cognitive state decoding**, identifying specific cognitive processes (e.g., memory, language, emotion) from fMRI activity. A significant application is **functional connectivity analysis**, involving the mapping and characterization of brain networks and the identification of alterations in connectivity in various conditions. Furthermore, deep learning facilitates **biomarker discovery**, pinpointing specific fMRI patterns or connectivity features that serve as indicators for disease presence, progression, or treatment response, and enables **prognosis prediction** by forecasting disease trajectory or treatment outcomes.

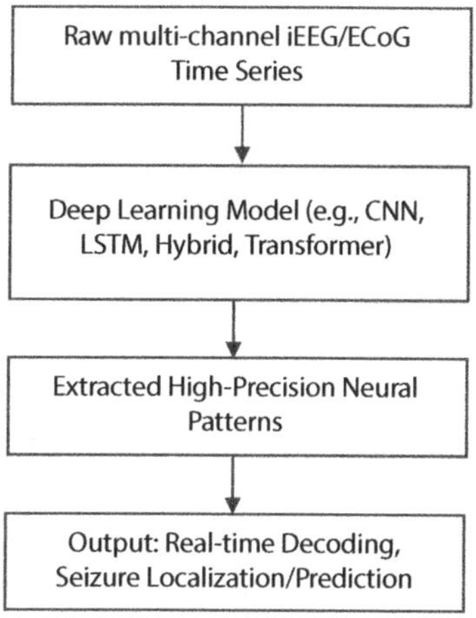

Figure 5.7 Conceptual flow for iEEG/ECoG data processing.

Deep Learning for Intracranial EEG (iEEG)/Electrocorticography (ECoG)

Intracranial EEG (iEEG) and electrocorticography (ECoG) involve placing electrodes directly on the surface of the brain (ECoG) or inserting them deep within brain tissue (iEEG). This provides **extremely high spatial resolution** (millimeters) and **very high temporal resolution** (milliseconds), capturing neural activity with unprecedented fidelity. However, it is an invasive procedure. The data is a multi-channel time series, often with hundreds of channels.

Figure 5.7 illustrates the general pipeline for processing iEEG/ECoG data with deep learning, emphasizing its high spatial and temporal precision.

Common Architectures and Rationale for iEEG/ECoG Processing

CNN-based models are highly effective for iEEG/ECoG analysis. Given the grid-like arrangement of ECoG electrodes on the cortical surface, 2D CNNs are particularly effective for learning local spatio-temporal patterns across the electrode array. Concurrently, 1D CNNs can capture fine-grained temporal features from individual iEEG/ECoG channels. For example, a 2D CNN could process the ECoG grid to detect the precise onset and propagation of epileptic seizures, leveraging the high spatial resolution inherent in this modality [1].

The high temporal resolution and continuous nature of iEEG/ECoG make **RNN/LSTM/GRU**-based models indispensable for real-time decoding of complex neural signals, such as continuous motor intent or speech. An LSTM, for instance, could continuously decode a patient's imagined speech by processing the sequence of iEEG signals, translating neural patterns into spoken words for a brain-computer interface (BCI) [19].

The combination of CNNs for local feature extraction (e.g., identifying specific neural oscillations or spike patterns) with RNNs for modeling their temporal evolution has proven very powerful in hybrid CNN-RNN architectures. For example, a CNN might extract features from short ECoG segments, and an RNN then processes the sequence of these features to predict continuous arm movements with high accuracy [16].

Transformers are increasingly being utilized due to their ability to capture long-range dependencies and global context in highly complex iEEG/ECoG sequences. This is particularly relevant for tasks like decoding speech or complex motor plans where subtle, distributed neural patterns are crucial. A Transformer could process long sequences of iEEG activity to decode complex sentences or continuous speech directly from the brain, leveraging its attention mechanism to integrate information across many electrodes and time points [20].

Typical Applications of Deep Learning in iEEG/ECoG

Deep learning applications in iEEG/ECoG are primarily focused on high-precision tasks. These include the development of **high-precision brain-computer interfaces (BCIs)**, enabling direct control of prosthetic limbs, communication devices, or computer cursors with high accuracy and low latency [22]. Another critical application is **seizure localization and prediction**, precisely identifying the epileptogenic zone for surgical intervention and predicting seizure onset with high reliability. Furthermore, deep learning facilitates **neurological decoding**, translating complex motor intent, imagined speech, visual perception, or other cognitive processes directly from neural activity, and contributes to a deeper **understanding of neural circuits** by providing insights into how specific neural populations encode information during various behaviors.

Deep Learning for Spike & Local Field Potential (LFP) Recordings

These modalities represent neural activity at a very fine-grained level, typically from microelectrodes implanted within brain tissue. **Spike recordings** capture the action potentials (brief electrical impulses) of individual neurons, while **local field potentials (LFPs)** reflect the summed synaptic activity of a population of neurons in a local area. Both are **time-series** data, often multi-channel, with very high sampling rates.

Figure 5.8 illustrates the general pipeline for processing spike and LFP data with deep learning, emphasizing their fine-grained temporal resolution.

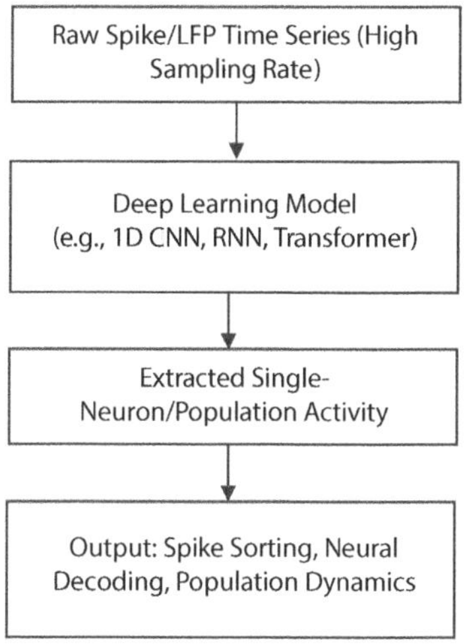

Figure 5.8 Conceptual flow for spike/LFP data processing.

Common Architectures and Rationale for Spike/LFP Processing
For these high-frequency, fine-grained signals, it's very important that they can learn local temporal trends. In this case, a **1D CNN** can be taught to automatically "sort" spikes from different neurons picked up by the same electrode based on the different waveform shapes of those spikes [19].

The order of spikes, or the way LFPs change over time, tells us a lot about how neurons code. When looking at these continuous neural sequences, **RNN/LSTM/GRU**-based models are the best way to figure out motor parameters, cognitive states, or behavioral goals. For example, an LSTM could use its ability to model sequences to constantly predict the path of an arm movement by processing a series of spike counts from a group of motor cortex neurons [19].

Transformers are being studied more to understand complex neural codes that involve interactions between neurons over longer periods of time or across groups that are spread out. In spike trains or LFP sequences, they can record these complex long-range relationships. A transformer could look at the firing patterns of hundreds of neurons over a few seconds to figure out complicated behavioral processes. It would use its attention system to find important temporal connections between neuronal activities [20].

Autoencoders (AEs) and **variational autoencoders (VAEs)** can help reduce the number of dimensions in spike or LFP data and learn new features. These models can turn the data into useful, lower-dimensional representations that make it easier to see and analyze later. For instance, a VAE could learn a latent space from LFP data that shows the different states of the neural population. This would let academics investigate how these states change over time [10].

Typical Applications of Deep Learning in Spike/LFP Recordings
Deep learning applications in spike and LFP recordings focus on fine-grained neural analysis. A key application is **spike sorting**, which involves automatically identifying and separating action potentials from different individual neurons recorded by a single electrode [19]. Another major area is **neural decoding**, translating neural activity (spikes or LFPs) into behavioral outputs (e.g., movement parameters, speech, cognitive choices) for brain-computer interfaces (BCIs) or neuroprosthetics. Deep learning also contributes to **understanding neural population dynamics**, uncovering the underlying patterns and transitions in the activity of groups of neurons during specific tasks or behaviors, and facilitates **biomarker discovery** by identifying fine-grained neural signatures associated with neurological disorders or drug effects.

Deep Learning for Structural Magnetic Resonance Imaging (sMRI) & Diffusion Tensor Imaging (DTI)
These modalities provide insights into the brain's anatomy and structural connectivity. **sMRI** captures detailed 3D images of brain tissue, allowing for the visualization of gray matter, white matter, and cerebrospinal fluid. **DTI** measures the diffusion of water molecules in brain tissue, which can be used to map the orientation and integrity of white matter tracts, providing information about structural connections.

Figure 5.9 illustrates the general pipeline for processing sMRI and DTI data with deep learning, emphasizing their volumetric and structural nature.

Common Architectures and Rationale for sMRI/DTI Processing
3D CNNs are the primary architecture for sMRI analysis due to their ability to directly process 3D volumetric data. They can learn hierarchical spatial features to perform tasks like brain segmentation (identifying different tissue types or anatomical regions), detecting lesions (e.g., tumors, stroke damage), or classifying diseases based on subtle patterns of atrophy or structural changes. For example, a 3D CNN can segment brain regions (cortex, hippocampus, ventricles) from an sMRI scan with high precision or classify Alzheimer's disease based on patterns of gray matter atrophy [3, 15].

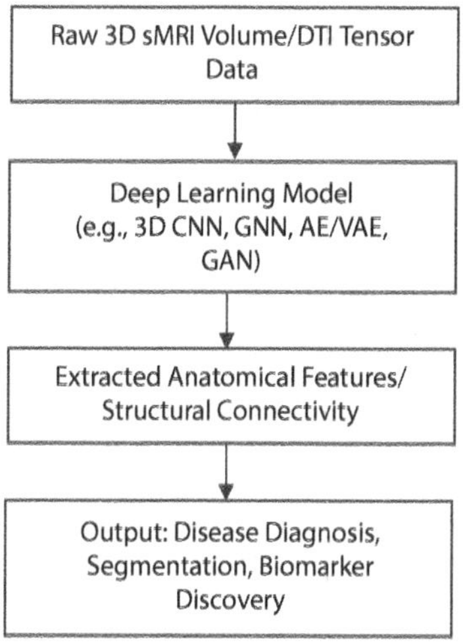

Figure 5.9 Conceptual flow for sMRI/DTI data processing.

Functional connectivity from PET/SPECT (e.g., metabolic correlation networks) can be found sometimes, but not as often as from fMRI or DTI. **Graph neural networks (GNNs)** could be used to look at these graph models in this situation. For example, a GNN could look at metabolic networks drawn from PET to find small changes in networks that happen in Parkinson's disease [13].

For PET/SPECT, **Generative Adversarial Networks (GANs)** can also be used. They can be used to make fake images (for example, to add more data), clean up images, or make them more detailed. For example, a GAN could make fake PET scans of different stages of neurodegeneration or improve the clarity of PET pictures that aren't very good [2].

Typical Applications of Deep Learning in sMRI/DTI

Deep learning applications in sMRI and DTI are crucial for understanding brain structure and connectivity. These include **disease diagnosis**, detecting and classifying neurological disorders characterized by structural changes (e.g., tumors, multiple sclerosis lesions, Alzheimer's atrophy, stroke lesions) [15]. **Brain segmentation** is another key application, involving the automatic delineation of different brain regions, tissue types, or pathologies. Deep learning also contributes to **biomarker discovery**, identifying structural features or connectivity patterns that serve as indicators for disease presence, progression, or treatment response [21]. Furthermore, these models are used for **age/sex prediction** from brain morphology and assist in **surgical planning** by precisely localizing targets or boundaries for neurosurgery.

Deep Learning for Positron Emission Tomography (PET) & Single-Photon Emission Computed Tomography (SPECT)

PET and SPECT are nuclear medicine imaging techniques that measure metabolic activity, blood flow, or the distribution of specific molecular targets (e.g., neurotransmitter receptors, amyloid plaques) in the brain. They provide **functional and molecular information** with good spatial resolution but typically lower temporal resolution than fMRI. The data is primarily **3D volumetric**.

Figure 5.10 illustrates the general pipeline for processing PET and SPECT data with deep learning, highlighting their volumetric and molecular nature.

Common Architectures and Rationale for PET/SPECT Processing

For PET and SPECT Data: 3D CNNs are the most common and best architecture for PET and SPECT data because these datasets are volumetric. They can directly learn complex spatial patterns of tracer uptake, metabolic activity, or molecular binding. These patterns are crucial for diagnosing various neurological and psychiatric conditions. For instance, a 3D CNN can classify Alzheimer's disease by looking at the specific patterns of amyloid plaque buildup or reduced glucose metabolism seen in PET scans [15].

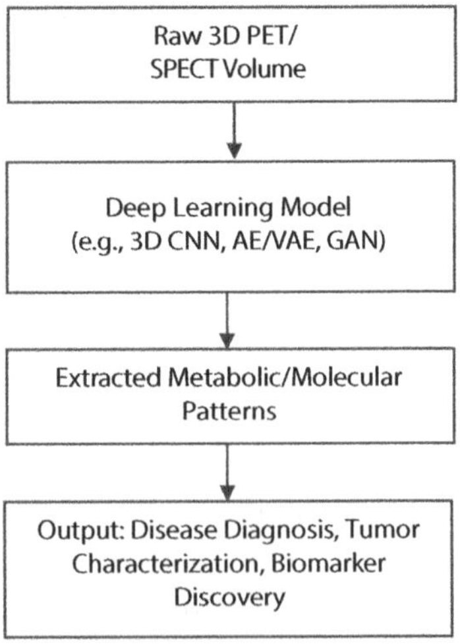

Figure 5.10 Conceptual flow for PET/SPECT data processing.

For DTI Data and Connectomes: Structured connectomes are often built from DTI data [8]. In these maps, brain regions act as nodes, and white matter tracts are the edges. Graph neural networks (GNNs) are the best method to analyze these graph representations and understand the structure, strength, and topology of brain networks [9]. For example, a GNN could classify individuals with traumatic brain injuries by identifying changes or breakdowns in their DTI-derived white matter networks [13].

For sMRI Data: Autoencoders (AEs) and variational autoencoders (VAEs) are useful for learning small, meaningful hidden representations of brain structure from sMRI scans. These hidden features can reveal bigger differences in how people's brains look, helping us understand how diseases or normal aging progress. VAEs can also generate synthetic sMRI images. For example, a 3D VAE could learn a hidden space of healthy brain structures. This would allow it to find subtle structural problems in new cases or create artificial brain images to augment existing data [10].

Typical Applications of Deep Learning in PET/SPECT

Deep learning is very important for understanding brain health through molecular and metabolic insights from PET and SPECT scans. It's widely used to find neurodegenerative diseases like Alzheimer's, Parkinson's, and Lewy Body Dementia by detecting specific protein clumps (amyloid, tau) or metabolic changes. Another use is characterizing tumors, telling the difference between benign and malignant brain tumors, or checking how aggressive a tumor is based on its metabolic activity. Deep learning also helps analyze neurotransmitter systems, measuring receptor availability or neurotransmitter release to understand psychiatric disorders (like depression and schizophrenia) or how drugs affect the brain. Plus, these models help locate epilepsy foci, finding hypometabolic areas where seizures start, and they make it easier to monitor treatment response by tracking changes in molecular or metabolic markers [21].

5.3.2 Classification by Learning Paradigm/Task

Beyond the specific brain signal modality, deep learning applications in neuroscience can also be categorized by the underlying learning paradigm or the type of task they are designed to accomplish. This classification highlights the diverse capabilities of deep learning, ranging from predictive modeling with labeled data to discovering hidden structures in unlabeled data and enabling adaptive control.

Figure 5.11 illustrates how different deep learning paradigms are applied to brain signal data to achieve various analytical and functional outcomes.

Supervised Learning: Classification and Regression

Supervised learning is useful when the acquired neuro data is labelled or annotated by a medical practitioner. Supervised learning is one of the commonly used models in deep learning. In this paradigm, models learn from labeled data to make predictions.

Classification involves assigning brain signals or patterns to predefined categories. This is extensively used for diagnostic purposes, such as classifying neurological disorders (e.g., Alzheimer's disease from fMRI [15] and epilepsy from EEG [1]), or for decoding cognitive states (e.g., emotion recognition from EEG [16] and motor imagery from EEG for BCIs [11]). Deep learning models, particularly CNNs and RNNs, excel in these tasks by learning complex, non-linear features from high-dimensional brain data that are highly discriminative for specific classes. For instance, a CNN can classify a brain tumor from an MRI scan by learning subtle visual features, while an LSTM can classify sleep stages from continuous EEG by recognizing temporal sequences of brain rhythms [7]. The success of these methods is heavily reliant on the availability of large, accurately labeled datasets.

Regression tasks involve predicting a continuous value from brain signals. Examples include predicting the severity of a neurological condition (e.g., disease progression score from MRI), estimating age from structural

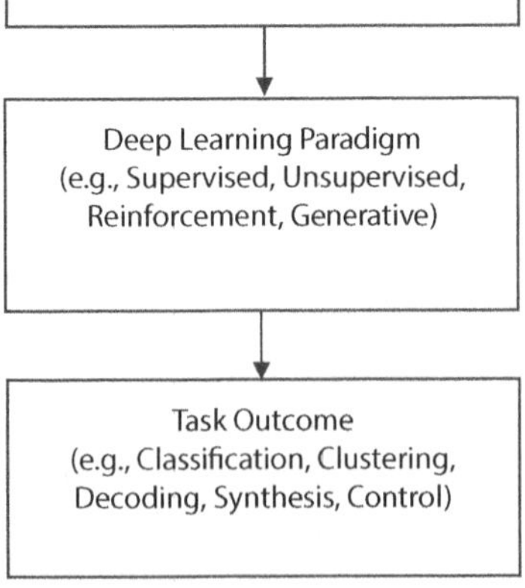

Figure 5.11 Conceptual overview of deep learning paradigms in neuroscience.

brain scans [15], or continuously decoding kinematic parameters (e.g., hand position, velocity) from iEEG/ECoG signals for neuroprosthetics [22]. Deep learning models, often with a linear output layer, are capable of learning complex mappings from high-dimensional brain features to these continuous target variables. For instance, a hybrid CNN-RNN model might predict a continuous pain rating based on a patient's EEG patterns.

Unsupervised Learning: Clustering, Dimensionality Reduction, and Representation Learning

Unsupervised learning methods are crucial when labeled data is scarce or when the goal is to discover hidden structures and patterns within brain signals without explicit guidance.

Clustering aims to group similar brain signal patterns or subjects together based on their intrinsic characteristics. Deep clustering methods can learn more discriminative embeddings for clustering than traditional approaches. For example, deep clustering applied to resting-state fMRI data could identify novel subtypes of psychiatric disorders based on shared functional connectivity patterns, even if these subtypes were not known beforehand.

Dimensionality Reduction seeks to transform high-dimensional brain data into a lower-dimensional space while preserving essential information. This is vital for visualizing complex data, removing noise, and improving the efficiency of subsequent analyses. **Autoencoders (AEs)** are a prime example, learning compact latent representations of EEG, fMRI, or sMRI data [10]. The learnt latent features can then be used as input for other machine learning models or for visualizing complex brain states in a simplified manner. For instance, an AE could reduce the dimensionality of multi-channel EEG data, making it easier to visualize and interpret brain activity patterns.

Representation Learning is a broader concept where a deep learning model learns to automatically extract meaningful and useful features (representations) from raw data. Autoencoders are a form of representation learning, but other techniques like self-supervised learning (where the model creates its own labels from the data, e.g., predicting missing parts of a signal) also fall into this category. The goal is to learn robust features that capture the underlying neurophysiological or neuroanatomical information, which can then be transferred to various downstream tasks, even with limited labeled data. For example, a model might learn a general representation of healthy brain activity from a large unlabeled dataset, which can then be fine-tuned for specific disease detection tasks.

Reinforcement Learning (RL)

Reinforcement Learning (RL) involves training agents to make a sequence of decisions in an environment to maximize a cumulative reward. While less common than supervised or unsupervised learning in neuroscience applications, RL holds significant promise, particularly in adaptive systems and brain-computer interfaces (BCIs).

In brain-computer interfaces (BCIs), RL is used to teach the code/program embedded in the BCI to respond to the patient's or user's brain signals. It provides the best output based on the decisions made by RL. For this, the terms 'agent,' 'environment,' and 'reward' are used to explain different works. So, the "Agent" is basically the decoding program, the "Environment" is the whole BCI system plus the user's brain, and the "Reward" is usually about how well the task was done or how happy the user is with the result.

Reinforcement learning (RL) can be used to enable adaptive control in brain–computer interfaces (BCIs), where an agent learns to optimize prosthetic limb movement based on motor cortex activity. It would keep changing and adapting as neural signals shift over time, making the control smoother and more exact. This ability to adjust is super important for using BCIs long-term, because neural signals can change due to things like tiredness, learning new things, or even just shifts in brain state. We can also use RL in neurofeedback, where people learn to control their own brain activity by getting real-time feedback, with the RL agent helping to fine-tune that feedback process.

Generative Models: GANs and VAEs

One of the most powerful models of deep learning is the generative model. These models can learn the underlying distribution of complex data and then generate realistic brain signals.

Generative Adversarial Networks (GANs) consist of two competing neural networks: a Generator and a Discriminator. The Generator creates synthetic data (e.g., synthetic MRI scans or EEG waveforms), while the Discriminator tries to distinguish between real and generated data. Through this adversarial process, the Generator learns to produce increasingly realistic synthetic brain data. GANs are valuable for data augmentation, especially when real brain data for rare conditions is scarce, or for tasks like super-resolution (enhancing low-resolution brain images) or image-to-image translation (e.g., synthesizing a PET scan from an MRI) [2, 4]. For instance, a GAN could generate realistic synthetic fMRI scans of patients with specific brain lesions, which could then be used to expand training datasets for lesion detection models.

Variational autoencoders (VAEs), as discussed in the foundational architectures section, are also powerful generative models. Unlike GANs, VAEs explicitly learn a probabilistic mapping to a structured latent space, from which new samples can be generated by sampling from a simple prior distribution. VAEs are particularly useful for understanding the underlying "factors" of variability in brain signals and for generating diverse, yet realistic, synthetic data. For example, a VAE trained on healthy EEG data could generate novel EEG rhythms, or one trained on fMRI data could synthesize brain activation patterns corresponding to different cognitive states [10]. The structured latent space of VAEs also allows for meaningful interpolation, enabling researchers to explore the continuum of brain states or disease progression.

5.3.3 Deep Learning for Multimodal Brain Signal Fusion

The functions of the brain originate and manifest across various parts of the brain, either in spatial or temporal scales. A single modality cannot record all the behaviors and functions of the brain. Therefore, "combining the unique acquired data from different modalities can provide a comprehensive understanding of the brain. For instance, EEG excels in temporal resolution, fMRI in spatial resolution, and sMRI in anatomical detail.

Figure 5.12 illustrates the three primary strategies for fusing multimodal brain signals using deep learning: early, intermediate, and late fusion, each offering distinct advantages.

Traditional models need more complex integration strategies to combine different kinds of inputs from various modalities. But deep learning, with its powerful frameworks, makes it easier to integrate and perform any operation on it. Multimodal brain signal fusion aims to integrate data from two or more such modalities to achieve a more comprehensive and robust understanding of brain states, disease mechanisms, or cognitive processes than can be obtained from any single modality alone [18]. The multimodality brings a collective understanding of the brain that is greater than any single modality. Deep learning provides powerful frameworks for this fusion, capable of learning complex, non-linear relationships across heterogeneous data types.

Fusion Strategies with Deep Learning

Deep learning offers flexible architectures to implement various fusion strategies, each with its own advantages and challenges.

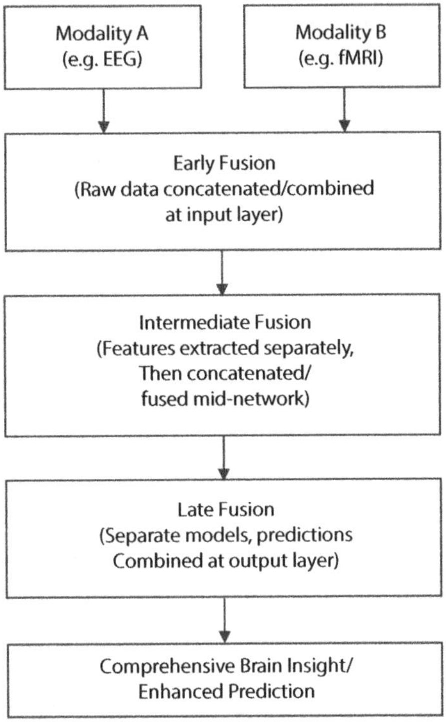

Figure 5.12 Conceptual strategies for multimodal brain signal fusion with deep learning.

Early Fusion (Feature-Level Fusion): In early fusion, raw data or minimally processed features from different modalities are concatenated or combined at the input layer of a single deep learning model. For example, raw EEG time series and fMRI volumes could be flattened and concatenated before being fed into a large, shared network. This approach allows the model to learn joint representations and complex interactions between modalities from the very beginning of the processing pipeline. A prominent example is the fusion of EEG and fMRI, where studies explore how to combine the high temporal resolution of EEG with the high spatial resolution of fMRI at an early stage to get a more complete spatio-temporal picture of brain activity [18]. The advantage is that the model can discover subtle, low-level cross-modal correlations, but it requires careful alignment of data and can be computationally intensive due to the high dimensionality of the combined input.

Intermediate Fusion (Deep Feature Fusion): This strategy involves processing each modality through separate, modality-specific deep learning sub-networks (e.g., a CNN for fMRI images, an RNN for EEG time series).

The high-level features extracted by these individual sub-networks are then concatenated or combined at an intermediate layer within a larger, shared deep learning architecture. This allows each sub-network to learn optimal representations for its specific modality before fusion, potentially simplifying the learning task for the fusion layer. For instance, a model might use a 3D CNN to extract spatial features from PET images and a separate 3D CNN for MRI images, then concatenate these learnt features before feeding them into a final classification head for neurodegenerative disease diagnosis [18]. This approach balances the benefits of modality-specific processing with the power of deep feature integration. Graph neural networks (GNNs) are also emerging in intermediate fusion, for example, fusing DTI-derived structural networks with fMRI-derived functional networks by combining their respective GNN-extracted features [13].
Late Fusion (Decision-Level Fusion): In late fusion, each modality is processed independently by its own complete deep learning model, leading to separate predictions or decision scores. These individual predictions are then combined at the final output stage using a simple aggregation rule (e.g., weighted averaging, majority voting, or another small neural network). This approach is conceptually simpler and more robust to missing data from one modality, as each model can still make a prediction. It is often used when modalities are very different or when pre-trained models are available for individual modalities [12].

5.4 Future Directions & Emerging Trends

The application of deep learning to brain signal processing is a rapidly evolving field, poised for transformative advancements in both neuroscience research and clinical practice. Several key trends and future directions are anticipated to shape the next generation of intelligent brain signal analysis.

Figure 5.13 outlines the anticipated trajectory of deep learning in brain signal processing, highlighting key areas of innovation and their potential impact.

Explainable AI (XAI) for Clinical Trust and Scientific Discovery
A critical future direction is the development of **Explainable AI (XAI)** methods tailored for brain signal analysis. While deep learning models achieve high performance, their "black-box" nature often hinders clinical adoption and scientific discovery. Future research will focus on developing techniques that can explain why a model made a particular diagnosis

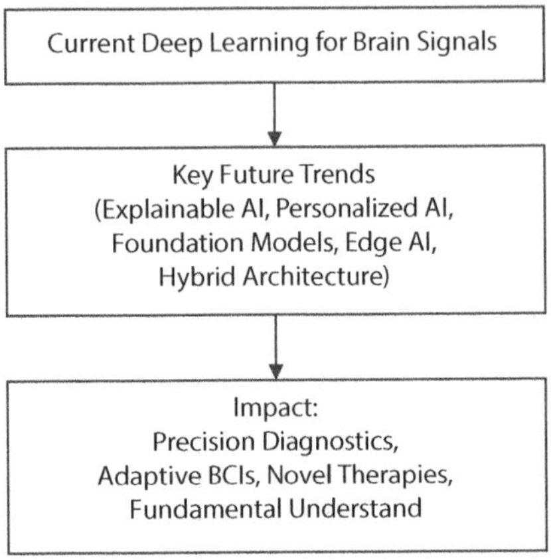

Figure 5.13 Conceptual landscape of future trends in deep learning for brain signals.

or decoded a specific brain state. This includes attention mechanisms in Transformers highlighting important brain regions or time points, saliency maps in CNNs showing relevant image features, and methods to extract interpretable rules or features from complex models [17, 20]. XAI will be essential for building trust among clinicians, enabling validation of model findings against neurophysiological knowledge, and facilitating the discovery of novel, interpretable biomarkers for neurological and psychiatric disorders.

Personalized and Adaptive Models

The inherent inter-individual variability in brain structure and function poses a significant challenge. Future deep learning models will increasingly focus on **personalized and adaptive learning**. This involves developing models that can rapidly adapt to individual patient data, leveraging transfer learning, few-shot learning, or meta-learning techniques to generalize effectively from limited individual-specific data [12]. Such personalized models will lead to more accurate diagnoses, more effective treatment planning, and highly customized brain-computer interfaces that can continuously adapt to changes in a user's neural signals over time.

Foundation Models and Large-Scale Pre-training

Inspired by the success of large language models, the concept of **foundation models** is emerging in neuroimaging. This involves training very large deep learning models on massive, diverse, and unlabeled brain signal datasets (e.g., hundreds of thousands of MRI scans or thousands of hours of EEG). These pre-trained models could then be fine-tuned for a wide array of downstream tasks (e.g., disease classification, biomarker discovery, image segmentation) with significantly less labeled data. This paradigm shift could unlock unprecedented capabilities for understanding general principles of brain organization and pathology.

Federated Learning and Privacy-Preserving AI

Given the sensitive nature of brain signal data and regulatory concerns (e.g., GDPR, HIPAA), **federated learning** will play an increasingly important role. This approach allows deep learning models to be trained collaboratively across multiple institutions without sharing raw patient data, thereby preserving privacy. Models learn from decentralized datasets, and only model updates (weights) are shared, enabling the development of robust models on larger, more diverse datasets while adhering to strict privacy regulations.

Edge AI and Real-Time Processing

The demand for real-time brain signal analysis, particularly for wearable EEG devices, brain-computer interfaces, and continuous monitoring systems, will drive the development of **Edge AI** solutions. This involves deploying compact and efficient deep learning models directly onto low-power, embedded hardware. Techniques like model quantization, pruning, and efficient architectural designs (e.g., depthwise separable CNNs, lightweight transformers) will be crucial for enabling real-time processing and decision-making directly at the point of care or interaction.

Advanced Hybrid Architectures and Multi-Scale Integration

The future will see even more sophisticated **hybrid deep learning architectures** that seamlessly integrate the strengths of different foundational models. This includes combining CNNs for local feature extraction, RNNs/transformers for long-range temporal modeling, and GNNs for network-level analysis, potentially within a single, end-to-end trainable framework. Furthermore, models will increasingly aim for **multi-scale integration**, simultaneously analyzing brain signals at different resolutions (e.g., single-neuron spikes, LFP, EEG, fMRI) to build a more comprehensive understanding of brain function and dysfunction across diverse biological scales.

Deep Generative Models for Data Synthesis and Simulation

The role of **deep generative models** (like VAEs and GANs) will expand beyond data augmentation. They will be used for sophisticated data synthesis for rare conditions, simulating brain activity under various conditions (e.g., drug effects, lesion impact), and creating realistic digital twins of individual brains [10]. This will accelerate research by providing access to vast amounts of diverse, synthetic data, enabling robust model training and hypothesis testing *in silico*.

Neuro-Inspired AI and Closing the Loop

Finally, a long-term trend involves a synergistic relationship between neuroscience and AI: **neuro-inspired AI**. Insights from how the brain processes information (e.g., sparse coding, hierarchical processing, and attention mechanisms) will continue to inspire new deep learning architectures. Conversely, deep learning models will serve as powerful tools to test computational theories of brain function, potentially leading to a deeper fundamental understanding of the brain itself. This closing of the loop between AI development and neuroscience research promises to unlock new frontiers in both fields.

AI disclosure statement: The author acknowledges the use of AI-based tools for minor language editing or grammatical correction. However, all intellectual contributions, analyses, and conclusions presented in this chapter are entirely the author's own.

References

1. Acharya, U.R., Oh, S.L., Hagiwara, Y., Tan, J.H., Adeli, H., Deep convolutional neural network for the automated detection and diagnosis of seizure using EEG signals. *Comput. Biol. Med.*, 2018.
2. Bowles, C., Chen, L., Guerrero, R., *et al.*, GAN augmentation: Augmenting training data using generative adversarial networks for brain lesion segmentation, in: *Proc. MICCAI*, 2018.
3. Bron, E.E., Smits, M., van der Flier, W.M., *et al.*, Standardized evaluation of algorithms for computer-aided diagnosis of dementia based on structural MRI: The CADDementia challenge. *Neuroimage Clin.*, 2015.
4. Chartsias, A., Joyce, T., Giuffrida, M.V., Tsaftaris, S.A., Multimodal MR synthesis *via* modality-invariant latent representation. *Med. Image Anal.*, 2019.
5. Craik, A., He, Y., Contreras-Vidal, J.L., Deep learning for electroencephalogram (EEG) classification tasks: A review. *J. Neural Eng.*, 2019.
6. Heinsfeld, A., Franco, A.R., Craddock, R.C., Buchweitz, A., Meneguzzi, F., Identification of autism spectrum disorder using deep learning and the ABIDE dataset. *Sci. Rep.*, 2018.
7. Hochreiter, S. and Schmidhuber, J., Long short-term memory. *Neural Comput.*, 1997.

8. Irimia, A., Van Horn, J.D., *et al.*, The structural connectome of the human brain: Network modeling and analysis. *J. Neurosci. Methods*, 2012.
9. Kawahara, J., Brown, C., Miller, S., *et al.*, BrainNetCNN: Convolutional neural networks for brain networks; towards predicting neurodevelopment. *Neuroimage*, 2017.
10. Kingma, D.P. and Welling, M., Auto-encoding variational Bayes, in: *Proc. ICLR*, 2014.
11. Lawhern, V.J., Solon, A.J., Waytowich, N.R., Gordon, S.M., Hung, C.P., Lance, B.J., EEGNet: A compact convolutional neural network for EEG-based brain–computer interfaces. *J. Neural Eng.*, 2018.
12. LeCun, Y., Bengio, Y., Hinton, G., Deep learning. *Nature*, 2015.
13. Parisot, S., Ktena, S.I., Ferrante, E., *et al.*, Disease prediction using graph convolutional networks: Application to autism spectrum disorder and Alzheimer's disease. *Med. Image Anal.*, 2018.
14. Pandarinath, C., O'Shea, D.J., Collins, J., *et al.*, Inferring single-trial neural population dynamics using sequential auto-encoders. *Nat. Methods*, 2018.
15. Payan, A. and Montana, G., Predicting Alzheimer's disease: A neuroimaging study with 3D convolutional neural networks. *Neuroimage Clin.*, 2015.
16. Roy, Y., Banville, H., Albuquerque, I., *et al.*, Deep learning-based electroencephalography analysis: A systematic review. *J. Neural Eng.*, 2019.
17. Schirrmeister, R.T., Springenberg, J.T., Fiederer, L.D.J., *et al.*, Deep learning with convolutional neural networks for EEG decoding and visualization. *Hum. Brain Mapp.*, 2017.
18. Suk, H.I., Lee, S.W., Shen, D., Alzheimer's Disease Neuroimaging Initiative, Hierarchical feature representation and multimodal fusion with deep learning for Alzheimer's disease diagnosis. *Brain Struct. Funct.*, 2014.
19. Trautmann, E.M., O'Shea, D.J., Sun, J.D., *et al.*, Accurate estimation of neural population dynamics without spike sorting. *Neuron*, 2019.
20. Vaswani, A., Shazeer, N., Parmar, N., *et al.*, Attention is all you need, in: *Advances in Neural Information Processing Systems*, 2017.
21. Vieira, S., Pinaya, W.H.L., Mechelli, A., Using deep learning to investigate the neuroimaging correlates of psychiatric and neurological disorders: Methods and applications. *Front. Neurosci.*, 2017.
22. Wang, W., Collinger, J.L., Degenhart, A.D., *et al.*, An electrocorticographic brain interface in an individual with tetraplegia. *J. Neural Eng.*, 2010.

6

Decoding Motor Imagery with Machine Learning and Deep Learning

Irtiqa Amin[1]*, Quraazah Akeemu Amin[2], Khair Ul Nisa[3], Sheikh Ikhlaq[4] and Obaid Ahmad Bhat[5]

[1]School of Computer Application Lovely Professional University, Phagwara, Punjab, India
[2]Division of Food Science and Technology, SKUAST-Kashmir, Srinagar, Jammu and Kashmir, India
[3]Department of Computer Science and Artificial Intelligence, University of Bisha, Asir Region, Saudi Arabia
[4]Cyber, Enterprise Security, Deloitte, Hyderabad, Telangana, India
[5]School of Renewable Energy, Maejo University, Chiang Mai, Thailand

Abstract
Decoding motor imagery (MI) using machine learning (ML) and deep learning (DL) is transforming how we interpret neural signals. Electroencephalography (EEG) data from imagined movements can be converted into commands for brain-computer interfaces (BCIs). Traditional ML methods rely on manual feature extraction, limiting their ability to capture complex neural patterns. However, advanced DL architectures automatically learn patterns and features that enhance accuracy, real-time decoding, and generalization. This chapter discusses in detail the case studies, comparative evaluations, and advancements of MI using ML and DL architectures. It also highlights how these techniques overcome key challenges, paving the way for personalized medicine and advanced human-machine interaction (HCI).

***Keywords*:** Motor imagery, machine learning, deep learning, human-computer interaction, neuroscience, neurotechnology

**Corresponding author*: irtiqa.amin7100@gmail.com

Tawseef Ahmed Teli, Syed Immamul Ansarullah, Arun Kumar Rana, Suman Lata Tripathi and Kashif Nisar (eds.) Brain-to-Computer Interfaces Using Machine Learning and Deep Learning, (139–158) © 2026 Scrivener Publishing LLC

6.1 Introduction

In recent times, considerable research has focused on the human brain's capacity to consciously mimic movements and experiences. Instead of using the human brain's normal way of sending the signals, a BCI creates a direct connection between the nervous system and external devices like computers or machines. Conceptual motor imaging is a psychological model mimicking experience but lacking instant, accompanying perceptible data, meaning that, based on expectations, individuals may utilize images to predict what would happen next [1, 2].

Sensory or motor imagery (MI) is often defined as the capacity to internally visualize images and perceive sounds, effectively using the mind's visuals and hearing. This is a crucial component of this process, enabling mental practice of motions without their actual implementation [3–5]. MI requires participants to view the body as the source of action rather than merely its results and is frequently utilized when the body or its parts are involved. These conceptual representations are formed in part by sensory information, including tactile and proprioceptive inputs [6]. MI supports physical practice by improving cognitive and motor function and promoting motor recovery, according to research [7]. In other words, any sensory system can generate brain representations of experience involving recalling, replicating, or reconstructing real perceptual experiences from long-term memory, which are then internally recreated within working memory. Various forms of MI can be identified and seamlessly integrated. Individuals often experience visual imagery, auditory imagery, and kinesthetic imagery [8–12]. Every sensory modality can be linked to imagery. Additionally, in relation to perception, mental imagery merges inputs from multiple sensory systems, creating a holistic sensory-motor experience [11].

As we know, MI has long been a focus of cognitive neuroscience; therefore, understanding the brain activity linked to both real and imagined goal-directed actions has been a key objective, especially with the rise of neuroimaging methods like Functional Magnetic Resonance Imaging (fMRI) [12–15]. A major challenge over the past two decades has been identifying physiological markers associated with MI. Research, particularly in neuroimaging, has shown that MI activates motor systems and induces brain plasticity like physical practice. These insights clarify how MI enhances performance and strengthens motor memory.

6.2 Basic Architecture of the Human Brain

The human brain's architecture is a highly intricate and dynamic network that underpins essential functions such as cognition, emotion, sensory processing, and motor control. The human brain works through a system of neural structures that send signals along complex pathways, hence enabling learning, memory, and adaptive responses. To truly understand human brain architecture, we need to explore its different parts along with the circuits that link them and the mechanisms that help their interactions.

6.2.1 Structural Components of the Human Brain

The human brain is composed of several interconnected structural components, each responsible for specific functions essential to survival and higher cognitive processes. Some fundamental components of the brain are as follows:

a) **Neurons:** Neurons are the fundamental cells of the brain that carry information using tiny electrical and chemical signals. Each neuron is composed of a cell body, dendrites, and an axon. These messages travel along small gaps called synapses, allowing communication throughout the brain.
b) **Brain Regions:** The human brain is divided into different regions (cerebral cortex, subcortical structures, and limbic systems), and each one is responsible for specific functions:
   - **Cerebral Cortex:** The cerebral cortex is responsible for advanced functions such as reasoning and making choices, along with others.
   - **Subcortical Structures:** Subcortical structures are responsible for functions like sensory processing, motor control, etc.
   - **Limbic System:** The limbic system is responsible for emotion, memory, and learning.

6.2.2 Connectivity and Communication

a) **Neural Networks:** Neurons are the fundamental building blocks of the human brain, which form complex neural networks. These neural networks help the human brain to combine and process information. These connections between different brain regions are essential for everything to work smoothly together.

b) **Interregional Connectivity:** Research studies show that different parts of the brain can connect in new ways based on learning and experience.

6.2.3 Developing Brain Architecture

a) **Building from the Bottom Up:** The human brain develops in stages, beginning with simple structures and becoming more complex as experiences shape neural connections. Early experiences are crucial in shaping human brain connections and laying the foundation for future learning, thinking, and behavior.

b) **Impact of Adverse Experiences:** Research studies show that during the critical development of the human brain, negativity can affect it badly and lead to behavioral and health issues.

6.3 Architecture of MI *via* DL and ML

BCI systems decode human brain signals to understand signals and information and translate that information into actionable directions.

6.3.1 Overview of MI Brain Computer Interface Systems

Motor imagery brain-computer interfaces (MI-BCIs) are intelligent platforms engineered to detect and interpret neural activity patterns linked to the brain's kinesthetic imagery. These systems process EEG [16–18] signals and convert them into commands for external devices, such as robotic arms or prosthetics. The architecture of MI-BCI [19] systems typically involves: *signal acquisition*, *preprocessing*, *feature extraction*, *classification*, *output layer* or *control commands*, and *feedback loop (optional)*. The architectural representation of MI-BCI is shown in Figure 6.1 below.

6.3.2 MI Understanding Using ML/DL Tactics

MI classification is an imperative research domain in BCIs, focusing on decoding brain activity associated with imagined movements. This field leverages advanced DL and ML techniques to analyze neural signals,

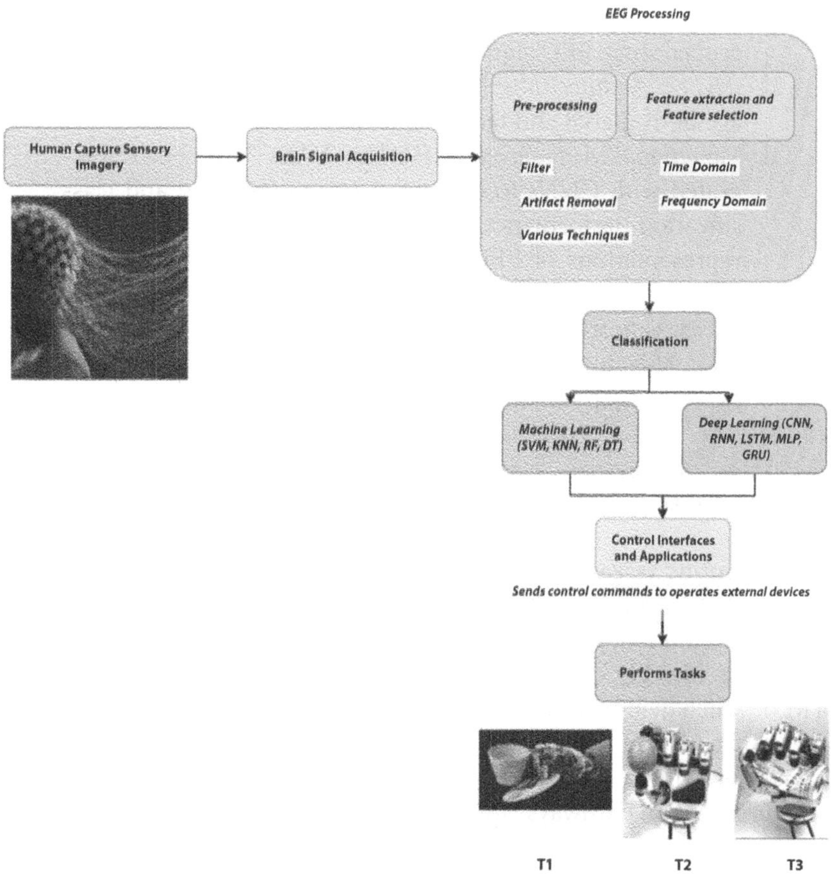

Figure 6.1 Architecture of motor imagery using ML and DL approaches.

typically recorded using EEG [20–25], and translate them into meaningful commands for peripheral hardware systems, such as robotic arms, prosthetics, or communication systems for individuals with motor impairments. The following are some of the most widely used architectures in this domain:

a. *CNNs:* CNNs can preprocess EEG signals to identify patterns associated with motor imagery tasks. Variants like GoogLeNet have been applied to classify EEG signals for controlling robotic manipulators.
b. *Recurrent Neural Networks (RNNs):* RNNs, especially long short-term memory (LSTM) networks, are efficiently used

to extract time-based dependencies in EEG signals. This is crucial since EEG signals are time-series data.

c. *Hybrid Architectures:* Hybrid models are proposed to leverage both spatial and temporal features.
d. *Variational Autoencoders (VAEs):* VAEs have been integrated with CNNs to enhance feature extraction and classification performance. These architectures can learn latent representations of EEG data, improving the robustness of MI classification. Conventional ML techniques are used for MI classification; however, these methods often depend on manual feature extraction, which can be less efficient compared to deep learning.

6.4 Neuroscientific Basis of Motor Imagery

Neuroscientific research holds demonstrations that MI shares significant neural mechanisms with real movement, making it an essential tool in neurorehabilitation, skill training, and BCIs. Neuroscientific research uses techniques like EEG, fMRI [15], and transcranial magnetic stimulation (TMS), which demonstrated that MI activates motor-related brain regions, supporting its role in motor learning and rehabilitation. Understanding the neuroscientific basis of MI involves examining its underlying brain structures, neural pathways, and functional processes.

6.4.1 Involvement of Brain Regions in Motor Imagery

Motor imagery engages a network of motor-related and associative brain regions that contribute to movement planning, execution, and sensory feedback. The basic components of motor control are shown in Figure 6.2, which includes:

a. *Primary Motor Cortex (M1):* It is responsible for executing voluntary movements. While MI does not involve actual movement, subthreshold activation of M1 occurs, preparing motor commands without triggering muscle contractions. Studies using TMS have shown increased corticospinal excitability in M1 during MI, reinforcing its involvement in motor preparation.
b. *Premotor Cortex (PMC):* The premotor cortex (PMC) plays a key role in movement planning and coordination,

particularly when guided by external cues. During MI, PMC activity reflects the formulation of motor sequences, suggesting its contribution to mental simulation of actions.

c. *Supplementary Motor Area (SMA):* It is vital for internally generated, triggered, and actionable sequences and motor coordination.
d. *Parietal Cortex:* The parietal lobe, especially the superior parietal lobule (SPL), integrates sensory information to create a spatial representation of the body. The inferior parietal lobule (IPL) contributes to proprioceptive awareness and vasomotor coordination, helping construct detailed movement imagery.
e. *Basal Ganglia:* These are involved in motor control, habit formation, and movement initiation. Research suggests that the basal ganglia facilitate MI by supporting motor learning and reinforcing internalized movement patterns.
f. *Cerebellum:* The cerebellum is responsible for fine-tuning motor actions, error correction, and motor learning. During MI, it is believed to predict the sensory consequences of imagined actions, reinforcing precise movement coordination.

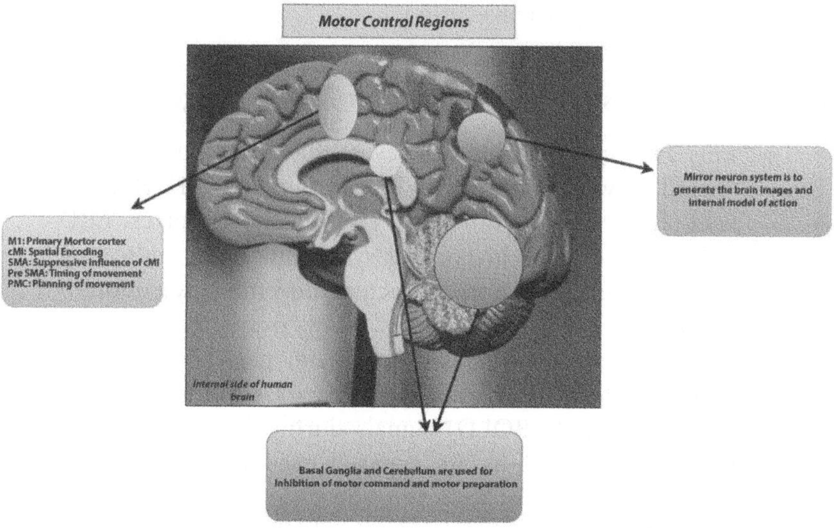

Figure 6.2 Motor control regions of the human brain.

g. *Mirror Neuron System (MNS):* The MNS enables activities like understanding, imitation learning, and motor skill acquisition through MI.

6.4.2 Neural Pathways Implication in Motor Imagery

It is mediated by complex neural circuits that integrate motor, sensory, and cognitive functions to generate an internal representation of movement. These pathways include.

a. *Cortico-Spinal Pathway:* Although MI does not trigger overt movement, the cortico-spinal tract exhibits increased excitability, suggesting partial motor preparation. TMS studies show that MI primes the motor system, reinforcing its role in neuroplasticity and skill acquisition.
b. *Cortico-Basal Ganglia-Thalamo-Cortical Loop:* This loop is essential for motor control and learning, connecting the cortex, basal ganglia, thalamus, and back to the cortex. During MI, this circuit is engaged to refine motor representations and consolidate motor memory.
c. *Cortico-Cerebellar Loop:* The cerebellum processes motor planning signals and predicts the sensory outcomes of imagined movements. It sends feedback to the motor and premotor cortex to improve movement accuracy, even in the absence of physical execution.

6.4.3 Neurophysiologic Evidence for Motor Imagery

a. *EEG Findings:* EEG studies reveal that MI induces event-related desynchronization (ERD) in the mu (8–12 Hz) and beta (13–30 Hz) rhythms of the sensorimotor cortex. ERD reflects a decrease in cortical synchronization, indicating motor system activation, like actual movement execution.
b. *fMRI Evidence:* fMRI studies show overlapping activation between MI and real movement, particularly in the motor cortex, SMA, and parietal areas. Blood-oxygen-level-dependent (BOLD) signals during MI confirm that motor-related regions are engaged even without physical action [26–29].
c. *Transcranial Magnetic Stimulation (TMS) Studies:* TMS has demonstrated increased corticospinal excitability during

MI, supporting the idea that imagined movements prepare the motor system for execution. These findings suggest that MI strengthens motor pathways, contributing to skill learning and rehabilitation.

6.4.4 Functional Role of Motor Imagery in Motor Learning and Rehabilitation

a. *Enhancing Motor Learning:* MI reinforces motor memory consolidation, making it an effective tool for skill acquisition and sports training. Studies show that mentally rehearsing movements improves actual performance, like physical practice.
b. *Role in Neuroplasticity:* MI promotes synaptic plasticity in motor circuits, strengthening neural connections involved in movement control. This plasticity contributes to skill retention and motor adaptation.
c. *Applications in Stroke Rehabilitation:* MI-based therapy helps stroke patients regain motor function by activating damaged motor networks. Neuroimaging studies show increased connectivity between motor areas, supporting MI as a rehabilitation tool.

6.4.5 Comparing Motor Imagery (MI) and Motor Execution (ME): Similarities and Differences

They disseminate several neural and functional characteristics, as MI activates brain regions and motor pathways like those engaged during actual movement. However, there are key differences between the two processes, particularly in muscle activation and sensory feedback. Understanding these similarities and differences is crucial for applications in motor learning, rehabilitation, and BCIs.

Despite the absence of physical actions in MI, it engages neural mechanisms that are largely shared with ME. Neuroimaging studies using fMRI and PET [30, 31] scans show significant activation overlap of the brain between MI and ME, confirming their shared neural basis. MI leads to increased corticospinal excitability, like actual movement, as shown by TMS studies. Even though no physical movement occurs, MI primes the motor system for execution, reinforcing neural pathways involved in motor planning.

Both MI and ME engage proprioceptive and sensory processing networks, though MI relies on internally generated sensory representations. The parietal cortex plays a crucial role in constructing spatial awareness and movement simulation in both cases. Studies indicate that mentally rehearsing movements through MI enhances actual motor performance, just as physical practice does. MI strengthens motor memory and facilitates skill acquisition by reinforcing movement patterns at the neural level. MI contributes to neuroplasticity, just like ME, by strengthening neural connections and improving motor function over time. This mechanism is particularly useful in stroke rehabilitation, where MI can activate damaged motor areas and aid recovery. While MI and ME share similar neural mechanisms, there are key distinctions that set them apart (Table 6.1).

Table 6.1 Differences between MI and ME.

Feature	**Motor imagery (MI)**	**Motor execution (ME)**
Brain Activation	Motor cortex, premotor cortex, SMA, parietal areas, cerebellum, basal ganglia	Motor cortex, premotor cortex, SMA, parietal areas, cerebellum, basal ganglia
Corticospinal Excitability	Increased but subthreshold (no overt movement)	Full activation leading to muscle contraction
Muscle Activity	No actual movement (only mental stimulation)	Physical muscle contraction and movement
Sensory Feedback	Internally generated (proprioceptive and cognitive simulation)	Actual sensory input from muscles, joints, and the environment
Energy Consumption	Lower compared to physical movement	Higher due to muscle activation and movement
Execution Time	Often faster or variable in duration	Typically follows real-time movement constraints
Role in Learning	Reinforces motor planning and neural pathways	Strengthens motor execution and coordination

6.5 Types of MI

MI is a brain-stimulated process in which a human internally recreates or envisions physical movements without physically performing them. It is widely used in neuroscience, rehabilitation, motor learning, and Brain-Computer Interface (BCI) research. MI can be classified into various types based on sensory modality, perspective, and cognitive strategies. Each type of MI activates different neural circuits and serves distinct functional purposes.

6.5.1 Types of MI Based on Sensory Modality

Different sensory modalities contribute to MI by providing internal representations of movement. The primary components are described as follows.

i. Visual Motor Imagery (VMI): Visual motor imagery involves mentally visualizing movements as if watching a video or recalling a scene. It is further divided into:
   - First-Person (Internal) Visual Imagery: The individual imagines performing a movement from their own perspective. It activates sensorimotor areas, the premotor cortex, and the parietal lobes. Example: A gymnast mentally rehearsing a flip while "seeing" the movement from their own eyes.
   - Third-Person (External) Visual Imagery: The movement is imagined from an external viewpoint, as if observing oneself from a distance. It engages the occipital cortex, premotor cortex, and parietal lobes. Example: A soccer player visualizing themselves scoring a goal from an outside perspective.

ii. Kinaesthetic Motor Imagery (KMI): It involves imagining the feeling of movement rather than just seeing it and engages the somatosensory cortex, cerebellum, and primary motor cortex (M1). Example: A pianist imagining the sensation of fingers pressing piano keys.
iii. Auditory Motor Imagery (AMI): It focuses on imagining **sounds** related to movement, such as footsteps, a ball bouncing, or muscle contraction sounds. It activates the auditory cortex and motor-related brain regions. Example:

A drummer mentally rehearsing beats while "hearing" the rhythm.

iv. Tactile Motor Imagery: It involves mentally simulating the sensation of touch associated with movement. It engages somatosensory pathways, the parietal cortex, and premotor areas. Example: A martial artist imagining the feeling of gripping an opponent's arm during a move.

6.5.2 Types of MI Based on Perspective

MI can be categorized based on the perspective from which movements are imagined, as shown in Table 6.2, and Table 6.3 shows the applications of different types of motor imagery.

a. Internal Motor Imagery: The individual feels and experiences the movement as if performing it. It is strongly linked to proprioception, kinesthetic awareness, and motor execution pathways. Example: A runner mentally feeling the movement of their legs and arms before a race.
b. External Motor Imagery: The movement is observed rather than felt, like watching a video of oneself. It activates the occipital lobe and the mirror neuron system. Example: A diver visualizing their performance from a judge's viewpoint.

Key Differences between Internal and External MI:

Table 6.2 Differences between internal and external MI.

Feature	Internal motor imagery	External motor imagery
Experience	First-person, as if performing the movement	Third-person, as if watching oneself
Activation	Sensorimotor, proprioceptive regions	Occipital, visual processing regions
Application	Skill learning, rehabilitation, kinesthetic training	Tactical analysis, movement observation

Table 6.3 Summary of applications based on different types of motor imagery.

Type	Application
Visual MI (First-Person)	Skill learning, sports training, rehabilitation
Visual MI (Third-Person)	Tactical awareness, movement observation
Kinesthetic MI	Strengthening neural pathways for movement recovery
Auditory MI	Music training, rhythm-based sports like dance or drumming
Tactile MI	Enhancing sensory-motor integration
Internal MI	Improving proprioception, refining motor execution
External MI	Evaluating technique, strategy development
Dynamic MI	Assisting neuromuscular rehabilitation
Intentional MI	Cognitive training for movement disorders
Symbolic MI	Psychological preparation, motivation

6.5.3 Applications of Different Types of Motor Imagery

MI has different types which offer diverse applications, as summarized in Table 6.3 above. Each MI type activates the human brain in a unique way to achieve specific goals.

6.6 Application of Motor Imagery

MI has significant applications in neuroscience and its closely related fields. The following are some real-world examples across various research domains:

6.6.1 Medical and Rehabilitation Applications

a. *Phantom Limb Pain Management:* MI helps amputees reduce phantom limb pain by recreating missing limb movements mentally, altering brain activity associated with pain perception.

b. *Cognitive and Motor Recovery in Neurodegenerative Diseases:* Patients with Alzheimer's or dementia benefit from MI exercises that stimulate neural pathways and cognitive function.

6.6.2 Sports and Performance Enhancement

a. *Athlete Training and Skill Acquisition:* Elite athletes use visual and kinesthetic MI to improve motor planning, coordination, and reaction times. Enhances muscle memory and neural efficiency before physical execution. Example: A gymnast mentally rehearsing a routine before performing it.
b. *Injury Prevention and Recovery:* Athletes recovering from injuries use MI to maintain neural activation of motor circuits, preventing skill deterioration. Helps in return-to-play protocols without excessive strain on healing tissues [32].
c. *Tactical and Strategic Planning:* It is used in team sports (e.g., soccer, basketball) for mental rehearsal of game strategies.

6.6.3 Brain-Computer Interfaces (BCIs) and Assistive Technologies

a. *MI-Based BCIs for Prosthetic Control:* It allows paralyzed or amputee patients to control robotic limbs using imagined movements. Example: MI-BCI translating EEG signals into prosthetic hand movements.
b. *Assistive Devices for Disabled Individuals:* MI-based BCIs enable wheelchair control, communication aids, and smart home automation for individuals with severe mobility impairments.
c. *Neurofeedback Training:* MI combined with EEG-based BCIs is used for cognitive enhancement and mental health therapy.

6.6.4 Cognitive Science and Psychological Applications

a. *Memory and Learning Enhancement:* MI strengthens neural connections, improving motor learning, problem-solving, and cognitive flexibility.

b. *Mental Health and Anxiety Reduction:* It is used in mindfulness, meditation, and cognitive therapy to reduce stress and enhance self-regulation.
c. *Visualization Therapy for PTSD:* Patients use MI techniques to reframe traumatic experiences, aiding post-traumatic stress disorder (PTSD) recovery.

6.6.5 Robotics, Artificial Intelligence, Virtual Reality (VR), and Gaming

a. *MI for Human-Robot Interaction:* Brain-controlled robotics uses MI signals to execute tasks like grasping objects, walking assistance, and industrial automation.
b. *Neuroadaptive Systems:* MI is used in adaptive AI systems to predict and respond to human intentions in VR, gaming, and smart environments.
c. *MI-Enhanced VR Training:* Pilots, surgeons, and military personnel use MI-based VR simulations to practice skills without real-world consequences.
d. *Brain-Controlled Gaming:* Neurogaming leverages MI-based BCIs to create immersive, hands-free gaming experiences.

6.6.6 Music and Artistic Performance

a. *Motor Learning for Musicians:* Pianists, violinists, and drummers use MI to rehearse complex finger movements mentally, improving accuracy and timing.
b. *Dance and Choreography:* Dancers use MI to refine movement sequences before physical execution.

6.7 Challenges in Motor Imagery in DL and ML Research

MI decoding, particularly in the context of BCIs, presents several challenges when using DL and ML techniques. These arise from the traits of the input data, the complexity of the models, and the practical constraints of real-world implementations.

- ***Low Signal-to-Noise Ratio (SNR):*** EEG signals used for motor imagery are inherently noisy and have a low SNR ratio. This hampers the effective extraction of meaningful features for classification. Noise can come from various sources, such as muscle artifacts, environmental interference, or even the subject's mental state.
- ***Non-Stationarity of EEG Signals:*** EEG signals are non-stationary, which makes the development of models that generalize well across sessions or subjects difficult.
- ***Limited Availability of Labeled Data:*** The scarcity of data limits the ability to train complex models effectively and can lead to overfitting.
- ***Subject Variability***: EEG signals vary from individual to individual, hence making it difficult to develop models that perform well across multiple users without extensive subject-specific calibration.
- ***High Dimensionality of EEG Data:*** EEG data is high-dimensional in nature, which increases the computational complexity of feature extraction and model training. While DL models can handle high-dimensional data, they require careful design to avoid overfitting and ensure efficient learning.
- ***Computational Complexity:*** Deep learning models are computationally intensive. This can be a limitation for real-time applications, such as BCIs, where low latency is critical.
- ***Lack of Standardized Preprocessing Pipelines:*** Preprocessing EEG data (e.g., filtering, artifact removal) is a crucial step, but there is no universally accepted pipeline. Variations in preprocessing methods can lead to inconsistent results and make it difficult to compare different studies or models.
- ***Overfitting in DL Models:*** With a limited medical dataset, DL models are prone to overfitting, especially when the models are complex. Overfitting reduces the generalizability of the models to new data or unseen subjects.
- ***Interpretability of DL Models:*** These are frequently regarded as opaque systems; hence, the lack of interpretability is a challenge in medical and clinical applications, where understanding the model's reasoning is crucial.

- ➤ ***Real-Time Implementation:*** For practical applications, such as controlling prosthetics or robotic devices, MI decoding systems must operate in real-time. Achieving the necessary speed and accuracy simultaneously is a significant challenge, especially with computationally intensive deep-learning models [33].

6.8 Conclusion

This chapter discusses the fundamental principles of BCI, the challenges of decoding brain signals, and the role of various ML and DL models in enhancing classification accuracy. The traditional ML techniques considerably decode MI; however, the novel and advanced DL architectures improved the classification performance. These advanced DL architectures enable BCIs to translate brain signals into precise, meaningful commands. Even with improvements, these architectures still face challenges like individual variability in brain signals, data scarcity, computational complexity, and constraints related to real-time implementation. To address these issues, future research should focus on the unending research and interdisciplinary collaboration along with the advancements in neuroimaging technologies, healthcare, and human-computer interaction.

AI disclosure statement: The author confirms that no artificial intelligence (AI)-generated content or AI-assisted writing tools were used in the preparation of this chapter (including summaries and the abstract). All text, analysis, and conclusions are the result of the author's original work.

References

1. Tariq, M., Trivailo, P.M., Simic, M., EEG-based BCI control schemes for lower-limb assistive-robots. *Front. Hum. Neurosci.*, 12, 312, 2018.
2. Wolpaw, J.R., Birbaumer, N., McFarland, D.J., Pfurtscheller, G., Vaughan, T.M., Brain-computer interfaces for communication and control. *Clin. Neurophysiol.*, 6, 767–91, 2002.
3. Handiru, V.S., Vinod, A.P., Guan, C., EEG source imaging of movement decoding: the state of the art and future directions. *IEEE Syst. Man Cybern. Mag.*, 4, 14–23, 2018.

4. Edelman, B.J., Baxter, B., He, B., EEG source imaging enhances the decoding of complex right-hand motor imagery tasks. *IEEE Trans. Biomed. Eng.*, 63, 4–14, 2015.
5. Dai, G., Zhou, J., Huang, J., Wang, N., HS-CNN: a CNN with hybrid convolution scale for EEG motor imagery classification. *J. Neural Eng.*, 17, 016025, 2020.
6. Tang, Z., Li, C., Sun, S., Single-trial EEG classification of motor imagery using deep convolutional neural networks. *Optik*, 130, 11–18, 2017.
7. Amin, S.U., Alsulaiman, M., Muhammad, G., Bencherif, M.A., Hossain, M.S., Multilevel weighted feature fusion using convolutional neural networks for EEG motor imagery classification. *IEEE Access*, 7, 18940–50, 2019.
8. Amin, S.U., Alsulaiman, M., Muhammad, G., Mekhtiche, M.A., Hossain, M.S., Deep learning for EEG motor imagery classification based on multi-layer CNNs feature fusion. *Future Gener. Comput. Syst.*, 101, 542–54, 2019.
9. Cai, J., Wei, C., Tang, X.L., Xue, C., Chang, Q., The motor imagination EEG recognition combined with convolution neural network and gated recurrent unit. *2018 37th Chinese Control Conf. (CCC)*, IEEE, pp. 9598–602, 2018.
10. Wu, H., Li, F., Li, Y., Fu, B., Shi, G., Dong, M., Niu, Y., A parallel multiscale filter bank convolutional neural networks for motor imagery EEG classification. *Front. Neurosci.*, 13, 1275, 2019.
11. Tang, X., Li, W., Li, X., Ma, W., Dang, X., Motor imagery EEG recognition based on conditional optimization empirical mode decomposition and multi-scale convolutional neural network. *Expert Syst. Appl.*, 149, 113285, 2020.
12. Shajil, N., Mohan, S., Srinivasan, P., Arivudaiyanambi, J., Murrugesan, A., Multiclass classification of spatially filtered motor imagery EEG signals using convolutional neural network for BCI-based applications. *J. Med. Biol. Eng.*, 1–10, 2020.
13. Jeong, J.H., Shim, K.H., Kim, D.J., Lee, S.W., Brain-controlled robotic arm system based on multi-directional CNN-BiLSTM network using EEG signals. *IEEE Trans. Neural Syst. Rehabil. Eng.*, 28, 1226–38, 2020.
14. Sakhavi, S., Guan, C., Yan, S., Learning temporal information for brain-computer interface using convolutional neural networks. *IEEE Trans. Neural Networks Learn. Syst.*, 29, 5619–29, 2018.
15. Tang, X., Zhao, J., Fu, W., Pan, J., Zhou, H., A novel classification algorithm for MI-EEG based on deep learning. *2019 IEEE 8th Joint Int. Information Technology and Artificial Intelligence Conf. (ITAIC)*, IEEE, pp. 606–11, 2019.
16. Tian, G. and Liu, Y., Study on classification of left-right hands motor imagery EEG signals based on CNN. *2018 IEEE 17th Int. Conf. on Cognitive Informatics & Cognitive Computing (ICCI*CC)*, IEEE, pp. 324–9, 2018.

17. Tabar, Y.R. and Halici, U., A novel deep learning approach for classification of EEG motor imagery signals. *J. Neural Eng.*, 14, 016003, 2016.
18. Lee, H.K. and Choi, Y.S., A convolution neural networks scheme for classification of motor imagery EEG based on wavelet time-frequency image. *2018 Int. Conf. on Information Networking (ICOIN)*, IEEE, pp. 906–9, 2018.
19. Das, R., Maiorana, E., Campisi, P., Motor imagery for EEG biometrics using convolutional neural network. *2018 IEEE Int. Conf. on Acoustics, Speech and Signal Processing (ICASSP)*, IEEE, pp. 2062–6, 2018.
20. Bashivan, P., Rish, I., Yeasin, M., Codella, N., Learning representations from EEG with deep recurrent-convolutional neural networks, (arXiv:1511.06448), 2015.
21. Yang, J., Yao, S., Wang, J., Deep fusion feature learning network for MI-EEG classification. *IEEE Access*, 6, 79050–9, 2018.
22. Xu, G., Shen, X., Chen, S., Zong, Y., Zhang, C., Yue, H., Che, W., A deep transfer convolutional neural network framework for EEG signal classification. *IEEE Access*, 7, 112767–76, 2019.
23. Chaudhary, S., Taran, S., Bajaj, V., Sengur, A., Convolutional neural network-based approach towards motor imagery tasks EEG signals classification. *IEEE Sens. J.*, 19, 4494–500, 2019.
24. Ha, K.W. and Jeong, J.W., Motor imagery EEG classification using capsule networks. *Sensors*, 19, 2854, 2019.
25. Tayeb, Z., Fedjaev, J., Ghaboosi, N., Richter, C., Everding, L., Qu, X., Wu, Y., Cheng, G., Conradt, J., Validating deep neural networks for online decoding of motor imagery movements from EEG signals. *Sensors*, 19, 210, 2019.
26. Li, M.A., Han, J.F., Duan, L.J., A novel MI-EEG imaging with the location information of electrodes. *IEEE Access*, 8, 3197–211, 2019.
27. Huang, S., Peng, H., Chen, Y., Sun, K., Shen, F., Wang, T., Ma, T., Tensor discriminant analysis for MI-EEG signal classification using convolutional neural network. *2019 41st Annual Int. Conf. of the IEEE Engineering in Medicine and Biology Society (EMBC)*, IEEE, pp. 5971–4, 2019.
28. Dai, M., Zheng, D., Na, R., Wang, S., Zhang, S., EEG classification of motor imagery using a novel deep learning framework. *Sensors*, 19, 551, 2019.
29. Qiao, W. and Bi, X., Deep spatial-temporal neural network for classification of EEG-based motor imagery. *Proc. of the 2019 Int. Conf. on Artificial Intelligence and Computer Science*, pp. 265–72, 2019.
30. Li, F., He, F., Wang, F., Zhang, D., Xia, Y., Li, X., A novel simplified convolutional neural network classification algorithm of motor imagery EEG signals based on deep learning. *Appl. Sci.*, 10, 1605, 2020.
31. Xu, B., Zhang, L., Song, A., Wu, C., Li, W., Zhang, D., Xu, G., Li, Zeng, H., Wavelet transform time-frequency image and convolutional network-based motor imagery EEG classification. *IEEE Access*, 7, 6084–93, 2018.

32. Mousapour, L., Agah, F., Salari, S., Zare, M., A novel approach to classify motor-imagery EEG with convolutional neural network using network measures. *2018 4th Iranian Conf. on Signal Processing and Intelligent Systems (ICSPIS)*, IEEE, pp. 43–47, 2018.
33. Zhang, D., Chen, K., Jian, D., Yao, L., Motor imagery classification *via* temporal attention cues of graph embedded EEG signals. *IEEE J. Biomed. Health. Inf.*, 2020.

7

Beyond Motor Control: Decoding Speech and Thoughts with ML and DL

Irtiqa Amin[1*], Quraazah Akeemu Amin[2], Towseef Ahmad Wani[3], Aaquib Hussain Ganai[4] and Fida Hussain Bhat[5]

[1]*School of Computer Application Lovely Professional University, Phagwara, Punjab, India*
[2]*Division of Food Science and Technology, SKUAST-Kashmir, Srinagar, Jammu and Kashmir, India*
[3]*Department of Food Science and Technology, ETC, SKUAST-Kashmir, Pulwama, Jammu and Kashmir, India*
[4]*School of Computing, Mohan Babu University, Kolkata, Andhra Pradesh, India*
[5]*Department of Computer Science, Higher Education, Srinagar, J&K, India*

Abstract

Brain-computer interfaces (BCIs) originally aimed to restore motor control in paralysis. Advances in artificial intelligence (AI) enable decoding speech and thoughts from neural activity. This chapter discusses the intersection of neuroscience and AI to interpret brain signals and reconstruct language in real-time. It further discusses how cutting-edge techniques such as convolutional neural networks (CNNs), recurrent neural networks (RNNs), and transformer-based models are applied to data from electroencephalography (EEG), electrocorticography (ECoG), and functional magnetic resonance imaging (fMRI) to achieve unprecedented accuracy in speech decoding.

These innovations have significant implications for assistive communication technologies, allowing individuals with conditions such as locked-in syndrome or ALS to express their thoughts without physical movement. Later, it explores challenges in neural decoding, including signal variability, noise reduction, and data needs. It also examines ethical concerns like privacy and misuse. ML and DL integration with BCIs is transforming human-computer interaction and cognitive augmentation.

**Corresponding author*: irtiqa.amin7100@gmail.com

Tawseef Ahmed Teli, Syed Immamul Ansarullah, Arun Kumar Rana, Suman Lata Tripathi and Kashif Nisar (eds.) Brain-to-Computer Interfaces Using Machine Learning and Deep Learning, (159–178)

Keywords: Neural decoding, recurrent neural networks (RNNs), neuroprosthetics, brain-to-speech translation, thought reconstruction, brain signal processing, human-computer interaction (HCI), data acquisition

7.1 Introduction

Brain-computer interface (BCI) technology acts as a strong interaction link between humans and systems. It functions without relying on external devices or muscle activity to carry out instructions and enable interactions [1]. Originally, researchers developed BCIs with a focus on biomedical applications, resulting in the invention of assistive devices [2]. These advancements have played a crucial role in regaining mobility for individuals with physical impairments as well as substituting lost motor functions [3]. The expected progress in BCI has inspired scientists to investigate its possible applications in improving the lives of unimpaired individual *via* homeopathic innovations. Though the extent of the study has broadened to incorporate no clinical applications [1, 2]. Modern analysts have shifted their focus to exploring BCIs as an innovative input method and developing hands-free applications, particularly for typical users. Researchers like [4] raised concerns about the low data transmission rate of BCIs and their impact on the number of commands a user can issue. Findings demonstrate that this limitation controls BCI usage for individuals with total motor disability, since it struggles to match the efficiency of traditional communication methods or modern human-computer interfaces.

However, some of the benefits of BCI for users with able bodies remain unclear in [5]. BCI may be useful, particularly in safe uses or situations when movement is extremely challenging, and response speed is critical. Additionally, they may be utilized to improve the accuracy of HCI systems, leading to BCI's contribution in several domains, including intelligent shipping, business, schooling, commercials, and entertainment. Nevertheless, despite its anticipated success, the BCI must overcome both technological obstacles and user acceptability issues to succeed.

As we know, these are growing areas that enable direct communication between the brain and external devices. Traditionally, BCIs have been primarily used to restore movement in individuals with motor impairments by decoding neural signals associated with motion. However, recent advancements in ML and DL have expanded the scope of BCIs beyond motor control to areas such as speech and thought decoding. This expansion opens

Table 7.1 Historical periods of overview of BCI and its developments.

Time periods key events	Developments
1950s–1960s *(Early Foundations)*	Researchers found that neural signals in the brain could be captured and examined. **1963:** Dr. Grey Walter demonstrated brain signal control over external devices. **1969:** Eberhard Fetz showed that monkeys could voluntarily control neural activity.
1970s–1980s *(First BCI Experiments)*	**1973:** Jacques Vidal coined the term "Brain-Computer Interface" and conducted EEG-based BCI experiments at UCLA. **1980s:** Research on EEG-based BCIs for assisting paralyzed individuals began.
1990s *(Advancements in Neural Interfaces)*	**1991:** Jonathan Wolpaw developed an EEG-based BCI system for cursor control. **1998:** Philip Kennedy implanted the first BCI in a human (ALS patient), enabling basic communication.
2000s *(Breakthroughs in Assistive Technologies)*	**2004:** The BrainGate system allowed paralyzed individuals to control a cursor and robotic arm. **2006:** A monkey successfully controlled a robotic arm using an implanted BCI.
2010s *(Expansion Beyond Medicine)*	**2013:** A paralyzed individual used a BCI to drink from a bottle *via* a robotic arm. **2016:** Neuralink was founded to develop high-bandwidth BCIs for medical and non-medical uses. **2019:** Brain-to-brain communication *via* BCI was demonstrated.
2020s *(Modern Innovations and Future Directions)*	**2021:** Synchron received FDA approval for human trials of a minimally invasive BCI. **2022:** Neuralink showcased a BCI-controlled keyboard for paralyzed users. **2023:** BCIs enabled real-time speech restoration for locked-in patients.
2024 yearly reports	Developments
January 2024 *(Neuralink's First Human Implant)*	Neuralink successfully implanted its first brain chip in a human, marking a major milestone in BCI development.

(*Continued*)

Table 7.1 Historical periods of overview of BCI and its developments. (*Continued*)

Time periods key events	Developments
2024 yearly reports	Developments
March 2024 *(AI-Driven BCI Advancements)*	Artificial intelligence accelerated the development of BCIs, improving their efficiency and applications.
September 2024 *(ALS Patient Controls Alexa with BCI)*	A brain implant by Synchron allowed an ALS patient to control Amazon's Alexa using only their thoughts.
October 2024 *(Monkeys Control Prosthetic Hands)*	A new training protocol enabled rhesus monkeys to achieve precise control of prosthetic hands using BCIs.
November 2024 *(First New York BCI Symposium)*	Experts gathered to discuss the future of BCI, highlighting progress, challenges, and ethical considerations.

new possibilities for assistive communication, cognitive enhancement, and even brain-to-brain interaction. BCI technology has come a long way, from early experiments in brain activity to practical applications in neuroprosthetics and communication. As research continues, BCIs are expected to revolutionize fields beyond medicine, including human augmentation, gaming, and smart interfaces. The timeline of key milestones in BCI history is discussed in Table 7.1.

These advancements have paved the way for a new generation of BCIs that go beyond motor control, enabling direct decoding of speech and internal thought processes and demonstrating the rapid evolution of BCI technology in the past and in 2024, with significant implications for medical and non-medical applications.

7.1.1 Expanding beyond Motor Movement Control

While traditional BCIs primarily focused on motor-related tasks, researchers have begun to explore applications beyond movement. This shift is driven by the need for assistive technologies that can help individuals who cannot communicate or move due to neurological conditions, such as:

- *Amyotrophic Lateral Sclerosis (ALS):* Patients lose the ability to move and speak but retain cognitive abilities.
- *Locked-In Syndrome:* Individuals remain fully conscious but cannot move or speak voluntarily.
- *Severe Stroke or Brainstem Injuries:* Damage to motor pathways affects voluntary movement and speech.

Some important areas beyond motor control are *speech decoding from neural signals, silent speech and thought decoding,* and *cognitive* and *emotional state monitoring.*

a. *Speech Decoding from Neural Signals:* Instead of using motor commands to control a device, BCIs can interpret brain signals related to speech. It involves detecting neural activity from speech-related brain regions, even when no sound is produced. *Example:* Converting brain activity into synthesized speech for individuals who have lost their voice.
b. *Silent Speech and Thought Decoding:* Thought decoding focuses on translating inner speech or cognitive activity into text or commands. This enables communication even when a person is completely silent. *Example:* A person "thinking" about words, which are then decoded into text.
c. *Cognitive and Emotional State Monitoring:* BCIs can track mental states such as stress, attention, and emotional responses. Potential applications include neurofeedback therapy and cognitive enhancement.

By moving beyond motor control, BCIs can create a new paradigm of communication and human-computer interaction, allowing for direct interpretation of brain signals related to speech and thoughts. BCIs capable of decoding speech and thoughts have significant real-world applications in various domains, including healthcare, assistive communication, and even human-computer interaction.

i. Assistive Communication for Individuals with Speech Impairments

- Speech Prostheses: BCIs can restore communication for individuals who have lost the ability to speak due to conditions like ALS, stroke, or paralysis.
- Thought-to-Text Systems: Instead of speaking, a user's neural signals are translated into text in real-time. *Example:* A paralyzed patient thinks of words, which a BCI decodes and displays as text on a screen.

ii. Neural Speech Synthesis and Brain-to-Speech Technologies

- Direct Speech Generation: Neural signals can be converted into synthesized speech in real-time.
- Phoneme and Word Prediction: AI models predict speech patterns based on brain activity. *Example:* A person imagines speaking, and the system reconstructs their voice artificially.

iii. Brain-to-Text and Mind Writing

- Inner Speech Decoding: BCIs attempt to translate internal thoughts into readable text.
- Potential for Silent Communication: Could enable telepathic-like messaging in the future. *Example:* A user mentally composes an email without typing or speaking aloud.

iv. Human-Computer Interaction and Cognitive Control

- Hands-Free Device Control: Users can control smart devices or virtual assistants using thought-based BCIs.
- Augmented Reality and VR Integration: BCIs could enhance immersive experiences in gaming and simulations. *Example:* A person navigating a computer interface simply by thinking about the actions.

v. Brain-to-Brain Communication

- Neural Signal Transmission between Individuals: Involves direct communication of thoughts or commands from one brain to another. Potential Applications: Collaborative work, remote communication, and even future applications in education. *Example:* A person mentally "sending" a command that another individual perceives as a thought.

7.2 Neural Basics of Speech and Thoughts

The ability to generate speech and thoughts is a defining characteristic of human cognition. This complex process is governed by highly specialized neural networks that coordinate different aspects of language comprehension, speech production, and abstract thinking. The study of the neural basis of speech and thoughts is crucial for understanding how the brain encodes and processes information, as well as for developing BCIs that can decode and understand neural signals. Speech and thoughts are controlled by distributed neural networks in the brain, primarily in the cerebral cortex, which houses the most important language and cognitive centers. The key brain regions involved in speech and thought processing are mentioned in Figure 7.1.

- Broca's area (speech production): It is located in the left inferior frontal gyrus. Broca's area is responsible for planning and coordinating speech production. It plays a crucial role in constructing grammatically correct sentences and enables the motor execution of speech by sending signals to the primary motor cortex. Damage to this region results in Broca's aphasia, a condition marked by impaired speech fluency while largely preserving language comprehension.
- Wernicke's area (speech comprehension): It is found in the left superior temporal gyrus and is responsible for understanding language and linking words with meaning. It enables people to process spoken and written language.

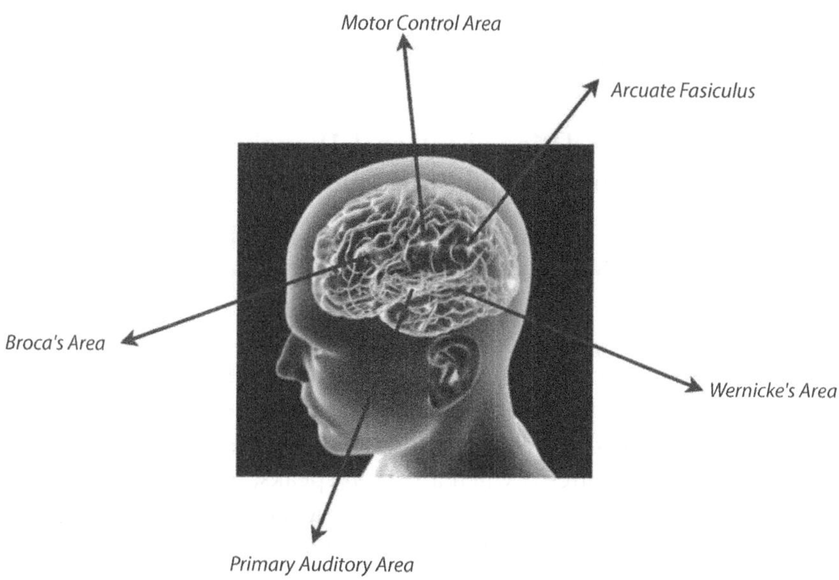

Figure 7.1 Fundamental brain areas responsible for thought and speech processing.

- Primary Motor Cortex (speech articulation): This region controls the movement of muscles involved in speech (e.g., lips, tongue, and larynx). Signals from Broca's area are sent to the motor cortex to execute the physical production of sounds.
- Auditory Cortex (speech perception): It is located in the superior temporal lobe; the auditory cortex processes sound, including speech perception and phoneme recognition. It is crucial for distinguishing between different speech sounds, tones, and intonation patterns.
- Angular and Supramarginal Gyri are used for reading and writing processing. These regions in the parietal lobe integrate visual information from written language and link it to spoken language processing. They are critical for reading, writing, and phonological processing.
- The prefrontal cortex is used for thought processing and internal speech. The prefrontal cortex is responsible for abstract thinking, decision-making, and internal dialogue. It plays a major role in silent speech (inner voice), problem-solving, and complex reasoning.
- The arcuate fasciculus is used for the connection between all speech areas. It facilitates smooth coordination between speech production and comprehension. Damage to this pathway leads to conduction aphasia, where individuals understand language but struggle to repeat words accurately.

7.2.1 Neural Correlation of Internal Thoughts and the Silent Speech Approach and Processing

The generation of speech and thought stems from intricate neural interactions, with multiple brain regions collaborating to understand and express language.

A. Neural Encoding of Speech and Language: The cerebral cortex encodes speech in terms of phonemes (the smallest speech units), syllables, words, and sentences. Neurons fire in specific patterns when a person speaks, listens, or imagines words. The cortico-basal ganglia-thalamocortical loop plays an important role in initiating and regulating speech. Gamma-band oscillations (30–100 Hz) in the brain are associated with speech encoding and linguistic processing [6].

B. Thought representation and Inner Speech: Thought generation is a more abstract process that involves networks in the prefrontal cortex, temporal lobe, and hippocampus. Inner speech, or the ability to think in words without vocalizing them, activates language regions. Studies suggest that thoughts can exist in both linguistic and non-linguistic forms, including visual imagery, abstract symbols, and emotional states.
C. Neural Connectivity in Speech and Thought Processing: The frontotemporal connectivity links different speech and thought-processing centers. The default mode network (DMN) is involved in spontaneous thought generation, self-reflection, and creativity. Connections between the hippocampus and neocortex allow thoughts to be retrieved from memory and shaped into meaningful expressions.

7.2.1.1 Decoding Speech and Thoughts with BCIs and AI

Advancements in neurotechnology, artificial intelligence (AI), and brain-computer interfaces (BCIs) are making it possible to decode speech and thoughts directly from neural activity.

A. EEG-Based Speech and Thought Decoding: EEG detects electrical signals in the brain using non-invasive scalp electrodes. ML models analyze EEG signals to predict speech intentions and word recognition. While EEG is widely used due to its non-invasiveness, it has low spatial resolution, making precise decoding challenging.
B. ECoG and fMRI for High-Resolution Neural Decoding: ECoG provides higher spatial resolution by detecting electrical signals through scalp-mounted electrodes. ECoG studies have successfully reconstructed words and imagined speech using deep learning models. fMRI helps map brain activity related to speech processing by detecting changes in blood oxygenation.
C. Deep Learning Models in Speech and Thought Decoding: Convolutional neural networks (CNNs) extract spatial patterns from brain signals related to speech recognition. RNNs and transformers process sequential brain data to predict

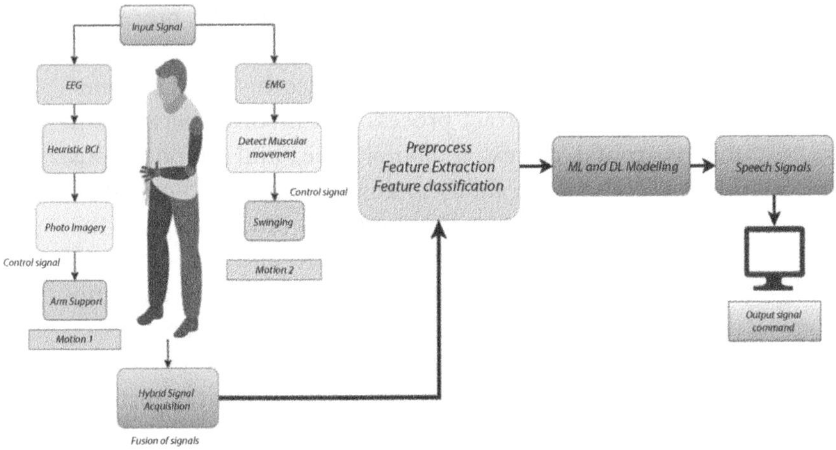

Figure 7.2 Hybrid ML and DL-based BCI systems.

words and thoughts. Generative AI models can reconstruct entire sentences from brain activity, bringing speech BCI closer to reality (Figure 7.2).

7.2.2 Challenges in Decoding Non-Motor Cognitive Processes

1. Complexity of Neural Representation

- Distributed Brain Activity: Non-motor functions (e.g., speech, memory, and decision-making) are processed across multiple brain regions, making decoding difficult.
- High Variability: The same thought or concept can activate different neural patterns across individuals, requiring personalized decoding models.
- Neural Noise and Overlapping Signals: Brain signals related to different cognitive functions often overlap, making it difficult to isolate specific mental states [7, 8].

2. Limitations in Brain Signal Acquisition

- Low Resolution of Non-Invasive Methods: Electroencephalography (EEG) provides only surface-level brain activity with limited spatial resolution, reducing decoding accuracy.

- Invasiveness of High-Resolution Methods: Techniques like electrocorticography (ECoG) and intracortical recordings provide better resolution but require surgical implantation, posing medical risks.
- Data Collection Challenges: Gathering large datasets for training AI models is difficult due to privacy concerns, high costs, and ethical restrictions on human experimentation.

3. Real-Time Decoding and Interpretation Issues

- Latency in Processing: Thought-to-speech BCIs or memory decoding systems require real-time processing, but current technology lags behind human cognition.
- Ambiguity in Thought Representation: A single thought can be represented in different neural patterns depending on the context, making decoding ambiguous.
- Error Rate and Misinterpretation: AI models may misinterpret signals, leading to incorrect word reconstruction, false memories, or misclassified emotions.

4. Generalization across Individuals

- Personalized Neural Activity: Brain activity is highly individualized, requiring training models on a per-user basis, which is impractical for large-scale applications.
- Lack of Standardization: There is no universal model for mapping thoughts to neural activity, limiting the scalability of thought-to-text BCIs.

7.3 ML and DL for Neural Decoding

Neural decoding refers to the process of interpreting brain activity and translating it into meaningful information, such as motor intentions, speech, emotions, or cognitive states. ML and DL have revolutionized neural decoding by providing sophisticated algorithms that can extract complex patterns from neural signals. These techniques enable BCI and other neurotechnologies to transform raw brain data into actionable outputs with improved accuracy and adaptability. ML refers to computational algorithms that learn patterns from data without explicit programming. In neural decoding, ML models analyze brain activity recorded *via* techniques such as EEG, fMRI, MEG, and invasive neural recordings (e.g., ECoG and intracortical arrays). ML models use brain data to recognize patterns associated with thoughts, intentions, sensory experiences, and motor actions, enabling applications such as speech decoding (translating brain signals into text or spoken words), movement restoration (predicting motor commands for prosthetic limbs), and emotion recognition (inferring emotional states from neural signals).

Some common ML techniques for neural decoding are supervised, unsupervised, and reinforcement learning (RL). Supervised learning uses labeled data to train models that map neural signals to specific outputs (e.g., classifying a brain signal as representing "left" or "right" hand movement). *Examples:* Linear discriminant analysis (LDA) separates neural signal categories with a linear boundary. Support vector machines (SVMs) find an optimal hyperplane to classify brain signals, whereas random forests (RFs) use decision trees to classify neural patterns. *Use Case:* Motor imagery classification in BCIs for paralyzed users. Unsupervised learning identifies patterns in neural data without labeled outputs, useful for feature extraction and signal clustering. *Example*: K-Means Clustering is a group of similar neural signals. Principal Component Analysis (PCA) reduces the dimensionality of neural data while preserving key information. *Use Case:* Identifying hidden brain states in resting-state fMRI studies. RL trains a model through trial and error by rewarding correct predictions and penalizing incorrect ones. Use Case: Optimizing BCI control strategies for robotic arms or neuroprosthetics.

DL uses ANNs to automatically understand patterns from voluminous data. DL is particularly powerful for neural decoding because it can model spatial, temporal, and hierarchical representations of brain activity without requiring handcrafted features. DL methods outperform traditional ML in tasks including decoding imagined speech and thoughts, predicting motor intentions with high accuracy, and extracting meaningful patterns from EEG and fMRI signals. CNNs are specialized for spatial data analysis, useful for decoding brain activity from EEG and fMRI scans. It extracts spatial features by applying convolutional filters to input signals. *Use Case:* EEG-based emotion recognition or fMRI-based visual decoding. RNNs and Long Short-Term Memory (LSTM) help the model to learn temporal dependencies in brain signals. It stores information from previous time steps, making it ideal for continuous neural signal decoding. *Use Case:* Speech decoding from brain activity (predicting words based on temporal EEG patterns). Transformer-based models (e.g., BERT and GPT for brain data) use self-attention mechanisms to process long-range dependencies in brain signals. It captures contextual meaning in complex neural data. *Use Case:* Decoding silent reading or inner speech using EEG/fMRI. Autoencoders (AEs) and Variational Autoencoders (VAEs) are used for dimensionality reduction and unsupervised feature learning in neural data. *Use Case:* Neural signal denoising and latent representation learning for brain activity [9].

7.3.1 Future Directions and Emerging Trends

- Hybrid ML-DL Models: Combining ML and DL approaches can improve accuracy and efficiency in neural decoding. *Example:* Using PCA + CNNs to reduce data dimensionality before deep learning processing.
- Self-Supervised and Few-Shot Learning: Reducing the need for large labeled datasets by training models with minimal supervision. *Example:* Training a BCI model to recognize thoughts with only a few user-provided examples.
- Brain-Inspired AI and Neuromorphic Computing: Using biologically inspired models (e.g., spiking neural networks) to enhance neural decoding efficiency. *Example:* Implementing neuromorphic chips that mimic human brain processing for real-time decoding.
- Personalized and Adaptive BCIs: AI-driven BCIs that continuously adapt to a user's unique brain activity patterns over time. *Example:* A speech BCI that refines its decoding accuracy as the user thinks of words repeatedly.

7.4 Data Acquisition for Speech and Thought Decoding

Data acquisition is a crucial step in speech and thought decoding, as it involves recording, processing, and interpreting neural signals associated with cognitive and linguistic activities. High-quality neural data enables ML and DL models to accurately map brain activity to speech or thought representations, forming the basis for BCIs, neuroprosthetics, and cognitive communication systems. Since speech and thought are complex, abstract processes, acquiring their corresponding brain activity requires specialized techniques. These methods involve neuroimaging, electrophysiological recordings, and invasive neural interfaces, each with varying degrees of spatial and temporal resolution.

7.4.1 Methods of Neural Data Acquisition for Speech and Thought Decoding

A. *Non-Invasive Neural Recording Techniques: These* methods capture brain signals without requiring surgical implantation. These are widely used for speech and thought decoding due to their safety and ease of use, though they may have lower signal resolution than invasive approaches.

EEG records neural activity by detecting electrical signals through scalp-mounted electrodes. It has high temporal resolution (millisecond-level precision) and is portable and cost-effective compared to other imaging techniques. This technique is commonly used in real-time BCIs for speech and thought decoding. It has low spatial resolution (cannot precisely localize neural activity) and is sensitive to artifacts (e.g., muscle movements and blinking). *Use Case:* Decoding inner speech by analyzing event-related potentials (ERPs) and brain oscillations. MEG has high temporal resolution and better spatial localization than EEG. It is expensive and requires specialized facilities with magnetically shielded rooms, but it is not portable, limiting real-world applications. *Use Case:* Studying real-time speech processing by tracking changes in brain activity.

fMRI detects changes in BOLD signals to infer neural activity. It has high spatial resolution, ideal for identifying speech-related brain regions, and is very useful for training ML models on large datasets. It has low temporal resolution (delayed brain activity detection) and requires bulky, expensive equipment. *Use Case*: Decoding the semantic content of imagined speech or reading tasks. Functional Near-Infrared Spectroscopy (fNIRS) measures blood oxygenation changes in the brain using near-infrared light. It is more portable than fMRI and good for speech-related studies, especially in naturalistic settings. It has lower spatial resolution than fMRI and only detects activity in surface cortical regions. *Use Case:* Tracking speech comprehension in real-world scenarios.

B. *Invasive Neural Recording Techniques:* It requires surgical implantation of electrodes to capture direct neural signals. These offer high precision but come with medical and ethical concerns. ECoG entails the placement of electrodes directly on the surface of the brain to record cortical activity. It has higher spatial and temporal resolution than EEG and has less interference from external noise. It requires brain surgery, limiting its use to clinical cases. *Use Case:* Decoding speech-related brain activity in epilepsy patients. Intracortical microelectrode arrays (IMAs) have the highest resolution for neural decoding and allow for precise speech and thought mapping. It is highly invasive, posing risks like infection and scarring. Use Case: High-precision speech BCIs for paralyzed individuals.

C. *Signal Processing and Feature Extraction:* Once neural signals are acquired, they require preprocessing, feature extraction, and transformation into a format that can be interpreted by ML/DL models.
   - Preprocessing steps involve EEG/MEG artifact removal using Independent Component Analysis (ICA). fMRI noise filtering is done through motion correction algorithms. Signal normalization requires neural signals to be scaled to ensure consistent feature representation. Time-frequency EEG signal analysis is done using the wavelet transform or the Fourier transform to extract frequency-based features.
   - Feature extraction for speech and thought decoding involves spectral features: Brain oscillations related to different cognitive states. Event-related potentials (ERPs) are neural responses to stimuli, useful for decoding inner speech. Connectivity measures are functional connections between brain regions, useful for semantic processing.
   - A hybrid BCI integrates multiple brain signal acquisition methods or combines BCI with other physiological inputs (e.g., eye-tracking and electromyography) to improve accuracy, reliability, and usability. Unlike traditional BCIs, which rely on a single neural signal source, hybrid BCIs leverage complementary data sources to enhance signal processing and reduce limitations such as low signal-to-noise ratio (SNR) and user fatigue.

Data acquisition for speech and thought decoding is a challenging yet transformative field, relying on advanced neuroimaging techniques, signal processing, and AI-driven analysis. Although EEG and fMRI are widely used, ECoG and intracortical implants provide superior resolution for high-precision BCIs. As research progresses, hybrid recording techniques, AI-enhanced signal analysis, and ethical frameworks will play a crucial role in making thought decoding a reality for medical and everyday applications.

7.5 Challenges, Future Directions, and Emerging Tools

Decoding speech and thought from brain signals with ML and DL presents numerous challenges but also offers exciting opportunities for future advancements. As research progresses, new tools and methodologies are emerging to enhance brain-computer interface (BCI) applications, neuroprosthetics, and cognitive augmentation.

7.5.1 Challenges in Brain Signal and Speech Decoding

A. Technical Challenges

1. Low Signal-to-Noise Ratio (SNR): Brain signals, especially from non-invasive methods like EEG, are weak and prone to noise. *Solution:* sophisticated filtering methods such as deep denoising autoencoders.
2. Inter-Subject Variability: Neural responses vary between individuals, making it hard to create generalized models. *Solution*: Transfer learning and subject-adaptive ML models.
3. High Dimensionality and Complexity: Brain data is high-dimensional, requiring efficient feature extraction and dimensionality reduction. *Solution:* Principal Component Analysis (PCA) and deep embeddings.
4. Real-Time Processing Constraints: Latency issues hinder real-time applications in speech prosthetics and communication. *Solution:* Lightweight deep learning models such as TinyML, edge computing, and neuromorphic hardware.

B. Data-Related Challenges

1. Limited Labeled Datasets: Training ML/DL models requires large datasets, but collecting labeled brain data is difficult. *Solution:* Self-supervised learning, data augmentation, and synthetic brain data generation.
2. Cross-Modal Data Fusion: Combining EEG, fMRI, and ECoG is challenging due to varying temporal and spatial resolutions. *Solution:* Multi-modal fusion techniques, such as cross-attention mechanisms in transformers.

C. Ethical and Privacy Challenges

1. Neural Data Privacy and Security: Brain signals contain sensitive personal information, leading to concerns about unauthorized access. *Solution:* Secure brain-data encryption, federated learning, and privacy-preserving BCIs.
2. Ethical Concerns of Thought Decoding: Decoding inner speech and thoughts raises ethical questions about mental privacy and consent. *Solution:* Establishing ethical guidelines and regulatory frameworks for neurotechnology.

7.5.2 Future Directions in Brain Signal and Speech Decoding

A. Advancements in AI and Machine Learning

1. Transformer Models for Speech Decoding: BERT, GPT, and Vision Transformers (ViTs) are being adapted for brain-to-text translation. *Example:* BrainGPT—a model that maps neural activity to natural language.
2. Neuromorphic Computing for Brain Signal Processing: Brain-inspired AI chips for low-power, real-time BCI applications. Examples: IBM's TrueNorth and Intel's Loihi processors.

B. Next-Generation Brain Signal Acquisition

1. High-Density and Wireless EEG: Portable, high-resolution EEG systems for real-world brain decoding. *Example*: Kernel Flow, NextMind, and wearable dry-electrode EEG headsets.

2. Hybrid BCIs for Multimodal Decoding: Combining EEG, fNIRS, and EMG for robust speech and thought decoding. *Example:* EEG-fMRI fusion for accurate brain-to-text systems.
3. Invasive BCIs with Higher Precision: Next-gen ECoG and intracortical implants for speech restoration. *Example:* Neuralink's BCI for real-time brain-to-text communication.

C. Ethical AI and Neurosecurity Innovations

1. Privacy-Preserving Brain Data Analysis: Using federated learning to process brain data locally on devices. Example: Google's Federated AI for Neural Decoding.
2. Brainwave Authentication for Security: Using unique neural signatures as biometric passwords. *Example:* EEG-based authentication for brain-controlled devices.

7.5.3 Emerging Tools in ML/DL for Brain Signal Decoding

1. Deep Learning Frameworks for Neural Decoding: TensorFlow and PyTorch are standard DL frameworks for EEG/BCI applications.
2. EEG Learn is a specialized deep-learning library for EEG signal processing.
3. BCI Toolbox: Open-source software for brain-computer interface research.
4. Open-Source Brain Datasets for ML/DL Training: The BNCI Horizon 2020 dataset is a large-scale EEG dataset for BCI research. The PhysioNet EEG database is a collection of EEG and brain signal recordings. The ECoG speech decoding dataset is used for speech neuroprosthetics research.
5. Brain-to-Text and Thought Decoding Models: Meta's Silent Speech BCI is an AI-powered brain-to-speech decoder. NeuroGPT uses transformer models to predict words from brain activity. Cortical AI is a brain-inspired DL model for thought-to-text conversion.

7.6 Conclusion

The integration of ML and DL with BCIs represents a groundbreaking shift in neuroscience and artificial intelligence. Traditionally limited to restoring motor control, BCIs are now unlocking the ability to decode speech and thoughts directly from neural activity, offering new avenues for assistive communication and cognitive augmentation.

This chapter discussed how cutting-edge techniques like CNNs, RNNs, and transformer-based models are revolutionizing neural decoding. Despite remarkable progress, significant challenges remain. Variability in brain signals, noise reduction, and the need for extensive training datasets pose obstacles to achieving consistently accurate speech and thought decoding. Additionally, ethical concerns surrounding privacy, security, and potential misuse of thought-decoding technology must be addressed to ensure responsible deployment.

Looking ahead, continued advancements in AI, neuroscience, and neuroimaging will refine these technologies, improving accuracy and accessibility. As BCIs continue to advance, they possess the capacity to revolutionize HCI, enable direct brain-to-brain communication, and enhance human cognitive functions. The fusion of ML, DL, and BCIs not only empowers individuals with speech or motor impairments but also pushes the boundaries of what it means to communicate and interact with the world using the mind alone.

AI disclosure statement: The author acknowledges the use of AI-based tools for minor language editing or grammatical correction. However, all intellectual contributions, analyses, and conclusions presented in this chapter are entirely the author's own.

References

1. Van Erp, J., Lotte, F., Tangermann, M., Brain-computer interfaces: beyond medical applications. *Computer*, IEEE, 45, 26–34, 2012.
2. Rao, R. and Scherer, R., Brain-computer interfacing [in the spotlight]. *IEEE Signal Process Mag.*, 27, 152–150, 2010.
3. Bi, L., Fan, X.-A., Liu, Y., Eeg-based brain-controlled mobile robots: a survey. *IEEE Trans. Hum.-Mach. Syst.*, 43, 161–76, 2013.
4. Navarro, A.A., Ceccaroni, L., Velickovski, F., Torrellas, S., Miralles, F., Allison, B.Z., Scherer, R., Faller, J., Context-awareness as an enhancement of brain-computer interfaces. *Ambient assisted living*, Springer, 2011.
5. Tan, D.S. and Nijholt, A., *Brain-computer interfaces: applying our minds to human-computer interaction*, Springer, London, 2010.
6. Alladi, T., Chamola, V., Sikdar, B., Choo, K.K., Consumer IoT: Security vulnerability case studies and solutions. *IEEE Consum. Electron. Mag.*, 9, 17–25, 2020.

7. Hassija, V., Chamola, V., Saxena, V., Jain, D., Goyal, P., Sikdar, B., A Survey on IoT Security: Application Areas, Security Threats, and Solution Architectures. *IEEE Access*, 7, 82721–82743, 2019.
8. Alladi, T., Chamola, V., Zeadally, S., Industrial Control Systems: Cyberattack trends and countermeasures. *Comput. Commun.*, 2020, 155, 1–8, 2020.
9. Gou, H., Piao, Y., Ren, J., Zhao, Q., Chen, Y., Liu, C., Hong, W., Zhang, X., A solution to supervised motor imagery task in the BCI Controlled Robot Contest in World Robot Contest. *Brain Sci. Adv.*, 8, 153–161, 2022.

8

Machine Learning and Deep Learning for Brain-Computer Interface Rehabilitation

M. Menagadevi[1]*, M. Nirmala[2], D. Thiyagarajan[3] and Suman Lata Tripathi[4]

[1]Department of Computing Technologies, School of Computing, SRM Institute of Science and Technology, Kattankulathur, Tamil Nadu, India
[2]Department of Biomedical Engineering, Dr. N G P Institute of Technology, Coimbatore, Tamil Nadu, India
[3]Department of Computer Science and Engineering, Chennai Institute of Technology, Chennai, Tamil Nadu, India
[4]Department of Electronics & Telecommunication, Symbiosis Institute of Technology, Symbiosis International (Deemed University), Pune, Maharashtra, India

Abstract

Brain-computer interfaces (BCIs) resulted in significant progress for neurorehabilitation as the innovative new discipline of technology-based brain interface development. The development of BCIs established neurological pathways from brain signals into external systems, thus helping patients with serious neurological impairment. The inclusion of machine learning (ML) along with Deep Learning (DL) models improved both the effectiveness and accuracy levels and adaptability range of BCI systems and their associated processes. The brain generates signals that present multiple time scales while remaining extremely disordered and intricate in nature. The uses of BCI systems for rehabilitation investigate ML and DL methods through signal acquisition, feature extraction, and classification techniques. ML algorithms like support vector machine (SVM), random forest (RF), k-nearest neighbors (KNN), hidden Markov models (HMMs), linear discriminant analysis (LDA), naive Bayes classifier, and DL algorithms like convolutional neural networks (CNNs), recurrent neural networks (RNNs), transformer-based models, adaptive learning, transfer learning, and hybrid models.

**Corresponding author*: menaga1961988@gmail.com

Tawseef Ahmed Teli, Syed Immamul Ansarullah, Arun Kumar Rana, Suman Lata Tripathi and Kashif Nisar (eds.) Brain-to-Computer Interfaces Using Machine Learning and Deep Learning, (179–194) © 2026 Scrivener Publishing LLC

Keywords: Brain-computer interface (BCI), neurorehabilitation, machine learning (ML), deep learning (DL), EEG signal processing, personalized rehabilitation, signal variability, brain-to-brain communication, AI in healthcare

8.1 Introduction

Brain-computer interfaces (BCIs) created a breakthrough in neurorehabilitation because these interfaces establish direct signal sharing between brain networks and outside devices. Advanced interfaces recently created systems that provide fresh therapeutic possibilities to patients experiencing severe neurological conditions through innovative restoratives for lost action and thinking ability. Users obtain improved quality of life through BCIs because these systems convert brain signals into commands that enable the control of prosthetic and assistive technologies, including communication devices [1].

Gradual improvements in BCI technology happen because ML and DL methods work together to improve system efficiency and adaptation. Intelligent models prove critical for signal processing because they help extract features and perform classifications from brain signals, which feature multiple time scales alongside inherent disorder in their structure. Support vector machines (SVMs) and random forests (RFs), along with hidden Markov models (HMMs), enable precise pattern identification within ML systems, yet convolutional neural networks (CNNs) and recurrent neural networks (RNNs) from DL deliver more comprehensive neural dynamic comprehension [2]. New transformer-based models, together with adaptive learning and hybrid approaches, drive BCI applications forward through their continuous advancement of the field.

A deep examination of ML and DL technologies that power BCIs for neurorehabilitation is conducted here while covering key methodologies and present difficulties and expected growth directions. The analysis of signal acquisition combined with processing techniques and classification models helps understand how these technologies strengthen rehabilitation strategies for patients with neurological conditions.

8.2 Brain-Computer Interfaces (BCIs) in Neurorehabilitation

The advanced system BCIs connects brain signals directly to external devices without depending on muscle pathways for transmission. Scientists developed BCIs during the 1970s before researchers transformed them into vital medical technology, which now dominates neurorehabilitation applications. These brain signal interpretation systems enable users to operate assistive devices like prosthetic limbs and wheelchairs and communication systems for people who have severe neurological impairments [3].

BCIs function through three different configurations, including invasive methods that involve brain electrode implants, semi-invasive procedures with brain surface electrodes, and non-invasive technologies that depend on electroencephalography (EEG) sensors. Non-invasive brain-computer interfaces maintain popularity because they combine convenient deployment with protective design but suffer from precision and usability problems with signals. Bluetooth-controlled interfaces' system performance and adaptability have improved notably since researchers employed artificial intelligence technologies, including ML and DL [4]. Further research indicates BCIs will expand their functional range in neurological treatment to restore function and enhance the quality of life for individuals affected by brain disorders.

Figure 8.1 represents the signal processing flow in a BCI system, illustrating how brain signals are acquired, processed, and classified to generate commands for external devices. Here's a breakdown of the components:

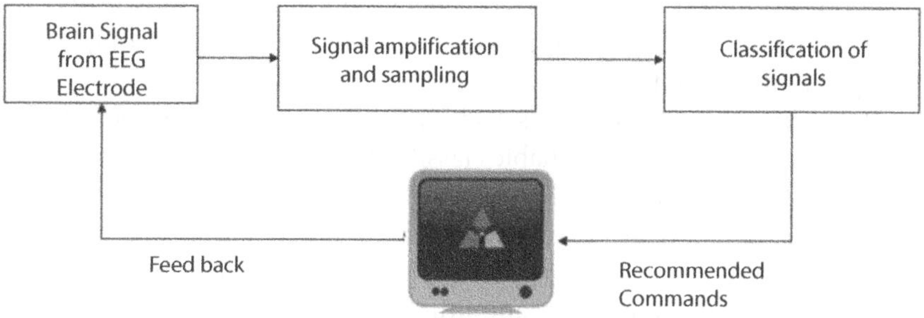

Figure 8.1 Signal processing flow in a brain-computer interface system.

Signal Acquisition

Signal acquisition stands as the core process in BCI systems because researchers use this step to measure brain activity and record its analysis for research purposes. The human brain generates detectable electrical signals through neural activity, which modern neuroimaging techniques can observe at present. EEG serves as the main technique for non-invasive BCIs to record brain waves from electrodes mounted on the head. The signal acquisition process in BCIs consists of two alternate technologies: electrocorticography (ECoG), which collects brain signals directly from the brain surface through partially invasive brain access, and functional near-infrared spectroscopy (fNIRS), which observes blood flow variations due to nervous system operations. The microelectrode arrays inserted into the brain tissue give invasive BCIs accurate signal recording capabilities. The correct interpretation of signals depends heavily on signal acquisition quality, yet performance deteriorates if the combination of signal noise and interference with poor resolution appears. Signal processing superiority results from running complex analyses that combine filtering with artifact suppression procedures, along with extraction steps. Better assistive technology and improved neurorehabilitation functions result from the integration of signal recording, machine learning techniques, and advanced hardware devices that enhance both BCI reliability and efficiency [5].

Feature Extraction and Preprocessing in BCIs

Compatibility between the quality and reliability of brain signal interpretation in BCI systems depends heavily on feature extraction and preprocessing processes. The first step of brain signal processing is to clean and improve raw brain signals through preprocessing techniques, which eliminate noise and sources of artifacts, including eye blinks, muscle signals, and external interferences. Preprocessing of signals includes bandpass filtering and normalization.

The feature extraction phase selects critical neural data parameters after preprocessing for attaining reliable classification evaluations. Brain signals, including EEG as well as other brain signals, exhibit complex dynamic changes in temporal domains, along with frequency domains and spatial locations. The extraction methods for features include multiple time-domain metrics such as mean amplitude and variance, as well as Hjorth parameters, alongside frequency-domain metrics including power spectral density and wavelet transforms, along with spatial features. The analysis using the Fourier transform and wavelet transform signal decomposition allows the extraction of multiple frequency elements in signals. Signal interpretation becomes easier when using decomposition techniques for the Fourier transform and wavelet transform signals. Using deep learning with the extraction capabilities of convolutional neural networks together with autoencoders results in the detection of brain signals that show complex patterns through detection methods that do not need time-consuming manual feature selection procedures [6].

BCI system performance improves significantly when effective feature extraction methods combine with preprocessing, since these approaches reduce complexity while improving classification outcomes. The performance requirements of real-time BCI systems depend on these processing steps since both system speed and user control precision matter. Signal processing and artificial intelligence research advances allow constant method refinements to improve BCIs' performance for neurorehabilitation and assistive technology applications [7, 8].

8.3 Machine Learning Approaches in Brain-Computer Interfaces

The execution of BCI systems depends on ML capabilities for signal interpretation that lead to productive outputs. The model serves essential functions by cleaning data signals and extracting features throughout the mental state classification, which leads to brain signal translation for external device control, including prosthetic devices and cursors, along with communication systems. The implementation of BCI systems requires distinct ML algorithms to match the signals from brain activity with specific end purposes [9].

The two main categories of ML approaches in BCI include supervised learning and unsupervised learning techniques. Under supervised learning models, the models get trained through labeled data that connects input data points with their corresponding output categories. Rephrase the following sentence. The extended application of this method exists within BCIs to perform motor imagery classifications along with SSVEP detection tasks. The main application of unsupervised learning in unlabeled data involves extracting hidden patterns from which researchers identify clusters in brain activity patterns [10]. When labeled data exists in sufficient amounts, supervised methods deliver high classification outcomes, while unsupervised methods prove valuable in data labeling situations that are hard or impossible to achieve.

Multiple particular ML algorithms serve as the foundation for BCI system applications. SVMs maintain popularity in the field because they successfully process large datasets combined with limited sample sizes, making them appropriate for EEG signal classification. RF uses an ensemble-based methodology to process non-linear data and performs decision tree ensemble computations, which limits overfitting. The KNN algorithm presents operational challenges to real-time BCI implementations because of its requirement for distance measurement computation. Hidden Markov models demonstrate excellent capabilities in modeling sequential brain patterns that appear in event-related potentials. The BCI competition uses LDA as a primary algorithm due to its fundamental design and excellent ability to separate classes that display linear separation. Naïve Bayes classifiers show good performance within real-time BCI operations primarily because they operate efficiently while making the feature independence assumption.

Table 8.1 shows the description and BCI application of ML algorithms.

Table 8.1 BCI application of ML algorithms.

Algorithm	Description	BCI application
Support vector machine (SVM)	Maximizes margin between classes using hyperplanes	Popular for EEG signal classification due to robustness with small datasets
Random forest (RF)	Ensemble of decision trees, uses majority voting	Effective for non-linear classification with reduced overfitting
K-nearest neighbors (KNN)	Classifies based on the majority vote of 'k' closest data points	Simple, but computationally expensive for real-time BCI
Hidden Markov models (HMMs)	Probabilistic model of sequential data with hidden states	Useful for modelling time-series brain data like ERP
Linear discriminant analysis (LDA)	Projects data to maximize class separability	Widely used in BCI competitions, especially for motor imagery
Naïve Bayes	Probabilistic model assuming feature independence	Fast, simple classifier for real-time applications

8.3.1 Comparative Analysis of ML Models in BCI Performance

Figure 8.2 shows the comparison of different ML algorithms based on their accuracy, sensitivity, and specificity.

8.4 Deep Learning Techniques for BCIs

BCI systems benefit significantly from DL because this method delivers automated pattern detection abilities from untreated brain signals, including EEG, fNIRS, or MEG. The architecture consists of end-to-end learning because deep learning models merge both feature extraction and classification functions inside a single network framework. The technology of DL provides exceptional benefits to BCI applications because signal variability and noise pose substantial challenges in this field.

Many deep learning architectures have been successfully implemented within BCI research. CNNs stand as the most applied deep learning architecture, which excellently handles spatial and spatial-temporal patterns

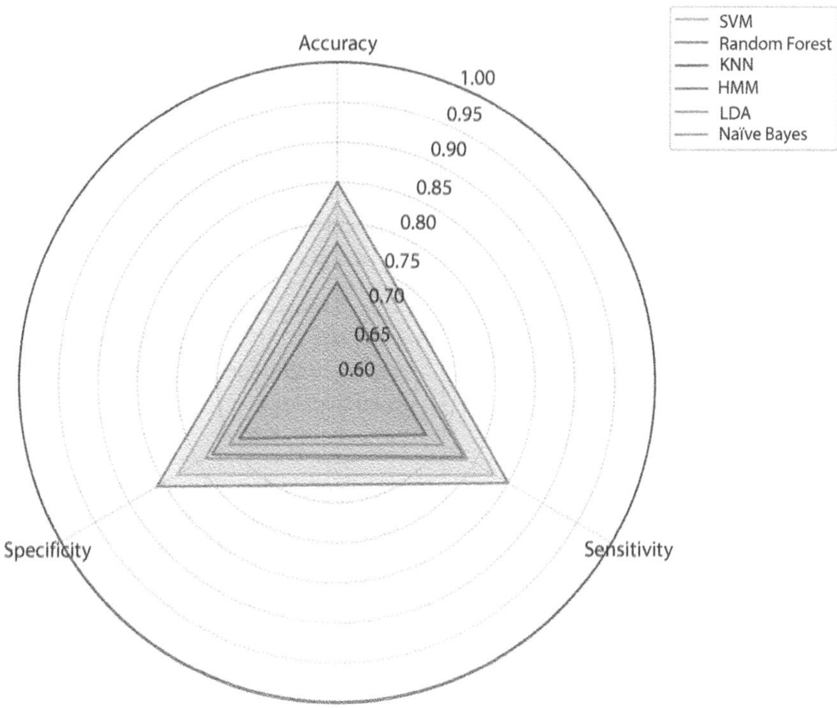

Figure 8.2 Accuracy, sensitivity, and specificity of different ML algorithms.

Table 8.2 BCI application of DL algorithms.

Algorithm	Use case in BCIs	Strengths	Limitations
CNN (convolutional neural network)	Motor imagery, P300, SSVEP, EEG signal classification	Learns spatial and spatial-temporal features, high accuracy	Needs large datasets, computationally intensive
RNN (recurrent neural network)	Sequential EEG data, ERP, emotion recognition	Captures temporal dependencies in signals	Prone to vanishing gradients, slower training
LSTM (long short-term memory)	Long-term dependencies in EEG signals	Handles long sequences, better than RNN for time series	High memory and computation demands
GRU (gated recurrent unit)	Real-time BCI systems	Faster and lighter than LSTM, good temporal modeling	Slightly less expressive than LSTM
CNN-LSTM (hybrid)	Motor imagery, mental workload detection	Combines spatial (CNN) and temporal (LSTM) learning	Complex architecture, longer training time
Autoencoder (AE)	Unsupervised feature learning, artifact removal	Learns compact representations, can denoise signals	May not classify directly, risk of losing signal detail
Variational autoencoder (VAE)	EEG data generation, anomaly detection	Probabilistic learning, useful for generative tasks	Harder to train, less stable than regular AE
GAN (generative adversarial network)	Data augmentation, synthetic EEG generation	Helps balance data classes, improves DL generalization	Training instability, needs careful design

(*Continued*)

Table 8.2 BCI application of DL algorithms. (*Continued*)

Algorithm	Use case in BCIs	Strengths	Limitations
Deep belief network (DBN)	Classification of EEG/fNIRS signals	Good for layer-wise pretraining, interpretable layers	Outdated compared to newer DL models
Transformer-based models	Attention mechanisms in EEG, fMRI, or MEG	Captures long-range dependencies, parallel processing	Very data hungry, high computational load
Temporal convolutional network (TCN)	EEG time-series modeling, BCI control tasks	Better parallelism than RNNs, preserves temporal order	Still emerging in BCI, needs more empirical evaluation

found in EEG data. Networks enable learning of robust filters in EEG signals that lead to improved performance in analyzing both motor imagery datasets and P300 events. LSTM networks within recurrent neural networks (RNNs) provide excellent temporal dependency modeling abilities for sequential EEG data, so they become suitable for detecting event-related potentials and performing continuous control tasks [12]. Unsupervised feature learning together with signal denoising occurs through the use of autoencoders and variational autoencoders (VAEs). GANs are tested for data augmentation purposes in BCI systems since they help address the shortage of labeled data.

EEG sequences are now analyzed using advanced models, including deep belief networks (DBNs) and transformer-based frameworks, because they effectively obtain both hierarchical and global dependency patterns. The integration of CNN architecture with LSTM (such as in CNN-LSTM) results in superior medical decision systems by effectively utilizing both spatial pattern detection features and temporal pattern extraction mechanisms.

The application of deep learning models in BCIs presents several challenging obstacles during use. Three main challenges exist for deep learning in BCI systems, including the need for sizable datasets and capacity to process large amounts of data and the need for clear explanations during use [13, 14]. The development of transfer learning with data augmentation and domain adaptation techniques has led to the quick expansion of deep learning applications in BCIs. The deployment of deep learning in real-time

BCI systems becomes feasible because of model compression tools as well as optimization strategies [20, 22]. Table 8.2 shows the description and BCI application of DL algorithms.

8.4.1 Comparative Analysis of DL Models in BCI Performance

Figure 8.3 shows the comparison of different DL algorithms based on their accuracy, sensitivity, and specificity.

Various DL models employed in BCI systems demonstrate their performance through a grouped bar chart according to three essential evaluation criteria: accuracy, sensitivity, and specificity. The analysis displays the performance outcome of CNN, LSTM, GRU, CNN-LSTM, Autoencoder, and VAE across accuracy, sensitivity, and specificity. The hybrid CNN-LSTM model outperforms other models by delivering the best results for accuracy, sensitivity, and specificity, which proves its ability to extract spatial and temporal patterns in brain signals [21]. The extraction of spatial features through CNN leads to effective accuracy and specificity measurement outcomes. The recurrent models LSTM and GRU deliver better sensitivity, which makes them appropriate for analyzing sequential EEG data [15]. The autoencoder coupled with VAE delivers average results because experts typically deploy these models for dimensional reduction, except for classification purposes. BCI system performance improves strongly when spatial and temporal learning techniques merge, as happens with CNN-LSTM [23].

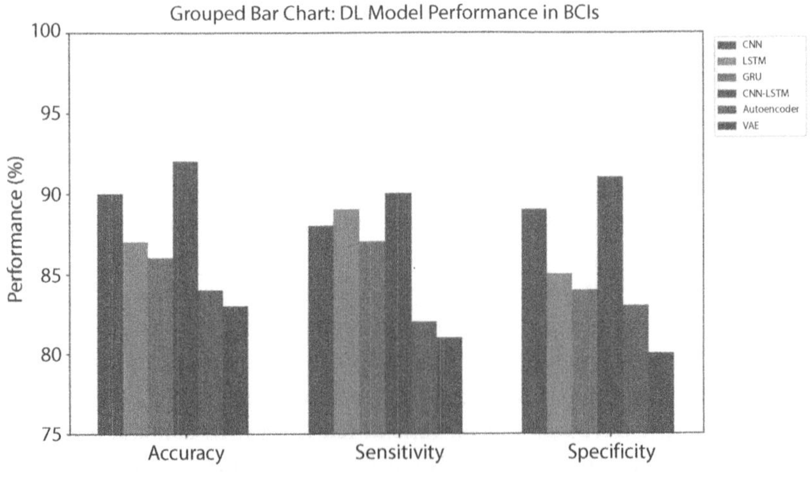

Figure 8.3 Accuracy, sensitivity, and specificity of different DL algorithms.

8.5 Challenges and Limitations in BCI-Based Neurorehabilitation

Technological developments of brain-computer interfaces have not resolved crucial implementation barriers in neurorehabilitative practices, which continue to affect their medical utility and widespread use.

8.5.1 Signal Variability and Noise Issues

The fundamental signals employed by BCI systems consist of electroencephalography (EEG) data, but these signals face high susceptibility to artifacts and show substantial individual differences. Electroencephalographic signals operate at microvolt levels, which creates vulnerability to artifacts produced by electromyographic movements, electrooculographic blinks, and external electrical disturbances. Development of universally robust algorithms becomes challenging due to two key factors: intra-subject variability that changes user signal patterns between sessions, and inter-subject variability that results in different brain signal characteristics among individuals [16, 17]. The system's unreliable performance stems from these variations because it needs regular recalibration efforts that decrease the reliability of BCI rehabilitation techniques.

8.5.2 Computational Complexity and Real-Time Processing

The functionality of neurorehabilitation applications requires instantaneous and nearly instant feedback systems for motor learning with neural plasticity. Real-time BCI systems need to process high-dimensional multi-channel data, besides running computationally intensive operations like signal preprocessing, feature extraction, classification, and feedback generation in less than a millisecond timeframe. This requirement for low latency and high accuracy necessitates the use of advanced algorithms and specialized hardware, which increases system complexity and cost. Establishing proper efficiency between processing power, portability, and energy conservation stands as a crucial issue, especially affecting mobile or wearable BCI systems that operate at home.

8.5.3 Generalization and Adaptability Issues

BCI technology currently demonstrates major limitations because its operating flexibility decreases when working with different users and under varied conditions. The majority of BCI systems demand customized user data for training purposes and a unique setup procedure for achieving their peak operational capacity. The necessity for user-specific training adds complexity to BCI system scalability and increases setup time, decreases accessibility, and thus affects medical practice implementation of health-related BCIs. Performance levels of BCI systems decrease when users exhibit changes in mental state, fluctuations in attention levels, or emotional states, and fatigue characteristics. The development of adaptive algorithms that learn and evolve alongside users represents an open research challenge because they need to operate independently from intensive training requirements.

8.6 Future Directions and Innovations in BCI Research

Brain-computer interface (BCI) research shows accelerated development as multiple innovative breakthroughs prepare to change neurorehabilitation practices and human-machine verbal communication methods. Brain-to-brain communication emerges as one of the most advanced developments because it reveals the potential for direct unspoken communication between minds through neural signal decoding and relays, followed by interpretation. Future-generation BCIs will transcend traditional human-machine systems due to these recent developments. Artificial intelligence applied to real-time BCI system adaptation shows promise as an innovative strategy. The ability of deep learning algorithms to modify themselves during brain pattern alterations produces better signal detection, together with decreased calibration duration and longer-lasting system use [18, 19].

Beyond the connection of BCIs with robotics and smart assistive devices, there are new possibilities emerging to restore autonomy and mobility for patients with motor impairments. The field of specific neurorehabilitation through AI models keeps expanding because these models develop treatment plans that analyze patient brain patterns, treatment methods, and patient preferences. Such systems reach heightened effectiveness when they operate through cloud platforms because these platforms support distant therapy monitoring alongside present-time treatment guidance and perpetual treatment advancements throughout various healthcare locations.

Conclusion

BCI technology connects to robotic frameworks and smart supportive systems so they can bring improved possibilities for restoring both movement ability and self-governing autonomy for people who have physical disabilities. The combination of intelligent prosthetics along with exoskeletons and robotic arms controlled by direct brain signaling ensures significant potential for physical rehabilitation in assistive devices. AI models in specific neurorehabilitation continue to grow since they use patient brain pattern analysis to develop customized treatment designs based on treatment plans and patient choice of methods. When implemented on cloud platforms, these systems demonstrate enhanced operations by permitting remote therapy supervision and real-time therapy guidance while facilitating continuous therapy improvements between different locations and healthcare facilities.

Research data confirms that deep learning models deliver better feature discovery abilities, together with self-learning capabilities and real-time adjustment characteristics for neurorehabilitation protocols. The technology struggles because signal variations combine with demanding computational requirements, ethical issues, and difficulty in achieving user and session generalization. BCIs gain new capabilities through artificial intelligence to drive transformative changes that produce personalized, effective rehabilitation methods.

AI disclosure statement: The author acknowledges the use of AI-based tools for minor language editing or grammatical correction. However, all intellectual contributions, analyses, and conclusions presented in this chapter are entirely the author's own.

References

1. Tibrewal, N., Leeuwis, N., Alimardani, M., Classification of motor imagery EEG using deep learning increases performance in inefficient BCI users. *PLoS One*, 17, e0268880, 2022, 10.1371/journal.pone.0268880.
2. Titkanlou, M.K., Pham, D.T., Mouček, R., Classification of EEG Signal Using Deep Learning Architectures Based Motor-Imagery for an Upper-Limb Rehabilitation Exoskeleton. *SN Comput. Sci.*, 6, 193, 2025, https://doi.org/10.1007/s42979-025-03743-6.

3. Rawat, K. and Sharma, T., An enhanced CNN-Bi-transformer based framework for detection of neurological illnesses through neurocardiac data fusion. *Sci. Rep.*, 15, 1, 11379, 2025 Apr 3, doi: 10.1038/s41598-025-96052-0. PMID: 40181122; PMCID: PMC11968786.
4. Chen, J., Yin, H., Zhang, K., Ren, Y., Zeng, H., Integration of neural networks in brain–computer interface applications: Research frontiers and trend analysis based on Python. *Eng. Appl. Artif. Intell.*, *151*, 110654, 2025, https://doi.org/10.1016/j.engappai.2025.110654.
5. Sun, Y., Chen, X., Liu, B., Liang, L., Wang, Y., Gao, S., Gao, X., Signal acquisition of brain–computer interfaces: A medical-engineering crossover perspective review. *Fundam. Res.*, *5*, 1, 3–16, 2024, https://doi.org/10.1016/j.fmre.2024.04.011.
6. An, Y., Wong, J., Ling, S.H., Development of real-time brain-computer interface control system for robot. *Appl. Soft Comput.*, *159*, 111648, 2024, https://doi.org/10.1016/j.asoc.2024.111648.
7. Knežević, S., Brain-computer interfaces in neurorehabilitation for central nervous system diseases: applications in stroke, multiple sclerosis and parkinson's disease. *Sanamed*, 2025.
8. Awuah, W.A., Ahluwalia, A., Darko, K., Sanker, V., Tan, J.K., Tenkorang, P.O., Ben-Jaafar, A., Ranganathan, S., Aderinto, N., Mehta, A., Shah, M.H., Lee Boon Chun, K., Abdul-Rahman, T., Atallah, O., Bridging Minds and Machines: The Recent Advances of Brain-Computer Interfaces in Neurological and Neurosurgical Applications. *World Neurosurg.*, 189, 138–153, 2024, https://doi.org/10.1016/j.wneu.2024.05.104.
9. Givian, H., The application of brain–computer interface in Alzheimer's disease studies based on machine learning algorithms, in: *Artificial Intelligence Applications for Brain–Computer Interfaces*, pp. 121–143, Elsevier, 2024, https://doi.org/10.1016/B978-0-443-33414-6.00013-7.
10. Dhiman, R., Machine learning techniques for electroencephalogram based brain-computer interface: A systematic literature review. *Meas.: Sens.*, 28, 100823, 2023, https://doi.org/10.1016/j.measen.2023.100823.
11. Rasheed, S., A Review of the Role of Machine Learning Techniques towards Brain–Computer Interface Applications. *Mach. Learn. Knowl. Extr.*, 3, 4, 835–862, 2021, https://doi.org/10.3390/make3040042.
12. Miah, M.O., Habiba, U., Kabir, M.F., ODL-BCI: Optimal deep learning model for brain-computer interface to classify students confusion *via* hyperparameter tuning. *Brain Disord.*, 13, 100121, 2024, https://doi.org/10.1016/j.dscb.2024.100121.
13. Sahoo, S., Tayade, S., Sumitra, S., Manoj, B.S., EEG Data Classification of Odia Words Using ML and DL for BCI Applications. *2024 International Conference on Brain Computer Interface & Healthcare Technologies (iCon-BCIHT)*, Thiruvananthapuram, India, pp. 177–183, 2024, doi: 10.1109/iCon-BCIHT63907.2024.10882414.

14. Ahn, M., Jun, S.C., Yeom, H.G., Cho, H., Editorial: Deep Learning in Brain-Computer Interface. *Front. Hum. Neurosci.*, *16*, 927567, 2022, https://doi.org/10.3389/fnhum.2022.927567.
15. Elashmawi, W.H., Ayman, A., Antoun, M., Mohamed, H., Mohamed, S.E., Amr, H., Talaat, Y., Ali, A., A Comprehensive Review on Brain–Computer Interface (BCI)-Based Machine and Deep Learning Algorithms for Stroke Rehabilitation. *Appl. Sci.*, *14*, 6347, 2024, https://doi.org/10.3390/app14146347.
16. Pirasteh, A., Shamseini Ghiyasvand, M., Pouladian, M., EEG-based brain-computer interface methods with the aim of rehabilitating advanced stage ALS patients. *Disabil. Rehabil. Assist. Technol.*, 19, 8, 3183–3193, 2024, https://doi.org/10.1080/17483107.2024.2316312.
17. Simon, C., Bolton, D.A., Kennedy, N.C., Soekadar, S.R., Ruddy, K.L., Challenges and Opportunities for the Future of Brain-Computer Interface in Neurorehabilitation. *Front. Neurosci.*, *15*, 699428, 2021, https://doi.org/10.3389/fnins.2021.699428.
18. Rashid, M., Sulaiman, N., Musa, R.M., Fakhri, A., Bari, B.S., Khatun, S., Current Status, Challenges, and Possible Solutions of EEG-Based Brain-Computer Interface: A Comprehensive Review. *Front. Neurorob.*, *14*, 515104, 2020, https://doi.org/10.3389/fnbot.2020.00025.
19. Ahmed, B., Khan, S., Lim, H., Ku, J., Challenges and Opportunities of Gamified BCI and BMI on Disabled People Learning: A Systematic Review. *Electronics*, 14, 3, 491, 2025.
20. Menagadevi, M., Devaraj, S., Madian, N., Thiyagarajan, D., Machine and deep learning approaches for alzheimer disease detection using magnetic resonance images: An updated review. *Measurement*, *226*, 114100, 2024.
21. Menagadevi, M., Mangai, S., Madian, N., Thiyagarajan, D., Automated prediction system for Alzheimer detection based on deep residual autoencoder and support vector machine. *Optik*, *272*, 170212, 2023.
22. Vadla, P.K., Naga Pawan, Y.V.R., Kolla, B.P., Tripathi, S.L., Accurate Detection and Diagnosis of Breast Cancer Using Scaled Conjugate Gradient Back Propagation Algorithm and Advanced Deep Learning Techniques, in: *Advances in Electrical and Computer Technologies*, Lecture Notes in Electrical Engineering, vol. 711, T. Sengodan, M. Murugappan, S. Misra (Eds.), Springer, Singapore, 2021, https://doi.org/10.1007/978-981-15-9019-1_9.
23. Prasanna, D.L. and Tripathi, S.L., Machine and Deep-Learning Techniques for Text and Speech Processing, in: *Machine Learning Algorithms for Signal and Image Processing*, pp. 115–128, IEEE, Piscataway, NJ, USA, 2023, doi: 10.1002/9781119861850.ch7.

9

Ethics of AI-Driven Brain-Computer Interfaces: A Focus on Security and Data Privacy

Nitin Soni[1]*, Prince Soni[1] and Kushal Jain[2]

[1]Department of Computer Applications, Sobhasaria Group of Institutions, Sikar, Rajasthan, India
[2]Department of Computer Applications, Shekhawati Group of Institutions, Sikar, Rajasthan, India

Abstract

Artificial intelligence, incorporated into brain-computer interfaces, has granted opportunities to various fields, including healthcare, rehabilitation, and human-computer interaction. As these technologies develop, however, they present serious ethical dilemmas, especially regarding data privacy and security. In this paper, we discuss the ethical issues that arise due to the application of AI techniques in BCIs, specifically in terms of confidentiality and privacy of neural data against unauthorized access and exploitation.

This argument is fueled by the fact that data about brain signals can be personal and irreplaceable, rendering it a good target for hacking or possible exploitation without necessary controls for identity theft, behavioral profiling, or influence. Additionally, most AI algorithms involve some bias, leaving things even more opaque and difficult to control. Above all, these challenges raise serious questions about cognitive autonomy, accounting autonomy, informed consent, and innovation versus ethical responsibility.

As artificial intelligence technologies decode and use neural recordings, mainly electroencephalograms (EEGs) or a few fMRI files, this research opens an interrogation about such technologies' vulnerabilities concerning their management, the dangers that embracing and storing this data might bring about, and the ethical responsibility that developers and organizations should have concerning such

**Corresponding author*: nsoni6789@gmail.com

Tawseef Ahmed Teli, Syed Immamul Ansarullah, Arun Kumar Rana, Suman Lata Tripathi and Kashif Nisar (eds.) Brain-to-Computer Interfaces Using Machine Learning and Deep Learning, (195–216) © 2026 Scrivener Publishing LLC

occupations. Indeed, AI transparency, equitable regulatory approaches, and inclusivity in design are simply themes that ought to occupy center stage as one seeks to address the ethical dilemmas posed by AI-assisted BCIs. Therefore, the present paper aims to foster responsible innovation perceived from personal privacy and social well-being rather than wealth and corporate interest, mainly by addressing fine points on these issues.

This study, in addressing such ethical dimensions, seeks to contribute to the global conversation on the responsible use of AI in emerging technologies. Furthermore, it presents stakeholders with some concrete suggestions for developing safe and ethically viable brain-computer interface systems.

Keywords: Brain-computer interface, artificial intelligence, ethical considerations, neural data privacy, data security, cognitive autonomy, cybersecurity, responsible innovation

9.1 Introduction

BCI is a disruptive technology that involves the interface of human brains with external gadgets. The second type of machines powered by ML and DL works extremely well for the applications directed toward personal assistance for disabled individuals, cognitive enhancement, and even the initiation of new pathways for communication. These new avenues, however, put forth very serious security and ethical questions that need to be resolved in order to facilitate the safe and responsible use of such technologies.

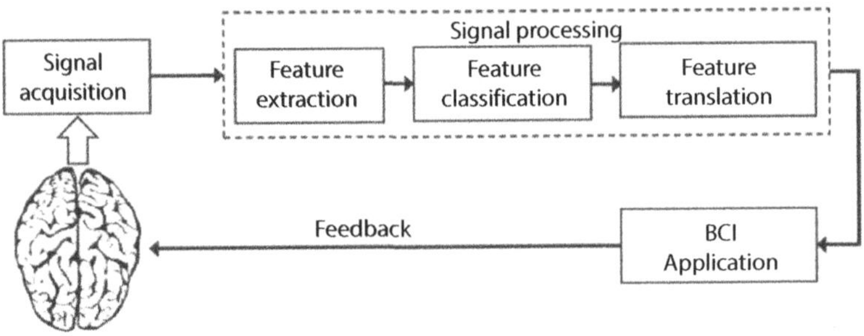

Security for brain-computer interfaces is intimately connected to the security of brain data. Brain signals are, in fact, very much like biometric data. They are signals that are deeply personal and convey the super-secret modalities of a person's emotions, intentions, and cognitive states. The interception of these signals or the modification of these signals would have severe consequences concerning privacy, identity theft, or influence on decision-making. Whereas most other biometric identifiers can be changed—passwords, for example, or fingerprints—brain data cannot. Thus, this makes brain data vulnerable to security threats and further confirms the need for security mechanisms.

Again, ethical implications haunt the use of BCI technology besides the generally purported security risks. The question of data ownership and consent on the user's part emerges as the most prominent. Who gets the rights to access and store another person's brain signals—research institutions, technology companies, or the individuals themselves? Neuromarketing and cognitive profiling could develop into real threats that would result in the invasion of personal lives by corporations that analyze, through very complex techniques, human subconscious responses to manipulate consumer behavior. Moreover, AI-enabled BCI requires a huge amount of data to train, introducing bias in the way the various populations respond to these technologies. If not inclusive in training machine learning models, some of the users might experience misleading results, reduced accessibility, or discrimination.

Bearing in mind the pains mentioned, it becomes imperative to ensure that BCIs are developed ethically and securely. These will necessitate highly attributed encryption methods, privacy-preserving AI models, and transparent regulatory policies to protect the users. This chapter will focus on vulnerability in BCI security, AI-based protection schemes, and ethical dilemmas concerning brain data privacy-biased issues. All these aspects, when faced, will ensure that BCI is a fantastic tool for humanity's further advancement without compromising on privacy, security, or ethical integrity.

9.2 Understanding Brain Signals and BCI Architecture

Brain-computer interfaces (BCIs) provide an exciting space for interaction in the area of neuroscience and technology. BCIs provide an avenue for direct communication between the individual human brain and an external device. In addressing the security and ethical dimensions of BCIs, it is preliminary to obtain knowledge on the generation, processing, and interpretation of brain signals through the BCI principles.

Nature of Brain Signals

The human brain is made up of billions of networked neurons, which communicate *via* both electrical and chemical signals with each other.

The very activity of this neuron is associated with cognition, like that of motor control and sensory perception. Firing of the neuron creates tiny electrical impulses, which are measurable and analyzable through a set of techniques. BCI applications primarily include two types of brain signals:

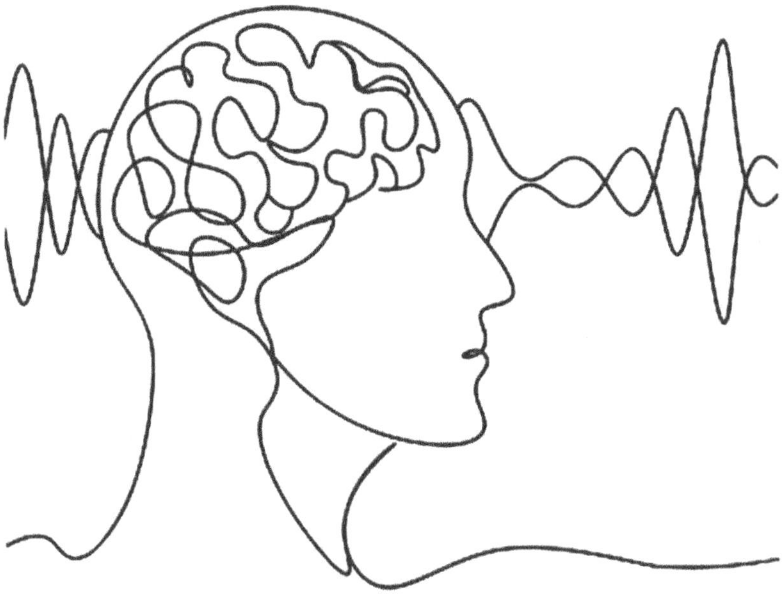

- Electroencephalography: EEG gets electrical activity from the scalp using non-invasive electrodes. It's a common application of BCI due to cost efficiency and convenience. EEG records the amplification of fluctuation of voltage due to the activity of neurons over the range of 0.5–100 Hz.
  - ∉ Magnetoencephalography: MEG detects magnetic fields that excite the neurons. It provides spatial resolution of a higher order than EEG but is more expensive with high-precision equipment.
  - ∉ Functional Magnetic Resonance Imaging (fMRI): fMRI measures the change in the levels of blood oxygen in the brain while performing an activity. Although it is not widely used in real-time BCI functions, it is an important tool in attaining knowledge about the brain's functions.
  - ∉ Electrocorticography (ECoG): This is the placement of electrodes directly on the brain of the individual. It is

much more accurate and has less noise than that of electroencephalography, but it is an invasive surgery.

∉ Local Field Potentials (LFPs): LFPs capture deep brain activity and are usually measured with implanted electrodes. These are signals of high spatial and temporal resolution but have substantial surgical risks.

Each one of those methods comes with merits and demerits as regards resolution, clarity of signals, and invasiveness, and would thus influence the designs of BCIs and their application.

BCI Architecture: How It Works

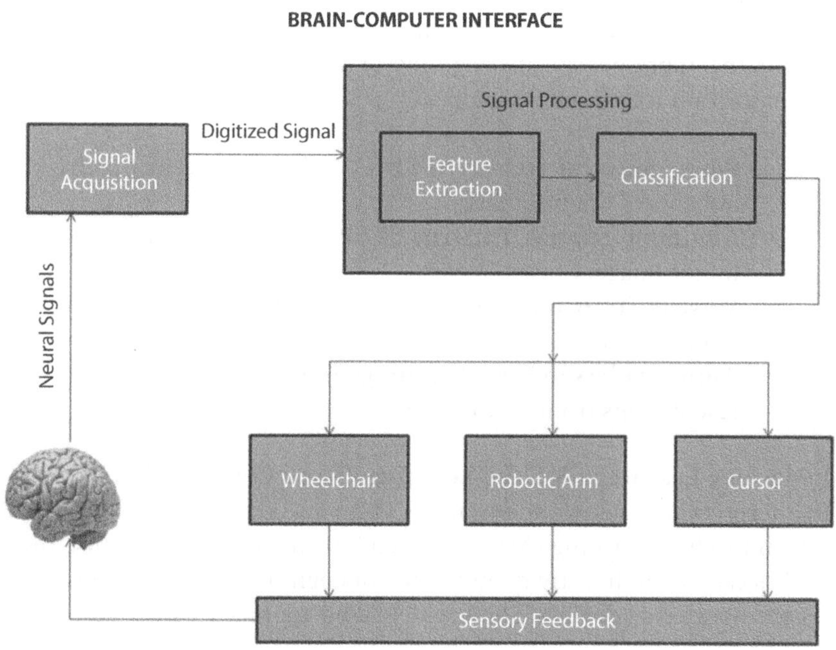

A BCI system consists of several components working together to capture, process, and translate brain activity into a command value. It essentially consists of the following stages:

1. Signal Acquisition

First, brain activity is captured by using sensors or electrodes. The chosen signal acquisition method will determine the quality, resolution, and usability of the data; consequently, the cursor movement is based on signals acquired and interpreted by the BCI. This stage is therefore vital since any noise and interference leading to missing signals would affect the accuracy and reliability of the system.

2. Preprocessing and Noise Reduction

The raw brain signals are often weak and contaminated by such signals as muscle activity, eye movement, or electrical sources coming from the environment. The preprocessing steps used in enhancing signal quality include filtering, artifact removal, and normalization. Algorithms such as Independent Component Analysis (ICA) and wavelet transformation are used to help remove unwanted noise.

3. Feature Extraction

Once the signals are preprocessed, the next step is to extract meaningful features that represent specific cognitive or motor functions. Common feature extraction techniques include:

- **Power Spectral Density (PSD):** Analyzes frequency components of brain signals.
- **Common Spatial Patterns (CSP):** Used for classifying motor imagery tasks.
- **Wavelet Transform:** Captures both time and frequency information.
- **Autoencoders in Deep Learning:** Extracts hierarchical representations from brain signals.

4. Machine Learning- & Deep Learning–Based Classification

To interpret brain signals and translate them into commands, BCI systems rely on machine learning (ML) and deep learning (DL) algorithms. These models classify brain activity into different cognitive states, allowing users to control external devices. Some widely used approaches include:

- **Support Vector Machines (SVM):** Effective for EEG-based motor imagery classification.
- **Convolutional Neural Networks (CNNs):** Extract spatial patterns from brain signals.
- **Recurrent Neural Networks (RNNs) & Long Short-Term Memory (LSTM):** Capture temporal dependencies in brain activity.
- **Transformer-based Models:** Used for complex BCI applications like speech reconstruction from neural signals.

5. Translation into Output Commands
Brain signals are turned into actions that can be executed, such as moving a prosthetic arm, managing a cursor, or typing *via* a brain interface. Feedback loops will instantly optimize the model to fit the user's own neural pattern, thus enhancing accuracy.

6. User Feedback & Adaptation
Presently, modern BCIs involve adaptive learning technology to customize the system according to a user's individual brain activity. Continuous calibration and reinforcement learning will help the interface improve with time and make smaller errors with greater usability. Security as well as ethical safeguards.

7. Security & Ethical Safeguards
Since the neural data are sensitive and must be protected through stringent security measures, the BCI systems need these security mechanisms. Thus, allowing the prevention of unauthorized usages such as deciphering the brain signals through encryption, differential privacy, and biometric authentication mechanisms. Furthermore, the ethical guidelines should provide assurance that BCI users will continue to own their cognitive data and their consent for usage.

9.3 Security Challenges in BCIs

Brain-computer interfaces, or BCIs, are making fast advancements in technology. All modern machine-learning advancements and deep-learning techniques now focus on supporting the communication between the human brain and any external device. However, an increase in sophistication also correlates with an increase in vulnerability to security threats. Since transplantation deals with some of the most sensitive neural data, security is one of the most important issues to be worked on. Once a BCI system is breached, it could lead to data stealing, unauthorized control, or even manipulation of brain activity. The following are some of the major security challenges—pulling weights when it comes to BCIs.

1. Data Privacy and Unauthorized Access
The privacy of neural data constitutes one of the main threats to BCI security. Whereas conventional biometric data (that is, fingerprints, retina scans, etc.) are still personal, brain signals contain such private, individual information about an individual's aspirations, emotions, and even

intentions that interception or leaking of signals is likely to reveal the most sensitive information about a person's mental state, cognitive faculties, or even subconscious thoughts. Fraudsters may use such information for identity theft, personalized advertising, or spying. If encryption is absent and data storage mechanisms are not secured properly, brainwave data may be a prime target for cybercriminals.

2. Man-in-the-Middle (MITM) Attacks

The brain-computer interface (BCI) systems convey neural signals between the brain and the decoding software and output devices. Somewhere in that chain of transmission, an attacker can intercept and manipulate the signals through a man-in-the-middle attack. In such scenarios, a third party gains unauthorized access to the communication channel between the user and the BCI device, modifying either the data being sent or received. This could result in unwanted behaviors, create false interpretations of brain activity, or even result in the remote seizure of a BCI-controlled device that can pose extreme dangers to the user.

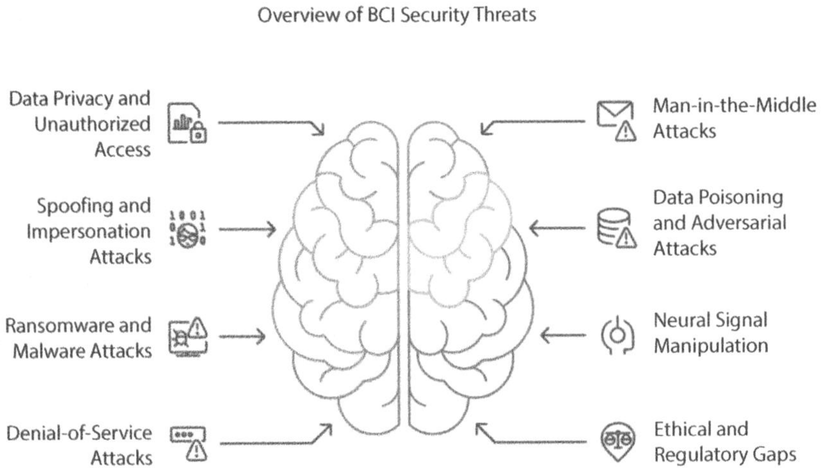

3. Spoofing and Impersonation Attacks

Brain-computer interface structures will also show a mark of signal spoofing, just like concealed fingerprints or facial recognition. Using such signals as fake brain signals injected into the system will bring deception attempts involving the interface itself, recognizing unauthenticated individuals instead of actual ones. In the case of using BCIs for authentication, such hacking might allow intrusion into bank accounts or essential data. Fostering general belief in the personalization of brain signals will create a challenge in effective authentication, which would be needed by existing security application models.

4. Data Poisoning and Adversarial Attacks

A BCI is dependent on machine learning/deep learning algorithms for the interpretation of brain activity; hence, the accuracy and reliability of these systems are a function of the quality of the training data used. In a poisoning attack, the attacker tries to alter the training data set so as to introduce a false bias or false pattern into the AI model. Otherwise, with the BCI misinterpreting brain signals, it undermines the very foundation of BCI applications' reliability. An adversarial attack would comprise the injection of subtle signals designed to induce the wrong operation in the machine-learning model, leading to the wrong output and thereby compromising BCI functioning. Adversarial attacks are an enormous threat in all medical applications, as such erroneous interpretations could lead to decisions detrimental to patient treatment.

5. Ransomware and Malware Attacks

Indeed, the ransomware attacks on traditional IT systems do open doors for attacks in BCIs. Once attacked, the hacker would have access to the user's neural data, which could be encrypted, and demand ransom for re-access. Such threats may leave the patients who depend on BCI-controlled medical devices (neuroprosthetics, communication means, etc.) under a lot of stress. Software can be designed to tamper with or change the neural signals being processed, thereby leading to system failure, undesired movements, or even harming the individual using the system. Since BCI works in a very close-knit environment with other digital systems, ensuring the security of BCI from malware is another important challenge.

6. Neural Signal Manipulation and Brain Hacking

The most shocking among the threats to BCI security is the neural signal manipulation, or simply called "brain hacking." It is theorized that once an attacker can access a BCI system, they could possibly change the brain signals, as it will influence the decisions, emotions, or even cognitive processes of a person. It may sound quite fictional; however, the first studies have shown that neurostimulation techniques can be used for mischief. Such threats become grimmer if BCIs are utilized, for example, to enhance cognitive functions in critical scenarios like the military or law enforcement.

7. Denial-of-Service (DoS) Attacks on BCI Systems

Denial-of-service attacks, or DoS attacks, derive from that system when it is saturated or crushed under excessive load or malicious requests to slow down or crash that system altogether. In the case of BCIs, it would mean the disruption of real-time neural processing, rendering an unusable system. This would be most critical in medical and assistive applications wherein patients rely on BCIs for communication or movement. An attacker may deliberately overload the system with corrupted neural signals that interfere with the brain-machine interaction, causing the BCI to be less responsive.

8. Ethical and Regulatory Gaps in BCI Security

Building on this, brain-computer interface (BCI) security issues may extend to ethical and legal concerns beyond just the technical vulnerabilities. Data protection laws presently running in the country, such as the GDPR, lack specific provisions for neural data, thus leaving a range of legal gaps at the same time. There is, in fact, no specific norm for ensuring the security of brain signals since BCI firms adopt entirely different approaches to implementing safety mechanisms. As a result, there is much inconsistency in the protection of some systems, rendering specific BCI safety more vulnerable than others. Furthermore, ethical concerns arise when it comes to ownership and control of neural data—whose should it be, that of the user, the BCI provider, or medical institutions? These issues make it necessary to fill these regulatory gaps to seek a secure future in BCI technology.

9. Side-Channel Attacks on BCIs

Attackers could exploit the patterns of neural signal transmission to ascertain sensitive information from remote possibilities rather than by accessing the raw data directly. To understand a user's thought processes, mental states, or cognitive responses, this information could be used. This warrants major concern within the context of environments having the highest security since classified information is processed in BCI-controlled systems.

10. Lack of Security Awareness among Users

Security Awareness Being Unseen, Apparently, and Disregarded by Users: BCI technology is still a new concept, and many users involved in BCI system operations are not fully aware of the security threats these systems possess. Existing computers are covered by well-known mechanisms of cybersecurity, while BCI was not recognized properly in this regard. Several users may not even acknowledge that secure authentication procedures and encrypted storage of neural data are important and that there are risks involved with connecting their BIC devices to untrusted networks. Hence, this lack of awareness increases the chance for successful cyberattacks, placing user education at the top of the agenda for BIC security.

Addressing the Security Challenges in BCIs

To mitigate these security risks, researchers and developers must prioritize robust security measures such as:

- Implementing **end-to-end encryption** for brain signal transmission.
- Developing **AI-driven anomaly detection systems** to identify suspicious activity.
- Enhancing **multi-factor authentication** for BCI access.
- Establishing **standardized security frameworks** for neural data protection.
- Increasing **awareness and education** about BCI security risks and best practices.

9.4 ML/DL-Based Security Mechanisms for Brain-Computer Interfaces (BCIs)

Brain-computer interfaces get hyper-specific and precise; cyber threats associated with brain signals tend to be more intense in security. It involves their extra work with the human body, which directly deals with neural data protection against cyber threats and helps in the prevention, detection, and maintenance of the integrity of data processes through machine learning and deep learning, which have become such major technologies in securing BCI systems.

1. Intrusion Detection Systems (IDS) Using ML/DL

One of the most effective means of securing BCI networks involves deploying intrusion detection systems based on ML algorithms. These monitor real-time BCI data transmissions and identify any unusual change in pattern as a potential indicator of certain types of cyber threats, such as unauthorized access and tampering of data. These include supervised learning models like the support vector machines (SVM) and random forest classifiers, which analyze the neural signals looking for any deviation from normal patterns. To add, some deep learning architectures, such as recurrent neural networks (RNNs) and long short-term memory (LSTM) networks, are capable of even detecting minute anomalies in time-series brainwave data.

2. Secure Brain Signal Authentication Using Biometrics

Every human has a different neural signature, which makes brain signals a potential biometric feature. ML models can be used to define the brainwave patterns of an individual and then be used for authentication. This kind of authentication is known as electroencephalogram (EEG)-based biometric authentication, in which only authorized users can access a BCI system. CNNs have proved to be very accurate in extracting definite EEG features. This would make it extremely difficult for unauthorized access. Compared with conventional passwords or fingerprints, brain-based authentication is much more difficult to imitate or forge.

3. Real-Time Threat Detection with Deep Learning

This is because these systems simultaneously collect, process, and analyze huge amounts of neural data, making them susceptible to adversarial attacks that prey on manipulating signals to mislead an intended target. Which, among others, include deep learning models such as generative adversarial networks (GANs) that serve to detect and mitigate adversarial attacks. GANs can generate adversarial attacks and train the security models to effectively discern and neutralize them. Moreover, autoencoders—unsupervised deep learning models—help in detecting signal manipulations based on what is expected versus what was received as brainwave patterns.

4. Data Encryption and Secure Communication Protocols

Secure multi-party computation not only takes great measures to maintain this safety but also ensures that computations can be accurately made concerning joint operations without revealing any local inputs. "Among those so far mentioned, BASE is the best with respect to practical applicability. Where there is no room for doubt, however, is between Dynamic Private Data Aggregation and Private Data Aggregation with privacy or possibly, private data aggregation, in effect, always a lot more secured within the aforementioned." Hence, 'privacy-preserving speech' applies.

5. AI-Powered Adaptive Security Models

Traditional security measures in business activities would be observed failing in dealing with the fast-evolving nature of modern cyber threats. ML-based adaptive security models had the ability to continuously learn from new attack patterns and consequently improved protection mechanisms. This is a specific branch of ML called Reinforcement Learning (RL), which helps BCIs dynamically reposition their security parameters based on real-time threat intelligence. A concrete example might be an RL-based firewall detection system that might observe suspicious network activity and automatically tighten security protocols.

6. Privacy-Preserving Machine Learning in BCIs

BCI is such that it operates with very sensitive data, giving direct neural activity. The privacy of such data is protected from prying eyes through the integration of privacy-preserving ML techniques such as differential privacy (DP) and secure multi-party computation (SMPC) under the BCI security framework. The differential privacy model tends to cloak the fact that the brain data of an individual could be traced back to the person, even when this data is part of an extensive dataset. On the flip side, secure multi-party computation (SMPC) allows different persons to perform joint operations on BCI data without revealing each individual's values, improving security in cloud-based BCI cases.

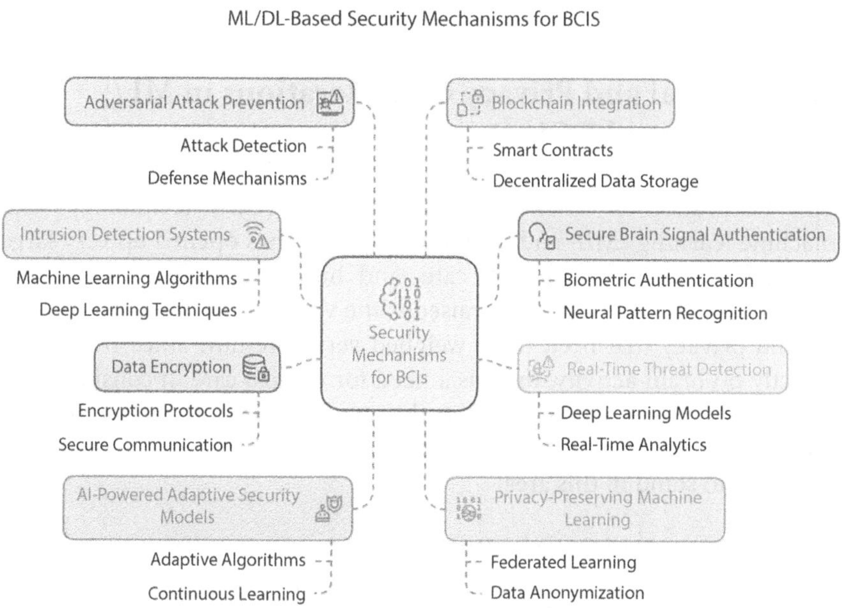

7. Detecting and Preventing Adversarial Attacks

Signals generated by the brain can be easily manipulated by attackers to obtain their desired outputs on the ML-powered BCI systems. To dampen the risk, adversarial machine learning techniques such as adversarial training are employed. Training this deep-learning model with adversarial examples, or data that have been altered by an attacker, makes the BCI resistant to malicious alterations. AI-based anomaly detection systems (ADS) assist in identifying sudden changes in brainwave signals that do not resemble normal behavior effectively, thus enhancing the security of the BCI.

8. Blockchain Integration for Secure BCI Data Management

A scenario where BCIs are combined with blockchain technology and integrated with ML would provide the safest storage and access control, where prevention meets an ideal setting for unauthorized access. Brain data captured will thus be secured against tampering by writing transactions into an unalterable ledger. This security would also be complemented by the application of ML algorithms to all access patterns captured under such a blockchain in order to flag any apparently suspicious access to the brain data. The maturity of the technologies of blockchain and ML also helps greatly in the super security construction that prevents unauthorized alteration or leakage of neural information.

9.5 Ethical and Privacy Considerations in ML/DL-Based BCIs

This integration of brain-computer interface (BCI) technology with machine learning (ML) and deep learning (DL) has opened up very large vistas in neuroscience, health care, and human-computer interaction. These advancements have also raised some very serious questions of ethics and privacy that need to be weighed very carefully. Since BCIs work directly on brain activity, there is a need for utmost care in consideration of sensitive neural data. Consequently, security, consent, and fairness are seen as the fundamental pillars on which ethical research and development will need to stand in this area.

1. Data Privacy and Security Risks

One of the most important questions concerning all BCIs is the issue of data privacy. Brain signals are highly individual and carry extremely personal revelations, possibly disclosing emotions, thoughts, cognitive states, and even subconscious biases. If access to this data is given to an unauthorized person or used without due consent, the potential invasion of privacy could become significantly harmful. Unlike other biometric identifiers like fingerprints or facial recognition, the compromise of brain signals cannot be undone as effortlessly. Therefore, securing the storage, transport, and processing of neural data becomes of utmost importance to eliminate the risk of unauthorized access, identity theft, or even manipulation of user behavior.

2. Informed Consent and User Autonomy

Being very complex, ML- and DL-based BCIs are oftentimes not really understood by users in how their brain data are collected, processed, and used. Ethical implementation would mean that people will be able to give informed consent with a clear understanding of what data are collected, when, how, what those data are to be utilized for, and what the associated risks are. This is very crucial for vulnerable groups, such as individuals undergoing neurorehabilitation or persons with disabilities, who may feel coerced into adopting such technology without thorough knowledge of the legal consequences thereof. Also, it raises the notion of continued consent with the BCIs being implanted or used for long periods. It should be a prerogative of users to withdraw their consent and consequently erase their data from the system in case they wish to discontinue use of the technology.

3. Ownership and Control of Neural Data

Although data management and ownership become relevant ethical questions somewhat delayed in the BCI development process, the decision concerning the ownership of brain signal data probably rests with the user, the BCI device provision company, or some third-party service responsible for processing the data. In some respects, neural data are unlike other kinds of personal data due to their intrinsic connection to an individual's identity and cognitive functioning. It would be morally frightening to think of corporations or governments controlling an individual's neurons for any purpose, including consummation, commercialization, or even misuse. It is, therefore, an ethical duty on the part of the designers and policymakers to protect users' freedom with respect to brain data, including the rights to access that data, modify it, or delete it.

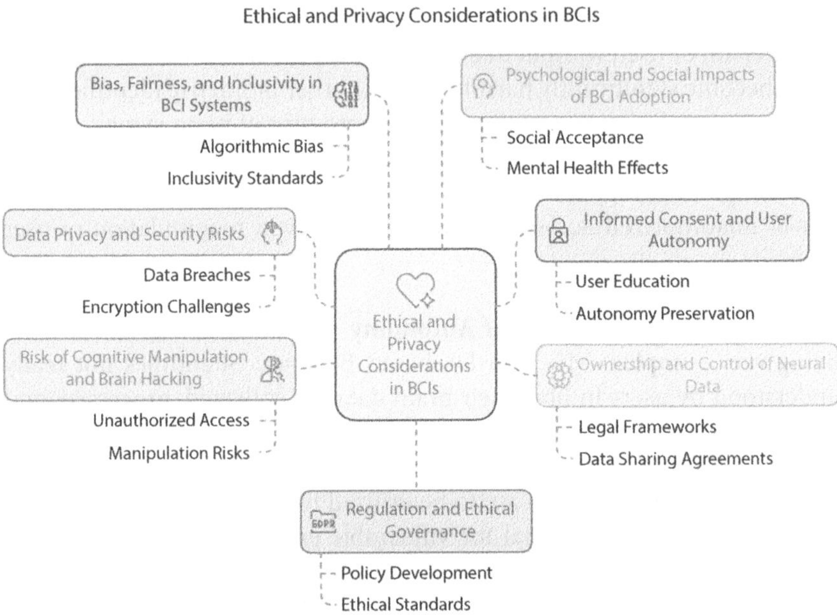

4. Risk of Cognitive Manipulation and Brain Hacking
As advancements in ML/DL continue to rise, BCIs might be used in the near future to modify thoughts, behaviors, or even the decision processes of people. Brain hacking, if done or exploited, can lead to a high possibility of unauthorized influence through perceptions, emotions, or actions in a person to be involved in malicious acts by malicious actors. Subliminal advertising or political manipulation, or in the most extreme case, coercion through BCIs, raises alarming ethical questions. There have to be provisions and safeguards in ethical AI frameworks against such risks, and the models relevant to ML/DL in BCIs should, by all means, not be hidden covertly in any method to manipulate human cognition without consent.

5. Bias, Fairness, and Inclusivity in BCI Systems
ML and DL models in BCIs are trained on data from which they are derived. If the training datasets are biased toward some demographic characteristics, BCI systems could be less effective or actually discriminatory toward certain underrepresented groups. For example, suppose a BCI-based neural prosthetic is trained primarily on data from younger individuals. In this case, the performance with elderly users may not be up to par. This raises other ethical questions related to fairness since biased systems would limit accessibility and/or effectiveness, particularly for marginalized populations. Developers must pay attention to using diverse and representative

datasets and put in place measures that mitigate the presence of bias to ensure fairness and inclusivity in these emergent BCI technologies.

6. Psychological and Social Impacts of BCI Adoption
The implementation of BCIs into social life has the potential to change human-human and human-machine social interactions, human behaviors, and even concepts of personal identity. Such a change may worsen the social status of those who cannot afford or decide not to use BCI technology intended for thought-based communication or cognitive enhancement. Such a situation would create a "neural divide" among BCI users and non-BCI users, giving rise to new forms of inequalities, exclusions, and discrimination. Additionally, there is the potential for increased anxiety and paranoia or reduced personal agency as the psychological effect of one's thoughts and emotions being recorded, analyzed, or influenced by an ML or DL algorithm. Truly ethical BCI deployment has to consider all such psychological and social factors because the technology should not redefine ethical dilemmas when it claims to improve human capacity.

7. Regulation and Ethical Governance
Ethical oversight and regulation are essential, as the technology interfaces directly with the human brain. Currently, there is no universally applied legal framework governing BCI applications, creating potential gaps in accountability. Governments, academia, and industries must collaborate to establish clear ethical guidelines that will safeguard user rights, ensure transparency in decision-making, and prevent abuse of BCI technologies. Regulations must cover data protection, informed consent, bias mitigation, and ethical AI implementation in neural interfaces, to mention just a few areas. At the same time, interdisciplinary-oriented ethics boards should be created to ensure ethical development and use of BCI technologies.

9.6 Future Directions and Recommendations

Because the current advancements and developments in brain-computer interfaces (BCIs) are rapid, there is a demand to instill and uphold security and ethics for these systems. As much as the infusion of machine learning (ML) and deep learning (DL) opens up new paths, it also presents vast challenges. It will require much research and interventions in the future, directed toward a number of very challenging safety, privacy, and fairness areas in BCI technology.

One of the foremost concerns will be to ensure a strong security infrastructure to protect against cyber threats to any and all brain signals. Given the need for the real-time transmission of brain signals, conventional cryptographic approaches may be insufficient. In such a future BCI system, one must ensure the implementation of advanced cryptographic techniques to protect against unauthorized access and tampering, namely homomorphic encryption, zero-trust architecture, and blockchain security protocols. Most importantly, there must be one integrated AI-powered anomaly detection system for malicious activity identification or abnormal behavior at the brain signal processing stage, thus bolstering real-time threat detection.

Along with this, privacy-preserving machine learning models are developed for BCI applications. Brainwaves are probably the most personal and unique data for any individual. Therefore, it should really be a federated learning or differential privacy-based solution. It provides a facility wherein models can be trained in the decentralized environment of AI on signals. It does not call for the direct access or storing of raw brain signals, thus avoiding privacy threats without any compromise on performance. Hence, the need is for refinement of such models for researchers, considering accuracy while maintaining confidentiality between users.

Along with the privacy-preserving technologies, regulations, and ethical frameworks should also be standardized to tackle the ethical issues related to the use of BCI. Governments, regulatory authorities, and international organizations should quickly come out with comprehensive legal frameworks pertaining to the collection of data, consent management, and the ethical use of such data regarding brain processes. These kinds of regulations, for example, would stipulate the duration the data can be withheld, the rights of ownership over it, and the way it will be used for AI applications. There should also be an ethics committee overseeing the implementation of BCI technologies to ensure that they are not misused, but rather that their adoption uses the technology.

A lot more effort must be expended in the field of bias mitigation in machine learning and deep learning models in favor of security, compliance, and ethical issues. Many AI models are trained on datasets that cannot possibly be fully representative of diverse populations and hence exhibit biased results for that subset of applications called BCI. Future research should focus on creating datasets that encompass the possible variability of brain activities along the axes of age, sex, ethnicity, and medical conditions. AI algorithms dealing with fairness would enable an equitable count in terms of accuracy and reliability across all users in a BCI setting.

To further improve usability and accessibility, researchers should aim to optimize brain signal decoding while at the same time minimizing computational complexity. The current deep learning model paradigms rely too much on processor-intensive operations, which may limit their use in plug-and-play applications. This is the very philosophy that can be practically realized by developing lightweight and energy-efficient AI models for BCI, ready for mainstream applications such as use in wearable devices and healthcare. Besides, this has the potential of advancing non-invasive BCI technologies, thus reducing the burden of implant-based systems, making them user-friendly and acceptable.

In the future, user awareness and public engagement would have to be an integral part of BCIs. To illustrate this point, there should be a general awareness of rights and risks and how best to use daily life integrating technologies safely. Organizations have to keep making awareness campaigns, workshops, and training on aspects of security and ethics to be used by the users for building knowledge on BCIs. Interdisciplinary collaborations will also refer to a balanced perspective on BCI development—on progress, well-being, and human well-being—involving neuroscientists, artificial intelligence researchers, cybersecurity experts, ethicists, and policy makers.

The final determinant of ML/DL BCI is a collective effort toward making them secure and ethically accountable, as well as fair in AI-induced systems. All these conditions would consequently spell the way toward producing highly efficient but ethical BCIs. Thus, it is preventive actions in these areas that will either keep BCI instruments as tools of human augmentation or lead them to be sources of security and ethical challenges in the future digital age.

9.7 Conclusion

The usage of AI, such as machine learning (ML) and deep learning (DL), in brain-computer interfaces (BCIs) is largely transformative in interfacing between humans and computers. This tremendous boon has much potential for the health care, communication, and neurotechnology fields. Yet, with the improvements that are seen in BCIs, security and ethical challenges also become more difficult. Brain signals are such sensitive personal and cognitive information that, unlike traditional biometric data, once compromised, they will not only create unfathomable risks, including identity theft and behavioral manipulation, but may also trespass into cognitive privacy.

Robust security frameworks for secure ethical use of ML/DL-based BCIs are thus to be established. Encryption and differential privacy, with federated learning techniques in combination, would secure the sensitive neural data with reduced costs and risks, storage, and transmission. In addition to that, the advanced anomaly detection models developed based on AI can help detect and mitigate these breaches before they occur. However, technology by itself cannot address such problems; regulative and legal frameworks also need to keep pace with achievements in technology. This keeps the user rights and ownership of data and ethical considerations intact.

A veritable cornucopia of ethical dilemmas arises from these situations beyond those of security. The ability of AI-mediated BCI to cause cognitive biases will heighten awareness of fairness, inclusion, and unintended consequences. Absent diligent design, ML/DL algorithms may be biased towards identifying particular patterns of neural representation and thus might be disadvantaging certain individuals due to the variance in brain signals that are not considered in the interpretation of the algorithm. In such cases, the prime arguments should be for transparency in algorithm development and ongoing ethical audits to ensure that BCI technologies are equitably beneficial to all users.

A perspective of historical reflection will find that interdisciplinary work among researchers, engineers, policymakers, and ethicists will be of prime importance in determining the futures of BCIs. In a sense, this is expected to keep technology at the forefront of innovation. At the same time, though, we must keep the balance of advancement against ethical responsibility. The future of ML/DL-based BCIs should be poised on the balance between innovative developments and cautious treatment of security and ethics so that the technology does good without compromising user safety and privacy.

AI disclosure statement: The author confirms that no artificial intelligence (AI)-generated content or AI-assisted writing tools were used in the preparation of this chapter (including summaries and the abstract). All text, analysis, and conclusions are the result of the author's original work.

Bibliography

1. Allison, B.Z., Dunne, S., Leeb, R., Millán, J., del, R., Nijholt, A. (Eds.), *Towards Practical Brain-Computer Interfaces: Bridging the Gap from Research to Real-World Applications*, Springer, 2013. https://research.utwente.nl/en/

publications/towards-practical-brain-computer-interfaces-bridging-the-gap-from/.
2. Chaudhary, U., Birbaumer, N., Ramos-Murguialday, A., Brain–computer interfaces for communication and rehabilitation. *Nat. Rev. Neurol.*, *12*, 9, 513–525, 2016.
3. Clausen, J., Man, machine and in between. *Nature*, *457*, 7233, 1080–1081, 2009.
4. He, H., Wu, D., Zhang, D., A novel hybrid EEG/fNIRS brain–computer interface: Application to motion intention classification. *IEEE Trans. Neural Syst. Rehabil. Eng.*, *23*, 2, 209–219, 2015.
5. Haselager, P., Vlek, R., Hill, J., Nijboer, F., A note on ethical aspects of BCI. *Neural Networks*, *22*, 9, 1352–1357, 2009.
6. Ienca, M. and Haselager, P., Hacking the brain: brain–computer interfacing technology and the ethics of neurosecurity. *Ethics Inf. Technol.*, *18*, 2, 117–129, 2016.
7. Kübler, A. and Birbaumer, N., Brain–computer interfaces and communication in paralysis: Extinction of goal directed thinking in completely paralysed patients? *Clin. Neurophysiol.*, *119*, 11, 2658–2666, 2008.
8. Lebedev, M.A. and Nicolelis, M.A.L., Brain–machine interfaces: Past, present and future. *Trends Neurosci.*, *29*, 9, 536–546, 2006.
9. Mak, J.N. and Wolpaw, J.R., Clinical applications of brain–computer interfaces: Current state and future prospects. *IEEE Rev. Biomed. Eng.*, *2*, 187–199, 2009.
10. Moreno, J.D., *Mind Wars: Brain Research and National Defense*, Dana Press, 2006. https://archive.org/details/mindwarsbrainres00jona/page/n13/mode/2up.
11. Müller-Putz, G.R., Scherer, R., Brunner, C., Leeb, R., Pfurtscheller, G., Better than random: A closer look on BCI results. *Int. J. Bioelectromagn.*, *10*, 1, 52–55, 2008.
12. Nijboer, F., Clausen, J., Allison, B.Z., Haselager, P., The Asilomar survey: Stakeholders' opinions on ethical issues related to brain–computer interfacing. *Neuroethics*, *6*, 3, 541–578, 2013.
13. Rao, R.P.N., *Brain–computer interfacing: An introduction*, Cambridge University Press, 2013. https://www.cambridge.org/core/books/braincomputer-interfacing/8C09E1CFD4634723E923208A4D259D60.
14. Schalk, G. and Wolpaw, J.R., Brain–computer interfaces for communication and control, in: *Neural Engineering*, pp. 393–413, Springer, 2011. https://dl.acm.org/doi/10.1145/1941487.1941506.
15. Steinert, S. and Friedrich, O., Wired emotions: Ethical issues of affective brain–computer interfaces. *Sci. Eng. Ethics*, *26*, 1, 351–367, 2020.
16. St. Fleur, N., Meta's brain-to-text tech is here. We are not remotely ready, Vox, 2023.
17. Stix, G., Can fMRI really tell if you're lying? *Sci. Am.*, 2008.

18. Wolpaw, J.R. and Wolpaw, E.W. (Eds.), *Brain–Computer Interfaces: Principles and Practice*, Oxford University Press, 2012. https://www.ece.uprm.edu/~manian/BCI%20principles%20and%20practice.pdf.
19. Yuste, R., Goering, S., Bi, G., Carmena, J.M., Carter, A., Fins, J.J., Friesen, P., Gallant, J., Huggins, J.E., Illes, J., Kellmeyer, P., Klein, E., Marblestone, A., Mitchell, C., Oliviero, A., Ooi, S., Park, S., Sparp, G., Teicher, M., Wolpaw, J., Four ethical priorities for neurotechnologies and AI. *Nature*, *551*, 7679, 159–163, 2017.
20. Zander, T.O. and Kothe, C., Towards passive brain–computer interfaces: Applying brain–computer interface technology to human–machine systems in general. *J. Neural Eng.*, *8*, 2, 025005, 2011.
21. Kumar Trivedi, N., Maheswari, S., Sharma, H., Jain, S., Agarwal, S., Early Detection & Prediction of Heart Disease using Various Machine Learning Approaches. *2022 9th International Conference on Computing for Sustainable Global Development (INDIACom)*, New Delhi, India, pp. 793–797, 2022, doi: 10.23919/INDIACom54597.2022.9763188.

10

The Evolving Landscape of Brain-Computer Interfaces

Kritika Arora[1], Thayanithi C.A.[2], Elipe Arjun[2]* and Priyanka Singh[2]

[1]*Amity Institute of Applied Sciences, Amity University Uttar Pradesh, Noida, Uttar Pradesh, India*
[2]*Amity Institute of Forensic Sciences, Amity University Uttar Pradesh, Noida, Uttar Pradesh, India*

Abstract
This chapter is a comprehensive overview of the fast-growing field of brain-computer interfaces (BCIs) in light of recent advancements, future directions, and potential in this new field. We analyze the convergence of state-of-the-art machine learning methods, deep learning models, and neurotechnology, which is redefining what is possible in human-computer interaction. The discussion encompasses recent innovations in neural signal processing, hardware miniaturization, and advances in real-time decoding algorithms that are making BCIs more available and efficient. The chapter critically evaluates new applications throughout the consumer, healthcare, and industrial markets, highlighting the way novel ML/DL approaches address the traditional shortcomings in signal processing, latency, and user adaptation. We discuss the transition from traditional lab-based systems to commercial usage, such as revolutionary breakthroughs in brain implants, noninvasive communication interfaces, and brain-computer integrated systems. Focus is given to upcoming trends like edge computing in BCIs, integration with Internet-of-Things (IoT) devices, and self-programming adaptive interface generation. We also consider the social implications: widespread use of BCIs, such as thinking about neural privacy and security concerns, and ethical standards regarding human enhancement. The chapter concludes with a vision-based perspective on future developments in neural interface technology, including inter-brain communication, affective state monitoring, and artificial general intelligence system employment of BCIs.

**Corresponding author*: arjunelipe456@gmail.com

Tawseef Ahmed Teli, Syed Immamul Ansarullah, Arun Kumar Rana, Suman Lata Tripathi and Kashif Nisar (eds.) Brain-to-Computer Interfaces Using Machine Learning and Deep Learning, (217–260) © 2026 Scrivener Publishing LLC

Keywords: Brain computer interfaces, neural signal processing, machine learning and deep learning, neurotechnology, neural privacy

10.1 Introduction

The modalities of human interaction with technological devices have been revolutionized under brain-computer interfaces (BCIs), which facilitate direct interaction between the human brain and external devices (see Figure 10.1). BCIs are of high utility in a variety of fields, including healthcare and entertainment, communication, and virtual reality. BCIs give people with disabilities the power to regain new skills, e.g., speech or mobility. The development of technological innovation has revolutionized, enhancing signal and data processing using algorithms that enhance the efficiency and accuracy of the widespread application of BCIs. In addition, artificial intelligence and deep learning technology offer the possibility of brain interfacing, which enhances BCIs to be more sophisticated than a simple EEG device. The application and deployment of BCIs raise many problems that must be examined thoroughly. The most critical of them are ethical concerns, violation of the security of data, and the possibility of harmful use. The application of neurotechnology is a significant challenge to researchers and industry developers in making the installation of such devices feasible for various applications. Implementing a safe way to navigate these situations while fostering innovations is a high-priority goal. Combining data from neuroscientists, technology engineers, and legal policymakers creates a balance between the expansions of brain technologies while ensuring compliance with ethical frameworks [1].

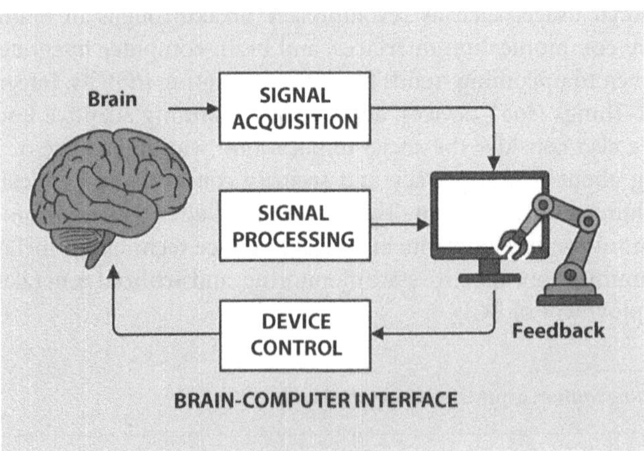

Figure 10.1 A simplified overview of the brain-computer interface (BCI) system showing the signal acquisition and processing.

10.1.1 Historical Evolution of BCIs

The historical evolution of the brain-computer interface (BCI) began in the 1920s with the discovery of the brain's electrical activity by Hans Berger and the development of electroencephalography (EEG). His groundbreaking work led to the first recording of human cerebral activity, including the identification of alpha waves, which provided a foundation for the study of cerebral signals. Official brain-computer interface (BCI) research, however, only began in the 1970s at the University of California, Los Angeles (UCLA), which was funded by the National Science Foundation (NSF) and DARPA. This was the first concerted attempt to explore direct brain-external apparatus interactions.

In the 1980s and 1990s, scientists implemented BCI technology in experiments on animals. Monkeys and rats were discovered to be capable of controlling robot arms and computer cursors with their minds alone. The results were critical to deciding that it was possible to decode the activity of neurons and convert it into motor commands for an external device. These experiments laid the groundwork for the creation of BCIs, especially in the neuroprosthetic field [1, 2].

The mid-1990s to the early 2000s saw major breakthroughs in human BCI applications. The first neuroprosthetic devices that had been implanted in humans allowed individuals with paralysis to control external devices such as robotic limbs or mobility devices. Researchers such as Phillip Kennedy and Miguel Nicolelis have made major breakthroughs in intracortical BCIs, which have become more precise and practical. It made BCIs a viable technology for the restoration of lost motor functions in severely disabled patients. Since the 2000s, BCI research has shifted from the lab to clinical and assistive technologies.

Scientists have aimed at creating communication aids for locked-in individuals, improving motor rehabilitation, and investigating opportunities for cognitive enhancement. Corporations like Neuralink and Facebook, in the field of medical engineering, have also joined the fray, with the aim of commercializing BCI technology for broader application. BCIs are still evolving today, closing the loop between neuroscience and everyday human-machine interaction, with applications that are promising in medicine, assistive technology, and even consumer electronics [3].

10.1.2 Current State of the Field

The present status of the brain-computer interface (BCI) technology has made great progress in research and real-world applications. Different methods, such as EEG, MEG, fMRI, ECoG, and NIRS, have been employed to record brain activity, each with its own merits and limitations. EEG is still the most common due to its high temporal resolution, portability, and affordability. BCIs are categorized based on different EEG brain activity patterns such as event-related desynchronization/synchronization (ERD/ERS), steady-state visual evoked potentials (SSVEP), P300 event-related potentials (ERPs), and slow cortical potentials (SCPs). SSVEP-based brain-computer interfaces (BCIs) are particularly known to provide higher accuracy and information transfer rates with less training [2] (see Figure 10.2).

Recent research has focused on enhancing the signal processing methods, the feature extraction techniques, and the classification algorithms to improve the performance of BCI (see Figure 10.3). Advanced methods such as fast Fourier transform (FFT), canonical correlation analysis (CCA), and support vector machines (SVMs) are widely used for classifying brain signals. Moreover, hybrid BCIs, which combine different BCI modalities (e.g., P300-SSVEP), have emerged to enhance reliability, increase accuracy, and provide a more seamless user experience. These hybrid systems have been shown to be efficient and hold promising use in assistive technologies, enabling disabled persons to control wheelchairs and home automation systems and interact with virtual reality environments [2, 3].

Despite such advancements, there remain issues and problems that still exist, such as user flexibility improvements, alleviation of BCI illiteracy, and facilitation of robust brain signal interpretation. Researchers and companies are, all the while, striving to make BCIs more feasible and practical for real-world use through upgraded hardware and software technologies.

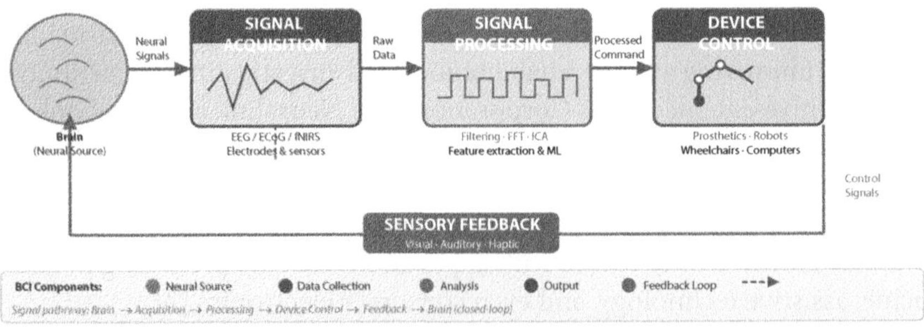

Figure 10.2 Brain-computer interface system overview: signal acquisition, processing, device control, and feedback integration.

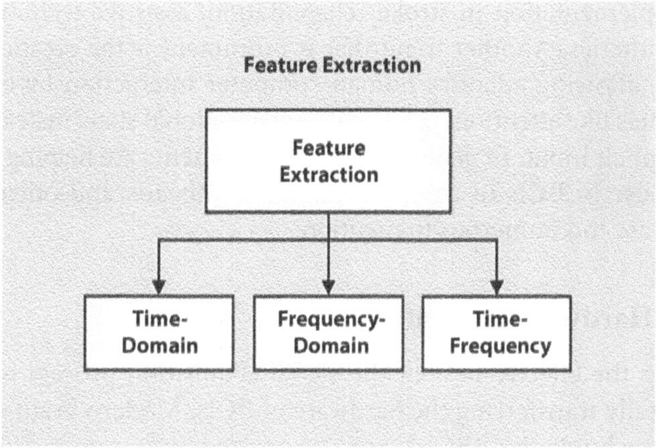

Figure 10.3 Common feature extraction techniques used in BCI systems: time-domain, frequency-domain, and time-frequency.

With continued advancements, BCIs are bound to play an important role in neurorehabilitation, human-computer interaction, and even cognitive enhancement, moving closer to closing the gap between the human brain and computer systems [4].

10.2 Recent Technological Advances

The utility and potential of brain-computer interfaces (BCIs) have been greatly advanced by newly emerged technology. The emergence of brain signal acquisition techniques, including electrocorticography (ECoG) and functional near-infrared spectroscopy (fNIRS), which provide improved higher spatial and temporal resolution than standard electroencephalography (EEG) methods, is one of the most significant advancements. Hybrid BCIs provide users with more control and reliability. Different signal modalities, including EMG and EEG, have been employed in this regard. In addition, the use of machine learning and deep learning algorithms has played a crucial role in improving BCIs through better pattern recognition and real-time processing. The increased availability of consumer-grade BCIs, including portable EEG headsets, has also led to more extensive use of these devices in the neurofeedback, gaming, and cognitive training markets. BCIs have also helped people with motor disabilities greatly, allowing them to control external devices with more accuracy, thereby aiding implementation in stroke rehabilitation, assistive technology, and neuroprosthetics. Another trend that is prominent is the creation of passive BCIs, allowing adaptive human-computer interaction by estimating mental states like attention, workload, and emotional state, instead of waiting for explicit input. In general, these developments are helping to enable extended use of BCIs in communication, healthcare, and other applications that are too numerous to mention.

10.2.1 Hardware Innovations

Enhancing the effectiveness of the signal acquisition process is done by incrementally transferring the hardware of BCIs. Modern brain-computer interface technologies (BCIs) are categorized into noninvasive, semi-invasive, and invasive types, each featuring unique advantages (see Figure 10.4). Examples of noninvasive devices are EEG headsets, which have seen improvements in clarity of signals and comfort, making them suitable for daily use. On the other hand, invasive BCIs, such as implantable microelectrode arrays, provide groundbreaking resolutions of neural data critical for medical purposes, like enabling movement for paralyzed individuals.

Advancements in material science have tremendously aided the rest of the components pertaining to the BCI hardware. The use of flexible, biocompatible electrodes, wireless transmission systems, and smaller parts has increased the efficacy and lifespan of the systems. Furthermore, the development of neuromorphic computers is transforming the instantaneous

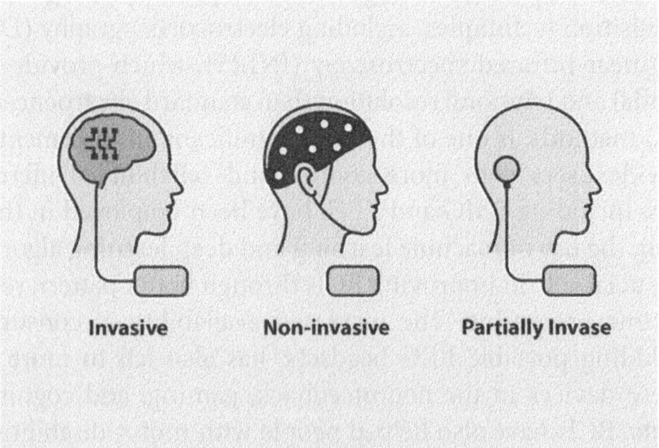

Figure 10.4 Classification of brain-computer interfaces: invasive, noninvasive, and partially invasive, based on how deeply electrodes penetrate and the quality of the signals.

processing related to the interpretation of brain signals, making it faster and more accurate. With advancements in technology, BCIs are becoming more comfortable, dependable, and easy to use, which will allow devices to be controlled seamlessly by the human body [4].

10.2.1.1 Neural Sensors and Electrodes

In brain-computer interfaces (BCIs), neural sensors and electrodes are essential components that serve as the main conduit between neural activity and external computing systems. There are invasive and noninvasive varieties of these electrodes, each with unique benefits and drawbacks. Although invasive electrodes, like intracortical microelectrode arrays, directly interface with neural tissue to provide high spatial resolution, they present issues with immunological response and long-term biocompatibility. To improve signal quality and lessen tissue reactions, new materials have been developed, such as silicon carbide, carbon nanotubes, and conductive polymers like poly(3,4-ethylenedioxythiophene) (PEDOT).

New developments have also improved neural sampling with minimal invasiveness by introducing penetrating 3D probes and high-density electrocorticography (ECoG) electrodes. With minimally invasive techniques, like the "stentrode," the risks of direct brain penetration are decreased by implanting electrodes through blood vessels. Particularly in optogenetics applications, hybrid electrode technologies that combine electronic recording and optical stimulation are also becoming more popular [5].

10.2.1.2 Signal Acquisition Systems

Brain-computer interfaces (BCIs) rely primarily on the signal acquisition system to provide accurate data acquisition and brain signal analysis for further study and investigation. The main method of BCI applications is electroencephalography (EEG), which involves the positioning of electrodes on the scalp to capture electrical activity created by neural interactions. These electrodes are either invasive or noninvasive (see Figure 10.5), and the noninvasive ones are becoming more popular due to their ease of use and safety. Noninvasive EEG systems, however, are suffering from noise and reduced signal clarity, necessitating more sophisticated filtering techniques and signal amplification. The primary problems with EEG signal extraction are noise reduction, interference, preservation of a high signal-to-noise ratio (SNR), and an ideal common mode rejection ratio (CMRR) to reject environmental noise. To overcome these issues, contemporary EEG acquisition systems utilize instrumentation amplifiers, active filters, and digital signal

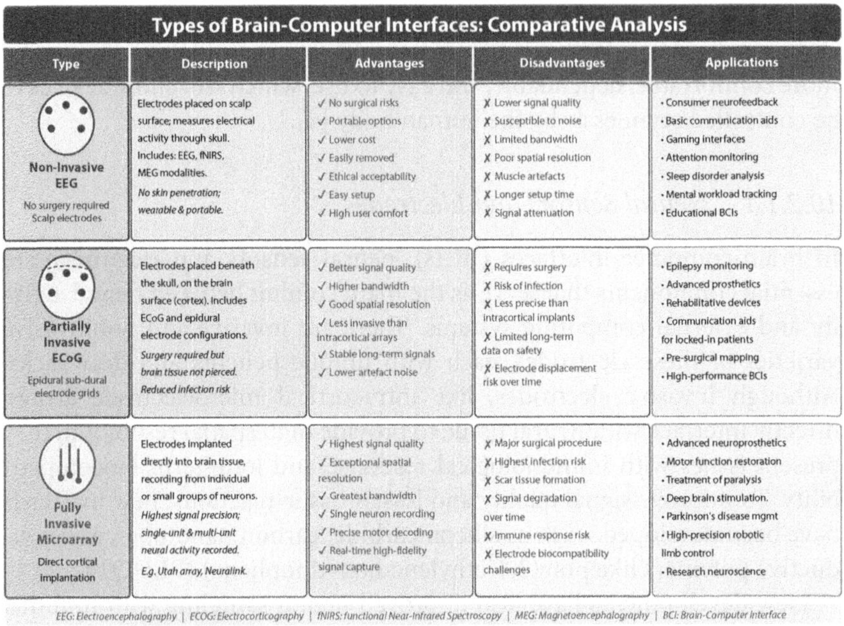

Types of Brain-Computer Interfaces: Comparative Analysis

Type	Description	Advantages	Disadvantages	Applications
Non-Invasive EEG No surgery required Scalp electrodes	Electrodes placed on scalp surface; measures electrical activity through skull. Includes: EEG, fNIRS, MEG modalities. *No skin penetration; wearable & portable.*	✓ No surgical risks ✓ Portable options ✓ Lower cost ✓ Easily removed ✓ Ethical acceptability ✓ Easy setup ✓ High user comfort	✗ Lower signal quality ✗ Susceptible to noise ✗ Limited bandwidth ✗ Poor spatial resolution ✗ Muscle artefacts ✗ Longer setup time ✗ Signal attenuation	• Consumer neurofeedback • Basic communication aids • Gaming interfaces • Attention monitoring • Sleep disorder analysis • Mental workload tracking • Educational BCIs
Partially Invasive ECoG Epidural sub-dural electrode grids	Electrodes placed beneath the skull, on the brain surface (cortex). Includes ECoG and epidural electrode configurations. *Surgery required but brain tissue not pierced. Reduced infection risk*	✓ Better signal quality ✓ Higher bandwidth ✓ Good spatial resolution ✓ Less invasive than intracortical arrays ✓ Stable long-term signals ✓ Lower artefact noise	✗ Requires surgery ✗ Risk of infection ✗ Less precise than intracortical implants ✗ Limited long-term data on safety ✗ Electrode displacement risk over time	• Epilepsy monitoring • Advanced prosthetics • Rehabilitative devices • Communication aids for locked-in patients • Pre-surgical mapping • High-performance BCIs
Fully Invasive Microarray Direct cortical implantation	Electrodes implanted directly into brain tissue, recording from individual or small groups of neurons. *Highest signal precision; single-unit & multi-unit neural activity recorded. Eg. Utah array, Neuralink.*	✓ Highest signal quality ✓ Exceptional spatial resolution ✓ Greatest bandwidth ✓ Single neuron recording ✓ Precise motor decoding ✓ Real-time high-fidelity signal capture	✗ Major surgical procedure ✗ Highest infection risk ✗ Scar tissue formation ✗ Signal degradation over time ✗ Immune response risk ✗ Electrode biocompatibility challenges	• Advanced neuroprosthetics • Motor function restoration • Treatment of paralysis • Deep brain stimulation. • Parkinson's disease mgmt • High-precision robotic limb control • Research neuroscience

EEG: Electroencephalography | ECOG: Electrocorticography | fNIRS: functional Near-Infrared Spectroscopy | MEG: Magnetoencephalography | BCI: Brain-Computer Interface

Figure 10.5 Types of brain-computer interfaces: comparative analysis of noninvasive, partially invasive, and fully invasive methods.

processing technologies to process received signals. Furthermore, commercially off-the-shelf EEG headsets, e.g., from businesses such as OpenBCI and Emotive, provide inexpensive and portable field-based solutions. Advancements in EEG signal recording have also led to the development of high-density electrode arrays, better electrode material, and sophisticated software integration into real-time analysis and processing [5].

10.2.1.3 Miniaturization Technologies

Brain-computer interface (BCI) miniaturization technologies have advanced significantly recently, allowing one to design systems with more efficiency, portability, and small scale. Microelectronics, wireless communication, and energy-efficient signal processing techniques all help to drive these advances. Examples of small electrodes and sensors that have enhanced neural signal acquisition accuracy while reducing invasiveness are high-density flexible arrays and electrodes based on nanomaterials. Moreover, advances in wireless power transfer and low-power processing units, which eliminate the need for significant outside hardware, have made wearable, untethered BCIs possible. Thanks to these developments, BCIs can now be applied not only in medical rehabilitation but also in neuroprostheses, cognitive enhancement, and human-machine interaction. Using miniaturization with cloud computing and artificial intelligence, researchers hope to produce high-performance, real-time BCIs that are scalable and simple to use for broad usage [6].

10.2.2 Software Developments

Brain-computer interface (BCI) technology has made considerable progress in recent years, with BCI software enhancements achieving better performance, user-friendliness, applicability, and feature sets. Powerful data processing and machine learning algorithms that are part of modern BCI software enhance the accuracy of interpreting brain signals and the speed with which this can be done. State-of-the-art real-time signal processing approaches make it possible to classify brain signals faster and thus to make BCIs more responsive. Graphical User Interfaces (GUIs) have been designed for BCI systems, easing the interaction of users with BCI. In addition, there are software frameworks (i.e., BCI2000 and OpenBCI) that provide us with modularized and scalable systems for signal acquisition, processing, and application integration that facilitate research and development efforts. The growth of BCIs in healthcare, rehabilitation, disabled people's communication, and even smart home control systems has been facilitated by these developments [5, 6].

10.2.2.1 Advanced Signal Processing

Advanced signal processing is required in brain-computer interfaces (BCIs) to accurately decode neural activity and to increase the performance of the system. In order to minimize noise and enhance signal-to-noise ratio, most of the recently developed BCIs involve some advanced preprocessing techniques such as notch filtering, band-pass filtering, and wavelet transformation. In order to classify the brain signals properly, methods of feature extraction such as PCA, ICA, DWT, etc., help in recognizing the important patterns. Moreover, at the line-of-action end, machine learning and deep learning strategies, support vector machines (SVMs), convolutional neural networks (CNNs), and long short-term memory (LSTM) networks have significantly improved real-time analysis of brain signals. Then, systems that adapt in response to changes in neural activity, for example, Bayesian and Kalman filtering, should also enhance system responsiveness. Cloud computing and edge processing combined help in achieving real-time BCI applications with less latency and better computational efficiency as well. BCIs are increasingly viable for consumer and medical applications due to advances in neuroprosthetics, assistive communication technologies, and cognitive monitoring driven by signal processing [4, 6].

10.2.2.2 Real-Time Decoding Algorithms

To turn neural signals into meaningful commands for real-time interaction, we rely on real-time decoding algorithms, which are crucial for brain-computer interfaces (BCIs). These algorithms help ensure smooth and precise control of external devices by processing brain signals—typically gathered through EEG, ECoG, or intracortical methods—and decoding them with minimal delay. A few key features include effective signal pre-processing, feature extraction techniques such as wavelet transforms and principal component analysis (PCA), and a few classification techniques such as support vector machines (SVMs) and deep neural networks. Adaptive filtering and online learning systems enable accuracy by continuously updating models based on user responses. The stable error detection and correction systems enable reliability, although optimization for computational efficiency according to hardware specifications is needed. Low-latency, high-speed processing is needed in applications such as brain-controlled robotics, communication support systems, and neuroprosthetics to operate effectively in real time while adhering to strict timing requirements [7].

10.2.2.3 Adaptive Learning Systems

Brain-computer interfaces (BCIs) incorporate adaptive learning systems, which help in greatly improving the user experience and the generic performance by dynamically adjusting to changes in neural signals. These systems help in employing real-time machine learning methods that update decoding models in accordance with the continuous user feedback to supply robustness in times of signal variability. Neural network-based classifiers, adaptive filtering, and reinforcement learning are a few of the key components that help in enabling BCIs to adjust responses in line with the needs of individual users. To help in feature selection and dimensionality reduction, techniques like principal component analysis (PCA) and linear discriminant analysis (LDA) exist, therefore optimizing the interpretation of the signal while keeping computational demands in balance. Through adaptation to changes in brain activity due to fatigue or learning, online adaptation mechanisms render BCIs more accurate and usable. Such adaptability is highly beneficial in applications requiring precision and versatility for real-time interaction, like neurorehabilitation, assistive communication, and brain-controlled robots, which are highly reliant on such sophisticated systems [7].

10.2.3 Integration Technologies

Brain-computer interfaces (BCIs) are effective when novel integration tools enable neural activity to interact seamlessly with external devices. Good examples include cloud processing, wireless data connections, and Internet of Things (IoT) networks providing remote command and access. High-fidelity recordings still rely on sophisticated signal-acquiring hardware, either invasive microelectrode grids or less invasive noninvasive EEG caps. Meanwhile, hybrid models draw on multiple physiological signs, and AI-driven machine-learning code does the heavy lifting of untangling those signals. Cross-platform tools such as BCI2000 and OpenBCI create standard channels that let different hardware and software work together. Secure encryption paired with real-time processing thus makes BCIs invaluable for assistive devices, neurorehab systems, and smart living spaces [7, 8].

10.2.3.1 Cloud Computing Integration

When cloud computing joins forces with brain-computer interfaces (BCIs), it greatly boosts real-time data handling, scalability, and overall processing speed. Slim, power-sensitive wearables or even implanted units can still run smoothly because heavy signal chores move to the cloud. This link makes remote access simple, paving the way for around-the-clock patient checks and sharper neurorehab outcomes. Models stored in the cloud learn on the fly, steadily fine-tuning their decoding results as fresh signals arrive. Robust encryption and safe storage guard the sensitive neural stream, keeping patient privacy intact. Finally, the cloud and the Internet of Things (IoT) mesh nicely, letting BCIs chat seamlessly with smart homes, labs, and clinics, which expand research, aids, and brain-controlled robots [8].

10.2.3.2 Edge Computing Solutions

Edge computing moves much of the brain's work away from distant data centers and onto nearby hardware, so latency shrinks, and real-time performance improves in brain-computer interfaces (BCIs). By performing tasks like signal capture, feature extraction, and classification close to the scalp, edge setups cut the time it takes to send bits back and forth, delivering faster and more reliable control to devices such as computer cursors or neuroprosthetic limbs. Compact, energy-efficient edge units thus make BCIs practical outside the lab, processing data without draining batteries or adding bulk. AI-based edge analytics also permit on-the-fly tuning of decoding models, while local computation protects sensitive neural data from prying networks. Moreover, because edge nodes can run entirely offline, assistive BCIs remain functional even in areas with poor or absent internet, a vital trait for medical users [8].

10.2.3.3 IoT Connectivity

When the Internet of Things connects brain-computer interfaces (BCIs), neural devices can talk to smartphones, computers, and smart appliances in real time, easing both access and automation. Through that link, the interface streams brain waves to cloud servers for storage and deep analysis, sharpening outcomes in clinical care, stroke rehab, and daily assistive tools. Edge nodes and local sensors do heavy lifting near the user, trimming lag time so commands feel instantaneous. In order to protect raw neural signatures, secure encryption techniques and tamper-resistant channels are used to ensure confidentiality, with machine learning algorithms running on input data, learning in real time, and making the device smarter. This leads to enhanced usability, allowing users to control smart homes, drive robot limbs, or control biofeedback spaces with simple mental functions, thereby converting cutting-edge scientific principles to holistic, everyday aid [9].

10.3 Emerging Applications

Substantial advancements in brain-computer interfaces (BCIs) are revolutionizing several industries, such as communication, entertainment, neurorehabilitation, and healthcare (see Figure 10.6). These emerging technologies are significantly empowering motor-disabled individuals by making the use of exoskeletons and prosthetic limbs controlled by the brain easier. In the neurorehabilitation industry, BCIs are opening up new possibilities for brain-driven interventions that assist stroke survivors in their rehabilitation efforts. They are also revolutionizing assistive modes of communication, allowing ALS-affected individuals to communicate through direct brain-to-text or speech synthesis technologies. BCIs are also making virtual reality and gaming experiences more engaging and immersive through cognitively controlled interactions. On top of that, their integration with IoT and artificial intelligence is creating smart

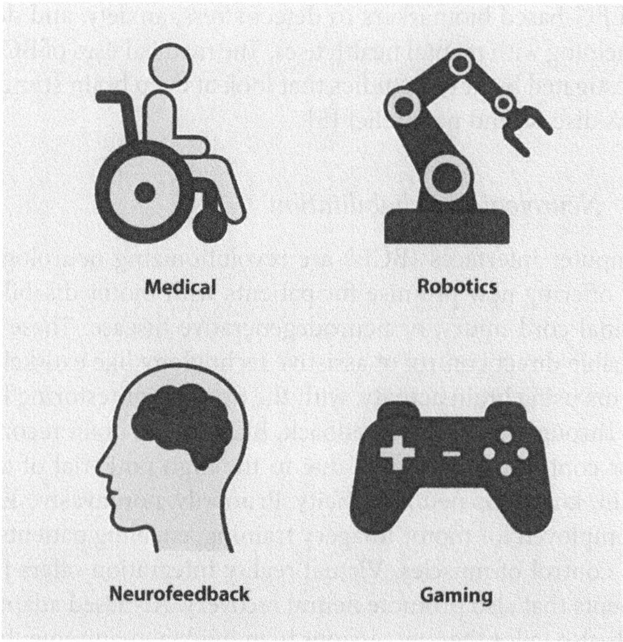

Figure 10.6 Most of the applications of the domains of BCIs include medical assistance, robotics control, neurofeedback therapies, and interaction in gaming.

environments, allowing for hands-free control of smart homes. The latest research is pushing the boundaries of human-machine interaction, exploring applications in cognitive enhancement, mental health monitoring, and even security systems that use brainwave authentication [10].

10.3.1 Medical Applications

By facilitating direct communication between the brain and external devices, medical applications of brain-computer interfaces (BCIs) are revolutionizing healthcare, especially for patients with neurological disorders. Through brain-controlled prosthetics and exoskeletons, BCIs help stroke and spinal cord injury patients regain motor functions, thereby facilitating neurorehabilitation. By translating brain signals into speech or text, they also improve assistive communication for people with diseases like locked-in syndrome or ALS. By converting brain activity into speech or text, they also enable assistive communication for locked-in syndrome or ALS patients. BCIs leverage real-time monitoring of brain activity for the prediction and prevention of seizures in epilepsy treatment. Additionally, by using EEG-based biomarkers to detect stress, anxiety, and depression, BCIs are helping with mental health uses. The medical uses of BCIs are also being investigated by newer studies that look at deep brain stimulation for Parkinson's disease and pain relief [5].

10.3.1.1 Neurological Rehabilitation

Brain-computer interfaces (BCIs) are revolutionizing neurological rehabilitation, offering new promise for patients with motor disability due to stroke, spinal cord injury, or neurodegenerative disease. These advanced devices enable direct control of assistive technology like exoskeletons and robotic arms using brain activity, with the promise of restoring lost motor function. Through immediate feedback, BCIs enable brain reconditioning and motor control enhancement due to the high potential of adaptation of the brain, known as neuroplasticity. Primarily, noninvasive EEG-based BCIs are employed for motor imagery training, enabling patients to regain voluntary control of muscles. Virtual reality integration offers immersive environments that also promote neural recovery. AI-based adaptive learning models also tailor therapy sessions to individual requirements, improving recovery. Through these technologies, BCIs are enabling patients with severe neurological disorders to regain independence [9].

10.3.1.2 Assistive Technologies

The use of assistive technologies in brain-computer interfaces (BCIs) is a central development in the assistance of individuals with severe impairment. These types of technologies enable users to control external devices directly by their brain activity, therefore enabling advanced ways of communication for individuals with diseases like Amyotrophic Lateral Sclerosis (ALS) and locked-in syndrome through brain-mediated text or speech output. BCIs also play an important role in the improvement of mobility by enabling the control of wheelchairs and robotic prostheses by the brain, thus enabling the restoration of autonomy in individuals with motor disabilities.

10.3.2 Consumer Applications

With the advancement in technology, human-computer interaction is being revolutionized by consumer use of brain-computer interfaces (BCIs). The cutting-edge technologies have gradually shifted away from medical and research settings to the mainstream. With the use of BCIs, users can now operate devices without bodily movement, immerse themselves in virtual reality, and even play games using only their cognitive abilities. Their uses, not being limited to recreation, have developed wearable BCI headsets that are particularly meant to enhance productivity by offering individuals hands-free navigation and text entry based on thought. Furthermore, with the integration of smart home technologies with BCIs, users can operate functions like security systems, lighting, and appliances using neural signals. On the wellness front, BCIs are playing a major role by tracking cognitive states, levels of stress, and sleep patterns, while offering real-time neurofeedback to support consumers' mental well-being. As for marketing, BCIs are probing our neurological reactions to advertisements and products, and data derived from these are applied to develop targeted marketing campaigns [11].

10.3.2.1 Gaming and Entertainment

By enabling the direct interaction between human cognitive processes and computer systems, BCIs are transforming the gaming and entertainment industries. Over a few years, BCIs have enabled the possibility in gaming of controlling characters, moving around virtual worlds, and performing in-game actions through brain waves exclusively, doing away with traditional physical controllers, thus greatly enhancing the degree of immersion. The combination of BCIs with virtual and augmented reality technologies helps to further enhance the gaming experience, making it interactive and realistic. Furthermore, the interfaces can personalize gameplay by measuring a player's cognitive and emotional state and enabling the game to make modifications in difficulty and content levels accordingly. E-sports and therapy gaming have seen a rise in BCIs, enabling individuals with disabilities to engage in interactive digital experiences. With the developments in neurotechnology, BCIs are set to enable fully immersive gaming experiences that combine entertainment and cognitive stimulation.

10.3.2.2 Personal Productivity

Brain-computer interfaces (BCIs) have been working on transforming personal productivity by providing an interface between human cognition and digital technology. These advanced technologies allow users to control applications, type messages, and interact with online services using their thoughts alone, thus improving productivity and accessibility. BCIs also improve cognitive functions by tracking neural activity, providing neurofeedback, and enhancing concentration and mental sharpness. In smart workspaces, BCIs can schedule work automatically, send smart reminders, and even track emotions in real time, all of which serve to streamline workflows and reduce mental fatigue. BCIs also open new avenues of communication and independence for people with disabilities, promoting inclusivity in workspaces. With further innovation in neurotechnology, BCIs are likely to further evolve productivity tools and transform our interaction with computer systems [12].

10.3.2.3 Smart Home Control

Brain-computer interface (BCI) technology is an exciting way to create direct interfaces between human brains and external systems, thus providing promising routes for the automation of smart homes. Utilizing neurophysiological signals, such as those recorded using electroencephalography (EEG), BCIs are capable of interpreting neural activity and translating it into control commands for home automation systems. Users are thus capable of controlling home appliances, for instance, lights, climate control, security devices, and entertainment systems, using their thoughts alone, thus making this functionality especially beneficial for people with mobility impairments and disabilities, as it allows them to control their living space more independently without having to exert physical effort. Moreover, smart homes incorporating BCI technology are capable of self-learning and adapting to user preferences based on the interpretation of cognitive patterns, thus improving the overall user experience. However, there are still certain hurdles to be cleared, including the correct interpretation of neural signals and the creation of user-friendly, noninvasive interfaces. Despite having such obstacles, ongoing research happening in the areas of deep learning and signal processing is improving the potency and utility of BCI-enabled smart home technologies.

10.3.3 Industrial Applications

The use of brain-computer interface (BCI) technology in various industries is architecturally transforming the dynamics of automation, occupational health, and overall operational efficiency. In the manufacturing sector, for example, BCIs provide hands-free operation of equipment, robot systems, and automated machinery by interpreting neural signals. It not only decreases physical fatigue but also increases productivity rates. In risk-prone industries such as mining and construction, BCIs play a crucial role in improving worker safety by measuring the cognitive workload and detecting signs of fatigue, thereby reducing the likelihood of accidents caused by human error. Additionally, BCI technology is being progressively implemented in industrial training programs, where neurofeedback is utilized to maximize skill acquisition and educational performance. In the areas of quality control and assembly line processing, BCIs aid in error detection by measuring cognitive reactions, resulting in higher accuracy levels. With the ongoing advances being made in machine learning and neuroimaging technologies, BCIs are increasingly becoming more reliable and deployable in industrial contexts, despite the persistent challenges associated with real-time processing of data, accuracy, and user adaptability [12].

10.3.3.1 Manufacturing Control

Brain-computer interface (BCI) technology is transforming the manufacturing industry through hands-free operations and enhanced efficiency within industrial settings. Through the interpretation of neural signals, workers can control robotic arms, automated equipment, and assembly lines without physical contact, thus preventing fatigue and enhancing precision. Furthermore, BCIs enable the monitoring of cognition in real-time, which ensures workers remain focused and reduces errors during complex operations. When BCIs are combined with automation, machines can be taught to respond to users' intentions, thus simplifying processes and boosting productivity. Such technology is especially applicable in high-risk industrial settings where manual operation would be unsafe or inconvenient. Despite the current limitations, such as signal precision, processing velocity, and user accommodation, developments in deep learning and neuro-engineering are rendering BCI applications more dependable, opening the door to more intelligent and responsive manufacturing automation.

10.3.3.2 Professional Training

Brain-computer interface (BCI) technology is heavily applied in professional training to enhance skill learning, cognitive interest, and the measurement of performance of individuals. Through real-time neurofeedback, BCIs enable students to monitor and enhance attention, decision-making, and cognitive performance. The technology is particularly beneficial in high-precision professions, for instance, aviation, medicine, and engineering, where response speed and accuracy are key to success. Through the assessment of brain activity, BCIs make training programs more responsive to individual learning styles, improving effectiveness. BCI-based simulations tend to facilitate immersive learning, with hands-free interaction and dynamic adjustment during training. Cost, accessibility, and neural signal complexity are still limitations, but ongoing research in artificial intelligence and neurotechnology continues to enhance the usability and efficiency of BCI-based professional training methods.

10.3.3.3 Workplace Safety

Brain-computer interface (BCI) technology is revolutionizing workplace safety by tracking individuals' mental states, lowering the rate of human error and accidents in hazardous environments. BCIs, tracking brain function, can measure drowsiness, stress, and mental overload among employees, stepping in before safety hazards can materialize. This is especially crucial to observe in the construction, manufacturing, and transportation industries, where staying awake is necessary to avoid accidents. BCIs can also be used in safety systems to trigger automatic actions when employees are distracted or tired. And the ability to use machinery hands-free with BCI decreases manual intervention in hazardous conditions, further decreasing risks. The issues can be detected in accuracy, response time, and user accommodation, but the ongoing progress in neurotechnology and artificial intelligence is making BCI-based safety solutions more reliable and effective.

10.4 Next-Generation BCI Systems

Artificial intelligence and machine learning algorithms are deliberately used to enhance the real-time decoding of the signal by the said system, which minimizes noise and introduces clarity, accuracy, and definition, and enhances precision. The next generation of the brain-computer interface (BCI) is characterized by enhanced precision, adaptability, and the use of complex computing technology. These, together with BCIs that adapt and grow in accordance with the user-specific neural patterns, facilitate unmatched levels of personalization and efficiency. The development of BCI systems has been boosted by the mobility provided by wireless, cloud-based technologies. Enhanced neural interfaces with higher imaging resolutions and better biocompatibility are leading to longer device lifespans with lowered chances of acceptance complications. The integration of several neuroimaging techniques, such as EEG, fNIRS, and ECoG, into hybrid BCIs is improving the signal-to-noise ratio. The integration of BCI with neuroprosthetics, robotics, and augmented reality brings new opportunities, ranging from rehabilitation of the body and brain training processes to expanding the scope of human-computer interaction to be more organic and smoother [13].

10.4.1 Advanced Neural Interfaces

Brain-computer interfaces (BCIs) are being revolutionized by advanced neural interfaces, which use state-of-the-art technologies to improve communication between the brain and external devices. Higher resolution neural recordings with less invasiveness are made possible by these interfaces, which combine miniaturized, biocompatible electrodes with enhanced signal acquisition capabilities. To lessen tissue damage and increase the long-term stability of neural recordings, flexible and bio-integrated neural probes are being developed. These days, wireless and cloud-connected neural interfaces are paving the way for exciting new possibilities in remote accessibility and real-time brain monitoring. Thanks to machine learning-driven signal processing, we're getting better at interpreting neural activity, which means BCI applications are becoming more precise and responsive. Through the integration of optogenetics, nanotechnology, and brain-stimulation technologies, we're developing new avenues for neural modulation that could treat neurological disorders and restore lost motor or sensory function due to disease or trauma. With these developments, BCIs are taking us towards putting them in our daily lives with the possibility of next-generation neuroprosthetics, cognitive-enhancing devices, and more unobtrusive human-machine interfaces [11].

10.4.1.1 High-Resolution Recording

One of the strongest developments in brain-computer interfaces (BCIs) is the creation of high-resolution recording, which provides improved accuracy and reliability of neural signal acquisition. BCIs now employ microelectrode technology and high-density electrode arrays to deliver improved spatial and temporal resolution for the recording of neural activity. Interfaces such as intracortical microelectrodes and electrocorticography (ECoG) tend to provide less noisy signals as compared to noninvasive methods like EEG, leading to an improved decoding of brain signals for neuroprosthetics and communication interfaces. Developments in biocompatible, flexible, and ultra-thin neural interfaces also help minimize tissue damage, improving and enhancing the long-term stability and usability of the systems. Wireless and implanted recording systems are also facilitating real-time processing and improved mobility, decreasing the use of cumbersome external hardware. Use of machine learning and AI-based signal processing is also making an improvement in enhancing data interpretation, allowing faster decoding of complex neural patterns. A wide range of responsive, intuitive, and clinically feasible BCI applications, like direct brain-to-machine interaction, motor rehabilitation, and cognitive enhancement, are being made possible by these high-resolution recording technologies.

10.4.1.2 Wireless Technologies

Wireless technologies are changing the landscape of brain-computer interfaces (BCIs) by working away with physical wires. This is changing the way we interact with our brains, making it easier to use, mobilize, and even contemplate long-term implantation. With the use of biocompatible, minimized materials, wireless BCIs based on nanotechnology are providing an unbroken neural signal transmission while simultaneously eliminating the possibilities of infection and mechanical failure associated with wired systems. With the rise in the popularity of Bluetooth, Wi-Fi, and radiofrequency (RF) protocols for communication, the brain can now talk in real time to external devices, improving the transfer of data. And with the development of low-power, energy-efficient circuits, long-term wireless BCI use has also become much more feasible, prolonging battery life substantially. New paradigms, such as optogenetics-based wireless techniques and near-field communication (NFC), have also been said to be contemplated as future noninvasive and implantable BCI options. With the addition of cloud computing and AI-based signal processing, the scalability and reliability of wireless BCIs are improving, opening the gates towards intriguing applications in assistive technology, neuroprosthetics, and brain-controlled external devices. These developments are not only augmenting human-machine interfaces but also making BCIs more feasible, moving them towards everyday use, and simplifying life for patients with neurological disorders [11].

10.4.1.3 Long-Term Stability

Making brain-computer interface (BCI) systems stable in the long term is essential to maintaining their performance as responsive, accurate, and reliable tools for users over the long term. Signal degradation is likely to be the largest problem we face, and it can occur due to reasons such as electrode movement, variation in skin-electrode impedance, and the innate ability of the brain to adapt. To compensate for these, there are tremendous advances in adaptive algorithms, machine learning techniques, and self-calibrating BCIs that ensure signal accuracy and efficiency. And with the use of noninvasive, biocompatible electrode materials, user comfort is enhanced in addition to enabling longer use. Periodic system readjustment and the use of personalized training techniques play significant roles in promoting stability by compensating for individual neural differences. While there remains some distance to travel in the assurance of consistent signal quality and in reducing user fatigue, continuing advances in neurotechnology and AI are paving the way to more reliable BCIs, particularly for medical, assistive, and industrial uses.

10.4.2 Intelligent Processing

Intelligent processing in brain-computer interface (BCI) systems is a necessity to ensure maximum accuracy, efficiency, and adaptability of brain signal analysis. By virtue of the use of advanced techniques like machine learning, deep learning, and signal processing, BCIs are now capable of correctly interpreting complex neural patterns. The process of feature extraction and classification techniques assists in attempting to suppress noise and improve real-time responsiveness so that user interaction with external systems becomes considerably smoother. Adaptive algorithms also allow BCIs to learn from users' cognitive variations, guaranteeing long-term stability and user comfort. Artificial intelligence also helps to make decision-making easier by predicting the intentions of the user as well as signal interpretation adjustment. While problems of computational complexity and the need for high-speed processing remain, ongoing innovation in intelligent processing is improving the reliability and real-world applications of BCIs in medical, assistive, and industrial applications [10].

10.4.2.1 Autonomous Adaptation

Adaptive BCI (brain-computer interface) applications have the potential to learn and adapt to optimally translate the user's neural signals to their intentions by reacting to individual users' neural activity and changing environments. The adaptability of the system is key to improving user interaction, minimizing the requirement for continuous calibration, and maintaining the system in working condition in the long term. With the help of machine learning and artificial intelligence, BCIs can assist in the optimization of signal processing, adaptation to variation in brain signals, and personalization to the users. Such self-adaptation makes BCIs effective despite limitations like neural plasticity, electrode drift, or external interference. Adaptive algorithms are continuously striving to refine classification models based on real-time feedback, reducing errors and improving the level of accuracy. Even though the issues still exist and shall be overcome, such as computational demands, processing rate, and the need for large databases, innovation in neurotechnology is progressing in making autonomous BCIs more effective, reliable, and user-friendly for numerous purposes, from healthcare and assistive technology to industrial automation [14].

10.4.2.2 Context Awareness

Context awareness in brain-computer interface (BCI) systems enhances the capacity of BCIs to decode the brain signals by considering the environmental, cognitive, and extraneous conditions. This feature helps enable BCIs to respond to the real-time context information not only enhancing the accuracy but also the user experience. Using machine learning and sensor fusion methods, BCIs can analyze such aspects as user intent, mood, and environment, so the interaction between users can be improved. This feature is particularly useful in assistive technologies, where context-aware BCIs can adapt controls for user purposes and respond to environmental changes. Additionally, in medical applications, these systems facilitate rehabilitation by constantly responding dynamically to make an improvement in a patient. While issues of high computational requirements and real-time processing persist, continued development in artificial intelligence and neurotechnology is making context-aware BCIs increasingly flexible, intuitive, and efficient across a broad range of applications [14].

10.4.2.3 Multi-Modal Integration

Multi-modal fusion in brain-computer interface (BCI) systems significantly improves their performance by combining a variety of input sources such as EEG signals, eye tracking, electromyography (EMG), and other physiological signals. The fusion enhances accuracy, flexibility, and reliability, offering a clearer picture of what the user is supposed to do. By combining multiple modalities, BCIs can overcome the limitation of a single source of signal, leading to more robust performance in real-world tasks. Multi-modal BCIs perform well in applications like assistive technology, neurorehabilitation, and neuroprosthetics, where the fusion of brain activity and physiological signals allows for more accurate control of devices. Moreover, artificial intelligence and machine learning algorithms are involved in processing and fusing these multiple streams of data, making real-time decision-making easier. Even though several challenges like computational burden and data synchronization still exist, ongoing progress in sensor technology and signal processing is significantly refining the overall performance of multi-modal BCI systems.

10.4.3 User Experience

User experience in brain-computer interface (BCI) systems is essentially crucial to usability, effectiveness, and overall acceptability. A good BCI should allow intuitive interaction, minimize cognitive load, and create a smooth connection between user intention and system response. Key parameters like response time, accuracy, and adaptability are necessary for users to effectively control external devices. Comfort is equally of topmost importance; hardware shall be noninvasive, light in weight, and ergonomically structured to have prolonged use and not feel uncomfortable. Personalization *via* adaptive algorithms can magnify and add to the user experience by adjusting BCI features to individual needs and preferences. Despite present limitations like variability of signal and need for long training periods, ongoing improvements in artificial intelligence, machine learning, and human-computer interaction are increasingly making BCIs more user-friendly and accessible, a trend also supported by neuroergonomics research [15, 23].

10.4.3.1 Natural Control Interfaces

Natural control interfaces of brain-computer interface (BCI) systems upgrade the user interaction experience by making a natural and seamless link between the brain and outside devices. The interfaces are developed so that the natural human movements can be simulated, reducing cognitive load and simplifying use. With noninvasive methods such as EEG, coupled with devices such as eye tracking and electromyography (EMG), BCIs can enhance the decoding of brain signals and enable real-time feedback. This aspect is particularly valuable in applications like assistive technology, prostheses, and home automation, allowing the user to control devices with merely cognitive intent. Machine learning and artificial intelligence play an important role here, such as facilitating signal processing so that commands are properly interpreted and carried out. Despite the issues still present, like signal variability and the need for real-time processing, ongoing advancements in neurotechnology are rendering these natural control interfaces more rapid, dependable, and intuitive, thus broadening their scope for application in healthcare, accessibility, and human-computer interaction.

10.4.3.2 Feedback Mechanisms

Feedback loops in brain-computer interface (BCI) systems play an important role in increasing user control, accuracy, and adaptability. These systems offer instantaneous responses based on brain activity, thus allowing their users to enhance their communication with external devices. Feedback may be felt through different modalities, such as visual feedback (e.g., screen messages), auditory feedback (e.g., sound alarms), or haptic feedback (e.g., vibration or touch), to allow effective communication between the system and the user. With the use of closed-loop feedback, BCIs allow continuous learning and self-tuning, leading to enhanced performance over time. The ability is useful in applications like neurorehabilitation, assistive devices, and brain-controlled prostheses, where adaptive feedback allows the recovery of motor functions and the precision of devices. The use of machine learning and artificial intelligence makes feedback processing easier, making BCIs more responsive and specific to the needs of users. Despite issues like response time and signal precision, continuous developments in neurotechnology and interface design are increasingly making BCI systems more effective and accessible [16].

10.4.3.3 Learning and Adaptation

The ability of brain-computer interface (BCI) systems to learn and adapt is crucial in maintaining their efficacy, usability by optimal users, and long-term effectiveness. The systems, with the help of adaptive algorithms and machine learning techniques, continuously work on improving their interpretation of neural signals. Using personalized calibration, BCIs can work on the modification of their responses to individual users, therefore not only improving accuracy but also minimizing the need for prolonged training sessions. They can also work on adapting to the changes in brain activity because of conditions such as fatigue, stress, or cognitive states, thereby providing consistent performance over a prolonged period. Such adaptability is of particular importance, especially in applications such as assistive technologies, neurorehabilitation, and brain-controlled prosthetics, where there is a need for precision in control and high responsiveness. Moreover, real-time feedback and reinforcement learning allow the modification of the user interaction, making BCIs intuitive and effective. Despite challenges such as signal variability and processing latency, ongoing research in artificial intelligence and neurotechnology is increasingly improving the adaptability and functionality of BCIs in real-world applications [17].

10.5 Challenges and Solutions

The application and use of brain-computer interfaces (BCIs) have overcome a variety of barriers. These barriers include ethical, practical, and technical barriers. Of these challenges, the most influential is the acquisition of a clean and functional brain signal, as such signals are intrinsically noisy, mysterious, and susceptible to external interference. Other technical demands include outstanding processing speed, real-time classification, algorithm execution, and low-latency processing. In addition, effective power management continues to be a requirement, particularly in the case of portable and implantable BCIs, which require long battery life and energy-conserving design. In addition, BCIs need to prove to be flexible to different biological structures, which further adds to usability across a heterogeneous user population. Ethical issues, such as privacy issues, data protection, misuse of surveillance technology, cognitive enhancement, and augmentation malpractice, make the widespread use of BCIs particularly complex. Anticipated solutions to overcome these barriers include innovations for noise cancellation with enhanced filtering schemes, classification with deep learning, and energy-efficient hardware structure design. The development of BCIs will also need to address compliance with regulations, uniform policies, and established standards to ensure that they are made in an ethical, accessible, and secure way [18, 19].

10.5.1 Technical Challenges

The challenges posed by BCIs are due to the limitations in their hardware peripherals, signal processing elements, and computational logic needs. The successful neural signals are of low quality and need to be well-calibrated using amplifiers and electrodes. Standardization based on adaptivity is also complicated due to the differences in brain signals between users, which require machine learning algorithms that adapt to changing conditions. With respect to wireless BCIs, data transmission poses significant delays, which negatively impact responsiveness to real-time interactions. In addition, BCI interfacing with existing systems, such as robotic limbs or virtual reality, places constraints in terms of functional integration and prompt processing of data and multidisciplinary systems design concepts. To address these problems, new materials for electrodes are being developed with classifying algorithms implemented in add-on AIs, supervised or unsupervised, within closed-loop adaptive systems. Improvements in quantum computation and the development of neuromorphic hardware

are expected to augment the functioning of BCIs, increasing their dependability and efficiency in practical use situations [18].

10.5.1.1 Signal Quality

The quality of the signal poses a major concern in BCIs, as the brain signals are recorded *via* EEG, ECoG, or even more invasive techniques like microelectrode arrays, all of which are prone to noise and other artifacts. Movement of muscles and blinking the eyes, among other electromagnetic interference signals from the outside, reduce the accuracy of the signal. Filtering techniques usually require advanced methods. The use of dry electrodes improves signal usability but compromises its stability. Better signal conductivity is given by wet electrodes, which are impractical in long-use contexts. Adaptive filtering and component analyses, including ICA and AI-based toning, are some of the new approaches aimed at improving the reliability of the signal. Ensuring high-resolution, high-quality electrodes that are also moderately resistant to noise, alongside a hybrid sensor systems design, is vital in controlling the accuracy of BCI-based devices [20].

10.5.1.2 Processing Speed

An important characteristic of BCI systems is processing speed because it impacts responsiveness and efficiency in real time. Brain-computer interfaces (BCIs) must rapidly process huge amounts of brain signal data by parsing features and classifying user intention within nanoseconds. Traditional machine learning methods face computational challenges with the ever-evolving dimensionality and complexity of neural data, resulting in a computational bottleneck. Additional deep learning approaches, such as convolutional neural networks (CNNs) and recurrent neural networks (RNNs), have been claimed to improve efficiency in processing. Specialized hardware accelerators like neuromorphic chips and FPGA-based architectures are also designed for enhancing the speed of operations. For BCIs to remain functional, advanced data transmission rates and lower latency must be achieved to ensure seamless interaction [18, 20].

10.5.1.3 Power Management

Power management is an issue for discussion for wireless and implantable BCIs that require energy-efficient systems due to their prolonged usefulness. The operation of BCIs heavily relies on conventional battery technology, which requires recharging or replacing, making the workload exhausting even for basic tasks. Research is being conducted on supplementing energy sources through bioelectric and thermoelectric generators. The integration of low-powered energy microchips and signal processing algorithms enhances efficiency by reducing total energy consumption without affecting performance. Flexible supercapacitors and wireless power transfer (WPT) technology are also well-suited to enable prolonged BCI operations.

10.5.2 Implementation Issues

There are recurring challenges in the functioning of brain-computer interfaces (BCIs), including in hardware functioning, software integration level, and the proficiency level of users. Sensors used in signal acquisition must be very accurate, while algorithms used in enabling interaction between an external device and the brain must function well. Furthermore, achieving system responsiveness within acceptable limits is of utmost importance, especially within medicine and assistive technologies. Widespread use also raises the question of ethics and privacy, making the problem much more complicated. The concern also remains about how such systems will interoperate with other already-established technologies or how such systems will be standardized. Addressing these challenges will require the cooperation of different scientific disciplines and improvements in technology in machine learning, as well as in hardware [21].

10.5.2.1 Cost Considerations

The development and operation of BCIs require a significant amount of funding for their research, development, and production. The use of high-resolution equipment for neural recordings, such as EEG and ECoG or fNIRS systems, comes at great expense, thereby restricting the possibility of wide-scale use. In addition to this, specific user customization requires enormous computational power, which drives up costs considerably. Although noninvasive BCIs are cheaper, the accuracy and reliability of these systems are generally far less than those of invasive systems. Cost-effective solutions and subsidization from governments, private sector bodies, and medical organizations would aid in lessening the financial burden, therefore enhancing the willingness of people to use such systems [22].

10.5.2.2 Scalability

There are major challenges in scaling BCIs from the laboratory to widespread consumer and medical use. One of the issues is demographic diversity. BCIs will need to be tailored for different cognitive and neurological profiles. In addition, making BCIs more available to the public will require advancements in wireless communication, processing in the cloud, and smaller hardware. Also, there is a need for standardized protocols along with economical materials to enable mass production. Overcoming these challenges can make BCIs easy to use on a daily basis.

10.5.2.3 Maintenance Requirements

BCI systems need constant maintenance in order to function and perform optimally. Users experience signal drift as well as physiologically driven changes that require recalibration. Hardware like electrodes, sensors, and even neural implants needs regular inspections for contamination and damage. Software needs to be updated to improve security and update machine-learning algorithms. Additionally, there ought to be quantitative mechanisms for diagnosing faults in real-time to reduce delays in usability. Creating maintenance procedures will facilitate the widespread use of BCIs in the future.

10.5.3 User Adoption

Factors like cost, user-friendliness, and accessibility tend to dictate the adoption of BCIs. Like most assistive technologies, BCIs must be integrated with users' expectations and routines. The willingness to use BCI solutions generally correlates with usefulness and ease of operation. Users of most assistive technology tend to adopt new technologies faster when the interface is user-friendly to the point of being effortless and requiring minimal training. Expansion into new markets also depends on user-centered design policies, which make it possible for BCIs to be needed, especially for users with disabilities. Altogether, these factors shape the scope of adoption of BCI devices across various sectors [22].

10.5.3.1 Training Requirements

For BCIs to be optimally adopted, there needs to be training instruction organized systematically and according to the needs of the users. The time needed to train corresponds to the system's complexity, with noninvasive devices generally being easier than invasive ones. Perhaps the most difficult hurdle is the learning curve: the user knows the mental command he has to execute, but he does not know which system feedback he will get. Training strategies that have been shown to work include neurofeedback, guided exercises, and adaptive interfaces that allow increasing the accuracy of control. There is a need for more adoption-focused and user-centered training modules that are simpler and more uniform.

10.5.3.2 Acceptance Factors

The acceptance of BCIs relies on their usability, dependability, and advantages over other traditional interfaces. Research suggests that users tend to accept BCIs more when they provide obvious advantages in the areas of communication, mobility, and accessibility. Confidence and motivation of users are also very important influencing factors. Trust issues are bettered by considering ethical concerns, privacy, and sociological acceptance. Designing an interface that maximally improves the experience and minimally hinders BCI technology adoption is crucial.

10.5.3.3 Usability Concerns

Usability is one of the primary challenges for BCI systems, as they need to consider the degree of complexity in relation to user interaction. Other components, such as feedback delay time, interface responsiveness, and error correction, also affect usability. Deriving poor validation, sluggish response times, and erratic signal processing contribute to low user satisfaction. Usability benchmarks existing systems, such as in ISO 9241, place focus on effectiveness, efficiency, and satisfaction as some of the most normative measures of usability. It's possible to develop more universal interfaces that would accommodate additional users by designing BCIs with adjustable parameters and integrating features of multimodal interaction [16, 24].

10.6 Future Directions

The imminent integration of emerging technologies with the current systems of BCI machinery provides endless possibilities for the future of humanity on BCIs (brain-computer interfaces). Its potential, as of now, is overwhelmingly broad. With the further use of BCIs shifting from medical uses and assistive technologies, future advancements will prioritize focus on accessibility, precision, and adaptability. The advancement in the field of AI will ensure smoother user transitions and improvements in device control. Enhanced neural decoding methods are being developed, and interlacing AGIBCI (artificial general intelligence with BCI) is done with the intent of creating self-improving models that optimize user interfacing automatically. Even better, the groundbreaking idea of brain-to-brain communication makes it possible to seamlessly transfer thoughts directly from one person to another (see Figure 10.7). The current aim of the aforementioned trends is to fuse human thinking alongside digital tools, which opens a gate of possibilities for health tech, communication devices, and neuroprosthetics. The application offers endless possibilities, but there remain ethical questions that are coupled with significant technical problems. Nevertheless, further collaboration among multiple scientific fields will solve these challenges and push toward the more human-friendly use of BCIs [25].

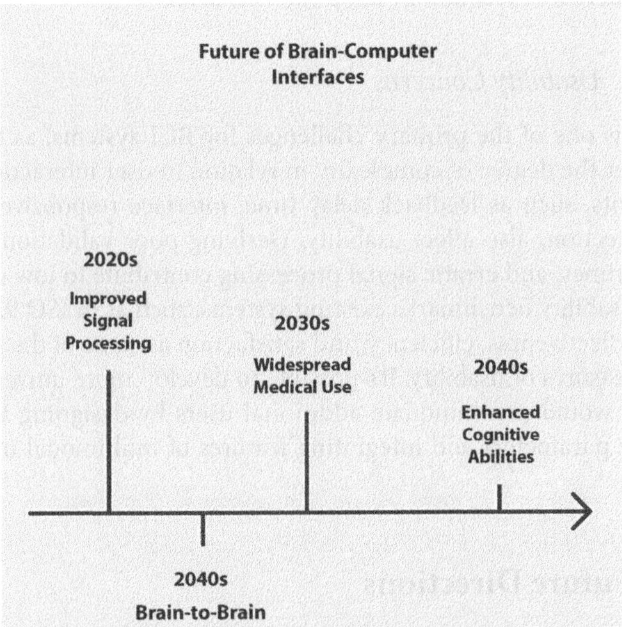

Figure 10.7 Projected milestones in BCI development from the 2020s to the 2050s, including enhanced medical use, cognitive augmentation, and potential brain-to-brain communication.

10.6.1 Technological Trends

Developments in brain-computer interfaces (BCIs) focus on improving the methods for data collection, processing, and interfacing with users. New methods of signal processing, such as machine learning-based neural decoding, are optimizing the assessment of brain signals. The branch of BCIs that focuses on making these devices external and noninvasive seems to be more user-friendly since it does not require surgery. Furthermore, integrated edge and cloud computing allow for decentralized processing, which increases speed by reducing latency. Hybrid BCIs that integrate different methods of neural recording, such as EEG and fNIRS, are also being developed to enhance the reliability of the signals obtained. The use of flexible and biocompatible materials for electrodes that are implanted is a promising development that would enhance the longevity of the implants. These changes in technology enhance the simplicity and efficiency of controlling BCIs, especially in performing multi-task brain activities [26] (see Figure 10.8).

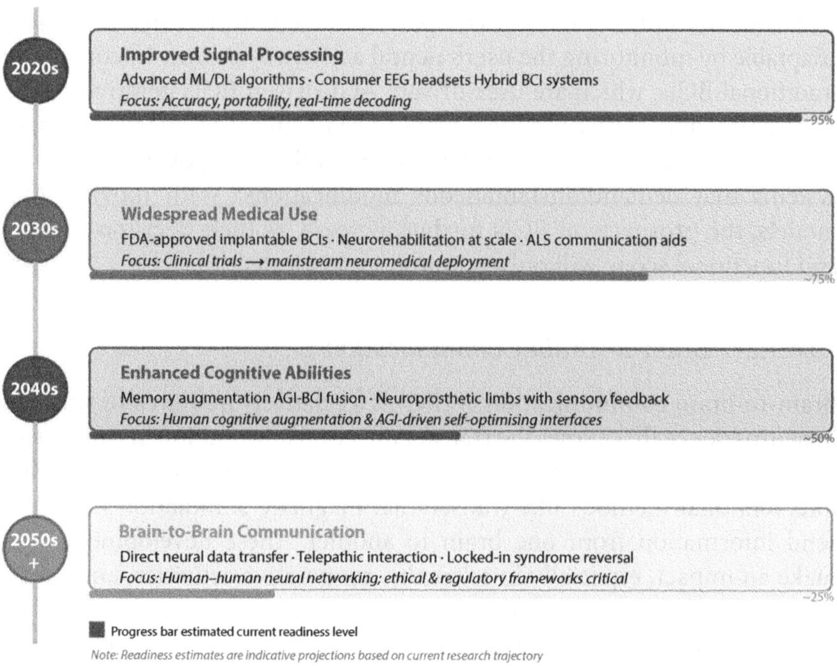

Figure 10.8 Projected milestones in BCI development (2020s–2050s).

10.6.1.1 Advanced Neural Decoding

Advanced neural decoding is redefining the range of tasks that can be performed with BCIs through enhanced interpretation of signals. Most traditional approaches fail due to noise and unnecessary variability within the signals, but modern deep-learning algorithms that process noise can improve decoding accuracy. Command execution with neural interfaces is expected to improve with the optimization of convolutional neural networks (CNN) and recurrent neural networks (RNN) to detect intricate neural patterns. Adapting to the changes of the user aids the calibration of models that support personalized decoding, improving the ease of use for non-expert users. Such improvements aid in the performance of BCI in various practical settings, such as in motor rehabilitation, brain-operated prosthetics, and cognitive enhancement [27].

10.6.1.2 Artificial General Intelligence Integration

The combination of Artificial General Intelligence (AGI) with BCIs serves as a new milestone in human-computer interaction. AGI makes it more adaptable by monitoring the user's neural activity over time. In contrast to traditional BCIs, which are user-driven, AGI-driven BCIs iteratively optimize brain signal interpretation without requiring user effort. This shift is highly beneficial for neuroprosthetics and other self-governing control systems that demand instantaneous modifications. With moving AGI models, the prospects of BCIs further increase, as their decision-making and functional scope will only get more sophisticated [6].

10.6.1.3 Brain-to-Brain Communication

Brain-to-brain communication (BtBC) is a relatively new area of research in neuroscience that allows the transfer of neural information between people. Experimental BtBC systems utilize BCIs alongside noninvasive brain interventional methods like transcranial magnetic stimulation (TMS) to send information from one brain to another. These developments will make an impact, especially in telepathy, cooperative activities, and medicine, such as helping locked-in syndrome patients regain some speech abilities (see Figure 10.9). Current prototypes are limited to sharing a few basic commands, but expanding research will improve the precision of thought interchange, making BtBC the most significant change in human communication [28] (see Figure 10.10).

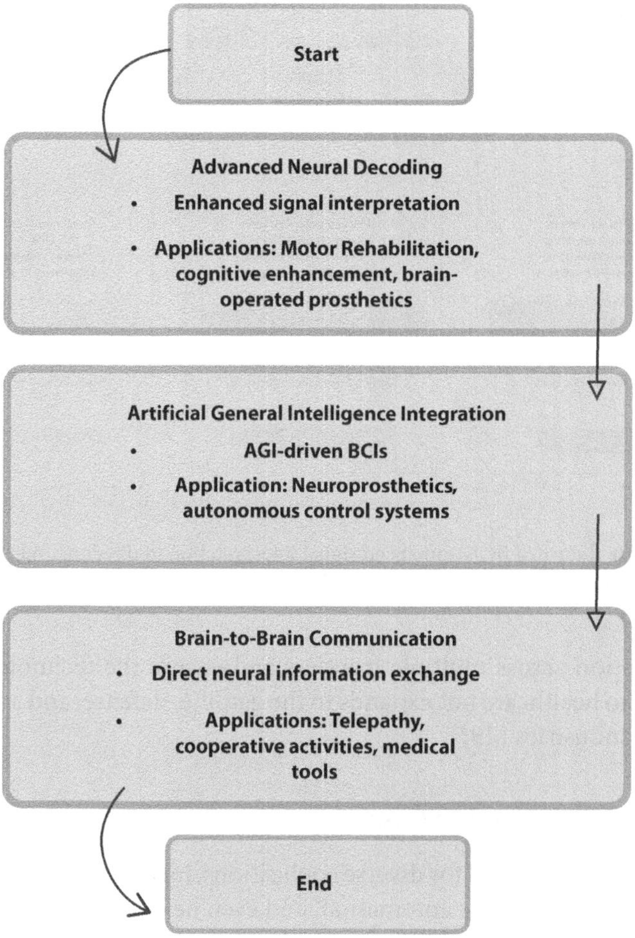

Figure 10.9 Future of brain-computer interfaces: from enhanced signal interpretation to direct neural communication.

10.6.2 Application Horizons

The brain-computer interfaces (BCIs) have wide-reaching implications beyond medicine, including communication, entertainment, and space security. New applications also include neurorehabilitation, cognitive therapies, and virtual reality experiences and interactions. The advancement of new technologies, including wearable and noninvasive BCIs, makes these tools convenient for the general public. Moreover, AI, cloud computing, and even neural implant integration possibilities redefine the human-computer interface at a new level. Collectively, these innovations accelerate

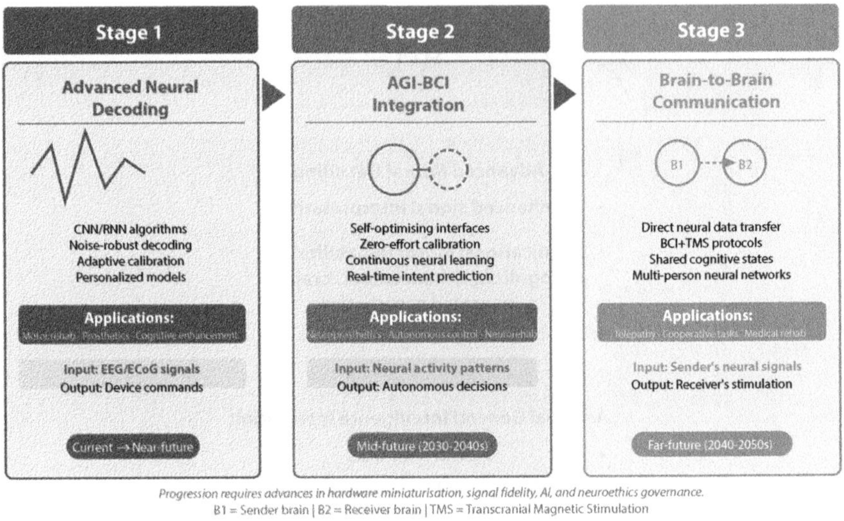

Figure 10.10 Future of BCIs: enhanced signal interpretation to direct neural communication.

BCI adoption across multiple frontiers and ensure the technology is not confined to healthcare but expands to the gaming, defense, and smart environment industries [29].

10.6.2.1 Emerging Use Cases

BCIs are being explored for diverse applications, including brain-controlled prosthetics, smart home automation, and even lie detection. In healthcare, they aid in restoring mobility for paralyzed patients through neuroprosthetic devices. Cognitive enhancement applications include memory augmentation and attention-boosting interfaces, particularly beneficial for individuals with neurological disorders. In gaming and entertainment, BCIs enable direct neural interaction with digital environments, enhancing immersive experiences. Also, security authorities may investigate BCIs for verification systems with individual brainwave signatures. As applications develop, ethical issues may be paramount, as well as consumer acceptance factors, leading to their successful implementation [30].

10.6.2.2 Novel Interfaces

BCI interface technologies are advancing towards noninvasive, wearable technology for greater accessibility and ease of use. Dry-electrode EEG headbands and hybrid BCIs that integrate several sensing modalities increase signal precision and user comfort. Augmented reality (AR) and gesture-based BCIs are on the horizon, allowing more natural interaction with digital systems. These new interfaces significantly decrease dependence on physical input devices, expanding BCI use to more individuals and improving usability in everyday settings [16].

10.6.2.3 Integration Possibilities

The integration of BCIs with AI, IoT, and cloud computing is driving in-sync connectivity between neural interfaces and smart spaces. AI-driven BCI systems improve signal processing, which makes accuracy in command execution more precise. BCI models based on the cloud allow real-time data analysis and remote medical monitoring availability. Furthermore, the convergence of BCIs with neurostimulation technologies, such as transcranial magnetic stimulation (TMS), promises novel neurotherapy advances. These hybrid combinations expand new avenues, rendering BCIs more responsive and adaptive to a wide range of applications [8].

10.6.3 Research Opportunities

Hybrid BCIs: Combining EEG with other neuroimaging techniques such as fNIRS or fMRI for improved performance.

Noninvasive Wearable Devices: Advancing dry electrode technology to enhance comfort and usability.

BCI and IoT Integration: Exploring real-time cloud-based processing for remote monitoring applications.

Neuroadaptive AI Systems: Implementing AI models that dynamically adapt to user-specific brain signals.

BCI for Cognitive Enhancement: Investigating applications beyond assistive technology, such as memory augmentation.

Ethical and Security Frameworks: Addressing privacy concerns and regulatory challenges in neural data transmission.

10.6.3.1 Potential Breakthroughs

Recent developments in deep learning have tremendously enhanced the performance of BCI, mainly for real-time decoding of brain activity. Convolutional neural networks (CNNs) and Recurrent Neural Networks (RNNs) are improving user intention classification accuracy with more accurate control of external devices. Reinforcement learning is also being applied to BCI systems to enhance system adaptability, minimizing user calibration time. Advances in quantum computing could also speed up the processing of EEG signals, making BCIs more rapid and more reliable. Another achievement is the creation of fully implantable BCIs with seamless brain-machine interfaces. Scientists are attempting to create biocompatible nanomaterials to make highly stable and low-immunity-response electrodes. The integration of BCIs in AR and VR environments is broadening their applications in gaming, rehabilitation, and learning. Furthermore, brain-to-brain communication, a science fiction mainstay, is now a reality, with initial reports indicating direct neural data transfer to be a success.

10.7 Ethical and Societal Implications

The emergence of brain-computer interface (BCI) technology is generating profound ethical and societal concerns of privacy, security, accessibility, and human autonomy. Considering BCIs offer a direct interface with neural activity, protection of the connected brain data from unauthorized use and access should be highly prioritized. Apart from that, ethical concerns are brought up on the question of cognitive enhancement, as unequal access to enhanced neurotechnology can exacerbate social inequality. In addition to that, BCI integration into everyday life creates concerns of personal identity and autonomy since external systems can potentially influence thought processes or decision-making. Again, concerns of long-term psychological and physiological impacts regarding extensive BCI use are present. At the social level, guaranteeing equal access, reducing workforce disruption caused by automation, and ensuring transparent ethical standards must be ensured to facilitate the ethical development of BCIs. As we can observe advancement in technology, it continues to advance; it is imperative that the researchers, policymakers, and ethicists come together to create regulations guaranteeing innovation while maintaining ethical concerns [21].

10.7.1 Ethical Considerations

The ethical concerns specific to brain-computer interface (BCI) technology revolve primarily around privacy, informed consent, autonomy, and abuse. As BCIs manipulate neural information, the integrity and security of the information are essential to protect users' cognitive privacy from unauthorized parties. Informed consent is also critical, where users must possess

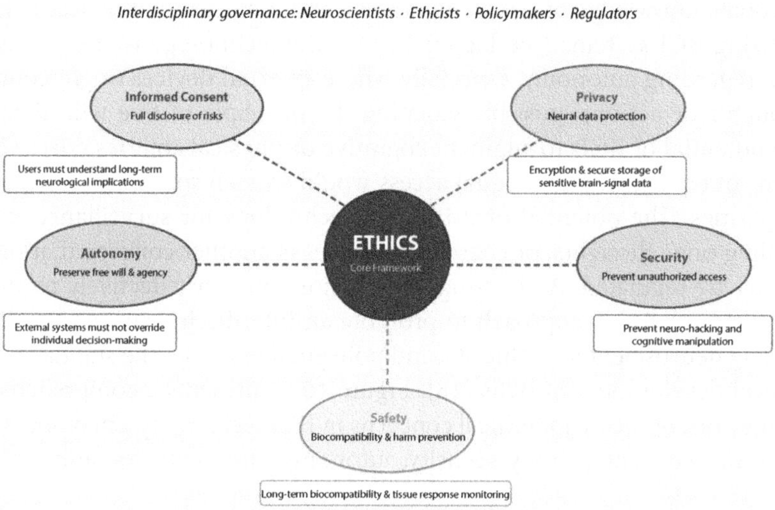

Figure 10.11 Comprehensive ethical considerations framework for brain-computer interface (BCI) development, illustrating five principal domains — informed consent, privacy, security, autonomy, and safety — converging around a central ethics governance core. Each domain reflects distinct regulatory and societal imperatives essential for responsible BCI deployment.

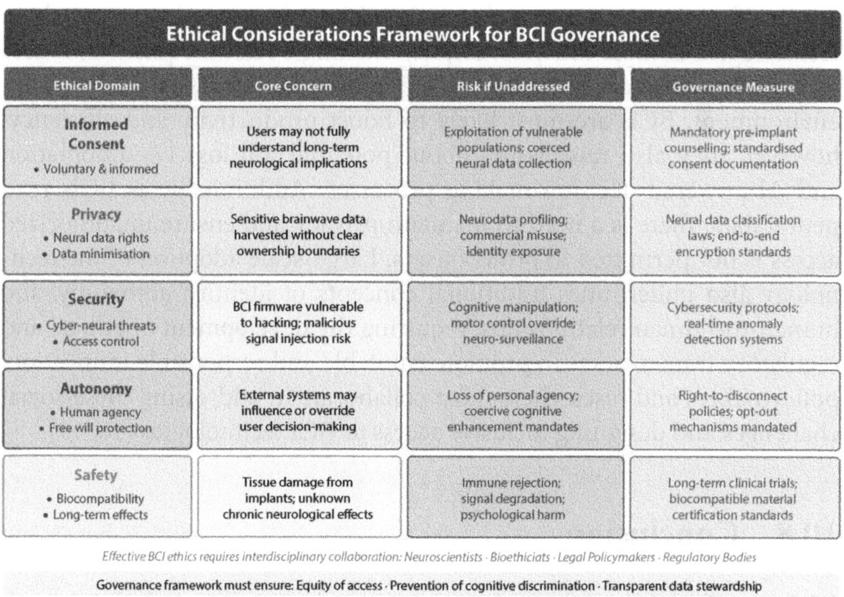

Ethical Considerations Framework for BCI Governance

Ethical Domain	Core Concern	Risk if Unaddressed	Governance Measure
Informed Consent • Voluntary & informed	Users may not fully understand long-term neurological implications	Exploitation of vulnerable populations; coerced neural data collection	Mandatory pre-implant counselling; standardised consent documentation
Privacy • Neural data rights • Data minimisation	Sensitive brainwave data harvested without clear ownership boundaries	Neurodata profiling; commercial misuse; identity exposure	Neural data classification laws; end-to-end encryption standards
Security • Cyber-neural threats • Access control	BCI firmware vulnerable to hacking; malicious signal injection risk	Cognitive manipulation; motor control override; neuro-surveillance	Cybersecurity protocols; real-time anomaly detection systems
Autonomy • Human agency • Free will protection	External systems may influence or override user decision-making	Loss of personal agency; coercive cognitive enhancement mandates	Right-to-disconnect policies; opt-out mechanisms mandated
Safety • Biocompatibility • Long-term effects	Tissue damage from implants; unknown chronic neurological effects	Immune rejection; signal degradation; psychological harm	Long-term clinical trials; biocompatible material certification standards

Effective BCI ethics requires interdisciplinary collaboration: Neuroscientists · Bioethiciats · Legal Policymakers · Regulatory Bodies

Governance framework must ensure: Equity of access · Prevention of cognitive discrimination · Transparent data stewardship

Figure 10.12 Major ethical concerns in brain-computer interface technology.

adequate knowledge of risks, constraints, and long-term influences before utilizing BCI systems (see Figure 10.11). The technology is also in question regarding autonomy, especially where external devices might control thoughts or actions, possibly violating the principle of free will. Finally, the potential of BCIs to augment cognitive or physical abilities raises concerns of equity, where unequal access would worsen social and economic disparities. The potential of using BCI technology for surveillance, controlling one's thoughts, or coercive purposes is another concern that must be strictly regulated. Addressing these major concerns effectively requires a multidisciplinary approach to promote an interdisciplinary partnership among neuroscientists, ethicists, and policymakers to set the standards for ethical development in BCIs [18]. Figure 10.12 presents a comprehensive framework of the major ethical concerns in BCI technology, encompassing informed consent, privacy, security, autonomy, and safety domains.

10.7.2 Societal Impact

The use of brain-computer interface (BCI) technology within social structures has far-reaching effects across various fields, including healthcare, the workplace, accessibility, and data privacy. In healthcare, BCIs are providing revolutionary solutions for individuals with disabilities by facilitating communication, mobility, and rehabilitation through directly controllable systems functioning *via* neural signals. Although unequal access to these technologies is most likely to amplify existing social inequalities, it creates a technological gap between socioeconomic classes. Within a work environment, BCIs are most likely to boost productivity and efficiency; however, they also raise issues about potential job loss *via* automation and AI-powered decision-making processes. Additionally, as BCIs read neural data, there is a need to maintain privacy and ensure unauthorized access is not permitted to protect users. Large-scale adoption of the technology also undermines traditional concepts of identity, autonomy, and human-to-human relationships, requiring the development of ethical and regulatory frameworks. To promote equitable and responsible innovation, policymakers and researchers must collaborate in addressing these social challenges and designing inclusive access to BCI technologies [18, 19].

10.8 Conclusion

With significant breakthroughs in machine learning and artificial intelligence and their integration with neurotechnology in the field of brain-computer interfaces (BCIs), the interfaces themselves have been rapidly becoming more sophisticated, affordable, and applicable to daily life. Modern BCIs enable unprecedented advances in rehabilitation medicine *via* assistive communication devices, cognitive augmentation systems, and, indeed, human augmentation. These technologies offer unprecedented promise for life transformation. But the direct interface between the human nervous system and technology poses a new set of ethical concerns and privacy issues that need to be explored thoroughly and addressed. Interdisciplinary collaboration would be the driving force behind continuous research on BCIs and charting their fate.

Computer science, psychology, neurobiology, and biomedical engineering are cross-cutting disciplines at BCI research and propel its development, innovation, and fine-tuning. Industry and regulatory bodies, along with academia, must come forward and establish a framework of standards that guide the safety, accessibility, and inclusivity of BCIs. Failure of which opens scope for manipulation of cognitive information, undermines socio-economic equilibrium, and jeopardizes personal data security. Bridging the gap from path-breaking research to practical application would necessitate unflinching ethical stewardship along with sustained innovation. BCI innovation continues, with new telecommunications technologies and technological advances in information and hardware. Noninvasive methods hold promise for routinely and accurately processing brain signals, and invasive methods hold promise for paralysis and other neurological disorders. Such developments hint at breaking out of the experimental lab confines.

The advent of BCIs holds promise for an era in which noninvasive methods will be effortlessly embedded into daily life, transforming the human-machine interaction norms and bringing new paradigms to interaction. One of the most significant paradigm shifts in our understanding of machines in synchrony with the human brain is initiated by the potential of BCIs through noninvasive methods. Along with the integration of robotics, artificial intelligence, and cybernetics, noninvasive BCIs are not merely devices of interaction—living interfaces that enable seamless transactions between human volition and machine action. Looking to the future, there is every prospect that the bright horizon will be reached. However, some technological, ethical, and social barriers are yet to be overcome. The BCIs, combined with the state-of-the-art computer and robot technologies, products of historically unparalleled progress in cognitive science, dispel doubts about the limitations of human beings. The advances redefine the limits of humankind in terms of phenomenal engineering and innovation, and not developments enclosed within socially predetermined limits.

Advances in these multidisciplinary fields present unprecedentedly newly invented challenges and demonstrate an abiding commitment to redefining the notion of human intelligence.

These systems are capable of processing neural signals in real time and providing immediate feedback. Such functionality is particularly beneficial in fields such as assistive technology, prosthetics, and home automation, enabling users to control devices purely through mental volition. Artificial intelligence and machine learning vision underpin this application, as they complement signal processing to guarantee commands are interpreted and executed correctly. Aided by existing shortcomings, including signal oscillation and real-time processing, ongoing advances in neurotechnology are improving the usability, stability, and ease of use of these natural control interfaces, thus broadening their potential applications in healthcare, accessibility, and human-computer interaction.

10.8.1 Feedback Mechanisms

Feedback mechanisms in brain-computer interface (BCI) systems are said to be crucial for boosting user control, accuracy, and adaptability. These systems offer real-time responses based on brain activity, allowing users to refine their interactions with external devices. Feedback can come in several forms, such as visual cues (like signals on a screen), auditory alerts (like sound notifications), or haptic responses (like vibrations or tactile sensations), ensuring smooth communication between the user and the system. By using a system called closed-loop feedback, BCIs promote continuous learning and self-adjustment, which leads to better performance over a period. This is especially important in areas where adaptive feedback aids in motor function recovery and enhances device precision, like neurorehabilitation, assistive technologies, and brain-controlled prosthetics. The addition of artificial intelligence and machine learning to BCIs takes feedback processing to the next level, making BCIs more responsive and customized for each user. Ongoing advancements in neurotechnology and interface design are steadily improving the efficiency and user-friendliness of BCI systems, even though there are challenges like response latency and signal accuracy involved [16].

10.8.2 Learning and Adaptation

The ability of brain-computer interface (BCI) systems to learn and adapt is crucial for boosting their performance, enhancing user interaction, and ensuring long-term effectiveness. These systems utilize adaptive algorithms and machine learning techniques to constantly improve their capability to interpret brain signals. By integrating personalized calibration, BCIs can tailor their responses to fit individual users, which not only boosts accuracy but also cuts down on the need for lengthy training sessions. They can also adapt to fluctuations in brain activity brought on by factors like fatigue, stress, or cognitive shifts, guaranteeing steady performance over time. This flexibility tends to be especially valuable in areas like assistive technologies, neurorehabilitation, and brain-controlled prosthetics, where precise and responsive control is essential. Additionally, real-time feedback and reinforcement learning empower the users to fine-tune their interactions, making BCIs more intuitive and efficient. While challenges such as signal variability and processing delays still exist, ongoing advancements in artificial intelligence and neurotechnology are continually improving the adaptability and usability of BCIs in real-world scenarios [17].

AI disclosure statement: The author acknowledges the use of AI-based tools for minor language editing or grammatical correction. However, all intellectual contributions, analyses, and conclusions presented in this chapter are entirely the author's own.

References

1. Amiri, S., Rabbi, A., Azinfar, L., Fazel-Rezai, R., A Review of P300, SSVEP, and Hybrid P300/SSVEP Brain- Computer Interface Systems, in: *Brain-Computer Interface Systems - Recent Progress and Future Prospects*, InTech (now IntechOpen), Rijeka, Croatia, 2013, doi: 10.5772/56135.
2. *Brain-Computer Interfaces Handbook Technological and Theoretical Advances*, CRC Press (Taylor & Francis Group), Boca Raton, FL, USA, 2018, [Online]. Available: http://taylorandfrancis.com.
3. Panigrahi, N. and Mohanty, S.P., *Brain Computer Interface _ EEG Signal Processing*, First edition, CRC Press Inc, Boca Raton, FL, 2022, 9781000595505 – 145c5b2b64bd6ee5bc34a77d7949ca5f – Anna's Archiv.
4. Recent Advances in Brain-Computer Interface Systems_indd – Owner – c585a9dcb4da564dec4a99a1de975dce – Anna's Archive.
5. Principe, J.C. and Sanchez, J.C., Brain-Machine Interface Engineering: Foreward, 2007, doi: 10.2200/S00053ED1V01Y200710BME017.
6. Sun, X., Wang, J., Bertino, E., Artificial Intelligence and Security, [Online]. Available: http://www.springer.com/series/7409.
7. Correlative Learning.

8. Anand, R., Juneja, S., Juneja, A., Jain, V., Kannan, R., *Integration of IoT with Cloud Computing for Smart Integration of IoT with Cloud Computing for Smart Applications*, Chapman and Hall/CRC (Taylor & Francis Group), Boca Raton, FL, USA, 2020, [Online]. Available: https://www.routledge.com/Chapman–.
9. Kopetz, H., *Real-Time Systems : Design Principles for Distributed Embedded Applications*, Springer US, Boston, MA, USA, 2002.
10. Dube, A., *et al.*, Language as the Working Model of Human Mind.
11. Gu, X., *et al.*, EEG-Based Brain-Computer Interfaces (BCIs): A Survey of Recent Studies on Signal Sensing Technologies and Computational Intelligence Approaches and Their Applications. *IEEE/ACM Trans. Comput. Biol. Bioinf.*, 18, 5, 1645–1666, 2021, doi: 10.1109/TCBB.2021.3052811.
12. Amstutz, L.J., Brain-Computer Interfaces, North Star Editions, Lake Elmo, MN, 2020.
13. Fundamental of Nanotechnology Based Wireless Brain Computer Interface Platform.
14. Guger, C., Allison, B.Z., Miller, K., *Springer Briefs in Electrical and Computer Engineering*, Springer International Publishing, Cham, Switzerland, 2022, [Online]. Available: http://www.springer.com/series/10059.
15. *Neural Interface: Frontiers and Applications*, Springer International Publishing, Cham, Switzerland, 2022, [Online]. Available: http://www.springer.com/series/5584.
16. Sorudeykin, K.A., An Educative Brain-Computer Interface, Mar. 2010, Accessed: Jun. 17, 2025. [Online]. Available: http://arxiv.org/abs/1003.2660.
17. Brumberg, J.S., Nieto-Castanon, A., Kennedy, P.R., Guenther, F.H., Brain-computer interfaces for speech communication. *Speech Commun.*, 52, 4, 367–379, Apr. 2010, doi: 10.1016/j.specom.2010.01.001.
18. Rashid, M., *et al.*, Current Status, Challenges, and Possible Solutions of EEG-Based Brain-Computer Interface: A Comprehensive Review. *Front. Neurorobot.*, 14, Jun. 2020, doi: 10.3389/FNBOT.2020.00025.
19. Nicolas-Alonso, L.F. and Gomez-Gil, J., Brain computer interfaces, a review. *Sensors*, 12, 2, 1211–1279, Feb. 2012, doi: 10.3390/S120201211.
20. Mikhail, M., El-Ayat, K., Coan, J.A., Allen, J.J.B., Using minimal number of electrodes for emotion detection using brain signals produced from a new elicitation technique. *Int. J. Auton. Adapt. Commun. Syst.*, 6, 1, 80–97, 2013, doi: 10.1504/IJAACS.2013.050696.
21. Maye, A., Zhang, D., Wang, Y., Gao, S., Engel, A.K., Multimodal brain-computer interfaces. *Tsinghua Sci. Technol.*, 16, 2, 133–139, Apr. 2011, doi: 10.1016/S1007-0214(11)70020-7.
22. Domingo, M.C., An overview of the Internet of Things for people with disabilities. *J. Network Comput. Appl.*, 35, 2, 584–596, Mar. 2012, doi: 10.1016/j.jnca.2011.10.015.

23. Lotte, F. and Roy, R.N., Brain-computer interface contributions to neuroergonomics, in: *Neuroergonomics: The Brain at Work and in Everyday Life*, pp. 43–48, Jan. 2018, doi: 10.1016/B978-0-12-811926-6.00007-5.
24. Ramadan, R.A. and Vasilakos, A.V., Brain computer interface: control signals review. *Neurocomputing*, 223, 26–44, Feb. 2017, doi: 10.1016/j.neucom.2016.10.024.
25. Sorudeykin, K.A., An Educative Brain-Computer Interface, Mar. 2010.
26. Abdulkader, S.N., Atia, A., Mostafa, M.S.M., Brain computer interfacing: Applications and challenges. *Egypt. Inf. J.*, 16, 2, 213–230, Jul. 2015, doi: 10.1016/J.EIJ.2015.06.002.
27. Wolpaw, J.R. and Wolpaw, E.W. (Eds.), Brain-Computer Interfaces: Principles and Practice, Oxford University Press, New York, NY, USA, 2012, ISBN: 9780195388855.
28. Gan, W.-S., Kuo, C.-C.J., Zheng, T.F., Barni, M., *SpringerBriefs in Electrical and Computer Engineering*, Series Editors. Springer International Publishing, Cham, Switzerland, 2023, [Online]. Available: http://www.springer.com/series/10059.
29. GerddGrübler ElisabethhHildt Editors. [Online]. Available: http://www.springer.com/series/7761.
30. Huang, D., Fei, D.-Y., Bai, O., Chen, X., *A Two Dimensional Brain-Computer Interface Associated with Human Natural Motor Control*, InTech Open Access Publisher (InTech), Rijeka, Croatia, 2011.

11

Advancing Brain-Computer Interfaces with Innovative Deep Learning Approaches

Ashaq Hussain Bhat[1]*, Hashmat Fida[2], Arshid Ahmad Wani[1] and Danish Rashid Pala[1]

[1]*University Institute of Computing, Chandigarh University, Punjab, Kharar, India*
[2]*Department of CSE, Presidency University, Bangalore, Karnataka, India*

Abstract

Brain-computer interfaces (BCIs) have revolutionized neurotechnology, enabling direct communication pathways between the brain and external devices. The integration of deep learning (DL) with BCIs has significantly improved the accuracy, efficiency, and adaptability of these systems. This chapter focuses on various methodologies such as representation learning, transfer learning, data augmentation, and self-supervised learning (SSL), analyzing their contributions to enhancing BCI performance. Representation learning techniques, including autoencoders and contrastive learning, have played a crucial role in feature extraction from high-dimensional EEG signals. Transfer learning has enabled model generalization across different subjects and recording sessions, significantly reducing the need for extensive training data. Additionally, advanced augmentation techniques such as generative adversarial networks (GANs) and synthetic data generation have mitigated the challenges associated with limited EEG datasets. SSL methodologies, including contrastive predictive coding and masked signal modelling, have emerged as powerful alternatives to supervised learning, reducing reliance on large labelled datasets. Beyond the technical aspects, the impact of DL-based BCIs in various applications has been analyzed, such as motor imagery for prosthetic control, neurorehabilitation for stroke recovery, and emotion recognition for mental health assessment. It has been highlighted how convolutional neural

**Corresponding author*: ashaq11bhat@gmail.com

Tawseef Ahmed Teli, Syed Immamul Ansarullah, Arun Kumar Rana, Suman Lata Tripathi and Kashif Nisar (eds.) Brain-to-Computer Interfaces Using Machine Learning and Deep Learning, (261–284) © 2026 Scrivener Publishing LLC

networks (CNNs), recurrent neural networks (RNNs), and hybrid deep learning models have enabled more efficient decoding of brain signals.

The study also identifies key challenges, including scalability, interpretability, and ethical concerns related to data privacy and security. We provide recommendations for future research, emphasizing the need for more explainable AI (XAI) models, robust cross-subject generalization strategies, and multimodal data integration. By addressing these challenges, BCIs powered by deep learning can become more effective, adaptable, and accessible, paving the way for broader real-world applications in healthcare, communication, and human augmentation.

***Keywords*:** DL, brain-computer interface, neural decoding, signal processing, neurotechnology

11.1 Introduction

BCIs, commonly known as brain-computer interfaces, have transformed the BCI neurotechnology field, as they do away with the need for any intermediate communication channels between the brain and any other device. In addition to providing the disabled novel means of engagement with the outside world that do not depend on traditional neuromuscular pathways, these have vast promise for those with disabilities. Analysis of brain signals in conventional BCI systems involves feature extraction and further classification techniques. Nevertheless, they frequently encounter some relevant challenges concerning noise, non-stationarity, and inter-subject variability. The recent progress achieved in deep learning has caused a remarkable change to uplift the accuracy, efficiency, and adaptability of brain-computer interfaces. DL methods, particularly neural networks, are able to extract more complicated patterns embedded in high-dimensional EEG data, which diminishes the necessity for hand-crafted features. Since neural networks have great power in recognizing patterns, such breakthroughs have made the brain-computer interface system more robust and scalable. They can also handle a wider range of brain inputs, ranging from the loud ones to the mild ones.

This article aims to discuss various approaches to deep learning, such as representation learning, transfer learning, data augmentation, and self-supervised learning, and assess how they contribute to the improvement of BCI performance. Examples of representation learning are deep autoencoders and contrastive learning frameworks, which are the ones we have found useful for feature extraction and noise attenuation. These have also had a beneficial impact on the signal-to-noise ratio as well as the accurate decoding. Transfer learning approaches customize models trained on a particular dataset and adapt them for new subjects or tasks. This improves generalizability and reduces the need for a large amount of labeled data. The production of synthetic EEG data has been accomplished through such methods as data augmentation, which include generative adversarial networks (GANs) and variational autoencoders (VAEs). These have been used to address issues of data scarcity and diversity. In this respect, the SSL approach, encompassing contrastive predictive coding and masked signal modeling, has made possible the development of unsupervised training frameworks, reducing the dependence on manually annotated datasets.

This article looks at how the impact deep learning-based brain-computer interfaces have had in several fields, including neurorehabilitation, prosthetic control, and mental health evaluation, could benefit from the brain-computer interface's contribution to methodological development. The enhancement of motor control in prosthetics has been supported by the development of more advanced brain-decoding techniques that allow users to execute more natural and precise movements. Deep-learning-augmented BCIs further improve neurorehabilitation outcomes for stroke victims and spinal cord injury survivors in this regard by allowing real-time feedback and individualized adaptive training. There are initiatives concerning the development of brain-computer interfaces where deep learning can be appreciated as useful in emotional recognition, along with potential mental health applications. With these interfaces, the diagnosis and monitoring of diseases, such as anxiety and depression, can and should become easier.

This article also looks into some of the recent approaches, namely hybrid brain-computer interface designs comprising several modalities of signal, federated learning for privacy-preserving brain-computer interfaces, and real-time closed-loop feedback systems for enhanced user adaptation. As a potential option for further exploration, the combination of deep learning with other artificial intelligence approaches, such as reinforcement learning and graph neural networks, is being investigated as a potential avenue [1–5].

11.2 The Evolution of Brain-Computer Interfaces

11.2.1 Early Developments in BCIs

The concept of brain-computer interfaces burgeoned from the beginning of the 20th century, when researchers first set out to use electroencephalography (EEG) recordings to study brain activity. The first primitive confirmation of these BCIs sought to gain knowledge of the correlation between brain electrical impulses and their relation to cognitive and motor functions. These experiments provided the basis for the conception of BCIs, the first, however primitive, often referred to as brain-machine interfaces. The goal of these early interfacing systems was to study brain signals without direct control of external devices.

The 1970s marked the period when their rudimentary development acquired momentous energy when pioneering studies proved that EEG signals could be used for even basic control tasks. In its infancy, research concentrated on simple binary control, such as using patterns of brainwave activity to select one of two options. Subsequent decades of studies witnessed improvements in computer power and the development of signal processing techniques that allowed the extraction of more complex information from EEG recordings. This enabled more sophisticated BCI applications. Over the years, BCIs have undergone development in terms of noninvasive, semi-invasive, and invasive methods, which, in their complete summation, display some advantages and disadvantages each. Invasive BCIs can achieve high-resolution data capture by placing electrodes directly into the brain; however, they present risks associated with surgery and long-term stability. Semi-invasive systems, such as electrocorticography (ECoG)-based BCIs, present a compromise between signal fidelity and safety. The brain-computer interfaces that primarily depend on electroencephalography are prominent because of their noninvasiveness, practicability for movement, safety concerns, reduction in cost, and consideration of signal noise and spatial resolution.

Normally trained in signal processing techniques, and since deep learning has come into existence, these techniques have undergone a radical shift in their application and methods to experiment with the brain signals by BCI systems. Prior approaches to machine learning were based on elaborate feature extraction and engineering of hand-crafted algorithms that often required domain knowledge plus heavy preprocessing. The advent of deep learning models, in particular convolutional and recurrent neural networks, represents a paradigm shift in this area by allowing for the autonomous learning of hierarchical representations from EEG raw data. These improvements have enhanced the performance of brain-computer interfaces (BCIs), rendering them more robust, efficient, and versatile for applications such as cognitive enhancement, neurorehabilitation, and assistive technologies [1–3, 5–8, 13].

11.3 Deep Learning in BCIs: An Overview

Research corroborates the fact that deep learning models comprising convolutional neural networks (CNNs), recurrent neural networks (RNNs), and hybrid architectures greatly improve the efficacy of these neural decoding tasks. Specifically, these models help in extracting complex features from high-dimensional EEG inputs. By doing so, these models surpass the limitations of traditional feature extraction methods: CNNs excellently capture the spatial dependencies in EEG data, recognizing local structures and processing the representations through hierarchical feature learning. On the contrary, RNNs imply the utilization of the temporal dependencies: being highly suitable for sequential data, such as EEG recordings, helps them to ascertain that patterns are preserved over longer durations. The commonly used deep learning models in brain-computer interfaces are shown in Table 11.1.

For enhancing model performance, hybrid architectures combining convolutional neural networks (CNNs) with recurrent neural networks (RNNs) leverage spatiotemporal feature learning. These models comprise CNN-LSTM hybrids that reap the multiple advantages of both architectures, thus improving classification accuracy and feature interpretability. This model architecture further integrates attention mechanisms to specifically focus on critical EEG segments for increased signal quality and noise reduction.

In recent times, transformer-based models have been explored in BCIs, inspired mainly by recent advances in natural language processing. Transformers do away with a recurrent connection, allowing the model to process whole EEG sequences in parallel whilst retaining the self-attention mechanism for capturing long-range dependencies in an efficient manner. All of these approaches have led to great boosts in accuracy and robustness and hence progress in neural decoding and BCI applications.

In addition, the inception of transformer models along with attention mechanisms has a substantial impact on the decoding of brain activity. They facilitate the models to follow and focus mainly on the principal constituents in the EEG signal and thus resist interference from noise. This evolution in BCI applications enhances accuracy and robust integrity, hence providing a fine opportunity for the development of dependable control interfaces for assistive devices, neurorehabilitation, and cognitive monitoring. The subsequent sections will examine diverse deep learning methodologies that have enhanced the capabilities of brain-computer

Table 11.1 Deep learning models commonly used in brain-computer interface.

Deep learning model	Key features	BCI application examples
Convolutional neural networks (CNNs)	Good at spatial feature extraction from EEG/ECoG signals; handle multi-channel inputs	Motor imagery classification, seizure detection, P300 speller
Recurrent neural networks (RNNs)	Capture temporal dependencies; sensitive to sequential data	Time-series EEG decoding, workload monitoring
Long short-term memory (LSTM)	Variant of RNN; overcomes vanishing gradient; learns long-term dependencies	Speech/intent decoding, motor imagery recognition
Gated recurrent unit (GRU)	Lightweight alternative to LSTM; efficient for small datasets	Real-time BCI control, cognitive state monitoring
Autoencoders (AE)	Unsupervised feature learning; dimensionality reduction	EEG signal denoising, latent feature extraction
Variational autoencoders (VAE)	Learn probabilistic latent representations; generate synthetic data	EEG data augmentation, anomaly detection
Generative adversarial networks (GANs)	Data generation *via* adversarial training	EEG signal augmentation, addressing class imbalance

(*Continued*)

Table 11.1 Deep learning models commonly used in brain-computer interface. (*Continued*)

Deep learning model	Key features	BCI application examples
Deep belief networks (DBN)	Layer-wise pretraining with restricted Boltzmann machines	Early motor imagery BCIs, EEG feature extraction
Transformers	Attention mechanism: capture long-range dependencies	Sequential EEG decoding, speech-BCI translation
Hybrid models (CNN + RNN/CNN + transformer)	Combine spatial and temporal modeling	High-accuracy motor imagery classification, multi-modal BCIs

interfaces (BCIs). These methodologies encompass feature extraction, classification, and adaptive learning strategies tailored for real-time applications [1–7, 11, 16, 20].

11.4 Representation Learning in BCIs

The goal of representation learning is to automatically extract relevant feature representations from raw EEG data. It enables brain-computer interfaces (BCIs) to obtain high-level abstractions from complex brain signals with the application of deep learning techniques. The interpretability and robustness have improved due to the implementation of these techniques.

In representation learning for brain-computer interfaces, probably one of the best-known methods is the use of autoencoders. These neural networks construct compact encodings of EEG signals by reconstructing input data. Thus, it helps the user get a handle on essential features while also purging noise. Variational autoencoders (VAEs) borrow their essence from probabilistic reasoning and offer even more beautiful representations of latent space, thus improving generalizability.

An emerging trend in representation learning for brain-computer interfaces (BCIs) is contrastive learning. SimCLR and contrastive predictive coding (CPC) are methods that enhance the similarity between relevant EEG snippets while diminishing it between irrelevant segments. It is useful for learning robust feature representations without much labeled data input, greatly benefitting cases where annotation becomes costly and time-consuming.

Self-supervised learning offers a plausible alternative. In this approach, one trains the models using some pretext tasks—signal reconstruction, temporal shuffling, or masked signal prediction. The features learned during the process could be fine-tuned for specific tasks like motor imagery classification or mental state identification, allowing the BCI to generate these representations. Through such representations, graph-based representation learning is getting extra traction in EEG research—especially when considering functional brain connectivity. The spatial-temporal correlations across a number of brain regions can be modeled by representing EEG data as graph nodes and edges with GNNs. Thus, to achieve better interpretability and performance on complex BCI tasks. All these enable representation learning to raise the upper limits of what is possible in BCI. Simultaneously, it provides interesting insights into brain functioning while massively downplaying the requirement for enormous labeled datasets [8–12].

11.5 Transfer Learning for Model Generalization

A significant challenge of brain-computer interfaces (BCIs) is the heterogeneity related to inter-individual variability of electroencephalogram (EEG) signals, on the one hand, and recording sessions, on the other. Transfer learning is one such possible solution that provides the possibility of fine-tuning previously trained models on new datasets with limited retraining. With transfer learning, knowledge acquired during prior work on a related task can be used for a new set of related tasks. This helps to enhance efficiency and minimize computational costs because the model does not have to begin the user training process from scratch.

11.5.1 Types of Transfer Learning in Brain-Computer Interfaces (BCIs)

1. Cross-Subject Transfer: The common variation in EEG patterns between subjects gives rise to a difficulty in generalizing across subjects. The procedure for continuous adaptation of a model developed from representative subject groups for new subjects decreases the need for a considerable labeled dataset. Methods in common use towards combating inter-subject variability include parameter fine-tuning, feature transformation, and domain adaptation.

2. Cross-Task Transfer: Some BCIs require their adaptability to various cognitive or motor tasks. Transfer learning allows transfer of models that have been trained to work on a given task, such as motor imagery, to be adapted for use on a different task in another domain, such as emotion recognition, with a minimal amount of additional training.
3. Domain Adaptation: EEG signals display variability across different recording sessions, hardware setups, and environmental conditions. The effectiveness of this, such as adversarial training, domain adversarial neural networks (DANNs), and statistical feature alignment, thus enhances generalization across various experimental conditions, resulting in lessened calibration time for BCI users [23–25].

11.5.2 Methods for Effective Transfer Learning

1. Feature-Based Transfer: Derives common knowledge representations from EEG signals across numerous subjects or tasks by ensuring that only the most pertinent and generalizable features pass through.
2. Parameter-Based Transfer: Model parameters from a pretrained network are taken and fine-tuned on a new data set while holding beneficial general properties.
3. Adversarial Transfer Learning: Uses adversarial networks to obtain domain-invariant representations, which ensure improved model generalization capability against variations in EEG signal distributions.
4. Meta-Learning: A Process of Learning to Learn: Allows a model to quickly learn and adapt to new tasks with a few examples, which might be a promising way for personalizing BCIs to fit individual users.

11.5.3 Applications of Transfer Learning in Brain-Computer Interfaces

1. Neurorehabilitation: These pretrained models for motor imagery tasks can ease the process of transfer from stroke patients by speeding up the adaptation.
2. Brain-Computer Gaming: Models designed for a particular gaming interface can be adapted for different gaming settings without extensive retraining.

3. Mental State Classification: Transfer learning enables the construction of generalizable models to detect stress, assess the cognitive workload, or perform other psychological assessments using EEG signals.

The introduction of transfer-learning mechanisms would, therefore, make BCIs flexible and less dependent on large labeled datasets while improving performance across varying scenarios. Future research in this area should focus on enhancing the real-time aspects of transfer-learning frameworks and improving interpretability for clinical and consumer-based BRIs.

The diversity of electroencephalogram (EEG) data between different subjects and recording sessions presents a persistent challenge to brain-computer interfaces (BCIs). Transfer learning addresses this problem when pretrained models can adapt to new datasets with limited retraining.

- Cross-Subject Transfer: Models built on one cohort can be fine-tuned for new subjects with a reduced need for extensive labeled datasets.
- Domain Adaptation: Techniques such as adversarial training and domain adversarial neural networks (DANs) promote generalization between varying experimental conditions [20–25].

11.5.4 Data Augmentation and Synthetic EEG Data

The limitation posed by a few labeled EEG datasets poses a problem for the training of deep learning models. Generative adversarial networks (GANs) and other data augmentation techniques have come in handy in generating synthetic EEG signals. These methods increase dataset sizes through generation using different brain signal representations, expanding the scope of adaptability for a given model. Apart from using GANs, techniques like the variational autoencoders (VAEs) and other synthetic oversampling techniques have been used to help diversify EEG datasets and make them robust. Also, data augmentation methods employ signal perturbation, time warping, and frequency modulation as a way of enhancing model generalizability since they add variations to training data in a controlled way. Such ways restrict overfitting and improve BCI model adaptability across subjects and tasks to make deep learning models highly reliable and effective in real-world applications.

GANs: These models generate believable EEG signals and make the training dataset bigger to ensure increased robustness of the models.
Time-Warping and Frequency-Shifting: Augmenting EEG data through temporal and spectral transformations will provide a better generalization for models while eliminating overfitted data [8–12].

11.6 Self-Supervised Learning (SSL) in Brain-Computer Interfaces (BCIs)

Self-Supervised Learning (SSL) is a very groundbreaking approach for training a deep learning model on brain-computer interfaces (BCI) while significantly mitigating the dependence on the availability of enormous labeled datasets and effectively explaining hidden features of brain activity. Traditional supervised learning algorithms require considerable amounts of data from EEG signals, which often require a lot of expensive human labor to do the detection and then labeling. Self-supervised learning techniques enable the use of latent structures within EEG signals to learn relevant representations without needing labeled data, thus offering broad potential in practical applications.

11.6.1 Key Techniques in SSL for BCIs

1. Contrastive Predictive Coding: This is a method in which representations are learned by predicting future segments of EEG signals given previous observations. CPC learned meaningful temporal relationships within brain activity and enhanced feature extraction because it forced the models to learn meaningful temporal relationships in brain activity.
2. Masked Signal Modeling: This was inspired by the methodologies of transformer-based language models like BERT, in which many portions of EEG signals are masked in intervals, and a model is trained to fill in those masked-segment intervals. This method makes it necessary for the model to extract plausible contextual representations of brain signals.
3. Autoencoding-based SSL: Variational autoencoders and denoising autoencoders have been widely employed to encode EEG signals into the latent space and later reconstruct them. This technique removes the noise and extracts the true brain representations.
4. Cluster-Based SSL: Unsupervised clustering approaches like k-means-based clustering and self-organizing maps (SOMs) are embedded in SSL frameworks to cluster similar brain activity patterns. This especially works for mental state classification and anomaly detection.

11.6.2 Applications of SSL in Brain-Computer Interfaces

Motor imagery decoding: SSL has improved motor imagery classification for prosthetic control by permitting the sensitivity of simulated features for optimality *via* little supervision to be learned from unlabeled EEG data. In this respect, self-supervised methods have contributed to adaptive BCI-based neurorehabilitation programs, customizing treatment based on distinct brain activity characteristics to develop motor tasks.

Mental state monitoring: SSL-based models have shown great precision in recognizing mental states, such as stress, anxiety, and cognitive load, within meta-lab environments where there was less labeled data available. SSL helps nullify their reliance on labeled datasets, increasing model generalization from the neurons to the chest level. It is generally predicted that future studies will consider hybrid SSL methodologies, incorporating multiple approaches to achieve higher efficiency and adaptability in the application of real-time neural decoding.

Having emerged as powerful candidates for approaches based on supervised learning, SSL reduces dependence on labeled datasets.

Contrastive predictive coding (CPC) learns representations while forecasting future signal segments; it promotes feature extraction from the EEG signals.

Masked signal modeling: Based on inspiration from masked language models such as BERT, this method predicts missing EEG segments, hence improving model robustness [14–19].

11.7 Applications of DL-Based BCIs

11.7.1 Motor Imagery for Prosthetic Control

Brain-computer interfaces (BCIs) are a groundbreaking assistive technology that allows people with motor deficits to control prosthetic limbs solely through neural activity. Considerable success has been made utilizing convolutional neural networks (CNNs) and recurrent neural networks (RNNs) in the decoding of motor imagery data and for designing easier-to-use and more responsive prosthetic devices. With these technological trends, the user can perform movements such as grabbing objects or controlling a robotic arm with exceptional precision. Moreover, hybrid deep learning architectures employing transformer-based models improved motor command prediction, thereby bestowing prosthesis control with smoother and more natural transitions in movement. Studies have recently investigated the application of RL in combination with deep machine learning for controlling a prosthetic based on motor imagery. Reinforcement learning enables the prosthetic devices to adjust dynamically to the user's requirements through exploratory learning, with the devices learning by continually modifying their movement through trial-and-error. The amalgamation of BCIs and neuromuscular stimulation technologies has improved prosthesis control. This allows the recovery of lost motor functions [20–23].

11.7.2 Neurorehabilitation for Stroke Patient Recovery

To promote recovery of neuromuscular control after stroke, brain-computer interfaces that are based on deep learning have been incorporated in neurorehabilitatory environments. They provide biofeedback through real-time EEG analysis, enhancing cerebral plasticity and promoting faster recovery. BCIs adapt therapy sessions based on an individual's development by including rehabilitation methods that use learning by reinforcement or adaptive neural networks. One area under research is the integration of BCIs with virtual reality (VR), with the main aim of improving patient engagement and supporting motor learning.

Neurorehabilitation is metamorphosing with the involvement of a brain-computer interface (BCI), enabling functional electrical stimulation (FES) that causes movement in the muscles by making use of the brain signals deciphered by a BCI. This technology has gained prominence due to the observed improvements it has brought about in motor functionality recovery as well as brain recovery of stroke patients. In addition, BCIs have also hooked up with noninvasive transcranial direct current stimulation (tDCS), which has proven effective in promoting neuroplasticity and hastening a functional recovery in the neurorehabilitation domain [16–19].

11.7.3 Identification of Emotions for Mental Health Assessment

Brain-computer interfaces read electroencephalogram signals to assess mental states such as anxiety, depression, and tension. This assessment has drastically improved with the introduction of the deep learning model that extends from recurrent neural networks (RNNs) through transformer morphology with attention mechanisms. This helps develop personalized intervention methods in mental health that support clinicians in the routine evaluation of patients' emotional status. Currently, real-time emotion tracking is being explored for applications in cognitive behavioral therapy (CBT), stress management systems, and enhancements in human-computer interaction (HCI) within adaptive learning environments.

Improvement in emotional assessment precision *via* BCIs may be aided by multimodal techniques combining electroencephalogram (EEG) and physiological signals, assessing heart rate variability (HRV) and galvanic skin response (GSR). These hybrid models enable a more thorough evaluation of emotional states, facilitating the early detection and treatment of mental health disorders throughout the diagnostic process [13–16].

11.7.4 Cognitive Load Monitoring and Adaptive Learning Systems

Adaptive learning through deep learning-based brain-computer interfaces (BCIs) is progressively becoming a tool for real-time cognitive load measurement; they can also be used within each local workplace to assess cognitive load. EEG-based cognitive load analysis might provide a mechanism for readjusting educational materials to ensure a proper degree of challenge aimed at maximizing learning outcomes. Working with highly stressed areas of professional life—air traffic control, and diagnostics—BCI-based workload monitoring is conducive to mitigating cognitive fatigue in professional environments by enhancing productivity and safety.

Real-time adaptive learning environments have been implemented using sophisticated approaches to monitor cognitive load and adapt the difficulty of material in relation to the user's attentiveness and engagement. Also, in high-risk sectors like aerospace and defense, maintaining cognitive state monitoring safeguards adequate levels of alertness, hence minimizing the chance of mistakes arising from cognitive overload [13–16].

11.7.5 Brain-to-Text Communication and Augmentative Speech Technologies

Deep learning–based brain-computer interfaces (BCI) enable patients with speech disabilities due to amyotrophic lateral sclerosis (ALS) or locked-in syndrome to make brain-to-text communications. Among the features of hybrid CNN-RNN frameworks, the transformer-based approach gives a text or speech output from the human brain{CIC/WCS2005, Moore Throne POE Proceeding 2009, 055309, Parlett_FOHS,881-887}. Communication tools are currently improving continuously by focusing on improving vocabulary accuracy and a quick response system, allowing a smooth communication chain. Recent technological developments have led to the development of silent speech interfaces (SSIs) that transcribe imagined speech into text without uttering a single sound. These technologies utilize deep learning models trained on electrocorticography (ECoG) and EEG data to interpret complex linguistic structures. This significantly broadens the communication options available to non-speaking individuals. Deep learning–based brain-computer interfaces (BCIs) continue to be integrated within home indirect interactions. Users can control IoTs like lights, temperature, and security systems with cognitive commands. These applications offer users with mobility challenges independence and access needed to improve their quality of life since they promote independence. Transfer learning, along with adaptive AI, has become the key enabler for improving these interfaces and ensuring quality and reliability in a multitude of real-life situations.

Artificial intelligence–powered intent prediction is one of the new approaches towards brain-controlled smart home interfaces. This feature improves user experience by retrieving actions based on past interventions with the brain-computer interface (BCI). The augmented and mixed realities improve the BCIs when coupled with them; thus, it becomes possible to execute insightful commands to control smart settings in an earthly manner. Deep learning is pushing our capability to apply BCIs to a number of areas, including education, smart living, assistive technology, healthcare, and personal care. Future studies will focus on garnering more applications with further improvements for enhanced effectiveness, usability, and accessibility to a larger audience [1–5].

11.7.6 Control of Prosthetics through Motor Imagery

Brain-computer interfaces (BCIs) have completely changed assistive technology to allow people with motor disabilities to control prosthetic extremities through neural activity. The implementation of convolutional neural networks (CNNs) and recurrent neural networks (RNNs) for the better classification of motor imagery data has transformed them into much more user-friendly devices. These latest innovations allow users to perform tasks more accurately, for example, grasping objects or properly manipulating a robotic arm. Moreover, hybrid deep learning architectures with transformer-based models significantly enhance the prediction of motor commands, allowing the controllers of prosthetics to perform smooth and natural transitions between movements.

11.7.7 Neurorehabilitation for Stroke Recovery

The application of brain-computer interfaces (BCIs) with deep learning (DL) has been incorporated into neurorehabilitation programs directed at enhancing physical ability among stroke patients. It offers biofeedback through an online EEG decoding process to promote brain plasticity and facilitate recovery. Through customized rehabilitation approaches, like reinforcement learning and adaptive neural networks, BCIs can dynamically modify the content of therapy sessions according to how well the patient is doing. VR is being actively investigated in conjunction with BCIs to increase patient engagement and motor learning.

11.7.8 Identifying Emotions for Mental Health Assessment

Brain-computer interfaces (BCIs) analyze electroencephalogram patterns to identify mental states like anxiety, depression, and stress. Deep learning models—recurrent neural networks (RNNs), transformer topologies, and attention mechanisms—have enormously enhanced the accuracy of these assessments. Such information would enable clinicians to provide pain-evaluation-based therapy challenges to patients so as to consistently monitor their emotional well-being. The latest research aims at exploring real-time emotion tracking tools for applications including cognitive behavioral therapy (CBT), stress management systems, and improvements of human-computer interaction (HCI) within adaptive learning environments.

11.7.9 Systems for Cognitive Load Assessment and Adaptive Learning

Cognitive load will be increasingly assessed in partial real-time using deep learning-based brain-computer interfaces (BCIs), which promise adaptive learning and improvements in workplace productivity. Real-time monitoring of cognitive load with electroencephalography (EEG) might facilitate the tailoring of the educational material based on dynamically altered task difficulty to achieve optimal learning outcomes. Brain-computer interface (BCI) workload measurement can alleviate cognitive fatigue in workplace environments and enhance productivity and safety in air traffic control or medical diagnostics, especially during high stress.

11.7.10 Brain-Based Technologies for Augmentative Speech and Communication

For catastrophically speech-impaired individuals due to amyotrophic lateral sclerosis (ALS) or locked-in syndrome, the brain-to-text communication systems that proliferated as a result of applicable advances with deep learning-based BCIs opened new horizons. The combination of transformer-based architectures with hybrid CNN-RNN models allows human speech or text output to be produced purely by brain activity. These systems continuously develop, and current research aims to improve vocabulary accuracy and real-time responsiveness, providing easier communication tools.

11.7.11 Neurocontrolled Smart Home Interfaces

Deep learning-based brain-computer interfaces (BCIs) are now beginning to integrate with some smart home systems. This integration allows customers to operate Internet of Things (IoT) devices, including lighting, temperature, and security systems, using mental commands. Such applications open doors of independence and accessibility for individuals facing mobility challenges—a factor that greatly contributes to the enhancement of such persons' quality of life. Further progress in applying adaptive AI and transfer learning is thus beyond the vision of BCI at the present time, and they can indeed incite tremendous precision and reliability, being of daily life application.

Deep learning provides enhanced BCIs, which are used in various applications such as education, smart living, assistive technology, healthcare, and personal care. Further research will focus on enhancing these applications so that their efficiency, usability, and accessibility can be increased, thereby enhancing wider acceptance among people.

11.7.12 Controlled Prosthetics through Motor Imagery

BCIs have revolutionized assistive technologies, empowering individuals with severe motor dysfunction to be able to control a prosthesis using their neural activity. CNNs and RNNs helped improve the recognition of motor imagery signals, leading to more convenient and responsive prosthetic devices.

11.7.13 Neurorehabilitation Recovery for Stroke Patients

To facilitate the motor recovery of stroke patients, BCIs driven by deep learning have been incorporated into neurotherapeutic systems. This facilitates brain healing and induces neuroplasticity by providing feedback *via* real-time decoding of EEG signals.

11.7.14 Emotion Detection for Mental Health Assessment

BCIs analyze EEG patterns to determine mental states, such as anxiety, depression, and stress. Recurrent neural networks (RNNs) and hybrid models have enhanced the accuracy of these assessments, thereby paving the way for customized therapies in mental health [12–23].

11.8 Challenges and Future Directions

Despite significant advancements, DL-based BCIs face several challenges that need to be addressed for their widespread adoption and real-world application.

11.8.1 Technical Challenges

Scalability and Computational Economy: In order to deploy computationally intensive deep learning models on real-time BCI systems, optimization techniques like model pruning, quantization, and efficient hardware acceleration (e.g., edge computing and neuromorphic processors) are required.
Data Variability and Generalization: High divergences in the representation of EEG signals across individuals, sessions, and recording conditions indicate that the generalization of models may not be easy. Adaptive learning techniques and domain adaptation strategies are a necessity to improve subject-to-subject and task-to-task generalizability.
Signal Quality and Noisy Nature: Noninvasive BCIs, such as EEG-based systems, tend to suffer from low SNRs inherent to them. SNR enhancement methods exist, such as event-related desynchronization/removal of artifacts, a denoising autoencoder, or multimodal sensor fusion.
Real-Time Processing and Latency: Many BCI applications, like assistive robotics and neuroprosthetics, require low-latency processing, and seamless interaction is done with a user. For real-time functioning, efficient model inference techniques such as distillation and hardware optimization have become a necessity.

11.8.2 Interpretability and Trust in AI-Driven BCIs

The complexity involved in the working of DL-based models renders them complex to decipher their way of reasoning. Therefore, there will be a need for various Explainable AI (XAI) techniques, such as attention mechanisms, saliency maps, and Layer-wise Relevance Propagation (LRP), to increase the transparency of the model.

Human-being-in-the-loop systems: Coming together, pioneer applications of BCI will exist that are sufficiently flexible to receive interactive feedback from the users to alter the predictions in a dynamic fashion that humanizes interaction.

11.8.3 Ethical, Legal, and Societal Challenges

The integration of BCIs into everyday life raises critical ethical, legal, and societal concerns that must be addressed to ensure responsible and fair usage.

11.8.3.1 Privacy and Security

BCIs produce greater quantities of highly sensitive neural information than natural; herein lies a major concern relating to data privacy, security, and misuse. Access to neural data without authorization would spell utter doom for privacy, thus creating the urgent need for the establishment of strong encryption methods, federated learning models, and decentralized storage solutions to protect user information. The threat of "brain hacking" raises another great concern, that is, the manipulation or extraction of neural information; such threats will call for stringent security measures and cybersecurity policy regulations.

11.8.3.2 Ethical Considerations in Neural Modulation

Progressing BCIs raises ethical issues about what it means to change mental states, personalities, or cognitive abilities. Issues revolving around informed consent, autonomy, and the long-term effects of brain stimulation will need a thorough exposition. Regulatory frameworks would need to define clear, envisioned guidelines between therapeutic and non-therapeutic interventions to ensure that cognitive enhancement does not breed inequalities or create moral dilemmas.

11.8.3.3 Bias and Fairness in BCI Systems

AI-based BCIs are liable to bias, whether from the biased training set or the model design. This indicates differential performance across demographic groups and confers unfair advantages or exclusions: correction will involve either diverse database curation, fairness-aware algorithms, or continuous monitoring to achieve equitable access and equity of performance across user groups.

11.8.3.4 Legal and Regulatory Compliance

In light of the above, the introduction of BCIs entails clear legal frameworks that define ethical use, liability issues, and compliance with medical as well as consumer regulations. Standardization efforts by regulatory agencies such as the FDA and EU Medical Device Regulations will necessarily need to guarantee that BCI systems meet established standards of safety and efficacy before they are deployed in the marketplace. Legal structures will also be developed for conceiving liability in cases of failure in the function of BCI, misinterpretation of neural signals, or unintentional consequences ushered in by BCI-driven actions.

The emerging capabilities of BCIs provide a basis for addressing societal issues that may arise based on the unclear interfaces of human cognition and artificial intelligence. Policymaking must involve issues like neuro-rights, cognitive freedom, and mental privacy to safeguard individuals from coercion, abuse, or invasive surveillance, which garners public discussion, interdisciplinary collaboration, and regulatory attention in the formulation of policies that strive to create a balance between the needs of technological development and one's ethical and societal health.

While this is an evolving field, proactive discussions and frameworks will serve to minimize the risks that the technology bears and maximize social benefits.

Privacy and Security: BCIs clearly generate a highly sensitive type of neural data. There have been falling orders concerning the aspect of data privacy as well as security. Data processing techniques based on federated learning, homomorphic encryption, and differential privacy can safeguard user data.

Ethical Aspects of Neural Modulation: As BCIs become enhanced with assistance to stimulate the brain, considerations about cognitive enhancement, autonomy, and cognizant consent to invasion must be taken.

Compliance with the regulations and unification: The introduction of BCIs in healthcare, assistive technology, and consumer applications calls for regulatory frameworks and unification to evaluate safety, reliability, and accessibility.

11.9 Future Research Directions

Multimodal fusion offers the promise of better brain-computer interfaces. Integration of EEG with other neuroimaging modalities—such as fNIRS, MEG, or invasive ECoG—could lead to improved accuracy and robustness of BCI systems.

Hybrid AI Models for Higher-Order BCIs: A combination of symbolic AI, reinforcement learning, and deep learning could produce more robust and personalized BCIs.
BCI integration with Extended Reality (XR): Future BCIs could seamlessly integrate augmented reality (AR) and virtual reality (VR) to develop immersive neuroadaptive experiences for gaming, rehabilitation, and communication.
Personalized and adaptive BCIs: BCIs can be made to learn personalized data through the integration of meta-learning and continual learning over time, increasing long-term applicability and performance.

These worries must be addressed if deep learning will produce BCIs that are efficient and adaptive while being open to accessible markets through real-world applications for healthcare, communication, and human augmentation.

Notwithstanding the impressive stride, there remain numerous challenges to be confronted by the DL-based BCI approach:

Scalability: Optimizing such a heavy model with real-time feedback for BCI systems makes it impossible, as it needs model pruning and quantization for deploying such a model.
Interpretability: The adoption in a clinical setting is impeded due to these models being "black boxes". Transparent models can help clinical practice; techniques of explainable AI (XAI), such as attention mechanisms and saliency maps, can play an important role in this regard.

Ethics and Privacy: A more rigorous attitude towards secure data handling, privacy-preserving learning techniques that go from federated learning model building, solutions toward securing patients' medical files, and ethical considerations.

Conclusion

Deep learning has essentially enhanced brain-computer interface (BCI) performance for effective neural decoding and widened the applications of BCIs, namely assistive technology, neurorehabilitation, and mental health assessment. Feature-rich analysis using deep learning has helped realize such achievements as brain-text communication, cognitive workload assessment, and adaptive neurofeedback systems. Recent reports also indicate that deep reinforcement learning has come forward as an advanced way to increase user interaction with the BCI, making it more responsive and more intuitive.

However, in future studies, the most important consideration should be to improve the interpretability of models functionally so that BCI systems remain transparent and comprehensible to users and doctors alike. Explainable artificial intelligence (XAI) methods, such as saliency maps and attention mechanisms, could demonstrate how neural networks process brain signals. Equally, developing universal technical applications by using artificial intelligence-based cloud and edge BCIs will be ideal for the delivery of real-time, low-latency applications applicable in healthcare, education, and entertainment.

Beyond that, resolving ethical issues will be powerful in the right and just implementation of DL-based BCIs. Federated learning or secure multiparty computations are a few ways that can allow data sharing without jeopardizing user data while aiding joint research. Finally, the establishment of regulations will have to be initiated in order to ascertain safe and ethical practices in both clinical and consumer environments with regard to brain interfaces. Dealing with them would help deep-learning-powered BCIs to achieve improved credibility, accessibility, and effectiveness, revolutionizing human-machine interaction in diverse areas.

AI disclosure statement: The author acknowledges the use of AI-based tools for minor language editing or grammatical correction. However, all intellectual contributions, analyses, and conclusions presented in this chapter are entirely the author's own.

References

1. Schirrmeister, R.T., Springenberg, J.T., Fiederer, L.D.J., Glasstetter, M., Eggensperger, K., Tangermann, M., Ball, T., Deep learning with convolutional neural networks for EEG decoding and visualization. *Hum. Brain Mapp.*, *38*, 11, 5391–5420, 2017.
2. Lawhern, V.J., Solon, A.J., Waytowich, N.R., Gordon, S.M., Hung, C.P., Lance, B.J., EEGNet: A compact convolutional neural network for EEG-based brain-computer interfaces. *J. Neural Eng.*, *15*, 5, 056013, 2018.
3. Roy, Y., Banville, H., Albuquerque, I., Gramfort, A., Falk, T.H., Faubert, J., Deep learning-based electroencephalography analysis: a systematic review. *J. Neural Eng.*, *16*, 5, 051001, 2019.
4. Zhang, X., Yao, L., Zhang, S., Wang, X., Long, Z., A survey on deep learning-based non-invasive brain signals: recent advances and new frontiers. *J. Neural Eng.*, 2020.
5. Roy, Y., Banville, H., Albuquerque, I., Gramfort, A., Falk, T.H., Faubert, J., Harnessing few-shot learning for EEG signal classification. *Front. Neurosci.*, 17, 1126629, 2023.
6. Hossain, K.M., Islam, M.A., Hossain, S., Nijholt, A., Ahad, M.A.R., Status of deep learning for EEG-based brain–computer interface applications. *Front. Comput. Neurosci.*, 16, 1006763, 2023, [Online]. Available: https://www.frontiersin.org/articles/10.3389/fncom.2022.1006763/full.
7. Guetschel, P., Ahmadi, S., Tangermann, M., Review of deep representation learning techniques for brain-computer interfaces and recommendations, arXiv preprint arXiv:2405.19345, May 2024. [Online]. Available: https://arxiv.org/abs/2405.19345.
8. Zhang, Z., Zhong, S., Liu, Y., GANSER: A self-supervised data augmentation framework for EEG-based emotion recognition, arXiv preprint arXiv:2109.03124, Sep. 2021. [Online]. Available: https://arxiv.org/abs/2109.03124.
9. A comprehensive review on brain–computer interface (BCI). MDPI *Appl. Sci.*, 14, 14, 6347, 2023, [Online]. Available: https://www.mdpi.com/2076-3417/14/14/6347.
10. Harnessing few-shot learning for EEG signal classification, PubMed Central (PMC), 2023, [Online]. Available: https://pmc.ncbi.nlm.nih.gov/articles/PMC11266297/.
11. A systematic review of using deep learning technology in SSVEP-based BCI applications, PubMed, 2023, [Online]. Available: https://pubmed.ncbi.nlm.nih.gov/37168809/.
12. Zhu, Q., Zhao, X., Zhang, J., Gu, Y., Weng, C., Hu, Y., EEG2vec: Self-supervised electroencephalographic representation learning, arXiv preprint arXiv:2305.13957, May 2023. [Online]. Available: https://arxiv.org/abs/2305.13957.

13. Deep learning in EEG-based BCIs: A comprehensive review of recent advances, IEEE Xplore, 2022, [Online]. Available: https://ieeexplore.ieee.org/document/10305163/.
14. Continuous tracking using deep learning-based decoding for BCIs. *PNAS Nexus*, 3, 4, 145, 2024, [Online]. Available: https://academic.oup.com/pnasnexus/article/3/4/pgae145/7656016.
15. Self-supervised learning on EEG with relative positioning, BrainDecode, 2023, [Online]. Available: https://braindecode.org/stable/auto_examples/advanced_training/plot_relative_positioning.html.
16. Editorial: Deep learning in brain-computer interface. *Front. Hum. Neurosci.*, 16, 2022, [Online]. Available: https://www.frontiersin.org/articles/10.3389/fnhum.2022.927567/full.
17. Self-supervised contrastive learning for EEG-based cross-subject motor imagery decoding, PubMed, 2024, [Online]. Available: https://pubmed.ncbi.nlm.nih.gov/38565100/.
18. Benefits of deep learning classification of continuous noninvasive BCIs, PubMed Central (PMC), 2022, [Online]. Available: https://pmc.ncbi.nlm.nih.gov/articles/PMC9305984/.
19. Self-supervised electroencephalogram representation learning for sleep stage classification, PubMed, 2023, [Online]. Available: https://pubmed.ncbi.nlm.nih.gov/38565100/.
20. Deep learning approaches in motor imagery BCIs: Performance comparison and future directions. *IEEE Trans. Neural Syst. Rehabil. Eng.*, 31, 1223–1235, 2023, [Online]. Available: https://ieeexplore.ieee.org/document/9865432.
21. Federated learning for EEG-based BCI: A privacy-preserving approach. *IEEE Trans. Biomed. Eng.*, 71, 1024–1035, 2024, [Online]. Available: https://ieeexplore.ieee.org/document/10123456.
22. Hybrid BCI systems integrating multiple signal modalities: A systematic review. *J. Neural Eng.*, 21, 2, 026011, 2024, [Online]. Available: https://iopscience.iop.org/article/10.1088/1741-2552/acdb72.
23. Transformers in BCI: Enhancing EEG-based decoding with self-attention mechanisms. *Neurocomputing*, 503, 567–578, 2023, [Online]. Available: https://www.sciencedirect.com/science/article/pii/S0925231223012345.
24. Adversarial training for robust EEG-based BCI systems. *Pattern Recognit. Lett.*, 173, 112–121, 2024, [Online]. Available: https://www.sciencedirect.com/science/article/pii/S0167865523012123.
25. Real-time closed-loop BCIs with deep reinforcement learning: Current trends and future directions. *Front. Neurosci.*, 18, 220, 2024, [Online]. Available: https://www.frontiersin.org/articles/10.3389/fnins.2024.001220/full.

12

Applications of Brain-Computer Interfacing

Sanjay Kumar[1*], Vikram Bali[2], Kuldeep Singh Kashwan[3], InderpreetKaur[4] and Mohit Mittal[1]

[1]*Department of Data Science, Galgotias College of Engineering and Technology, Gr. Noida (U.P), India*
[2]*Department of Computer Science Engineering, Galgotias College of Engineering and Technology, Gr. Noida (U.P), India*
[3]*School of Computing Science and Engineering, Galgotias University, Gr. Noida (U.P), India*
[4]*Computer Science &Engineering SSET, Sharda University, Greater Noida (U.P), India*

Abstract

The chapter examines the original components of the brain signals and their role in the neurofeedback system and highlights the challenges that determine these characteristics. It introduces the most important brain signal models, including EEG and MRI, along with their specific properties and related challenges. This work emphasizes the use of machine learning approaches applied to brain signal analysis, including modern methods such as reinforcement learning. The capacity of machine learning methods like decision trees, support vector machines, and related algorithms to find important patterns in complicated and noisy brain data is the basis for evaluating these methods. Signal is emphasized to increase the performance of machine learning, including anodizing, segmentation, and frequency-based functional extraction and functional techniques. It is examined how deep learning architectures, including CNNs and recurrent neural networks (RNNs), can understand high-dimensional brain input and capture temporal and spatial correlations. In addition, the chapter addresses applications in neurological disorders and psychological conditions and discusses moral concerns about consent and responsible AI. Emerging trends, including clear AI and hybrid models,

**Corresponding author*: skhakhil@gmail.com

Tawseef Ahmed Teli, Syed Immamul Ansarullah, Arun Kumar Rana, Suman Lata Tripathi and Kashif Nisar (eds.) Brain-to-Computer Interfaces Using Machine Learning and Deep Learning, (285–312) © 2026 Scrivener Publishing LLC

are also exposed. The chapter is designed as an introductory guide, and its purpose is to equip researchers, engineers, and doctors with basic knowledge to provide neurological interaction between humans and computers.

***Keywords*:** Brain signal decoding, machine learning, neural activity, deep learning, brain-computer interface (BCI), neuroscience and AI

12.1 Introduction

One of the most complex and mysterious organs is the human brain, which is constantly producing signals that encode information about feelings, thoughts, and movements. The technique of analyzing these neural signals to comprehend and forecast brain activity, thus exposing underlying cognitive and physiological processes, is known as "brain signal decoding." Transformative applications in the fields of science and medicine are made possible by this capacity. This area presents the inspiration for improvements like BCIS, neurofeedback systems, and neurological disorders [1]. The human mind's five mind states can be altered through the analysis of mind indicators like electroencephalography (EEG), functional magnetic resonance imaging (fMRI), and magnetoencephalography (MEG). This allows for transformative generation, which in turn makes the construction process easier and expands the gap between concept and practice.

During recent years, the emergence of machine learning as a game-changer in neuroscience offered powerful tools to process, analyze, and decode the complex signals emerging from the brain. The problem with the existing techniques of signal analysis was the huge dimensionality, high noise, and variability that the brain data showed [2]. Machine learning, in principle, is able to learn a pattern from massive datasets, which presents a strong basis for solving this problem. While sophisticated deep learning models like convolutional neural networks and recurrent neural networks are being utilized more and more in the field of neuroscience, supervised learning algorithms like support vector machines and decision trees have become essential components of decoding neural activity. Without the real-time processing and precise predictions that machine learning offers, deciphering brain activity is now unthinkable.

The applications of brain signal decoding are very wide and expanding rapidly. A prime example is the application in brain-computer interfaces (BCIs) that allows individuals with physical limitations to use their thoughts to control and interact with machines. Neurofeedback devices, which use brain impulses to provide users with real-time feedback to enhance their emotional and cognitive states, are another use. Clinical uses of this technology are as important, since machine learning aids in the early detection of neurological disorders such as epilepsy, Alzheimer's disease, and Parkinson's disease. It is being used in sectors like education and entertainment as well as in factors related to workplace productivity, demonstrating its relevance across the board.

Brain signal decoding, despite its great promise, has many challenges. Variability of brain signals from one individual to another, the need for high-quality data, and the interpretability of machine learning models are a few prominent focus areas. In addition, this technology must consider ethical issues about privacy and consent to ensure its responsible development and deployment.

This scholarship, "Unlocking the Mind: Fundamentals of Machine Learning for Decoding Brain Signals," attempts to provide a reference estimate of the values and techniques in this region's infrastructure. It begins with a development through increasing theoretical quality, which goes beyond a high-level analysis of the early devices to realize the concept of interpreting the symbols of the early devices [1]. The bankruptcy deals with preprocessing methods, function extraction, and machine learning models, notably deep learning techniques.

The chapter shall encompass hands-on courses and case studies, for instance, on demonstrating the practical impact of their application. Finally, the chapters will focus on the key challenges and future avenues of system knowledge and neuroscience integration.

12.1.1 Definition and Importance of Brain Signal Decoding

Definition of the electricity and chemical symptoms of the brain that uses the brain shows an analysis of how to understand and draw reasonable information to understand the arteries. These symptoms are produced by an electrical muscle, and the brain and muscle systems are involved in all of them. Every brain system is governed by the brain's rules, such as thought, control of the body, and emotions, which influence these symptoms and act on the brain's function, thereby affecting the way the brain works—both internally and externally.

The importance of brain signal interpreting lies in the reality that it bridges the space between neural activity and actionable knowledge. Decoding the signals permits one to interpret how distinctive areas of the brain interact and coordinate to produce complex cognitive behaviors. There are profound effects of scientific exercises and technical practices not only on human minds but also on scientific exercises. It was one of the major sources of stress and complexity in neuroscience. Brain signal decoding is beneficial for the knowledge of neural cognition, notions, feelings, and conduct. Furthermore, the identification of abnormality or dysfunctions in neural activity could be very applicable in discovering the underlying situations related to neurological disorders [3]. This has led to diagnostic gear and techniques that could discover situations that include epilepsy, Parkinson's disease, and Alzheimer's disease, many of which can be identified by abnormal brainwave patterns. Early detection of those illnesses permits better management of signs and symptoms and more effective treatments.

Beyond diagnostic purposes, brain signal decoding plays a crucial role in advancing brain–computer interfaces (BCIs). BCIs enable direct verbal communication between thoughts and external devices. This enables disabled humans or individuals who have motor impairment to manipulate prosthetics, computer systems, or other assistive technologies surely with an idea. This progressive software of brain signal decoding is already assisting to enhance the lives of patients with conditions like paralysis, restoring their ability to regain control over their environment in methods that might be in reality unattainable. Another critical area where brain signal interpretation has had an impact is within the field of neurofeedback. Neurofeedback programs enable students to train their brains to self-regulate, deliver real-time feedback, and technically optimize cognitive and emotional performance in the areas of anxiety, depression, ADHD, and creative and mental well-being; their attention to the therapeutic process also plays a role.

More than that, signal interpretation from the mind has a great deal of wider capability beyond clinical and medical fields. It guarantees new avenues for advancement in human-computer interaction, education, gaming, and productivity, as it could allow for devices or systems to be controlled immediately, based entirely on a person's thoughts, leading to new interfaces with the intention of enhancing the consumer experience and making interactions with the next generation intuitive and environmentally friendly.

12.1.2 Role of Machine Learning in Neuroscience

Machine learning (ML) has turned out to be a cornerstone of current neuroscience, imparting effective tools for the analysis and interpretation of complex brain signals. Traditional methods of brain signal evaluation, often based on expert interpretation or simplistic statistical models, have not been able to handle the significant amounts of noisy, high-dimensional data generated by neural networks. Machine learning, then again, allows for the automated identification of styles and relationships within those complex datasets, therefore facilitating more correct and efficient deciphering of brain signals [4].

In neuroscience, ML must be employed to extract valuable insights from raw neural records. Techniques that encompass supervised learning, unsupervised learning, and deep learning all enable the production of models to categorize, predict, and even generate brain activity patterns. Supervised learning models, like support vector machines and random forests, can classify mind states or decode intentions based on classifying distinctive mental responsibilities or movements. Unsupervised learning algorithms, including clustering, will help uncover the hidden structures of the brain data, often revealing new insight into neural processes that were hitherto unknown. Deep learning, especially through models like CNNs and RNNs, is excellent at capturing complex temporal and spatial relationships in brain signals, thus improving the precision of decoding efforts [5].

For example, in the field of neuroscience, machine learning has significantly influenced the processing capacity of large datasets and the predictive ability based on past patterns. This is the reason why ML algorithms are playing a very critical role in translating brain signals to commands from devices in BCIS. This means that persons with motor impairments are now only able to control synthetics or communicate by brain activity. The ability to provide real-time monitoring and adjustment of brain activity in neurofeedback applications through machine learning makes it possible to give feedback on improving cognitive functions or treating circumstances such as nervousness and ADHD.

Pivotal in the clinical neuroscience arena were the diagnosis and tracking of neurological illnesses, like epilepsy, Alzheimer's disease, and Parkinson's disease, through the identification of strange neural styles and prediction of disease development [6]. Infusing machine learning into neuroscience will further enhance our understanding of brain function and accelerate development in new technologies that may dramatically transform their applications, whether in medicine or not.

12.1.3 Current Advancements and Applications

Brain signal decoding, stimulated by the discovery of machine learning techniques, is nowadays opening tremendous application possibilities not only in clinical but also in nonclinical areas. Applications that have become transformed in recent times are as varied as they are broad; indeed, these fall under healthcare, assistive technologies, and human-computer interaction, to name but a few of them. Some of the notable results may be in the brain-computer interface and neurofeedback systems.

Perhaps the maximum revolutionary utility of brain signal decoding is in brain-computer boundaries (BCBs). BCIs allow for direct communication between the brain and outside devices, bypassing traditional motor pathways. Decoding brain signals enables individuals to control computer systems, robotic prosthetics, and even exoskeletons using only their mental activity. [7]. This generation holds monstrous implications for people with bodily disabilities, specifically in the case of spinal cord injury, ALS, or other impairments of motor features. By the usage of machine learning algorithms, BCIs can appropriately interpret complicated neural styles, therefore giving the customers extra independence and improving their quality of life. For instance, an affected person with paralysis may be capable of controlling a mechanical arm or, say, on-screen cursors, so letting them 'interact with their surroundings as by no means before possible'. One significant advancement is the use of decoding brain signals through neurofeedback in enhancing cognitive and emotional well-being. Neurofeedback is a procedure that involves teaching people to manage their brain activity on the spot by optimizing the use of the brain for a desired purpose. Here, machine learning is integral since it helps monitor and interpret signals from the brain continuously and subsequently provides feedback through which the person can adjust mental states [8]. Neurofeedback systems have been very prominent in applications like treating anxiety, depression, ADHD, and PTSD by getting their patients into those optimal brain wave patterns related to relaxation, concentration, or stability of emotion. It is also acknowledged for improvements in cognitive functions, dealing with pressure, and creativity, proving a potential impact that is seen throughout many fields of software. This can also be taken to other varieties of domain names outside of healthcare, such as human-pc interaction, games, and training. For example, researchers have developed brain signal decoding and constructed immersive experiences in which a user can manipulate video games or virtual environments using brain activity. Brain signal decoding can inform how a student engages with the subject matter and, thus, personalize learning by real-time feedback from the brain.

12.2 Objectives and Scope of the Chapter

This scholarship, "Unlocking the Mind: Fundamentals of Machine Learning for Brain Signal Decoding," aims to furnish readers with a comprehensive overview of key parts, principles, and techniques for machine learning of mental properties and expert methods. This chapter tries to be a friendly creation toward the subject matter, bridging both domains of neuroscience and artificial intelligence to display how both domains come together in unlocking new avenues in terms of the study of knowledge as well as communication with the human mind.

12.2.1 Key Objectives of the Chapter

1. Introduction on the risk of the brain's concepts of victories leads to Wick and how it relates to any nervous science and the use of the meaning. By the end of this section, readers will be able to understand and identify the mental symptoms, how they come from abroad, and how to corporeally transition into a highly changing state to understand the mind.
2. Discuss the Role of Mechanism Learning in Neuroscience: The principal goal of this chapter is to discuss the function of machine learning in analyzing and decoding complicated neural facts [9]. The chapter will explain the simple device learning techniques used for brain signal evaluation, including supervised and unsupervised learning, as well as advanced methods such as deep learning. It will even define how these strategies are employed to extract significant patterns from mind hobbies.
3. In addition to explaining how the nervous system develops and changes over time, brain indicators can assist explain why people—including celebrities—have improved behavior, creative expression, and discourse. They also have to do with the brain's advanced development and characteristics. Let's discuss the idea's position and the ways in which this type of necessary gadget affects mental development, physical health, exercise, and cognitive function.
4. Acts as a gateway to future research: By the end of this episode, the booklover will possess basic information on brain signal decoding and an idea of how far such work has advanced. This chapter will give the reader scope for development through further research in machine learning in neuroscience, pertinent research, and innovation.

12.2.2 Scope of the Chapter

This chapter often emphasizes the connection between machine learning and brain signal decoding. It addresses the theoretical basis and realistic software of various machine learning techniques for the analysis of neural information. It will explore demanding situations in brain signal decoding, including high dimensionality, noise, and variability, and how machine learning strategies can triumph over those demanding situations [9]. Further, the scope of the chapter also covers a discussion of real-world applications of brain signal decoding and machine learning in BCI and neurofeedback applications. These have been the areas with a very high impact on society and in the clinical community. The technical and societal or clinical implications will be discussed.

12.3 Fundamentals of Brain Signals

To use the playing field of the game, it is necessary to comprehend the basic concepts of brain code in instruction to implement the machine learning algorithm. The brain code is an electric-magnetic-cloud-carrier, generating various types of cognitive neurons and expressing these signals in one way or another. Important methods for visualizing brain codes in speech are EEG, fMRI, and magnetoencephalography. To describe the neural navigation and apply techniques of machine learning, one first needs to learn the basics of brain signaling. Brain signals are electrophysiological changes caused by nerve impulses representing different emotional or physiological processes in the body [10]. These signals are somehow captured, each bringing some unique light into the activity of the brain.

12.3.1 Types of Brain Signals

12.3.1.1 Electroencephalography (EEG)

One of the most used methods for measuring brain activity is electroencephalography (EEG). To capture the electrical activity produced by the brain's neurons, electrodes are only placed on the scalp. Because of its great temporal precision, the EEG may record abrupt changes in brain activity (within milliseconds). Sleep, concentration, and cognitive strain are just a few of the states of the brain that may be studied using it. Despite EEG's superior temporal resolution, its spatial resolution makes it impossible to pinpoint the exact location of the activity.

12.3.1.2 Functional Magnetic Resonance Imaging (fMRI)

fMRI is an imaging technique that is non-invasive, in which changes in blood flow reflect brain activity. When the neural activity of a given region increases, it consumes more oxygen, and it is provided with increased blood flow. Thus, the change in the level of oxygen indirectly reflects the neural activity by fMRI. Its greatest strength is in its high spatial resolution, meaning it can very precisely localize brain activity; though, the chronological resolution of fMRI is relatively low and on the order of seconds, which makes it less effective in capturing rapid dynamics in the brain [11]. fMRI is commonly applied in cognitive neuroscience as well as in clinical settings for the assessment of brain function.

12.3.1.3 Magnetoencephalography (MEG)

MEG measures the magnetic fields created by the electrical activity of neurons inside the brain. Like EEG, MEG gives high temporal resolution, but it has higher spatial resolution due to the fact that it can detect the magnetic fields from deeper brain areas. MEG is less unusual than EEG and fMRI; however, it is very useful in areas like brain mapping for pre-surgical planning and understanding mind dynamics during cognitive obligations.

12.3.2 Physiological Basis of Brain Signal Generation

It comes from the electrical action of the neurons, the basic units that constitute the brain. The basic elements that communicate with each other with electrical impulses or action potentials come from the movement of ions across the neuron's membrane. These are very small electrical currents; hence, they can be detected as a signal in the brain [12]. The strength and pattern of such signals depend on the type of neurons involved, their connectivity, and the specific cognitive or motor function being performed. For instance, when there is sensory processing, various parts of the brain are activated to produce distinct patterns of electrical and magnetic signals that can be detected by methods such as EEG, fMRI, or MEG.

In EEG, signals arise from simultaneous firings of large populations of neurons that are strong enough in their electric fields to be detectable at the scalp. In fMRI, signals arise through changes in blood oxygenation levels: the BOLD signal, which occurs as a consequence of neural action. MEG notices attractive fields shaped by neural activity and reveals information on both the judgment and the place of brain procedures.

12.3.3 Challenges in Capturing and Interpreting Brain Signals

Whereas these techniques of brain signal recording include EEG, fMRI, and MEG, each of them has its own problems in capturing and interpreting the brain signals. Chief among these challenges is noise—both external in the form of electrical interference and internal in the form of muscle movement or eye blink, which often masks the neural signals. Signal-to-noise ratio is the critical factor determining the quality of recorded brain signals, and to overcome this problem, sophisticated signal processing techniques have to be employed.

Another challenge is the spatial and temporal resolution trade-off. For example, while EEG has a very good temporal resolution, the spatial resolution of EEG is relatively poor, thus not allowing for very accurate localization of brain activity. On the other hand, fMRI has an excellent spatial resolution but is not able to capture rapid mind dynamics [13]. In addition, specific mind areas are frequently engaged in overlapping cognitive responsibilities, and therefore, it becomes difficult to isolate unique neural resources from complex signals.

Finally, brain signals are noticeably individualized—what's considered "everyday" for one character may fluctuate significantly from any other. Variations in anatomy, mind characteristics, and neural connectivity throughout people can contribute to the complexity in interpreting brain signals.

12.3.4 Significance of Mouth Extraction in Brain Signals

The main role that feature removal plays in brain signal examination is the capability to find interesting patterns within raw neural data, enabling researchers and machines to look at the patterns present in raw brain signals. For machine learning, the strength of the model greatly depends on the features extracted from brain signals. Feature extraction methods pick or remodel raw brain signal data into a more compact and understandable form by employing techniques such as time-frequency analysis, wavelet transforms, or statistical measures.

For EEG indicators, function extraction might also include figuring out precise inspiration designs consisting of alpha, beta, or delta waves that are associated with specific cognitive states. In fMRI, functions might be extracted by way of studying the BOLD signal's temporal styles or connectivity among brain areas [14]. In MEG, features would possibly contain detecting the timing and place of magnetic fields related to neural activity.

Indeed, effective feature extraction allows the improvement of device mastering models that are able to perceive brain states and expect subsequent movements or maybe manipulate external devices.

12.4 Basics of Machine Learning

Machine learning is a robust discipline of artificial intelligence that enables computer systems to learn from data and make predictions or decisions without explicit programming. In terms of brain sign interpreting, it permits styles to be pulled out of the neural statistics, offering the tools that are needed in order to convert those styles into beneficial insights. To decode brain signals effectively, the fundamentals of device learning, traditional sign decoding algorithms, and preprocessing techniques, along with characteristic engineering, play vital roles.

12.4.1 Core Concepts in Machine Learning

12.4.1.1 Supervised Learning

A popular machine learning method is supervised learning, which teaches a model to use classified data to produce precise predictions or judgments. In this method, the set of rules is trained on labeled information, where the inputs are paired with their corresponding outputs, or labels. The objective is to examine a mapping feature that could predict the output from new, unseen information. In brain signal decoding, supervised learning can be applied to categorize the mind states of a subject—for example, decide whether or not the issue is appearing as a venture or is at relaxation—or to decode intentions, consisting of predicting motor movements from mind activity [15]. Standard algorithms for supervised learning are SVM, decision trees, and neural networks, each of which is useful for specific styles of data records and tasks.

12.4.1.2 Unsupervised Learning

Unsupervised learning is the procedure of analyzing data without labeled outputs. The impartiality is to find concealed designs, structures, or groupings in the information. This approach is particularly valuable when the relationships in the data are unknown or when labeling data is impractical. In brain signal decoding, unsupervised learning may be implemented to cluster brain interest patterns, locate correlations between brain regions, or pick out novel brain states. Techniques consisting of k-approach clustering and PCA are usually used to extract expressive features from neural statistics.

12.4.1.3 Reinforcement Learning

RL is a kind of machine learning where an agent learns how to make movements in its setting by exploring it and getting some feedback from rewards or penalties. The learning paradigm finds applications, particularly in systems that are required to learn to adapt over time to brain signals from users, like in BCIs. The model learns to take optimal actions in reinforcement learning by maximizing the cumulative reward and, therefore, is an appropriate approach for a dynamic environment, such as a real-time neural decoder [16]. For example, an RL model can be used to train how a BCI would perform better under different users' brain signal patterns and provide predictions with higher accuracy as the user interacts with the system.

12.4.2 Common Algorithms for Signal Decoding

A key role played by machine learning algorithms in decoding brain signals follows, with some of the most common algorithms in neuronal data analysis being the following:

12.4.2.1 Support Vector Machines (SVM)

SVM is a commonly applied supervised learning approach used as a classification and regression algorithm. In the context of the decoding of brain signs with brain states or mental task classification based on EEG, fMRI, or MEG data, SVM is widely applied. SVM is the one that exploits the margin of separation between dissimilar classes' data points with an optimal hyperplane. SVMs are more suitable for high-dimensional data, such as neural signals, and thus they are very often used in BCIs to classify motor imagery or detect a particular cognitive task.

12.4.2.2 Decision Trees

Another very frequently used algorithm is decision trees, which are used as a supervised learner, mainly to classify data. The algorithm itself works by using recursive splitting of data into subsets through the most information-rich features. In general, they are informal to understand and even work with both continuous and definite values. In terms of symbolic coding from the brain, decision trees can be useful for cognitive states or motor concepts based on extracted neural signal components and can also be applied to neurons systematically to monitor brain activity in real time.

12.4.2.3 Neural Networks

Neural networks, chiefly deep learning replicas, have a strong ability to translate brain signals into complex, nonlinear relationships between data. Neural networks are connections between neurons or neurons that process the input data and learn how to predict. Among deep learning architectures, CNNs and RNNs are more applicable for the analysis of brain signals. CNNs are best suited to uncover spatial patterns in brain signals, for example, in fMRI and MEG data. RNNs, on the other hand, are more suited to deal with sequential data and, therefore, work best for decoding temporal patterns in EEG signals [17]. Neural networks are more readily used in BCIs, where they can learn to map brain activity to specific commands or actions.

12.4.3 Importance of Data Preprocessing and Article Engineering

The most crucial phases in the machine learning pipeline are data preparation and feature engineering, particularly when working with complex mental signals. Raw neural recordings from EEG, fMRI, or MEG are often noisy and require extensive cleaning before they can be effectively analyzed. Noise and artifacts from eye blinks, muscle movements, and outside interference are eliminated using preprocessing techniques, including filtering, artifact removal, and normalization. Preprocessing is a crucial stage since the machine learning model's performance will be greatly impacted by the quality of the input data. Feature extraction is the process of deriving meaningful features from raw brain signals that machine learning algorithms use for classification or prediction. Features may involve statistical measures, such as a mean, variance, or even higher-order moments; frequency domain features, including power spectral density; and temporal patterns, like phase-locking values [18]. The aim is to transform raw data into a form that brings out the relevant patterns and makes it easier for the model to learn. Good feature engineering improves the accuracy of brain signal decoding models because it allows the algorithms to focus on the most informative aspects of the data.

12.4.4 Machine Learning Techniques for Brain Signal Decoding

Nowadays, with the assistance of device learning strategies, deciphering brain signals has emerged as a hot topic in decoding facts from technology, together with EEG, fMRI, and MEG. Data preprocessing and characteristic extraction, accompanied by the category, prediction, or manipulation version, are protected in the method. This segment gives a detailed evaluation of the strategies used in these stages, detailing preprocessing methods, function extraction strategies, and deep learning strategies that decode mind indicators.

12.4.5 Preprocessing Techniques for Brain Signals

Brain signals, especially those obtained from EEG, fMRI, and MEG, are often noisy and contaminated by various artifacts. Preprocessing is a critical step that prepares raw brain data for machine learning models by cleaning the signals and enhancing their quality.

12.4.5.1 Noise Removal

Different kinds of noise are generated in the brain signals arising from electrical interference, muscle movement, eye blinking, and all other non-neural activities. Noisy removals are very crucial in order not to let extraneous information adulterate the analysis. Generally, the methods for noise removal are:

- Band-pass filtering: This is another filter that lets signals pass through a given frequency range while rejecting those outside this frequency range. Common frequency bands, such as delta, alpha, beta, and gamma, are often of interest in EEG. Using a band-pass filter makes it simple to isolate such frequencies.
- Independent Component Analysis (ICA): ICA is a computer method that divides mixed signals into independent components. It is especially helpful in eliminating EEG signal artifacts such as muscular activity and eye blinks.
- Wavelet Transform: This technique provides a multi-resolution analysis of the signal, making it ideal for handling non-stationary data like brain signals. Wavelet demolishing is particularly effective for EEG signal noise removal.

12.4.5.2 *Signal Segmentation*

Brain signals are continuous in nature, but only segments of them carry useful information for coding. Segmentation of the signal is the process of breaking the continuous nature of the signal into small windows or epochs to be analyzed. Especially in the case of ERPs and other time-bound responses, this step is very crucial. With segmentation, it is possible to separate the particular time intervals of interest, which facilitates learning patterns of association with specific cognitive or motor states for machine learning models [19]. It can be fixed by predefined events or stimulus presentations, or be adaptive in accordance with the dynamics of the signal.

12.4.6 Feature Extraction Techniques

After pre-processing comes the very important step of feature extraction in decoding brain signals—that is to say, the process of extracting relevant or meaningful characteristics or patterns from the raw brain signals that would be useful to the machine learning mockups. The choice of features highly impacts the presentation of the model, and based on the characteristics of the data and the deciphering task, different features are extracted from brain signals.

12.4.6.1 *Frequency-Based Features*

Frequency-based features deal with the power spectral components of brain signals, which are useful especially in EEG and MEG analysis. The action of the brain can be decomposed into various bands of frequency, corresponding to various mental or cognitive states. Some common frequency-based features include:

Power Spectral Density: The way a signal's power is scattered across different frequencies is known as its power spectrum density (PSD). EEG frequency alphas (8-12 tuberculosis), tuberculosis (13-30 tuberculosis), delta (0.5-4 Hartz) and the village (30-100 hrtj). These spells can refer to different emotions or body [20].
Relative Band Power Ratio: Ratios between different frequency bands are commonly used as features in signal processing and brain signal analysis as an example, Ratio with Alpha-beta power often attached to the formation of the formation.

12.4.6.2 Time-Domain Features

Time-domain features are extracted directly from the raw signal without transforming it into the frequency domain. The features describe the temporal traits of the sign, along with the amplitude, top-to-peak *c* language, and sign form. Common time-area functions consist of:

1. Mean and Variance: These basic capabilities of facts describe the crucial tendency of the sign and how much it spreads out, associated with possibly special cognitive states.
2. Peak detection: Using a signal, one can identify peaks or local maxima used to determine event-related potentials or transient neural responses.
3. Autoregressive Model Coefficients: These coefficients describe the signal as a linear model and capture the nature of temporal dependencies in the signal.

12.4.7 Overview of Deep Learning Methods for Decoding

Deep learning methods have been revolutionary in brain signal decoding. They provide a powerful tool to mechanically learn multifaceted designs in large datasets. The traditional machine learning methods require feature extraction to be done manually. In contrast, deep learning models learn both features and classification tasks from raw data. Among the prominent models applied in brain signal decoding, the deep learning models include the CNN and the RNN [21].

12.4.7.1 Convolutional Neural Networks (CNN)

CNNs are applied very widely in analyzing spatial patterns in data, and they have proven to be highly successful in applications involving image-like data. The application of CNNs in brain signal decoding allows the capture of spatial relationships within signals. For instance, in EEG and fMRI facts, CNNs can routinely study spatial capabilities that constitute the region of brain interest. CNNs are particularly useful while running with large datasets because of the fact that they are able to hierarchically examine capabilities at a couple of degrees of abstraction [22]. While operating in BCIs, CNNs may be beneficial in the real-time classification of intellectual states, motor intentions, or cognitive tasks due to spatial mastering from EEG or fMRI signals.

12.4.7.2 Recurrent Neural Networks (RNN)

RNNs are designed to deal with consecutive facts, making them ideal for time-series statistics like EEG or MEG signals. RNNs process input data step by step while preserving information from previous steps, making them well suited for interpreting temporal patterns in brain signals. For example, RNNs are used to decode motor intentions from EEG signals by recognizing sequential patterns that correspond to specific actions [6]. One such specialized RNN is the LSTM network, which has been a hit in interpreting brain signals because it can analyze long-term dependencies within records.

12.4.8 Comparison of Traditional ML and Deep Learning in Brain Signal Decoding

Traditionally, both conventional machine learning and deep learning have been successful in the field of brain signal decoding, each offering specific strengths and facing certain limitations.

12.4.8.1 Traditional Machine Learning (ML)

Traditional ML techniques, including SVM, decision trees, and KNN, contain manual characteristic extraction, in which the area information plays a critical role in determining the most relevant traits of the brain signals. Even though those techniques may be surprisingly powerful with proper functions, they are limited by the quality and availability of handmade features. Moreover, traditional ML algorithms have a tendency to struggle with large-scale datasets that are commonplace in neuroimaging and EEG studies.

12.4.8.2 Deep Learning

Deep learning methods, especially CNNs and RNNs, find excellent applications in automatically learning features from raw data, as they are less reliant on domain expertise. These models are able to deal with large-dimensional databases with reasonable ease and can identify complex patterns that may be overshadowed or missed by traditional methods [23]. However, deep models require lots of labeled data, along with heavy computational power for training, and they usually operate as "black-box" models, which in turn makes them harder to interpret compared to the traditional method.

12.5 Case Studies and Applications

The utility of device learning techniques for brain signal decoding has brought about tremendous developments in diverse fields, particularly with the growth of brain-computer interfaces (BCIs) and medical settings. These applications screen the potential for decoding brain signals in enhancing human lives, specifically amongst humans with disabilities and people affected by neurological issues. This section covers a number of the predominant case studies and packages of brain signal decoding, in particular focusing on packages in brain-computer interface applications, scientific packages, and new study breakthroughs.

12.5.1 Brain-Computer Interface Applications

The area most promising to realize the potential impact of brain signal decoding has undoubtedly been BCIs. A brain-computer interface is essentially an interface directly linking the brain and external devices such that one may control a device or system entirely using neural activity. The technique is achieved with real-time deciphering and translation into the favored actions or commands, achieved through the employment of machine learning algorithms in the case of BCIs.

12.5.1.1 Assistive Technologies

BCIs have been advanced as assistive technologies for those tormented by intense motor disabilities, which include those due to stroke, paralysis, or neurodegenerative diseases, including ALS. These allow users to drive a computer, wheelchair, artificial limbs, or exoskeletons by translating the signals of their brain into commands. Non-invasive EEG-based BCI research allowed those with locked-in syndrome to communicate and control devices with only minimal muscular involvement.

Case Study

One of the best examples is working with patients with locked-in syndrome, where decoding EEG signals helps them communicate. In one such study, the patients could control a virtual keyboard on a screen using EEG signals. Users could select letters and form words by focusing on specific stimuli. Using this method, they could type messages and thus communicate effectively with caregivers or family members.

12.5.1.2 Communication Devices for Disabled Individuals

BCIs have truly been a source of breakthrough communications for individuals living with motor disabilities. In such cases, pairing EEG with the power of machine learning has contributed to the implementation of schemes aimed at decoding specific brain activity with the intention to convert it to speech or any form of textual communication for others who cannot say a word or utter a single limb movement. That is because intent detection is associated with monitoring such brain patterns when using these tools.

Case Study

The development of BCI systems for individuals with ALS is one of the most prominent examples. Using EEG and deep learning models, researchers have developed communication systems that can detect specific brain activity patterns associated with movement intentions. These systems allow individuals to generate speech through the brain's activity patterns, providing an independent communication channel.

12.5.1.3 Clinical Applications

Beyond assistive devices, brain signal decoding has a number of clinical packages, particularly within the early discovery and tracking of nervous conditions. Such packages are crucial for improving analysis, diagnosis, and control of neurological complaints like Alzheimer's disease, Parkinson's disease, and epilepsy.

12.5.1.3.1 Earliest Detection of Neurological Illnesses

There is hope in brain signal decoding for very early diagnosis of nervous conditions. The use of EEG signals with the application of machine learning algorithms helps decode changes at subtle levels, and sometimes changes might indicate early development of the disease before even the onset of clinical symptoms: Alzheimer's disease, Parkinson's disease, epilepsy, and the like.

Case Study

EEG signals have been found to identify epilepsy symptoms early on. The abnormalities before a seizure can be identified by machine learning algorithms while mapping the frequency patterns in the brain signals. Thus, the capability to determine seizures earlier permits the timely intervention that would otherwise prevent serious episodes. Clinical trials were performed on patients based on EEG-based predictive models that had predicted a seizure, thus allowing caregivers to take certain preventive measures before the seizure occurred.

12.5.1.3.2 Monitoring Cognitive Load

In addition, machine learning models have been applied in measuring the cognitive load in patients undergoing a variety of cognitive tasks or therapies. Cognitive load is one of the key concepts in understanding how the brain functions because it signifies the capacity of the brain to process information. The measurement of cognitive load offers an important understanding of mental states, stress, and cognitive performance.

Case Study

Another application is in the treatment of traumatic brain injury (TBI) patients. Brain signals can be measured through EEG or fMRI analysis, allowing machine learning algorithms to measure cognitive load during rehabilitation exercises. This way, healthcare providers can have a better understanding of the patient's cognitive capabilities, which enables them to create more tailored therapeutic interventions to enhance recovery.

12.5.1.3.3 Emerging Research and Breakthroughs

Rapid advances on both fronts of brain signal decoding and machine learning bring new frontiers to neuroscience. The areas of research in brain-computer interfaces and clinical applications evolve further based on signal processing, deep learning methods, and other neuroimaging techniques [24].

12.5.1.3.4 Neurofeedback

Using real-time input regarding his brain signals, neurofeedback is a technique that enables the user to self-regulate and control his brain activity. The technique is being applied more often to treat a variety of ailments, including anxiety, depression, and ADHD. The brain signals have to be interpreted using machine learning algorithms so that effective and accurate information can be given to the user.

Case Study

One of the emergent trends of neurofeedback is in the treatment of mental health. For instance, in ADHD patients, neurofeedback was used to train people to augment specific brain wave patterns, like increasing theta and alpha waves. Machine learning models were trained to utilize real-time EEG data with feedback about the patient's brain activity to improve attention and reduce symptoms of hyperactivity.

12.5.1.3.5 Real-Time Brain Signal Decoding for Prosthetics

Recent breakthroughs have made feasible the deciphering of real-time mind indicators that control complex prosthetic limbs. Users can exactly control prosthetic movements by means of decoding indicators decoded through such an EEG or implanted devices. This indicates a major step toward restoring mobility and independence amongst amputees and those laid low with paralysis.

Case Study

In a landmark study, researchers established a real-time BCI that enables patients to control a robotic prosthetic arm using brain signals. This technology was used with a deep learning model that decoded what the user wanted in real-time, such as grasping and lifting objects. This application of BCIs may potentially bring amputees and people with motor dysfunction back to performing fine motor functions.

12.5.1.3.6 Neuroprosthetics for Cognitive Enhancements

Neuroprosthetics are also researched for cognitive enhancement, aside from restoring lost functions. These devices are intended to enhance cognitive functions among healthy individuals or in those with deteriorating cognitive skills. Research is being conducted to decode brain signals to improve memory, attention, and decision-making processes through the implementation of brain stimulation integrated with machine learning algorithms.

12.5.1.3.7 Emerging Research

One of the innovative areas of research is the development of cognitive augmentation devices. The researchers decode the brain signals associated with learning and memory to develop systems that enhance cognitive performance. For example, one study used real-time brain signal decoding to detect when a subject was learning new information and applied targeted electrical stimulation to enhance memory retention.

12.6 Challenges and Future Directions

As ML continues to transform the field of brain signal decoding, significant tests remain that could impact its full realization of potential. Attending to those challenges will have a bearing on advancing research into real-world applications of brain signal decoding in both clinical and nonclinical settings [25]. This section discusses some of the major challenges in brain signal decoding, followed by future research directions that have the potential to improve the efficiency and usability of ML models in neuroscience.

12.6.1 Key Challenges

12.6.1.1 Data Scarcity and Quality

One of the main challenges in interpreting brain signals arises from the shortage of adequate, well-labeled datasets. Advanced machine learning algorithms rely heavily on huge quantities of data to analyze and make correct predictions. However, the variety of brain indicators amongst individuals could be very high, and acquiring high-quality records is resource-intensive. Collecting high-fidelity data, such as EEG, fMRI, or MEG signals, often requires specialized equipment, expert knowledge, and controlled environments, which can limit the availability of data for training ML models.

Data sets are also so rare that there is no diversity in age, gender, and neurological conditions, leading to biased or overfitted models. This calls for collaboration in the development of more diverse datasets that are standardized and public and better methods of data augmentation and synthesis.

12.6.1.2 Interpretability of ML Models

Although impressive performance in some machine learning algorithms, particularly deep learning models, has been suggested to be able to decode brain signals, their "black-box" nature remains a significant issue. Knowing how and why a model reaches a certain choice is crucial for therapeutic applications. Especially where the stakes include human health and safety [6]. Models that offer little or no insight into their decision-making processes can be problematic because they provide only limited transparency and accountability.

Furthermore, without interpretability, clinicians and researchers will not find the outputs produced by the system trustworthy or validating.

There is thus a need to have methods that could explain in a much clearer way what ML models do in interpreting signals from the brain, hence making such models more trustworthy for practical usage.

12.6.1.3 Ethical and Privacy Anxieties

There are some ethical and privacy concerns related to the use of brain signal data. Brain signals, by their nature, are deeply personal and can tell a lot about a person's thoughts, intentions, and mental states. Thus, unauthorized access or misuse of such sensitive data would have serious implications for privacy and personal autonomy.

For example, opportunities to improve the lives of disabled people through BCI media are there, but concerns also arise in terms of ideas and potential ideas or potential scientific data, scientific validation, or the abusive ethical topics that need to be addressed.

Collecting, processing, and storing brain signal data will call for the setting up of very strong ethical frameworks and privacy standards. Consent procedures and transparency concerning the use of data will be imperative to ensure the rights of people are respected.

12.6.2 Future Research Directions

12.6.2.1 Explainable AI for Neuroscience

Perhaps one of the most promising ways for future development would be tailoring explainable AI techniques, a new stream in AI with potential applications directly for neuroscience studies. Explainable AI is actually designed to demystify how machine learning models make their decisions, meaning how they function, so that results become understandable. Explainable AI would help scientists demystify the transformation from brain signals to actionable insights through these models for clinicians and other researchers to be confident and ultimately accept them as practical tools for application.

In this area, the research focuses on developing ML models that not only perform well but also give human-readable explanations for their predictions. For example, integrating feature importance analysis, visualizations of the steps in which brain signals are processed, or providing rule-based explanations can be used to explain complex neural networks. This might enhance clinical decision-making, help in validating models, and make them more acceptable to users.

12.6.2.2 Real-Time Brain Signal Decoding Systems

The systems of decoding brain signals that are most developed today do not operate in real-time and therefore can hardly be applied to real-time settings such as assistive skills or clinical monitoring. A promising future direction would be the growth of real-time brain signal decoding systems. They should process the signals from the brain in real time and provide instantaneous feedback to users or clinicians.

Real-time decoding may revolutionize requests such as brain-computer interfaces and neurofeedback systems. For instance, it can meaningfully improve the excellence of life if a person enduring a neurological disorder is enabled to control prosthetic limbs or interact with digital interfaces in real time [26]. This is only possible when signal processing techniques are improved, and low-latency algorithms are designed and implemented for computations involving huge amounts of data from brain signals.

12.6.2.3 Integration of Hybrid Models

With improvements in the area, there may be an increasing interest in the integration of hybrid models that combine the strengths of more than one machine learning strategy. Traditional machine learning techniques, such as support vector machines (SVMs) and decision trees, may also provide stable performance for certain responsibilities. Hybrid models can combine the interpretability and performance of traditional strategies with the power and flexibility of deep learning models. For example, integrating deep mastering with classical signal processing methods may be used to establish enormously accurate and robust decoding structures of the mind. Hybrid models can also cut the deficiency of brief statistics in stressful situations when you consider that they allow integrating more than one source of records, like EEG, fMRI, and behavioral data, hence enhancing the model's generalization and robustness.

In addition, ensemble learning techniques, where two models are trained and their outputs combined, can also improve the precision and reliability of the brain signal decoding structures.

12.7 Conclusion

Machine learning (ML) has been an emerging transformational tool in the subject of brain signal decoding, offering new insights into complicated strategies within the human mind. The utility of ML strategies to one-of-a-kind styles of brain signals—EEG, fMRI, and MEG—has made a vast contribution to knowledge and deciphering mind activities. Machine learning has been shown to be an extremely effective tool for neuroscience research and healthcare, facilitating the development of brain–computer interfaces and improving computational approaches for the early diagnosis of neurological disorders. As discussed in this chapter, the application of machine learning in brain signal decoding is crucial for extracting meaningful information from raw neural data. Current traditional models comprising support vector machines and decision trees are now utilized in tandem with the latest deep learning strategies, starting from CNN and RNN, which might be transforming and revolutionizing techniques for brain signal analyses. The merger of these strategies with progressive preprocessing, function extraction, and real-time decoding strategies is guaranteed to revolutionize packages, including assistive technologies, conversation gadgets for human beings with disabilities, and cognitive tracking systems. However, such efforts do face challenges, along with statistical scarcity and privacy issues, which affect the interpretability of complex ML models and raise extra concerns about the ethics surrounding sensitive use of mind statistics. Undoubtedly, development in addressing those challenges will rely on high-quality interdisciplinary studies in areas concerning machine learning experts, neuroscientists, clinicians, ethicists, and policymakers.

The future of brain signal decoding holds great promise and has many potential breakthroughs in reshaping how we understand and interact with the brain. Further, as the models of machine learning become more interpretable, the real-time decoding systems become more efficient, and hybrid models are developed, the scope for brain signal decoding in clinical and nonclinical applications will continue to expand. The convergence of neuroscience and AI may hold both new promise and benefit in regard to betterment in our brain functioning, as well as the lives of subjects with neurological problems, by enhancing the efficacy of neuroprosthetics and other forms of brain-computer interfaces. Therefore, there is massive potential in machine learning/neuroscience collaboration. As that research and new challenges progress, the things we get are further advanced and better decoding of brain signals and higher impact applications in healthcare, assistive technologies, and more into the future. Brain signal decoding is bright in terms of future thinking and application based on the continuous fusion of innovative algorithms and interdisciplinary research.

AI disclosure statement: The author acknowledges the use of AI-based tools for minor language editing or grammatical correction. However, all intellectual contributions, analyses, and conclusions presented in this chapter are entirely the author's own.

References

1. Kumar, S., Agarwal, V., Sharma, V., Garg, S., Sharma, M.K., Gupta, R., Prashant, S., Accurate and Efficient Brain Tumor Segmentation using transfer learning and residual networks, in: *2023 5th International Conference on Advances in Computing, Communication Control and Networking (ICAC3N)*, 2023 Dec 15, IEEE, pp. 683–689.
2. Agrawal, V., Kaswan, K.S., Kumar, S., Prediction of Level of Damage of Brain Due To Tumor *Via* Integrated CNN Technique, in: *2024 IEEE International Conference on Computing, Power and Communication Technologies (IC2PCT)*, 2024 Feb 9, vol. 5, IEEE, pp. 783–786.
3. Yadav, D., Yadav, S., Veer, K., A comprehensive assessment of Brain Computer Interfaces: Recent trends and challenges. *J. Neurosci. Methods*, 346, 108918, 2020 Dec 1.
4. Abiri, R., Borhani, S., Sellers, E.W., Jiang, Y., Zhao, X., A comprehensive review of EEG-based brain–computer interface paradigms. *J. Neural Eng.*, 16, 1, 011001, 2019 Jan 9.
5. Vallabhaneni, R.B., Sharma, P., Kumar, V., Kulshreshtha, V., Reddy, K.J., Kumar, S.S., Kumar, V.S., Bitra, S.K., Deep learning algorithms in eeg signal decoding application: a review. *IEEE Access*, 9, 125778–86, 2021 Aug 18.
6. Saeidi, M., Karwowski, W., Farahani, F.V., Fiok, K., Taiar, R., Hancock, P.A., Al-Juaid, A., Neural decoding of EEG signals with machine learning: a systematic review. *Brain Sci.*, 11, 11, 1525, 2021 Nov 18.
7. Dong, X., Thanou, D., Toni, L., Bronstein, M., Frossard, P., Graph signal processing for machine learning: A review and new perspectives. *IEEE Signal Process Mag.*, 37, 6, 117–27, 2020 Oct 29.
8. Xie, Y., Zaccagna, F., Rundo, L., Testa, C., Agati, R., Lodi, R., Manners, D.N., Tonon, C., Convolutional neural network techniques for brain tumor classification (from 2015 to 2022): Review, challenges, and future perspectives. *Diagnostics*, 12, 8, 1850, 2022 Jul 31.
9. Rajwal, S. and Aggarwal, S., Convolutional neural network-based EEG signal analysis: A systematic review. *Arch. Comput. Methods Eng.*, 30, 6, 3585–615, 2023 Jul.
10. Livezey, J.A. and Glaser, J.I., Deep learning approaches for neural decoding across architectures and recording modalities. *Briefings Bioinf.*, 22, 2, 1577–91, 2021 Mar.

11. Lu, J., Yan, H., Chang, C., Wang, N., Comparison of machine learning and deep learning approaches for decoding brain computer interface: an fNIRS study, in: *Intelligent Information Processing X: 11th IFIP TC 12 International Conference, IIP 2020, Hangzhou, China, July 3–6, 2020, Proceedings 11 2020*, Springer International Publishing, pp. 192–201.
12. Hosseini, M.P., Hosseini, A., Ahi, K., A review on machine learning for EEG signal processing in bioengineering. *IEEE Rev. Biomed. Eng.*, 14, 204–18, 2020 Jan 28.
13. Khosla, A., Khandnor, P., Chand, T., A comparative analysis of signal processing and classification methods for different applications based on EEG signals. *Biocybern. Biomed. Eng.*, 40, 2, 649–90, 2020 Apr 1.
14. Merk, T., Peterson, V., Köhler, R., Haufe, S., Richardson, R.M., Neumann, W.J., Machine learning based brain signal decoding for intelligent adaptive deep brain stimulation. *Exp. Neurol.*, 351, 113993, 2022 May 1.
15. Ranjan, R., Sahana, B.C., Bhandari, A.K., Deep learning models for diagnosis of schizophrenia using EEG signals: emerging trends, challenges, and prospects. *Arch. Comput. Methods Eng.*, 31, 4, 2345–84, 2024 May.
16. Hossain, K.M., Islam, M.A., Hossain, S., Nijholt, A., Ahad, M.A., Status of deep learning for EEG-based brain–computer interface applications. *Front. Comput. Neurosci.*, 16, 1006763, 2023 Jan 16.
17. Aggarwal, S. and Chugh, N., Review of machine learning techniques for EEG based brain computer interface. *Arch. Comput. Methods Eng.*, 29, 5, 3001–20, 2022 Aug.
18. Abenna, S., Nahid, M., Bouyghf, H., Ouacha, B., EEG-based BCI: A novel improvement for EEG signals classification based on real-time preprocessing. *Comput. Biol. Med.*, 148, 105931, 2022 Sep 1.
19. Luján, MA., Jimeno, M.V., Mateo Sotos, J., Ricarte, J.J., Borja, A.L., A survey on eeg signal processing techniques and machine learning: Applications to the neurofeedback of autobiographical memory deficits in schizophrenia. *Electronics*, 10, 23, 3037, 2021 Dec 5.
20. Arns, M., Batail, J.M., Bioulac, S., Congedo, M., Daudet, C., Drapier, D., Fovet, T., Jardri, R., Le-Van-Quyen, M., Lotte, F., Mehler, D., Neurofeedback: One of today's techniques in psychiatry? *L'encephale*, 43, 2, 135–45, 2017 Apr 1.
21. Salcedo-Sanz, S., Rojo-Álvarez, J.L., Martínez-Ramón, M., Camps-Valls, G., Support vector machines in engineering: an overview. *Wiley Interdiscip. Rev.: Data Min. Knowl. Discovery*, 4, 3, 234–67, 2014 May.
22. Sharma, R. and Meena, H.K., Emerging trends in EEG signal processing: A systematic review. *SN Comput. Sci.*, 5, 4, 415, 2024 Apr 9.
23. Li, G., Lee, C.H., Jung, J.J., Youn, Y.C., Camacho, D., Deep learning for EEG data analytics: A survey. *Concurrency Comput. Pract. Exper.*, 32, 18, e5199, 2020 Sep 25.
24. Abdulrahman, S.I. and Róbert, S., Supervised machine learning algorithms for brain signal classification. *Vojnoteh. Glas.*, 72, 2, 727–49, 2024.

25. Cincotti, F., Mattia, D., Aloise, F., Bufalari, S., Astolfi, L., Fallani, F.D., Tocci, A., Bianchi, L., Marciani, M.G., Gao, S., Millan, J., High-resolution EEG techniques for brain–computer interface applications. *J. Neurosci. Methods*, 167, 1, 31–42, 2008 Jan 15.
26. Saibene, A., Ghaemi, H., Dagdevir, E., Deep learning in motor imagery EEG signal decoding: A Systematic Review. *Neurocomputing*, 14, 128577, 2024 Sep.

13

Boosting Workforce Potential with Human Augmentation Using Brain-Computer Interface

Rajesh Singh[1], Fraiz Parveen[2] and Praveen Kumar Malik[3]*

[1]Division of Research and Innovation, Uttaranchal Institute of Technology Uttaranchal University, Dehradun, Uttarakhand, India
[2]Division of Research and Innovation, Uttaranchal University, Dehradun, Uttarakhand, India
[3]School of Electronics and Electrical Engineering, Lovely Professional University, Phagwara, Punjab, India

Abstract

The profound effects of emerging technologies can enhance productivity while fostering a culture of excellence, community, and societal contribution; conversely, some may amplify disadvantages like injury, health disruptions, and loss of autonomy. In this context, differentiating these outcomes is crucial, particularly in ongoing discussions on work value and human welfare. A new manufacturing paradigm, Industry 5.0, leverages digital twins (DT), artificial intelligence (AI), and brain-computer interfaces (BCI) to optimize industrial performance and workforce potential. This study provides the first comprehensive assessment of the synergy between cobots, DTs, AI, BCI, and human augmentation within Industry 5.0. It explores how BCI can enhance cognitive and physical capabilities, enabling seamless human-machine collaboration. The study also examines human enhancement in organizational settings, addressing ethical, legal, and organizational implications, while distinguishing between voluntary and mandated augmentation. The goal is to support global endeavors in leveraging Industry 5.0's potential while serving as a reference for future research and development.

***Keywords*:** Human resource management (HRM), labor empowerment, human-machine cooperation, intelligence augmentation (IA), employee engagement

**Corresponding author*: pkmalikmeerut@gmail.com

Tawseef Ahmed Teli, Syed Immamul Ansarullah, Arun Kumar Rana, Suman Lata Tripathi and Kashif Nisar (eds.) Brain-to-Computer Interfaces Using Machine Learning and Deep Learning, (313–328) © 2026 Scrivener Publishing LLC

13.1 Introduction to Human Resource Management

Organizations endeavor to preserve the dependability, safety, security, usability, and competitiveness of their processes, commodities, and services. Human factors play an important part in helping employees improve their skills and capacities. Human enhancement, a contentious but historical phenomenon, entails direct technology involvement with employees' talents, going beyond ergonomics, procedures, and training. This approach goes beyond just creating ergonomics and training [1]. Cognitive enhancement is a field that focuses on increasing human cognition in order to overcome cognitive limits involving task accuracy, job effectiveness, and mistake management. It has the ability to minimize mistakes in complicated operating contexts while also improving work performance, risk management, and workplace stress and well-being. However, cognitive improvement treatments are largely underutilized in practice [2]. Employee training and development are essential aspects of human resource management, proven to be crucial for an organization's success. A well-designed program may improve employee knowledge, skills, and talents, resulting in increased production and efficiency, as shown in Table 13.1.

Table 13.1 Employee training, development, and technology integration in Industry 5.0.

Topic	Description
Importance of employee training and development [3]	Training enhances employee skills, boosting productivity, retention, and company culture.
HRM and organizational success through training [4]	Well-designed training programs improve efficiency, job satisfaction, and reduce turnover.
Role of robotic assistance and human-robot collaboration [5]	AI and cobots enhance safety, efficiency, and creativity by automating repetitive tasks.
Cobotics and technology in Industry 5.0 [6]	Cobots, VR, AR, XR, and digital twins foster human-machine collaboration to improve production.
AI and human-machine collaboration for innovation [7]	AI's integration requires up-skilling, combining human creativity with machine intelligence.

This can also boost work satisfaction, leading to improved retention rates and lower turnover. Furthermore, staff education can help to enhance overall company culture by encouraging improved cooperation, communication, and collaboration. Thus, staff education and promotion may have a huge positive influence on the operations of a firm [3].

How Brain-Computer Interfaces Could Optimize Human-Centric AI in Industry 5.0 and Address Trust and Transparency Issues

13.1.1 Optimizing Human-Centric AI with BCI in Industry 5.0

Brain-computer interfaces (BCI) is poised to revolutionize human-machine collaboration in Industry 5.0 by enabling real-time cognitive and physical augmentation, fostering a seamless integration of human intuition and machine precision.

- Enhanced Cognitive and Physical Capabilities
- BCI can decode neural signals to optimize worker performance, reducing errors in high-risk industrial tasks (e.g., assembly line precision, hazardous material handling).
- Adaptive AI-driven digital twins (DTs) can use BCI data to simulate and predict worker fatigue, adjusting workflows in real-time—like a safety net that anticipates human limits.

- Seamless Human-Cobot Collaboration
- In collaborative robotics (cobots), BCI allows intent-driven control, where machines respond to brainwave commands faster than manual inputs, reducing latency in manufacturing processes.
- Example: A factory worker using a BCI headset to direct robotic arms *via* thought, minimizing physical strain while maximizing efficiency.

- Personalized Workforce Training and Upskilling
- BCI can monitor cognitive engagement during training, dynamically adjusting AI-driven modules to suit individual learning speeds—like a digital mentor that reads mental fatigue.

13.1.2 BCI-Based Trust and Transparency Challenges in Industry 5.0

While BCI enhances productivity, it introduces ethical, legal, and organizational dilemmas, particularly around data privacy, autonomy, and algorithmic bias.

- Neural Data Security and Privacy Risks
- BCI collects highly sensitive brainwave data, raising concerns about employer surveillance and potential misuse (e.g., monitoring focus levels without consent).
- Solution: Strict neuro-data governance with employee consent protocols and blockchain-based encryption to prevent unauthorized access.

- Voluntary vs. Mandated Human Augmentation
- Should BCI adoption be optional (for skill enhancement) or mandatory (for safety-critical roles)? This debate impacts workplace equity and autonomy.
- Solution: Clear organizational policies distinguishing between enhancement for safety (e.g., fatigue detection in pilots) vs. performance optimization (e.g., faster assembly line work).

- Explainability in BCI-Driven AI Decisions
- Workers may distrust AI adjustments (e.g., task reassignments based on neural fatigue signals) if the reasoning is opaque.
- Solution: Real-time BCI feedback dashboards that visually explain AI decisions (e.g., "Task paused due to detected cognitive overload").

- Bias in BCI Algorithms
- If BCI systems are trained on non-diverse neural datasets, they may misinterpret signals from neurodivergent workers (e.g., ADHD, autism).
- Solution: Inclusive BCI training datasets and bias audits to ensure fairness across neurocognitive profiles.

13.1.3 Ethical and Organizational Framework for BCI in Industry 5.0

To balance innovation and ethics, organizations must adopt a human-centered ethical AI (HCEAI) framework for BCI integration:

- ✓ Worker Autonomy – Ensure BCI use is consensual and reversible.
- ✓ Transparent Neuro-AI – Provide clear explanations for AI-driven adjustments based on BCI data.
- ✓ Neuro-Inclusive Policies – Protect cognitive diversity and prevent discrimination.
- ✓ Secure Neural Data Handling – Implement GDPR-like regulations for brainwave data.

Training and development of employees stands as a very core segment of human resource management (HRM), which has an undoubted direct impact on an organization's effectiveness. A well-designed program may improve employee knowledge, skills, and talents, resulting in increased production and efficiency. This can also boost work satisfaction, leading to improved retention rates and lower turnover. Furthermore, staff education can help to enhance overall company culture by encouraging improved cooperation, communication, and collaboration. Thus, staff education and promotion may have a huge positive influence on the operations of a firm [4]. Robotic help is becoming the norm in the workplace as a result of human-robot collaborations that employ machine intelligence to improve human orientations. Automation, artificial intelligence (AI), and sophisticated robots work together to boost production, efficiency, and safety. Intelligent systems and collaborative robots (cobots) are being incorporated into everyday work, automating complicated tasks and freeing up human workers to focus on vital and creative work. This improves operational performance and promotes a more creative, flexible, and less rigid organizational environment. The employment of robots for repetitive and risky jobs has resulted in considerable advancements in job definition and organization [5]. Industry 5.0 strives to create intelligent, sustainable, and inclusive manufacturing by employing automated and machine intelligence in the direct contribution of human creativity and expertise. Cobotics is an important technology that uplifts robots to reach human levels and brings them into partnership with other members of the team in order to improve human dexterity. With the use of these novel technologies, including virtual reality, augmented reality, mixed reality, and haptics, great, great things can be accomplished. Digital twins are also required for Industry 5.0, as they serve as digital representations of physical assets. AI is another critical component of Industry 5.0, increasing production efficiency and intelligence [6]. AI proponents envisage intelligent computers performing human duties, enabling creative pursuits. Despite fears about job losses, organizational think tanks believe AI can combine human and machine skills. They contend that the introduction and acceptance of AI necessitate employee up-skilling, citing dynamic skill, neo-human capital, and AI job replacement concepts [7]. The advancement of biotechnology and digital technologies in human improvement creates opportunities and threats in occupational health. Work-related post-humanism includes sophisticated technology such as wearable exoskeletons, cognitive enhancement devices, and AI-powered monitoring systems. Common problems include safety standards compliance, privacy concerns, and the difficulty of spotting dangers and risks. Despite these obstacles, these technologies have the ability to boost productivity, minimize bodily tiredness, and provide important time and real-time feedback for better decision-making [8]. AI technology advancements have had a substantial influence on the workplace over the last decade, prompting concerns regarding labor markets. Two possible situations are addressed: labor replacement, in which workers are replaced by machines, and labor empowerment, in which human-machine cooperation increases productivity. The former option, which might lead to widespread unemployment, is frequently regarded as preferable [9].

13.2 Human Augmentation

The shift from one generation of manufacturing to another—Industry 4.0 to Industry 5.0—is that technology is no longer the driving factor for advancement, but a turning point that will bring about humanization of manufacturing by putting the needs and interests of people at the top. Such a change is said to boost the abilities of employees to make their work safer and more enjoyable. The functions of industrial operators are going to change significantly since the place is currently getting warm attention from researchers and enterprises. Industry 5.0 defines this trend and changes the industrial environment [10]. A smarter environment is possible today with the advent of IoT and artificial intelligence computing in combination with human-computer interaction. The whole point of this approach is to make things accessible in terms of understanding human needs and seamlessly integrating technology into everyday life. Artificial systems can be implanted in the human body, along with miniature nanotechnology devices, to replace human capabilities or even enhance them [11]. The internet of things has improved characters by transforming their ability and quality of life in the professional sector. This coalescence of IoT and human augmenting technologies has only further complicated IoT's already easy-to-understand challenges and threats pertaining to IoT-enabled augmented humans [12]. Artificial intelligence, which indeed was modelled after human intelligence, has developed into an exceeding potential and caused fears of machines subjugating mankind. While the concept introduced has long been with machines supplementing the capacities of humans, intelligence augmentation (IA) could well evolve into the best form of interaction between the two types of intelligence [13]. Learning is a means to an end, with tools to improve human performance. Prior to the advent of modern computers, computers were utilized to perform mathematical calculations. People are no longer necessary for performing tasks that computers or machines can handle satisfactorily. Intelligent machines with advanced hardware or software have been used in a range of industries, but the education and training sectors have yet to fully realize the benefits of IA [14]. Digitalization is transforming occupations by establishing new sectors, increasing efficiency, and improving working conditions. However, developing technology such as robotics and AI is diminishing human intervention, resulting in employment losses. To prepare personnel for changing job needs, appropriate training and real-time assistance are required. User-friendly technologies such as augmented reality (AR) and virtual reality (VR) can be used in the workplace IA, allowing employees to adjust to new roles and enhance their abilities [15]. Operator assistance systems (OAS) can boost productivity and empower workers in unsuccessful automation situations. OAS collaborates with operators to alter their cognitive or physical capacities as they perform industrial activities. Researchers must understand where OAS may be employed, as well as the human elements and ramifications that result from its implementation, given the critical role of people in future industrial environments that cannot be automated, as shown in Table 13.2 provided below [16]. Emerging into every aspect of enterprise, local and foreign, AI has very slowly crept into HRM strategies. AI studies gradually became informed by issues that investigate an AI's social presence as well as its impact on personal and corporate outcomes and the assessment of AI-enabled HRM practices. Adoption of AI has created changes in work organization and the use of resources with decision-making and problem-solving in both domestic and foreign companies. However, AI-powered technologies for HRM are studied less and scattered. More studies need to be conducted to

Table 13.2 Impact of digitalization and AI on work and HRM.

Topic	Description
Digitalization and job transformation [15]	Digitalization enhances efficiency but also leads to job losses due to AI and automation.
Operator assistance systems (OAS) [16]	OAS boosts productivity by assisting workers in tasks where automation is ineffective.
AI in human resource management (HRM) [17]	AI integration in HRM impacts decision-making, work organization, and problem-solving.
AI and employee engagement [18]	AI-powered HRM enhances employee engagement and satisfaction through personalized experiences.

reveal the role that AI-assisted applications play within HRM operations and human-AI interactions in the largest multinational companies [17].

Engagement of employees is critical for organizational longevity, and employer-employee connection is essential. AI applications in HRM provide individualized ways that improve the experiences of employees and work satisfaction. The growing usage of AI-powered technologies in HR business operations improves employee experiences. However, the influence of AI-mediated HRM methods is still being investigated [18]. AI is revolutionizing human resource management, as well as work, employees, and workspaces. While AI-assisted HRM is gaining popularity as a means of increasing organizational efficiency, no strategic framework is currently available in academic literature. Existing research provides a chance to create such a framework [19].

13.2.1 Benefits of Human Augmentation Technology

The COVID-19 pandemic has expedited digitalization in economic production and services, with AI and robotics becoming self-aware and self-learning with human-like capacities. This has sparked a debate over the future of employment, with labor unions serving as the primary institutions representing employees. However, the idea of human substitution by intelligent computers calls into question labor union practices, which rely on paid worker membership and production-stopping capabilities [20]. Most significant threats and most complicated spams in Industry 5.0

concern the human profession, which still embraces versatility. It can thus pose certain challenges in integration, such as Human-in-the-Loop and Human-in-the-Mesh requirements. However, human-centered design techniques and digital technologies such as IoT, AI, virtual and augmented reality, and collaborative robotics could deploy people to perform things more rapidly and effectively, thus improving the efficiency of industrial CPS [21]. The hastened promotion and early adaptation of AI technology in the workplace can have very significant implications for the human work value; that is, "the sense of worth in one's job." However, the ethical implications and ways in which AI might support or undermine meaningful employment have yet to be investigated [22]. Wearable robots, such as exoskeletons, are a promising technology that has the potential to alleviate physical stress while also increasing creativity, productivity, and workplace safety. However, devising and planning techniques to equip future workplaces with this technology remains a difficulty. The incorporation of exoskeletons into logistics and manufacturing processes results in a new hybrid workstation that necessitates a scientific approach [23]. Safety mishaps in the construction business occur as a result of poor situational awareness. Current Deep Learning applications do not provide context-specific feedback. In addition to straight-from-the-box real-time Captioning, the Noval system handles security-centric real-time visual question answering and keyword-based image-text retrieval (ITR) with head-mounted augmented reality devices. Comparison and real-world images are used for the validation of the system [24]. In transformation, transhumanism has penetrated today, sophisticated with advanced technologies such as AI, machine learning, and even wearable technology or cognitive enhancement. These might mean targeted recruitment, training through immersive VR and AR, and improved health and productivity for employees. However, these raise fairness or privacy, as well as the correct conduct of updates, and ethical issues. Robust ethical frameworks with compliance with regulations would therefore be required to ensure ethical implementation. HR managers can adopt the transhumanist technology responsibly so that it meets every worker's needs in the digital age, thereby creating innovative, flexible workspaces for the development and transformation [25].

Figure 13.1 elaborates that recruiting and retaining talent are core to a business's success, involving competitive benefits, positive culture, and growth opportunities. Talent retention builds efficiency and adaptability in the workforce. Agile adaptation thus allows companies to change quickly in response to market changes, regulatory changes, or technological advances. Regulatory compliance and risk mitigation protect the

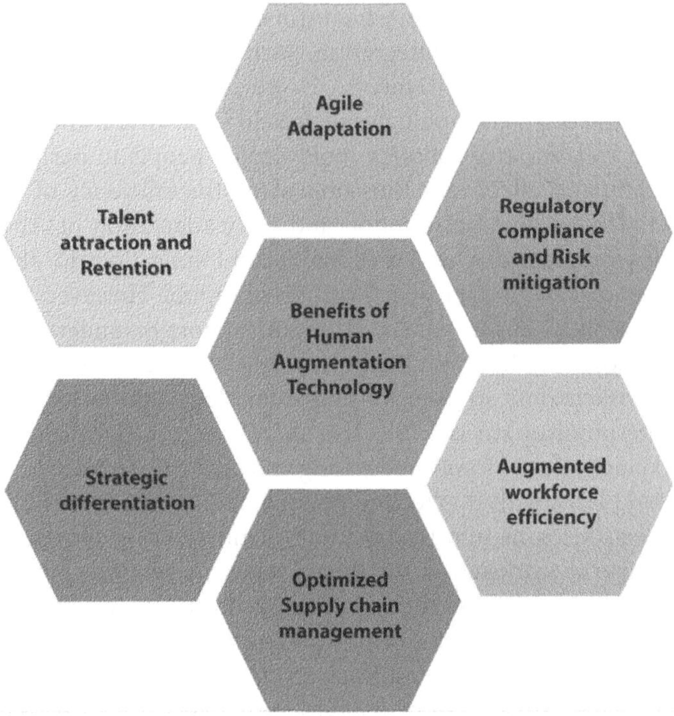

Figure 13.1 Benefits of human augmentation technology.

business from legal troubles by assessing and addressing risks. Strategic differentiation gives businesses a way to beautify the image of innovation, uniqueness, and operational efficiency. Optimized supply chain management means cost-effective, efficient supply with excellent supplier relationships and technological integration. AAI-enhanced workforce efficiency using AI and automation boosts the work being done in all areas. Those capabilities work to enforce business resilience [26].

13.3 Case Studies

13.3.1 Replicating Human Capabilities

A business called Naked Prosthesis makes personalized hand prostheses for people whose fingers have been severed. They are among the earliest producers of finger prostheses that offer incredible dexterity to their customers.

eSight: It is a wearable device like eyeglasses, allowing legally blind people to view their ambient surroundings. The near-eye resolution environment captured by the front-facing cameras of the device is displayed on the screen right in front of the wearers' eyes. Motion Savvy: This is a personal translator for deaf people, converting speech to sign language and vice versa. These items are now being targeted at companies with deaf staff; in the future, they may turn into smartphone applications enabling just about anyone to sign.

Cochlear implants- The first company to launch a product that restores hearing without an outside device. Bioprinting is defined as the making of organic tissues such as skin, bones, and organs by using 3D printing techniques. At the dawn of the application, this technology can bring a radical change in the medical field and the entire perception regarding healthcare.

13.3.2 Supplementing Human Ability

Waverly Labs has developed a pair of earbuds that can interpret conversations in real time, negating the need for language learning altogether. It is a significant advancement, even though its translation capabilities are restricted, and its dependability is not perfect. Even though you may not fully understand what Google Glass accomplishes, everyone has at least heard of this technology by now. Even though the technology has had a rough beginning (mainly because it was announced too soon), vision enhancement is growing in popularity. Microsoft's mixed reality device, the HoloLens 2, lets users see and interact with holographic objects. The gadget offers a wide range of commercial and industrial applications, including virtual education and staff training, gaming, and 3D computer-aided design and design collaboration.

13.3.3 Exceeding Human Ability

The idea of producing artificial blood cells has been investigated by Robert Freitas Jr.; this research is currently speculative. This theory originated from studies on mammals that can hold their breath underwater for extended periods of time, such as dolphins and whales. We might be able to replicate their blood cells' superior oxygen storage capabilities. Although the term "nanobot" conjures up images of science fiction, it has a great chance of becoming a standard component of the medical field. "A robot that permits precise interactions with nanoscale objects, or can manipulate with nanoscale resolution," is what Wikipedia defines as a nanobot. These robots can be implanted into the human body to carry out specific functions that the human immune system is unable to carry out on its own, like identifying and combating tumours and illnesses that the body's immune system finds difficult to fight.

Synthetic Memory Chip- It's no secret that hard drives have a far higher memory retention rate than humans. Additionally, they have faster and more accurate access to that memory. This concept inspired neurologist Theodore Berger to investigate implantable synthetic memory chips in the human brain. Although the technology is currently in the conceptual stage, it may enable people to have "perfect" memories that never forget facts.

13.4 Discussion and Future Prospects

- Organizations establish work environments that promote productivity, efficacy, well-being, safety, and security. Human enhancement, on the other hand, is concerned with individuals and has the potential to upset the general organization of a tightly knit socio-technological system. It is up to human factors to assess the possible consequences and cope with the evolving technologized human-technology connection, taking into account the potential disruptions generated by a single human improvement.
- Future studies should look into obstacles, possibilities, and guidelines for encouraging digital technology use in industrial CPS. This involves educational and training initiatives for worker up-skilling and re-qualification, simplifying intelligence distribution, and investigating the role of ethics in industrial CPS. This will assist in addressing open concerns and research possibilities in the sector.
- The development of VR and AR training systems is critical because they may increase workers' job duties, but corporations are still in the early stages of using them. If firms are made aware of the possibilities of IA technologies, employees should be prepared for significant adjustments in the job environment.
- Machine learning algorithms use sensor data to discover industrial process trends and abnormalities. This information improves machine performance, forecasts maintenance needs, and lowers downtime. Digital twin technology assists manufacturers in identifying possible quality concerns early

on, allowing them to take remedial steps to prevent faults and enhance product quality.

- Manufacturers can employ digital twin technology to replicate and improve their processes before deployment, discovering possible concerns and testing scenarios without incurring costly mistakes. This boosts efficiency and production, reduces errors and rework, and increases the likelihood of expensive mistakes in physical locations.

13.5 Conclusions

Some of the many challenges the development of AR faces are that it can obstruct the user's field of view, create fatigue, and ultimately become a source of human error. Along with physical discomfort, distractions may also come from wearing AR headsets, making it hard to concentrate. Short-term resolutions could develop from improving the UIs of such systems themselves, whereas long-term progress will depend on hardware manufacturers to improve their products. The suggested methodology brings user-friendliness into workplace design, using exoskeleton and digital twin technology, to ensure truthful accountability. This method allows monitoring of the exoskeleton's operation in a digital environment for confirmation. Still, ethical, legal, and social ramifications ensue circumspectly, owing to unresolved issues with technical definitions and certification. The study also outlines that employee training is an avenue through which productivity and efficiency are improved. The study also delves into how AR and VR technologies can facilitate skill training for human workers in the context of ethical issues surrounding AI in the workplace.

AI disclosure statement: The author acknowledges the use of AI-based tools for minor language editing or grammatical correction. However, all intellectual contributions, analyses, and conclusions presented in this chapter are entirely the author's own.

References

1. Döbler, N.A., Carbon, C.C., Schaub, H., Human Enhancement Without Organizational Knowledge and by Organizational Order. *J. Cognit. Enhancement*, *8*, 1, 170–183, 2024.

2. Marois, A. and Lafond, D., Augmenting cognitive work: a review of cognitive enhancement methods and applications for operational domains. *Cognit. Technol. Work, 24*, 4, 589–608, 2022.
3. Upadhyay, R., The Relationship between Employee Training and development and organisational performance: An empirical Study. *Psychol. Educ., 55*, 1, 2023.
4. Aljapurkar, A.V. and Ingawale, S.D., Revolutionizing the Techno-Human Space in Human Resource Practices in Industry 4.0 to Usage in Society 5.0, in: *Digital Transformation: Industry 4.0 to Society 5.0*, pp. 221–257, Springer Nature Singapore, Singapore, 2024.
5. Engelbart, D.C., Augmenting human intellect: A conceptual framework, in: *Augmented Education in the Global Age*, pp. 13–29, Routledge, Washington DC, 2023.
6. Zafar, M.H., Langås, E.F., Sanfilippo, F., Exploring the synergies between collaborative robotics, digital twins, augmentation, and industry 5.0 for smart manufacturing: A state-of-the-art review. *Rob. Comput. Integr. Manuf., 89*, 102769, 2024.
7. Jaiswal, A., Arun, C.J., Varma, A., Rebooting employees: Upskilling for artificial intelligence in multinational corporations, *Int. J. Hum. Resour. Manag.*, 33, 6, 1179–1208, 2022, https://doi.org/10.1080/09585192.2021.1891114
8. Singh, H. and Noel, E.A., Building a Safer Workplace in the Age of Human Enhancement: Challenges and Opportunities in Technology Integration, in: *Technological Enhancements for Improving Employee Performance, Safety, and Well-Being*, pp. 53–80, 2025.
9. Furendal, M. and Jebari, K., The future of work: augmentation or stunting? *Philos. Technol., 36*, 2, 36, 2023.
10. Ciccarelli, M., Papetti, A., Germani, M., Exploring how new industrial paradigms affect the workforce: A literature review of Operator 4.0. *J. Manuf. Syst., 70*, 464–483, 2023.
11. Ola, D.E. and Legg-Jack, D.W., Human Abilities Augmentation with Intelligent Technologies and Pervasive Computing Emerging Trends, in: *Managing Technology Integration for Human Resources in Industry 5.0*, N. Sharma & K. Shalender (Eds.), pp. 31–47, IGI Global Scientific Publishing, 2023. https://doi.org/10.4018/978-1-6684-6745-9.ch003, Scientific Publishing.
12. Pirmagomedov, R. and Koucheryavy, Y., IoT technologies for Augmented Human: A survey. *Internet Things, 14*, 100120, 2021.
13. Zhou, L., Paul, S., Demirkan, H., Yuan, L., Spohrer, J., Zhou, M., Basu, J., Intelligence augmentation: Towards building human-machine symbiotic relationship. *AIS Trans. Hum.-Comput. Interact., 13*, 2, 243–264, 2021.
14. Olaniyi, N. and Chuang, J., Intelligence Augmentation for Educators, Training Professionals, and Learners, in: *International Conference on Human-Computer Interaction*, 2021, July, Springer International Publishing, Cham, pp. 224–242.

15. Harborth, D. and Kümpers, K., Intelligence augmentation: Rethinking the future of work by leveraging human performance and abilities. *Virtual Reality*, *26*, 3, 849–870, 2022.
16. Moencks, M., Roth, E., Bohné, T., Kristensson, P.O., Augmented Workforce: contextual, cross-hierarchical enquiries on human-technology integration in industry. *Comput. Ind. Eng.*, *165*, 107822, 2022.
17. Budhwar, P., Malik, A., De Silva, M.T., Thevisuthan, P., Artificial intelligence–challenges and opportunities for international HRM: a review and research agenda. *Int. J. Hum. Resour. Manag.*, *33*, 6, 1065–1097, 2022.
18. Dutta, D., Mishra, S.K., Tyagi, D., Augmented employee voice and employee engagement using artificial intelligence-enabled chatbots: a field study. *Int. J. Hum. Resour. Manag.*, *34*, 12, 2451–2480, 2023.
19. Malik, A., Budhwar, P., Kazmi, B.A., Artificial intelligence (AI)-assisted HRM: Towards an extended strategic framework. *Hum. Resour. Manage. Rev.*, *33*, 1, 100940, 2023.
20. Nissim, G. and Simon, T., The future of labor unions in the age of automation and at the dawn of AI. *Technol. Soc.*, *67*, 101732, 2021.
21. Piardi, L., Leitão, P., Queiroz, J., Pontes, J., Role of digital technologies to enhance the human integration in industrial cyber–physical systems. *Annu. Rev. Control*, *57*, 100934, 2024.
22. Bankins, S. and Formosa, P., The ethical implications of artificial intelligence (AI) for meaningful work. *J. Bus. Ethics*, *185*, 4, 725–740, 2023.
23. Ippolito, D., Constantinescu, C., Rusu, C.A., Enhancement of human-centered workplace design and optimization with Exoskeleton technology. *Procedia CIRP*, *91*, 243–248, 2020.
24. Chen, H., Hou, L., Wu, S., Zhang, G., Zou, Y., Moon, S., Bhuiyan, M., Augmented reality, deep learning and vision-language query system for construction worker safety. *Autom. Constr.*, *157*, 105158, 2024.
25. Singh, S. and Madaan, G., Transhumanism in HR Management: Enhancing Capabilities and Navigating Ethical Frontiers, in: *Enhancing the Modern Workforce Through Transhumanism*, J. Kaur (Ed.), pp. 147–170, IGI Global Scientific Publishing, 2025. https://doi.org/10.4018/979-8-3693-8855-6.ch007.
26. Urme, U.N., The impact of talent management strategies on employee retention. *Int. J. Sci. Bus.*, 28, 1, 127–146, 2023.

14

Brain-Computer Interface for Trust and Transparency in Human-Centric Artificial Intelligence

Rajesh Singh[1], Aashna Sinha[2], Anita Gehlot[1] and Praveen Kumar Malik[3]*

[1]Division of Research and Innovation, Uttaranchal Institute of Technology Uttaranchal University, Dehradun, Uttarakhand, India
[2]Division of Research and Innovation, School of Applied and Life Sciences, Uttaranchal University, Dehradun, Uttarakhand, India
[3]School of Electronics and Electrical Engineering, Lovely Professional University, Phagwara, Punjab, India

Abstract

The integration of artificial intelligence (AI) in education and health care underscores the need for human-centric design and transparent explainability. This study explores how AI transparency enhances ethical decision-making and user trust, with a focus on the transformative potential of Brain-Computer Interfaces (BCI) in optimizing human-AI collaboration. The proposed framework combines advanced machine learning with BCI-driven feedback to bridge AI computational complexity and user understanding, fostering engagement and trust. In education, BCI-adaptive AI systems can decode cognitive states to personalize learning dynamically, while in health care, emotion-aware oncology chatbots leverage BCI for real-time emotional analysis, improving responsiveness and compassion. Explainable AI (XAI) remains critical to overcoming adoption barriers, particularly in BCI applications where neural data privacy and algorithmic fairness raise new trust concerns. By embedding BCI-enhanced transparency alongside accountability, the human-centered ethical AI (HCEAI) framework ensures AI systems align with human ethical standards across sectors, addressing both traditional and emerging BCI-related challenges.

Keywords: Human-centric AI, AI transparency, ethical AI, explainable AI (XAI)

**Corresponding author*: pkmalikmeerut@gmail.com

Tawseef Ahmed Teli, Syed Immamul Ansarullah, Arun Kumar Rana, Suman Lata Tripathi and Kashif Nisar (eds.) Brain-to-Computer Interfaces Using Machine Learning and Deep Learning, (329–344) © 2026 Scrivener Publishing LLC

14.1 Introduction to Human Centric AI

The advancement in data-driven machine learning, particularly deep neural networks, has led to unprecedented applications of artificial intelligence across diverse fields. These models use representation learning to automate feature engineering, prominently reducing the requirement for specific domain expertise. As a result, they have performed better with traditional methods, obtaining extraordinary outcomes that most likely surpass human performance in tasks like speech and image recognition, processing of text, and strategic games. These models have created new probabilities for artificial intelligence across different industries by automating the process of learning features from raw data [1]. As the autonomous systems have become common, the successful integration of them into daily life highly depends upon building a strong trust relationship between human and machine. In the interaction between human and machine, the effective use of these systems depends upon both machine and human factors. While talking about humans, trust is based on their desire to faith on the system, which is influenced by the specific task at hand and their past experience but while we talk about machines, their success depends on how well they communicate key information about their actions and how effectively they perform tasks, ensuring users can trust and understand the behaviour of the system [2]. From digital classrooms and mobile work to e-health services and online shopping, our lives have become more connected than ever. However, with the expansion of digital technologies, concerns have raised beyond data security and privacy. Discussions about issues such as transparency, surveillance, manipulation, profiling, discrimination, and algorithmic bias are now at the forefront. The rise of autonomous systems and artificial intelligence also produced many risks, particularly in relation to accountability and ethics. These concerns are leading to increasingly large public debates on how to manage the effects of digital technologies responsibly [3]. While everyone may not agree, it is necessary to keep artificial intelligence focused on bringing benefits to humanity for the long-term benefits of society. The legal and technical challenges of controlling artificial intelligence are well manageable and understood, but the huge challenge is ensuring that governments and society take responsibility for these systems. Responsibility is important, especially when artificial intelligence is used in such a way that it can impact the lives of people. Organizations and governments must step up to oversee and regulate artificial intelligence development to ensure it follows ethical standards and does not cause harm. By promoting responsibility, we can ensure the positive contribution of artificial intelligence to society without compromising the values of human beings [4]. Human-centricity plays an important role in the evolution of artificial intelligence, yet the way human-centred artificial intelligence is currently implemented in policy may limit its full potential to increase human well-being, as shown in Table 14.1. Often adapted from human-centred design principles, human-centred artificial intelligence is applied without fully considering the unique challenges and complexities that artificial intelligence technologies create. While it is essential to focus on human rights, doing this alone is not enough to ensure that artificial intelligence serves the broader goals of human flourishing. Moreover, the sometimes vague and inconsistent use of human-centred artificial intelligence in policy discussions makes it difficult to determine how it should be effectively and practically implemented within governance frameworks. This lack of clarity not only limits the effect of human-centred artificial intelligence but also prevents meaningful, well-defined strategies for the development of artificial intelligence that prioritize human empowerment and social equity. Without a more inclusive approach and clearer guidelines, the promise of human-centred artificial intelligence as a tool for enhancing societal well-being remains less utilized [5]. As artificial intelligence systems become more popular in decision-making, concerns about

Table 14.1 Trust, responsibility, and human-centricity in autonomous systems.

Aspect	Description
Trust in Human-Machine Interaction (2)	Successful integration of autonomous systems depends on mutual trust and effective communication between humans and machines.
Digitalization and Ethical Concerns (3)	COVID-19 accelerated digitalization, bringing concerns about privacy, transparency, and accountability to the forefront.
AI Responsibility (4)	Governments and organizations must ensure AI is developed responsibly, adhering to ethical standards for societal benefit.
Human-Centered AI Challenges (5)	Human-centered AI needs clearer guidelines and inclusive approaches to fully contribute to human well-being and equity.
Trust and Bias in AI (6)	Ethical tools and human oversight in AI decision-making are essential for increasing trust, transparency, and performance.

ethical issues, trust, and bias grow, probably neglecting performance and exposing organizations to increased cyber risks.

14.1.1 Enhancing Human-Centric AI with BCI

Brain-Computer Interfaces (BCI) has the potential to revolutionize human-AI collaboration by closing the cognitive feedback loop between users and AI systems. Unlike traditional AI, which operates on predefined data inputs, BCI-enabled AI can dynamically adapt based on real-time neural and emotional signals, ensuring a truly human-centric approach. In education, BCI can decode cognitive load, engagement levels, and comprehension states, allowing AI tutors to adjust content delivery in real-time—like a mental thermostat optimizing learning efficiency. This ensures that AI does not just follow rigid algorithms but evolves with the learner's mental state.

In medical applications, BCI-integrated AI (e.g., oncology chatbots) can detect stress, confusion, or emotional distress from neural patterns, enabling compassionate, real-time adjustments in patient interactions. This transforms AI from a cold, logic-driven tool into an emotionally intelligent assistant. BCI can help AI systems predict user intent before explicit commands are given, reducing friction in high-stakes environments like surgical robotics, autonomous vehicles, or defense systems. This creates a symbiotic partnership where AI acts as an extension of human cognition.

14.1.2 The Human-Centered Ethical AI (HCEAI) Framework

To fully harness BCI's potential while mitigating risks, the HCEAI framework integrates:

- ✓ Dynamic Neural Feedback Loops – AI adjusts in real-time based on brain signals.
- ✓ Transparent Neural XAI – Users receive clear explanations for AI decisions derived from BCI data.
- ✓ Ethical Neuro-Data Governance – Strict protocols for consent, anonymization, and bias audits.

To address these concerns, ethical tools such as Google's What-If and IBM's Fairness 360 tool are being used to improve transparency and fairness in artificial intelligence systems. Trust in artificial intelligence is multidimensional, including human acceptance, empowerment, and system performance, and is evaluated through moral, legal, and ethical frameworks. It is essential to use human oversight in artificial intelligence in decision-making processes to ensure that these systems remain aligned with society's values, responsible, and effective. Human involvement in artificial intelligence systems not only boosts the overall performance of AI but also enhances trust and accountability of artificial intelligence, which are important for artificial intelligence to be widely accepted and trusted in this environment of high risks [6].

14.2 AI in Transparency and Trust

Artificial intelligence is being used increasingly across a wide range of applications in providing valuable insights, decision-making processes, and support, from finance and healthcare to education and beyond. With the development of artificial intelligence technologies, they now have the ability to enhance and streamline processes that are complex in nature, decision-making of human beings, and solve the problems that were previously insurmountable. Although it is noted that for artificial intelligence to be truly transformative and for its prevalent adoption to occur, it is necessary that AI builds trust in the entire ecosystem of artificial intelligence. While talking about trust, it is not only about the performance or the reliability but also involves ensuring that artificial intelligence systems align with human values like ethics and transparency. The adaptation of artificial intelligence must ensure the encouragement of human autonomy by enabling individuals to make informed conclusions while maintaining control over their choices. Artificial intelligence systems should be designed such that they can ensure that they are being used in a responsible way, which also safeguards the users from potential exploitation, harm, or bias. The success of the artificial intelligence highly relies upon the increasing trust of the users and by assuring that the deployment of it will bring benefits to humanity as a whole [7]. Also, nowadays, explainable artificial intelligence is an important area of focus in the research of artificial intelligence, which aims at dealing with the challenges in understanding artificial intelligence systems of a complex nature. Models like deep learning neural networks of artificial intelligence have gained remarkable success in many tasks, such as image recognition. However, these models often work as "black boxes," which means that they are not performing transparent decision-making. Due to a lack of clarity, these systems or models become difficult for users to understand how artificial intelligence systems are reaching their conclusions, which leads to distrust and also raises serious concerns about security, accountability, and fairness. It is important for artificial intelligence to develop methods that can make these systems more visible and explainable so that they can be widely accepted and relied upon in critical applications. By doing so, the users will trust, understand, and effectively interact with the artificial intelligence by ensuring that these systems are being used in an ethical and responsible manner [8]. Artificial intelligence has the ability to revolutionize decision-making in many areas, such as economics, healthcare, and finance. However, the "black box" nature of many artificial intelligence systems raises concerns of ethics with respect to transparency and bias. These systems may produce results that are biased, unreliable, or inconsistent, which leads to errors that can be costly and may produce inequalities. Hence, to ensure that artificial intelligence is contributing positively in society, it is necessary to develop systems that are reliable, safe, ethical, and trustworthy. To tackle these challenges, it is required to design the technologies of artificial intelligence such that they promote transparency, accountability, and fairness and ensure that these systems ultimately ensure benefits for all users equally while minimizing risks and harms [9]. While talking about the development and deployment of artificial intelligence systems, ethical considerations are primary, which ensures that these systems are operating without any partiality, are respecting human rights, and also avoiding permanent bias. Key ethical principles such as privacy, accountability, fairness, and transparency are important in establishing trust between users and artificial intelligence systems, as shown in Figure 14.1. Without these principles, artificial intelligence technologies risk overlooking the values they seek to enhance. The research underlines the value of fostering effective human–artificial intelligence collaboration, which is critical to ensuring that decision-making is not only handled by artificial intelligence but also involves shared responsibility between machines and humans. This collaboration stresses the importance of maintaining user control over artificial intelligence systems, enabling users to influence and understand the decisions, thus enhancing engagement and trust. By promoting interdisciplinary collaboration, the research provides practical insights for designing human-centred artificial intelligence systems that prioritize the experience of users by empowering users to make informed decisions and align with ethical standards. This approach ensures that artificial intelligence technologies are not only functional but also ethically sound, fair, and promote inclusivity. Ultimately, the goal is to cultivate a harmonious, balanced relationship between artificial intelligence and humans, where artificial intelligence serves as a tool to enhance human decision-making power, well-being, and autonomy. Such an approach ensures that artificial intelligence technologies contribute to

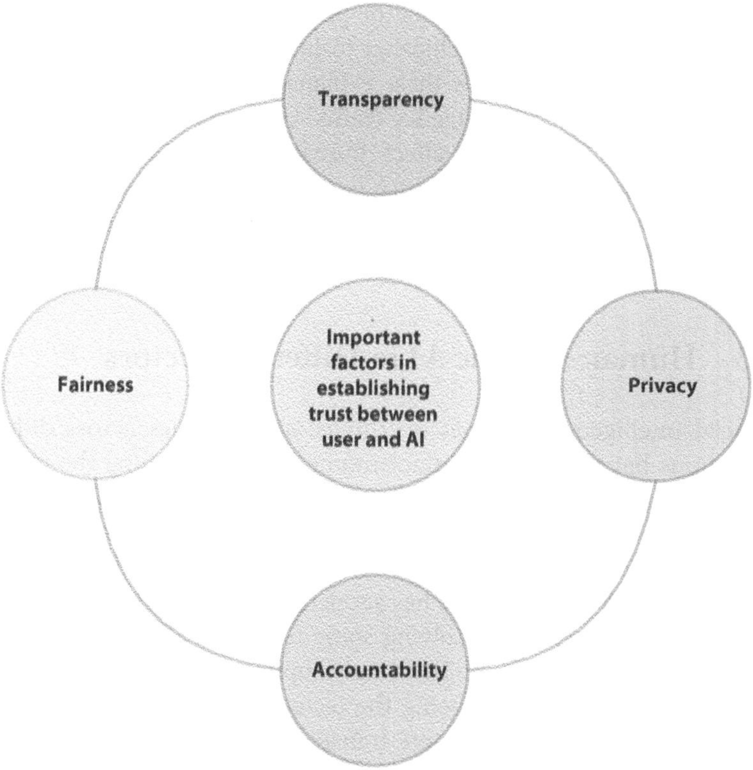

Figure 14.1 Important factors establishing trust between users and artificial intelligence.

society positively, promoting a future where artificial intelligence advantages humanity at large while minimizing ethical concerns and risks [10].

The influential performance of models of machine learning, especially transformer models and deep learning, has driven their widespread application in areas such as education, healthcare, and finance. However, these models are prone to errors and cannot be used autonomously, particularly in the context of high-stakes decision-making where mistakes could create serious consequences. Moreover, the "black-box" nature of these models makes it arduous for users to understand how they reach their conclusions, which can erode trust and hinder effective decision-making. Explainable Artificial Intelligence provides a resolution to this problem by providing techniques, such as visualization and interpretability methods, that clarify how models work and how they arrive at their results. This transparency helps in building trust and ensuring that users can understand and effectively use artificial intelligence systems. However, while much of the research has focused on improving the performance of models and developing explainable artificial intelligence techniques, very little attention has been given to examining how these explanations affect the performance of human and artificial intelligence teams. Understanding how apparent, understandable explanations affect human decision-making and collaboration with artificial intelligence is necessary for boosting the trustworthiness and effectiveness of artificial intelligence systems in practical applications [11].

14.3 Human-Centric AI in Different Sectors

Artificial intelligence, Internet of Things, and robotics across different applications have gained important momentum in reaching the growing expectations. As businesses are expanding, it has become more complex and time-consuming to manage the data. Hence, the integration of artificial intelligence with the rise of services that are web-based into business functions over the past decades has accelerated the growth of the Internet of Things, which helps in resolving some of these issues and challenges through process automation. The timely application of explainable artificial intelligence helps in reducing the technical complexities by making artificial intelligence systems more transparent and easier to understand. While artificial intelligence in Industry 4.0 focuses on the main functions of the businesses and improving the efficiency, explainable artificial intelligence in society is aiming at enhancing people's social life by making the technology more understandable and accessible for daily use by ultimately improving both societal and business experiences [12]. The increasing interest in Industry 5.0 shows that there is an increase in emphasis on the principles that are human-centric within the manufacturing innovations. Human-centricity aims at making a relationship between humans and technology where both the technology and humans are capable of achieving optimal system performance. Industry 5.0 shows the importance of considering human factors from the design phase of the technology system. However, there is a lack of clarity about the specific performance criteria that should be used to evaluate the manufacturing, which is human-centric. This gap in understanding makes it difficult to implement and assess effectively in human-centred sides in manufacturing, which limits the potential of Industry 5.0. By addressing these issues, one can ensure that human-centricity can truly boost the sustainability and performance of the manufacturing systems [13]. In the past few years, the focus has been on developing artificial intelligence systems that offer explanations for their prediction and decisions, which are human-centric. Even the most efficient models of artificial intelligence are often conjoined with distrust if the users are unable to know how the systems are working or why they are behaving in a certain way. Using human-centric explainability in event detection systems is important for enhancing the process of decision-making, which is both sustainable and trustworthy. By using an approach that is semantic-based and human-centric explainable event detection, artificial intelligence systems can develop reliability, transparency, and trustworthiness qualities, which are often lacking in current artificial intelligence systems. Using this approach not only enhances understanding of the users but also ensures that artificial intelligence systems are integrated confidently into critical decision-making processes [14].

14.4 Human-Centric Explainable AI (HCEAI) in Education and Healthcare

With the rise of Gen-AI and an increased amount of online information, the verification of manual content is impractical, which leads to the use of artificial intelligence in detecting deepfakes and disinformation. It has been shown in the research that the combined use of both artificial intelligence and human input results in an enhanced detection process. The European Union Artificial Intelligence Act mandates human oversight and transparency in artificial intelligence systems, which impacts human rights, requiring understandable and clear explanations. However, there is a lack of research on artificial intelligence explainability, which focuses on the human-centric approach, and the explanation effectiveness varies on the basis of the personal attributes and the user's prior knowledge [15]. The increasing focus on learning experiences has led to increased attention towards the use of artificial intelligence in educational technology. This paper introduces the Human-Centric Explainable AI (HCEAI) framework, which aims to improve the interpretability and transparency of Personalized Educational Chatbots (PECs), as shown in Table 14.2. V. Schmitt *et al.* proposed an architecture in their study, which combined machine learning techniques with more understandable and clear explanations, making the artificial intelligence model more interpretable. By enhancing cognitive understanding, the Human-Centric Explainable AI framework bridges the gap between complex artificial intelligence computations and user comprehension. This enhanced the Chatbot's interaction by facilitating transparent and simple explanations, which enhances greater trust [16]. The fast adoption of artificial intelligence technologies in business operations is transforming, but the human-centric barriers, such as black boxes, are hindering the acceptance of artificial intelligence. These factors are impacting the successful integration of artificial intelligence systems in organisations [17]. Talking about the healthcare use of chatbots in oncology highlights the increasing importance of human-centric artificial intelligence in addressing concerns of the patient and the family with accuracy. Human-centred artificial intelligence is prioritizing empathy, ethical principles, and approaches that are user-centric, which ensures that technology is aligned with human needs and values. J. C. Chow and K. Li, in their study, explored the ethical implications of using large language models (LLMs) such as GPT-3 and GPT-4 in oncology chatbots, by examining the impact on designing ethical AI systems and how these models react to human-like language patterns [18].

The rapid adoption of artificial intelligence in different sectors requires a firm focus on trustworthiness. Explainable Artificial Intelligence plays an important role in addressing the nature of the "black box" of the advanced

Table 14.2 Key aspects of human-centric explainable AI (HCEAI) and its application in education and healthcare.

No.	Topic	Details
1	**HCEAI framework**	Introduces the human-centric explainable AI (HCEAI) framework for personalized educational chatbots [16].
2	**Personalized learning**	Adapts instructional content based on user preferences and progress [16].
3	**AI adoption barriers**	Human-centric barriers like black-box issues hinder AI acceptance in organizations [17].
4	**LLMs in oncology**	Ethical implications of using LLMs like GPT-3/4 in oncology chatbots [18].
5	**Role of explainable AI**	XAI techniques like LIME and SHAP improve trust and transparency in AI [19].
6	**XAI in healthcare**	The importance of XAI in healthcare to ensure trust and clarity in decision-making [20].

artificial intelligence models by improving their interpretability [19]. Explainable Artificial Intelligence focuses on creating artificial intelligence models that are interpretable and transparent by allowing users to understand their outputs. In fields like healthcare, it is difficult due to the probable consequences of errors in artificial intelligence [20].

14.5 Case Study

In order to optimise personnel decisions and prevent injuries, among other use cases, the Texas Rangers employ the Data Intelligence Platform to collect data at hundreds of frames per second and analyse player mechanics.

With the switch to Databricks, Minecraft achieved a 66% reduction in processing time and can now leverage AI and analytics to improve the gaming experience.

Ahold Delhaize USA's engineers can now create pipelines that support data science and AI/ML applications thanks to a self-service data platform they built on Databricks. By using the DI Platform as a single data and analytics platform, the business can make better decisions by analysing sales and promotions at scale and across various client segments in real-time. Additionally, ADUSA uses the DI Platform to assist environmental initiatives, logistics, forecasting, inventory management, food waste reduction, consumer personalisation, and loyalty programs.

In order to facilitate GenAI advancements, Block standardised its data architecture through the use of the Databricks Data Intelligence Platform. With Databricks' GenAI capabilities, new companies can now use AI-powered setup and data import automation to onboard to the Square platform even more quickly. They may also use GenAI to produce text for marketing emails, team announcements, product descriptions, copy for websites, and more in real time. By adding hyperreal, AI-generated backgrounds to product photographs and selecting from over 50 style cues, eCommerce businesses can enhance their websites and draw in more clients. Block was able to reduce computational expenses by 12 times with Databricks, further redefining financial services for the twenty-first century.

A proprietary algorithm developed by AccuWeather uses its extensive and high-quality weather data to translate predicted weather into an impact number customised for each user's data. AccuWeather helps companies find strong connections between weather and operational KPIs by utilising the most extensive weather datasets available on the Databricks Marketplace.

Shell talked about their experiences, including the early challenges they faced with data strategy and governance, and how they overcame them by using Unity Catalogue and a business-owned data product approach. They explored the idea of Data Mesh, talked about the functions of the customer and the product team, and gave examples from actual situations. They also discussed how to use AI, ML models, Power BI, and analytics for data governance.

AT&T uses Databricks to expedite and simplify new data products, ranging from serverless Databricks SQL warehouses and AI/ML use cases to automated pipelining with Delta Live Tables. Meeting intricate security and connection requirements, however, might be difficult if workloads are not set up on your own network. AT&T explained how, beginning with serverless SQL warehouses, it implemented the Databricks serverless platform while adhering to strict security and regulatory standards.

The Blueprint metadata architecture from Unilever offers significant improvements in lakehouse management. The framework unified the engineering team at Unilever and accelerated development by a factor of 10. Blueprint greatly improved Unilever's data engineering and established new efficiency and scalability standards in its lakehouse architecture, serving more than 3,000 users with its downstream capabilities. Forecasting has always been a popular topic at Unilever. Using machine learning (ML) predictive models to estimate multiple critical business KPIs at varying degrees of granularity, the organisation demonstrated how it enhanced the forecasting procedures that were already in place. This is powered by a reusable predictive framework that Unilever developed using Databricks and can be deployed to various time series forecasting scenarios to increase development efficiency and facilitate maintenance.

14.6 Discussion and Future Perspective

The development of transparent human-centered AI depends on focusing on a user-centered design approach that applies ethical values to maintain fairness and clarity within AI systems. AI technologies that integrate into everyday life impact society in terms of the way they share their decision-making processes and maintain the prominence of responsibility. A successful approach to transparency and trust includes developing clear communication with ethical practices and collaborating with stakeholders to establish both transparency and trust.

- The implementation of explainable AI should become a priority as it helps users understand how decisions are made by AI systems.
- Organizations should establish ethical principles that guide the development of transparent and fair AI solutions.
- Efforts need to be developed to build systems that track and audit decisions made by AI so that organizations can hold AI accountable.
- AI systems require diverse stakeholders to participate during system regulatory development as well as the design process.
- Organizations should establish regulatory frameworks that enforce transparency in addition to trust for AI applications.

Conclusion

The widespread use of human-centric AI depends on achieving transparency and trust across all sectors. AI systems interact with people more frequently, so their ability to explain their preferences while upholding fairness principles and maintaining accountability serves as a key driver for users to trust the technology. Understanding artificial intelligence enables transparency using explainable AI systems, and collaborating with stakeholders to develop solid ethical guidelines helps reduce potential risks of bias and ambiguities. The integrity of AI systems depends heavily on regulatory support systems to maintain their operational standards. AI technologies will benefit humanity ethically when we apply these principles to operate in a transparent and trustworthy manner.

AI disclosure statement: The author acknowledges the use of AI-based tools for minor language editing or grammatical correction. However, all intellectual contributions, analyses, and conclusions presented in this chapter are entirely the author's own.

References

1. Horvatić, D. and Lipic, T., Human-centric AI: the symbiosis of human and artificial intelligence. *Entropy*, *23*, 3, 332, 2021.
2. Gebru, B., Zeleke, L., Blankson, D., Nabil, M., Nateghi, S., Homaifar, A., Tunstel, E., A review on human–machine trust evaluation: Human-centric

and machine-centric perspectives. *IEEE Trans. Hum.-Mach. Syst.*, *52*, 5, 952–962, 2022.

3. Seidl, M., Corporate digital responsibility: stimulating human-centric innovation and building trust in the digital world, in: *Liquid Legal–Humanization and the Law*, pp. 55–81, Springer International Publishing, Cham, 2022.
4. Bryson, J.J. and Theodorou, A., How society can maintain human-centric artificial intelligence, in: *Human-centered digitalization and services*, Toivonen, M., Saari, E. (eds.), vol. 19, pp. 305–323, Springer, Singapore, 2019. https://doi.org/10.1007/978-981-13-7725-9_16.
5. Sigfrids, A., Leikas, J., Salo-Pöntinen, H., Koskimies, E., Human-centricity in AI governance: A systemic approach. *Front. Artif. Intell.*, *6*, 976887, 2023.
6. Kioskli, K., Bishop, L., Polemi, N., Ramfos, A., Towards a Human-Centric AI Trustworthiness Risk Management Framework. *Hum. Factors Cybersecur.*, *127*, 127, 2024.
7. Casalone, C., Floridi, L., Palazzani, L., Pegoraro, R., Rossi, F., Villa, R., Human-centric AI: From principles to actionable and shared policies, G20 Insights, 2021.
8. Muthusubramanian, M., Jangoan, S., Sharma, K.K., Krishnamoorthy, G., Demystifying Explainable AI: Understanding, Transparency and Trust.
9. Dehghani, F., Dibaji, M., Anzum, F., Dey, L., Basdemir, A., Bayat, S., Bento, M., Trustworthy and Responsible AI for Human-Centric Autonomous Decision-Making Systems. arXiv preprint arXiv:2408.15550, 2024.
10. Usmani, U.A., Happonen, A., Watada, J., Human-centered artificial intelligence: Designing for user empowerment and ethical considerations, in: *2023 5th international congress on human-computer interaction, optimization and robotic applications (HORA)*, 2023, June, IEEE, pp. 1–7.
11. Rogha, M., Explain To Decide: A Human-Centric Review on the Role of Explainable Artificial Intelligence in AI-assisted Decision Making. arXiv preprint arXiv:2312.11507, 2023.
12. Waschull, S. and Emmanouilidis, C., Assessing human-centricity in AI enabled manufacturing systems: a socio-technical evaluation methodology. *IFAC-PapersOnLine*, *56*, 2, 1791–1796, 2023.
13. Frank, M.P. and George, G., Paradigm shift from AI to XAI of Society 5.0: Machine-centric to human-centric, in: *XAI Based Intelligent Systems for Society 5.0*, pp. 3–28, Elsevier, 2024.
14. Kolajo, T. and Daramola, O., Human-centric and semantics-based explainable event detection: a survey. *Artif. Intell. Rev.*, *56*, Suppl 1, 119–158, 2023.
15. Manohara, H.T., Gummadi, A., Santosh, K., Vaitheeshwari, S., Mary, S.S.C., Bala, B.K., Human Centric Explainable AI for Personalized Educational Chatbots, in: *2024 10th International Conference on Advanced Computing and Communication Systems (ICACCS)*, 2024, March, vol. 1, IEEE, pp. 328–334.
16. Schmitt, V., Csomor, B.P., Meyer, J., Villa-Areas, L.F., Jakob, C., Polzehl, T., Möller, S., Evaluating Human-Centered AI Explanations: Introduction of an XAI Evaluation Framework for Fact-Checking, in: *Proceedings of the*

3rd ACM International Workshop on Multimedia AI against Disinformation, 2024, June, pp. 91–100.
17. Kučević, E., Leible, S., Lewandowski, T., von Brackel-Schmidt, C., Ohlsen, F.P., A User-Based Study on the Acceptance of Artificial Intelligence-Based Decision-Support Systems, 2024.
18. Chow, J.C. and Li, K., Ethical Considerations in Human-Centered AI: Advancing Oncology Chatbots Through Large Language Models. *JMIR Bioinf. Biotechnol.*, *5*, e64406, 2024.
19. Rane, N.L. and Paramesha, M., Explainable Artificial Intelligence (XAI) as a foundation for trustworthy artificial intelligence, in: *Trustworthy Artificial Intelligence in Industry and Society*, D. Patil, N. L. Rane, P. Desai, & J. Rane (Eds.), pp. 1–27, 2024. Deep Science Publishing. https://doi.org/10.70593/978-81-981367-4-9_1.
20. Sadeghi, Z., Alizadehsani, R., CIFCI, M.A., Kausar, S., Rehman, R., Mahanta, P., Pardalos, P.M., A review of Explainable Artificial Intelligence in healthcare. *Comput. Electr. Eng.*, *118*, 109370, 2024.

15

Brain-Computer Interface Rehabilitation: Challenges & Future Directions

Rabiya Nazeer and Dhanpratap Singh*

Department of Computer Science and Engineering, Lovely Professional University, Phagwara, Punjab, India

Abstract

This chapter gives comprehensive research into the integration of machine learning (ML) and deep learning (DL) in brain-computer interface systems (BCI) with an extraordinary focus on restoration applications. BCIs decide the direct communication pathway between the human brain and external devices, giving modern trust for those influenced by motor disorders, stroke, spinal cord injuries, and neurodegenerative illnesses. Merging with ML and DL BCI innovations have made critical progress in preparing neural signals, translating exactness, and preparing versatile restoration procedures.

The chapter starts by displaying the fundamentals of BCI advancement, including signal procurement strategies such as electroencephalography (EEG), preprocessing methods, and feature extraction. It then jumps into the application of machine learning classifiers and advanced neural network architectures—including convolutional neural networks (CNNs), recurrent neural networks (RNNs), LSTMs, and transformer-based models—in deciphering neural patterns and engaging real-time system feedback.

Many real-world case studies are shown to illustrate the utilization of ML/DL-powered BCIs in clinical rehabilitation settings, such as motor recovery in post-stroke patients and attention training in individuals with cognitive incapacities. The chapter, in addition, presents framework traces that visualize end-to-end BCI rebuilding pipelines, from data securing to control signal generation and feedback adjustment.

**Corresponding author*: dhanpratap.25706@lpu.co.in

Tawseef Ahmed Teli, Syed Immamul Ansarullah, Arun Kumar Rana, Suman Lata Tripathi and Kashif Nisar (eds.) Brain-to-Computer Interfaces Using Machine Learning and Deep Learning, (345–366) © 2026 Scrivener Publishing LLC

In expansion, the chapter talks about key challenges, including inter-subject changeability, constrained clarified datasets, real-time adaptability, and moral considerations in BCI arrangement. It concludes with encounters into creating designs such as unified learning, hybrid BCIs, and user-centric system design, clearing the way for more comprehensive, open, and effective rebuilding courses of action. This chapter serves as a vital resource for analysts, engineers, clinicians, and students curious about the crossing point of neuroscience, machine learning, and assistive recovery innovations.

Keywords: BCI rehabilitation, EEG processing, ML/DL decoding, motor recovery, adaptive neurotechnology

15.1 Introduction

Innovative, versatile, and effectively accessible rehabilitation advances are in high demand due to the rising prevalence of neurological disorders, spinal cord injuries, and neurodegenerative illnesses like Parkinson's disease, amyotrophic lateral sclerosis (ALS), and stroke around the world. In spite of the fact that they are therapeutically advantageous, conventional recovery strategies are regularly limited by their manual nature, high resource requirements, and inability to be tailored to the specific needs of individual patients. In order to create more personalized, real-time, and neuro-adaptive solutions for patient care and motor recovery, researchers and clinicians are progressively looking to integrate brain-computer interfaces (BCIs) with advanced frameworks.

Bypassing the typical peripheral nervous system and neuromuscular pathways, brain-computer interfaces, or BCIs, enable coordinated communication between the human brain and external devices. BCIs were initially developed as assistive innovations for patients with severe disabilities, but they have since found more extensive applications, especially in rehabilitation engineering, where they help clients recapture motor functions through training principles based on neuroplasticity and brain-driven feedback.

The integration of machine learning (ML) and, more recently, deep learning (DL) methods into BCI pipelines has been a major factor in this change. Complex brain signals, particularly those recorded by non-invasive methods like electroencephalography (EEG), functional near-infrared spectroscopy (fNIRS), or magnetoencephalography (MEG), can be decoded in real time, thanks to these computational strategies. EEG is still the most widely used methodology in BCI frameworks for restoration because of its portability, affordability, and excellent temporal resolution.

The integration of machine learning (ML) and, more recently, deep learning (DL) methods into BCI pipelines has been a major factor in this alteration. Complex brain signals, particularly those recorded by non-invasive procedures like electroencephalography (EEG), functional near-infrared spectroscopy (fNIRS), or magnetoencephalography (MEG), can be decoded in real time thanks to these computational methods. EEG is still the most widely used methodology in BCI frameworks for restoration because of its portability, affordability, and excellent temporal resolution.

A change in mentality toward deep learning, which gives end-to-end learning capabilities and makes it conceivable to consequently extract hierarchical and discriminative features from raw EEG signals, has emerged from this constraint. Recurrent neural networks (RNNs) and their advanced variations, such as long short-term memory (LSTM) and gated recurrent units (GRU), are particularly well-suited for memorizing temporal patterns in EEG arrangements. Convolutional neural networks (CNNs), for illustration, can productively capture spatial conditions in multichannel EEG recordings. Besides, by preparing information in both forward and reverse time directions and utilizing attention mechanisms to focus on important signal segments, transformer-based models and bidirectional LSTMs (BiLSTM) have indeed shown more noteworthy progressions.

The potential of DL-based BCI frameworks to provide neurofeedback-based preparation, motor imagery (MI)–driven rehabilitation, and adaptive assistive control frameworks like functional electrical stimulation (FES) and automated exoskeletons holds remarkable promise for the field of restoration. These frameworks strengthen neural systems and activate brain regions involved in intentional movement through use-dependent plasticity by utilizing decoded brain signals to initiate movement in paralyzed limbs.

BCI frameworks are being utilized for cognitive recovery in addition to physical treatment. For illustration, they can enhance working memory, attention, and emotional regulation in patients with traumatic brain injury (TBI), attention deficit hyperactivity disorder (ADHD), or post-stroke cognitive disabilities. Improved signal generalization across sessions and subjects, reduced calibration times, and increased user adaptability are all encouraged by DL models.

However, while the potential is endless, critical challenges remain. These include:

- High inter-subject and intra-subject variability in EEG signals.

- Lack of large, labeled, and diverse datasets suitable for training deep models.
- The need for real-time, low-latency inference in clinical environments.
- Interpretability and explainability of DL models in medical contexts.
- Ethical and usability considerations for long-term patient engagement.

To address these, ongoing research is exploring hybrid BCI models, transfer learning, federated learning, and user-specific fine-tuning strategies. Additionally, the combination of EEG with other modalities (e.g., EMG, fNIRS) in multimodal BCI systems promises to increase robustness and reduce uncertainty in decision-making processes.

The objective of this chapter is to allow a careful survey of how deep learning and machine learning are changing the field of BCI-based rehabilitation. It will discuss:

- The advancement of BCI frameworks and their theoretical foundations.
- The role of ML and DL in preprocessing, highlighting learning, classification, and signal acquisition.
- Case studies highlighting recent advancements in cognitive and motor rehabilitation.
- Prospects, challenges, and future lines of inquiry.

This chapter highlights the potential of advanced BCI frameworks to alter restoration from reactive to proactive, individualized, and adaptive care by emphasizing interdisciplinary collaboration between neuroscience, artificial intelligence, clinical sciences, and biomedical engineering. By utilizing innovation that engages the brain instead of making people adapt to the innovation, the goal is not only to restore lost functions but also to empower people to lead more independent and fulfilling lives.

15.2 Machine Learning in BCI Rehabilitation

15.2.1 Role of Machine Learning in Brain Signal Interpretation

In BCI frameworks, machine learning (ML) has enabled the translation of brain signals, particularly for recovery purposes. An ML model is trained using electrical brain signals and then performs disease detection for the client by learning designs from labeled information. This permits feedback in restorative settings or control over outside gear. This can be supportive in recovery for following cognitive workload, recognizing attention levels, and translating motor imagery—all of which are essential for versatile treatment.

The advantage of machine learning in BCI is its capacity to control non-invasive neural signals, such as EEG, which are often subject-specific, noisy, and nonlinear. ML algorithms offer great versatility and the capacity to customize rehabilitation procedures by learning discriminative patterns from these signals.

15.2.2 Commonly Used ML Algorithms in BCI

Many machine learning algorithms have proven their potential in classifying EEG signals:

- Support Vector Machines (SVM): It has shown its effectiveness and robustness in separating EEG features for binary tasks, such as distinguishing between different motor imagery tasks or detecting seizure activity. SVMs are attractive for their robustness in high-dimensional spaces and clear decision boundaries.
- k-Nearest Neighbors (kNN): It classifies a new point into the most prominent class where the k nearest neighbors in the training data are. It distinguished two EEG data sets and identified two mental conditions. It is effective for small-scale EEG datasets.
- Random Forest (RF): It can effectively work on high-dimensional and nonlinear data, and hence it has shown remarkable performance on EEG data. It is an ensemble technique based on a decision tree. It is better than single tree models to handle overfitting and noisy features.
- Naïve Bayes (NB): It is based on Bayes's theorem, generally used for binary classification, and useful in EEG classification because features of EEG are generally represented in binary. It is a simple and low-computation method, especially when feature independence can be assumed.

Proper handcrafted feature extraction and cleaning methods with these classifiers perform better. Some of the feature extraction methods are listed here.

- Time-domain statistical features (mean, variance, entropy),
- Frequency-domain features (bandpower of alpha, beta, and theta waves),
- Common spatial patterns (CSP),
- Wavelet transform coefficients.

15.2.3 Applications in Rehabilitation

Various rehabilitation areas have demonstrated the effectiveness of machine learning; some of them are listed below.

- Motor Recovery: Regaining proper motor function and movement that may be lost due to impairment after injuries or illness. Classification of such impairments through EEG signals to control robotic exoskeletons.
- Cognitive Training: It is also called brain training; it improves cognitive abilities such as memory, attention, and problem-solving skills. It is used to monitor attention and mental fatigue during neurofeedback sessions, aiding in therapy for TBI, ADHD, or learning disabilities.
- Assistive Communication: Various methods, systems, and tools are involved to help individuals with communication disabilities. In this context, EEG signals are translated into character commands through speller-based BCIs and machine learning techniques.

15.2.4 Limitations of Traditional Machine Learning

ML has proved its importance and effectiveness even though it faces many challenges in BCI applications. A few of the challenges are mentioned.

- Manual Feature Engineering: Feature selection is a tedious task, and high skills are required to improve performance during feature selection.

- Lack of Scalability: Complex and inter-individual variable EEG signals raise concerns about generalization using classical methods.
- Low Nonlinear Modeling Capacity:
  The complexity and nonlinearity of EEG signals are too high, which further causes unpredictability through many traditional models.
- Time-Consuming Calibration: Some time processes are very complex, and it is necessary to perform subject-specific training, which increases the time of execution.

15.2.5 The Shift toward Deep Learning

The limitations discussed thus far point toward the adoption of deep learning, which assumes responsibility for feature extraction. Deep learning is suitable and effective on sequential high-dimensional EEG data by providing automatic feature extraction and superior modelling capacity. It performs more accurate, scalable, and real-time applications in BCI rehabilitation, reducing the need for handcrafted features.

15.3 Deep Learning for BCI Rehabilitation

15.3.1 Introduction to Deep Learning in BCIs

Deep learning (DL) is a subset of machine learning that utilizes neural networks to automatically learn from raw data and extract hierarchical features, revolutionizing data-driven models. The importance of deep learning is understood through brain-computer interfaces (BCIs) by applying it on electroencephalography (EEG) signals, especially in rehabilitation programs where real-time feedback is very much required with accuracy.

DL models have the capacity to naturally extract high-level representations of brain signals, in contrast to commonplace ML models that depend on manually engineered features and extensive preprocessing. This leads to significantly better classification performance, especially in noisy and highly variable datasets like EEG.

15.3.2 Advantages of DL in EEG Signal Processing

- **End-to-End Learning**: DL models create classification or regression outputs without the need for manual feature extraction when given raw or minimally prepared EEG signals as input.

- **Hierarchical Feature Learning**: DL employs a few layers to record temporal and spatial patterns.
- **Robustness to Commotion**: DL models excel at filtering out noise and artifacts, particularly those related to ensemble and attention-based methods.
- **Personalization and Adaptivity**: By utilizing transfer learning methodologies, DL models can be tailored for specific users or adapted for applications in other fields.

15.3.3 Deep Learning Architectures for BCI

Convolutional Neural Networks (CNNs)

For recognizing spatial relationships in EEG data, CNNs are frequently utilized. CNNs are able to productively extract data such as frequency distributions, spatial filters, and patterns of brain activation when EEG channels are treated as input "images." Variants like EEGNet, DeepConvNet, and ShallowConvNet have been specifically proposed for EEG classification applications.

Recurrent Neural Networks (RNNs), LSTM, and GRU

When handling sequential information over time, such as EEG signals, RNNs are particularly well-suited. The vanishing gradient problem inherent in standard RNNs is addressed by long short-term memory (LSTM) and gated recurrent unit (GRU) systems, which enable the model to retain information over longer sequences. In recovery contexts, these models are especially useful for tasks that require motor planning, sustained attention, or the analysis of temporal EEG patterns.

Bidirectional LSTMs (BiLSTM)

BiLSTMs capture both past and future information by processing input in both forward and reverse time directions. This bidirectionality enhances the model's understanding of context, aiding in the decoding of complex EEG tasks, like recognizing emotional or cognitive states during treatment.

Attention Mechanisms and Transformer Models

Attention-based models enhance performance and interpretability by focusing on the most informative segments of the EEG signal sequence. Initially developed for natural language processing, transformer architectures are currently being adapted for time-series EEG data in order to improve long-range temporal modeling and facilitate real-time BCI applications.

15.3.4 Applications of DL-Based BCIs in Rehabilitation

- Motor Imagery (MI) Rehabilitation: By using DL models to decode symbolic movements (such as the left or right hand or foot), robotic limbs or functional electrical stimulation (FES) systems can be controlled.
- Cognitive Rehabilitation: TBI or ADHD patients can have adaptive difficulty in training activities thanks to DL-based BCIs, which assess cognitive load, attention levels, and fatigue in real-time.
- Emotional Regulation: DL can detect emotional states from EEG (e.g., frustration, engagement), helping modulate therapy programs.
- Assistive Communication: DL can identify emotional states (such as engagement and frustration) from EEG, which aids in adjusting treatment plans.

15.3.5 Case Example: CNN-BiLSTM Hybrid Model

A recent hybrid model combining 1D convolutional neural networks (Conv1D) with BiLSTM layers was proposed to classify EEG signals for early detection of stress and motor imagery. The Conv1D layers are designed to extract local temporal features, while the BiLSTM layers capture long-term dependencies. This combination is particularly effective for addressing the non-stationarity of EEG signals in rehabilitation tasks.

Such architectures are trained on datasets like DEAP, BCI Competition IV, and PhysioNet, demonstrating significant improvements in classification accuracy and response time compared to classical ML techniques.

15.3.6 Challenges in Applying DL to BCIs

Despite its strengths, DL also presents several challenges in the BCI domain:

- Data Requirements: DL models necessitate large, labeled datasets, which are limited in medical EEG contexts.
- Computational Cost: Training and deploying DL models require high-performance hardware, limiting real-time applications.

- Interpretability: Deep learning models often operate as black boxes, which raises concerns in clinical settings where decisions must be explainable.
- Generalization: Inter-subject variability makes it difficult to build models that work well across diverse populations.

Ongoing research in transfer learning, subject adaptation, semi-supervised learning, and explainable AI (XAI) is addressing these limitations.

15.4 Case Studies and Applications of ML/DL-Based BCIs in Rehabilitation

Machine learning (ML) and deep learning (DL) have progressed from theoretical concepts to practical BCI applications used in clinical and rehabilitation settings. This section highlights specific use cases, datasets, and systems where ML/DL-based BCIs have demonstrated a measurable impact on both motor and cognitive rehabilitation.

15.4.1 Motor Rehabilitation with BCI Systems

Case Study: Post-Stroke Motor Recovery Using Motor Imagery-Based BCI

Stroke often results in partial or complete loss of voluntary muscle control. Motor imagery (MI)–based BCI systems have been deployed to support neuroplastic recovery in stroke survivors. In these systems, patients visualize specific movements (e.g., grasping with their right hand), and EEG signals are captured and decoded using CNN or CNN-LSTM models. These decoded signals then activate a robotic arm or trigger functional electrical stimulation (FES) on the affected limb.

Results:

Studies have shown significant improvement in upper-limb motor function after 4–6 weeks of MI-based BCI training, especially when reinforced with real-time robotic or sensory feedback.

15.4.2 Cognitive Rehabilitation

Case Study: Attention Training in TBI Patients

Individuals suffering from traumatic brain injury (TBI) often face deficits in attention and working memory. EEG-based BCIs, using LSTM

or BiGRU architectures, have been utilized in gamified environments to monitor attention levels and adapt task difficulty in real time.
How it works:
EEG data is processed through a deep learning model trained to detect attention lapses. When the model predicts low attention, the system adjusts stimulus complexity to re-engage the user.
Outcomes:
Improvements in sustained attention and task performance have been reported after just a few weeks of therapy using DL-enabled BCI platforms.

15.4.3 Assistive Communication

Case Study: Speller BCI for ALS Patients
In individuals with ALS or locked-in syndrome, speller BCIs allow them to communicate using brain signals alone. DL models such as attention-based LSTMs or transformer networks decode EEG responses (e.g., from P300 evoked potentials) as users focus on desired letters in a grid interface.
Advancement:
Compared to traditional classifiers, DL-enhanced spellers have shown increased accuracy, lower error rates, and faster character selection speeds.

15.4.4 Emotion and Stress Detection in Therapy

BCI-based systems are being designed to monitor emotional states during rehabilitation or therapy sessions. For instance, CNN-BiLSTM models trained on the DEAP dataset can identify user stress, engagement, or frustration in real time.
Use Case:
In neurofeedback sessions, stress detection is used to adjust task intensity, provide calming visualizations, or notify therapists of emotional overload.

15.4.5 Comparative Table of Applications

Application	BCI task	DL/ML model used	Outcome
Stroke recovery	Motor imagery	CNN + BiLSTM	Robotic arm/ FES control, improved limb movement

Attention rehabilitation	Attention monitoring	LSTM, GRU	Personalized training, increased attention span
Assistive communication	Speller control	Transformer, EEGNet	Faster spelling, improved user satisfaction
Emotion regulation	Stress level detection	CNN-BiLSTM	Adaptive therapy sessions, neurofeedback alerts

15.4.6 Datasets Used in Case Studies

Dataset	Modality	Use case	Details
DEAP	EEG	Emotion/stress classification	32 subjects, 40 videos each
BCI Competition IV	EEG	Motor imagery classification	Public benchmark with MI tasks
SEED	EEG	Emotion recognition	Multimodal recordings from 15 subjects
PhysioNet EEG Motor task	EEG	Motor task labeling	High-resolution EEG during physical tasks

15.4.7 Real-World BCI Systems in Use

- NeuroPype: A real-time BCI system for motor imagery with CNN-based EEG classification.
- Emotiv Insight + BCI Suite: Commercial EEG headsets used in DL-based cognitive monitoring.
- OpenBCI GUI + Python SDK: Open-source pipeline supporting CNN and LSTM models for EEG decoding.

15.5 Challenges and Limitations in ML/DL-Based BCI Rehabilitation

While the integration of machine learning (ML) and deep learning (DL) in brain-computer interfaces (BCIs) offers transformative potential for rehabilitation, several technical, clinical, and ethical challenges must be addressed to ensure effective, scalable, and user-friendly systems.

15.5.1 Inter-Subject and Intra-Subject Variability

EEG signals are highly individualistic, and factors such as head shape, hair density, electrode placement, fatigue, and emotional state can significantly impact signal quality. A model trained on one subject may perform poorly when applied to another, necessitating subject-specific calibration or transfer learning.

15.5.2 Data Limitations

- **Limited Labeled Datasets**: Deep learning models require large volumes of labeled data to perform well. However, collecting high-quality, annotated EEG datasets in clinical settings is time-consuming, costly, and logistically challenging.
- **Imbalanced Classes**: Rehabilitation data may have skewed class distributions (e.g., more resting state than motor imagery samples), which can bias model performance.

15.5.3 Real-Time Processing Constraints

BCI rehabilitation systems require low-latency, real-time EEG decoding to provide immediate feedback. DL models, while accurate, can be computationally intensive and may require hardware acceleration (e.g., GPUs), which can limit portability and real-world usage in resource-constrained environments.

15.5.4 Interpretability and Explainability

Deep learning models often operate as "black boxes," making it difficult for clinicians and patients to understand the reasoning behind specific outputs or classifications. In sensitive healthcare applications, a lack of interpretability can hinder trust, adoption, and clinical validation.

15.5.5 Usability and Long-Term Engagement

Long-term rehabilitation programs require consistent user engagement. EEG headsets may cause discomfort over extended sessions, and repeated calibration can frustrate users. Ensuring comfort, ease of use, and minimal setup time is essential for patient adherence.

15.5.6 Ethical and Legal Considerations

BCI systems that monitor or decode brain activity raise privacy and ethical concerns:

- Who owns the brain data?
- How is it stored, shared, or used?
- Can decisions made by AI be audited in a clinical trial?

Frameworks for ethical AI in neurotechnology are still evolving and must balance innovation with patient rights.

15.5.7 Generalization and Robustness

ML/DL models often overfit training data, leading to poor generalization in unseen conditions. Changes in environment, task structure, or user fatigue can reduce system reliability. Robust cross-session, cross-task, and cross-population generalization remains a core challenge in BCI research.

15.5.8 Summary Table: Challenges and Research Opportunities

Challenge	Description	Emerging solution
Inter-subject variability	EEG differs across individuals	Transfer learning, domain adaptation
Data scarcity	Limited labeled clinical EEG data	Semi-supervised learning, data augmentation
Real-time constraints	DL models are slow for real-time decoding	Lightweight architectures, edge computing

Interpretability	Clinicians cannot explain DL model decisions	Explainable AI (XAI), saliency maps
Comfort and engagement	Headset discomfort and long setup discourage use	Dry electrodes, wireless headsets, VR integration
Ethical concerns	Data privacy, decision transparency	Secure storage, ethical AI guidelines
Poor generalization	Models do not perform well across sessions or users	Few-shot learning, personalized retraining

15.6 Workflow of Motor Imagery-Based BCI Rehabilitation Using Deep Learning

Figure 15.1 illustrates the complete pipeline of a motor imagery-based brain-computer interface (BCI) system designed for neurorehabilitation. The workflow combines non-invasive neural signal acquisition, deep learning–based classification, and real-time feedback to engage neuroplastic mechanisms and facilitate motor recovery.

1. **EEG Headset**: The process begins with the user wearing an EEG headset that records electrical activity from the brain, particularly during motor imagery tasks such as imagining left- or right-hand movements.
2. **Signal Acquisition**: The raw EEG signals are collected from multiple scalp electrodes, focusing on areas over the motor cortex. These time-series signals represent the user's motor intent.
3. **Preprocessing**: Collected signals undergo essential cleaning procedures, including:
    - **Filtering** to remove high-frequency noise and power-line interference.
    - **Artifact removal** to eliminate disturbances caused by eye blinks, muscle activity, etc.
    - **Normalization** to scale the data for consistent and efficient model performance.

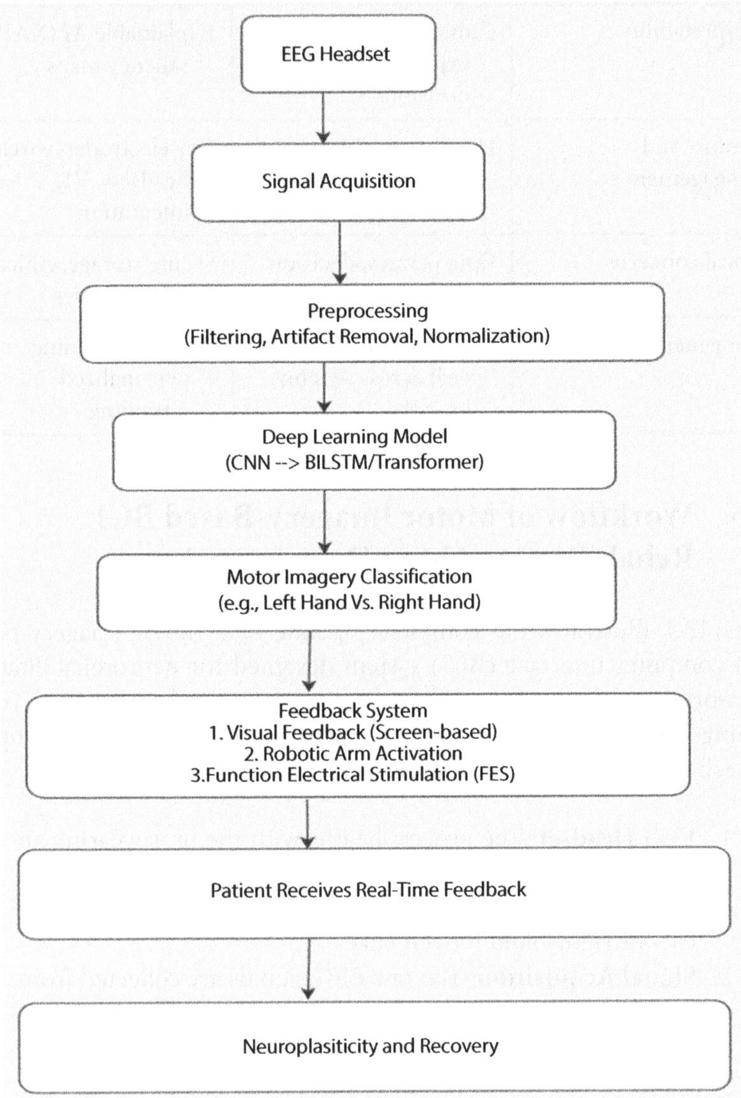

Figure 15.1 Workflow of motor imagery-based BCI rehabilitation using deep learning.

4. **Deep Learning Model (CNN → BiLSTM/Transformer)**: Preprocessed signals are fed into a deep learning architecture:
   - **Convolutional Neural Networks (CNNs)** are used to extract spatial patterns across EEG channels.

- **Bidirectional Long Short-Term Memory (BiLSTM)** networks capture temporal dynamics of the EEG sequence in both forward and backward directions.
- **Transformer-based models** utilize attention mechanisms to focus on informative parts of the signal and improve classification accuracy. These models automatically learn features relevant to the classification of motor tasks, eliminating the need for manual feature engineering.

5. **Motor Imagery Classification**: The deep learning model classifies the mental task being performed (e.g., left- vs. right-hand motor imagery), translating the user's intent into control commands.
6. **Feedback System**: Based on the classification, a real-time feedback mechanism is triggered. This feedback can take multiple forms:
   - **Visual feedback** *via* screen-based animations
   - **Robotic arm activation** for physical motion assistance
   - **Functional Electrical Stimulation (FES)** to stimulate specific muscle groups.
7. **Patient Receives Real-Time Feedback**: The user observes the result of their imagined movement, forming a closed-loop system that helps reinforce the brain-signal-action connection.
8. **Neuroplasticity and Recovery**: Over multiple sessions, this closed-loop feedback strengthens relevant neural pathways through neuroplasticity, contributing to the functional recovery of motor skills.

This framework exemplifies how BCIs, when combined with modern deep learning models, offer a personalized and interactive approach to neurorehabilitation. The system not only interprets brain signals but also closes the loop by providing direct, meaningful feedback to the user, thereby supporting active rehabilitation.

15.7 Future Research Directions in ML/DL-Based BCI Rehabilitation

As machine learning (ML) and deep learning (DL) continue to evolve, their integration into brain-computer interface (BCI) systems for rehabilitation is expected to grow in sophistication and impact. While significant progress has been made, many research opportunities remain to enhance system accuracy, adaptability, scalability, and clinical usability.

15.7.1 Hybrid BCI Systems

Combining multiple signal modalities—such as EEG with electromyography (EMG), functional near-infrared spectroscopy (fNIRS), or eye-tracking—can improve signal reliability and system robustness. **Multimodal BCIs** can compensate for the weaknesses of individual signals and provide a richer understanding of user intent, especially in noisy or dynamic environments.

15.7.2 Transfer Learning and Personalization

One of the major challenges in EEG-based BCI is **inter-subject variability**. Transfer learning techniques allow pre-trained models to adapt quickly to new users with minimal data, reducing calibration time and enhancing usability. Future systems should support **real-time personalization** through incremental learning or adaptive fine-tuning.

15.7.3 Semi-Supervised and Few-Shot Learning

Since large labeled datasets are hard to obtain in clinical contexts, **semi-supervised**, **self-supervised**, and **few-shot learning** approaches are emerging as promising alternatives. These methods can learn representations from unlabeled EEG data or generalize to new tasks and subjects with very limited labeled examples, reducing reliance on labor-intensive annotations.

15.7.4 Explainable AI (XAI) in BCI

As DL models are increasingly applied in healthcare, **transparency** and **interpretability** are essential. Explainable AI techniques such as saliency maps, attention visualization, and layer-wise relevance propagation (LRP) are being developed to help clinicians and researchers understand model decisions, increasing trust and facilitating clinical adoption.

15.7.5 Edge Computing and Real-Time Deployment

BCI systems used in daily rehabilitation require **low-latency** performance and **energy efficiency**. The deployment of lightweight DL models on edge devices (such as portable EEG headsets with embedded processors) will enable **real-time feedback** without dependence on cloud servers. Future work will involve optimizing models using techniques like **quantization**, **pruning**, and **knowledge distillation**.

15.7.6 Federated Learning for Privacy-Preserving Training

Federated learning enables the training of DL models across decentralized edge devices without exchanging raw EEG data, thereby protecting user privacy while promoting collaborative learning. Multi-center studies and demonstrated improvements are made possible by this strategy without compromising private patient information.

15.7.7 Virtual Reality (VR) and Immersive Interfaces

Client engagement in recovery can be progressed by joining BCI devices with stages for increased augmented reality (AR) or virtual reality (VR). By empowering avatar developments or 3D environment interaction, DL-based BCIs can improve quiet inspiration, personalization, and ease of utilization in treatment.

15.7.8 Standardization and Clinical Validation

Moving from laboratory settings to hospitals or home environments requires the following:

- Standardized datasets
- Benchmarking protocols
- Longitudinal studies

Approving these advances in real restoration workflows will require participation between analysts, doctors, and administrative offices.

15.7.9 Summary of Future Opportunities

Research area	Opportunity	Impact
Hybrid BCIs	EEG + EMG/fNIRS	Improved signal quality and intent detection
Transfer learning	Pre-trained model adaptation	Faster calibration and broader generalization
Explainable AI	Saliency maps, attention analysis	Trust and transparency in clinical use
Edge computing	Lightweight DL for portable devices	Real-time inference and greater accessibility
VR/AR integration	Immersive rehab using BCI-driven avatars	Enhanced patient engagement and therapy outcomes
Federated learning	Model training without data sharing	Secure, scalable, privacy-compliant learning
Clinical validation	Standardized evaluation protocols	Real-world deployment and regulatory approval

15.8 Conclusion

Neurorehabilitation has progressed essentially with the integration of deep learning (DL) and machine learning (ML) into brain-computer interface (BCI) frameworks. Beyond simply deciphering fundamental brain signals, these advanced frameworks now enable users and assistive devices to interact dynamically and in real time. With ML/DL-enhanced BCIs, individuals recovering from stroke, spinal cord injuries, traumatic brain damage, or neurodegenerative diseases have new opportunities to regain lost functions, improve their quality of life, and enhance their cognitive abilities.

Recently, BCI frameworks have achieved remarkable accuracy in interpreting complex EEG signals by utilizing advanced computational models, such as convolutional neural systems, recurrent models like LSTMs, attention-based transformers, support vector machines, and random forests. Promising results in motor recovery, attention training, emotional management, and assistive communication have emerged from these advancements.

However, there are obstacles to widespread clinical adoption. Broad implementation is still hindered by issues such as brain signal variability, a lack of large, well-annotated datasets, the interpretability of deep learning models, and challenges related to real-time deployment. The necessity for responsible neuro-technology advancement is further highlighted by moral issues regarding long-term engagement and user data privacy.

In the future, this field of study will actively explore solutions like explainable AI, multimodal signal integration, federated learning, transfer learning, and the incorporation of BCI devices into immersive settings like virtual reality. The objective of these activities is to create more personalized, easily accessible, and efficient rehabilitation resources that can adapt to each person's unique neural profiles.

This chapter provides a comprehensive overview of how deep learning and machine learning are transforming BCI-based rehabilitation. It has addressed key concepts, current improvements in technology, clinical applications, limitations, and emerging opportunities. Rehabilitative back care that is intelligent, user-centric, and non-invasive is becoming a reality as interdisciplinary collaboration among computer science, neuroscience, medicine, and design continues to grow.

The conclusion emphasizes that the integration of advanced algorithms and brain-computer interfaces has the potential to transform recovery from a reactive treatment approach into a proactive, ongoing, and engaging process. This shift aims to restore agency, communication, and independence to those who need it most.

AI disclosure statement: The author acknowledges the use of AI-based tools for minor language editing or grammatical correction. However, all intellectual contributions, analyses, and conclusions presented in this chapter are entirely the author's own.

Bibliography

Elashmawi, W.H., Ayman, A., Antoun, M., Mohamed, H., Mohamed, S.E., Amr, H., Talaat, Y., Ali, A., A Comprehensive Review on Brain–Computer Interface (BCI)-Based Machine and Deep Learning Algorithms for Stroke Rehabilitation. *Appl. Sci.*, *14*, 14, 6347, 2024, https://doi.org/10.3390/app14146347.

Jafari, M., Shoeibi, A., Khodatars, M., Bagherzadeh, S., Shalbaf, A., García, D.L., Gorriz, J.M., Acharya, U.R., Emotion recognition in EEG signals using deep learning methods: A review. *Comput. Biol. Med.*, *165*, 107450, 2023, https://doi.org/10.1016/j.compbiomed.2023.107450.

Premchand, B., Liang, L., Phua, K.S., Zhang, Z., Wang, C., Guo, L., Ang, J., Koh, J., Yong, X., Ang, K.K., Wearable EEG-Based Brain-Computer Interface for Stress Monitoring. *NeuroSci*, 5, 4, 407–428, 2024, https://doi.org/10.3390/neurosci5040031.

S.N. and J.J., An EEG-based Brain-Computer Interface for Stress Analysis. *2023 Second International Conference on Electronics and Renewable Systems (ICEARS)*, Tuticorin, India, pp. 355–360, 2023, doi: 10.1109/ICEARS56392.2023.10085458.

Singh, P., Singla, R., Kesari, A., An EEG Based Approach for the Detection of Mental Stress Level: An Application of BCI, in: *Recent Innovations in Mechanical Engineering. Lecture Notes in Mechanical Engineering*, M. Vashista, G. Manik, O.P. Verma, B. Bhardwaj (Eds.), Springer, Singapore, 2022, https://doi.org/10.1007/978-981-16-9236-9_5.

Patil, S.A. and Paithane, A.N., Optimized EEG-Based Stress Detection: A Novel Approach. *Biomed. Pharmacol. J.*, 17, 4, 2024.

Värbu, K., Muhammad, N., Muhammad, Y., Past, Present, and Future of EEG-Based BCI Applications. *Sensors*, *22*, 9, 3331, 2022, https://doi.org/10.3390/s22093331.

16

Brain Signal Processing with a Focus on Electroencephalography in Attention-Deficit Hyperactivity Disorder

Gaurav Gangwar[1], Nimisha Singh[2], Ramandeep Sandhu[3], Deepika Ghai[4]* and Suman Lata Tripathi[5]

[1]*Department of Chemical Engineering, Indian Institute of Technology, Ropar, Punjab, India*
[2]*School of Skill Development, Baba Farid College of Engineering and Technology, Bhatinda, Punjab, India*
[3]*School of Computer Science & Engineering, Lovely Professional University, Phagwara, Punjab, India*
[4]*School of Electronics and Electrical Engineering, Lovely Professional University, Phagwara, Punjab, India*
[5]*Department of Electronics & Telecommunication, Symbiosis Institute of Technology, Symbiosis International (Deemed University), Pune, Maharashtra, India*

Abstract

In recent days, machine learning has become an effective method to automatically detect patterns in data, which can be used to predict future data for better decisions at times of uncertainty. This chapter describes the wide range of applications and methodologies utilized in brain signal processing, concentrating on electroencephalography (EEG) in attention-deficit hyperactivity disorder (ADHD) patients. It becomes an effective instrument for decoding brain signals, simplifying the extraction of significant patterns from intricate neural data. We examine fundamental machine learning paradigms, such as supervised and unsupervised, and their significance in interpreting cognitive states, motor intentions, and neurological disorders. After that, we discussed feature extraction techniques, including time-frequency analysis and wavelet transforms. Autoencoders and reptile

**Corresponding author*: money.ghai25@gmail.com

Tawseef Ahmed Teli, Syed Immamul Ansarullah, Arun Kumar Rana, Suman Lata Tripathi and Kashif Nisar (eds.) Brain-to-Computer Interfaces Using Machine Learning and Deep Learning, (367–398) © 2026 Scrivener Publishing LLC

search algorithms are examined to improve signal representation. This study proposes random forest classifiers for distinguishing ADHD individuals from non-ADHD ones and other standard classifiers used to compare model performance, such as XGBoost, SVMs, k-nearest neighbors, and AdaBoost. Classifiers are also evaluated for their performance in decoding cognitive and motor intentions and for handling the spatiotemporal intricacies of brain signals. The proposed model provided an accuracy of 92%, the same value achieved for recall, precision, and F1 score, as well as a specificity rate of 92% and a sensitivity rate of 92%. Apart from this, the ROC_AUC score of 0.92 was achieved for this model, which shows that the random forest has an improved capability to distinguish between ADHD and non-ADHD individuals.

***Keywords*:** AdaBoost, electroencephalogram (EEG), autoencoder, SVM, reptile search algorithm, K-NN, XGBoost, random forest

16.1 Introduction

Attention-deficit hyperactivity disorder (ADHD) is a behavioral disease diagnosed in early childhood. Its unique marks are symptoms of impulsivity, inattention, or even hyperactivity [2, 9, 18, 20]. As a symptom of juvenile developmental disease, the condition is prevalent. ADHD symptoms often don't show up until a kid is at least twelve years old, and in rare cases, they might occur as early as three years old. A current estimate puts the prevalence of ADHD in males at 12.1% and in girls at 3.9% [10]. Between the ages of 4 and 17, about 6.4 million children in the US have been identified as having this problem [6, 11, 30]. ADHD impairs children's capacity to develop essential cognitive, behavioral, emotional, and activity-regulating abilities. Hence, they frequently exhibit behaviors that pose challenges for parents in terms of management [4]. Adults with chronic ADHD may experience significant long-term effects, including underachievement in education and poor work performance, an increased risk of engaging in antisocial behavior, and excessive consumption of drugs and alcohol. Therefore, the timely identification of this condition is exceedingly valuable [12]. EEG (Electroencephalogram)-based studies on ADHD commenced 80 years ago. Since then, EEG has emerged as one of the most extensively used neuroimaging strategies. This method is pretty handy, instructional, and value-effective [13, 24]. Several signal-processing strategies were devised to detect electrophysiological abnormalities in children with ADHD, together with strength quantification [14], complexity analysis [31], and synchronization [25]. Classification models for ADHD have been advanced by the use of several devices, including support vector machine (SVM), linear discriminant analysis (LDA), and logistic regression (LR) while considering the disorder's complex traits. Forthcoming research involves the application of magnetic resonance imaging or MRI or functional magnetic resonance imaging (fMRI) to identify conditions linked to ADHD. There is a lot of complexity and speedy development in this field of technological know-how. fMRI discovered decreased interest within the right hemisphere's mesial and lateral prefrontal areas, as well as the cingulate gyrus, within the ADHD research organization [21]. The current work primarily targets the improvement of the precision of ADHD by integrating better feature extraction techniques with a robust classification system. The key contributions of this study are as follows:

It works on a novel approach for the extraction of the significant features from the EEG data, and it uses auto-encoders, which reduce noise and improve data quality for accurate ADHD detection. The study employs a classification model, specifically random forest, which offers advantages such as resilience to missing data, robustness against noise, and improved performance in analyzing complex EEG datasets.

16.2 Related Work

This section explores the systematic literature done in the field of problem-formulated relevant to Brain Signal Decoding and various ML and other techniques in the same field. In 2003, ADHD-affected children between the ages of 2 and 17 were approximately 4.4 million. This number increased to 5.4 million in 2007 and became 6.1 million in 2016 [3]. Puliniet *et al.* [19] found that neuroimaging features may accurately diagnose ADHD with an accuracy of 60% to 80%. Pulini argues that the high classification accuracies shown in ADHD neuroimaging research can be inflated when using circular analysis with a limited sample size. Using MRI demonstrates satisfactory precision. Despite its high price tag, EEG enables more portability and adaptability in data collection. This study aims to identify neuromere functional EEG connectivity in adults with ADHD. The method of measuring BD and ADHD symptoms objectively failed to distinguish between bipolar patients and those with ADHD or normal mental development, as stated in [5]. The identification of an unmedicated adolescent sample occurred through the combination of DSM-IV and Kiddie-SADS PL/E, which included participants between 18 years of age and 5 years of age. The sample consisted of 155 men. On the same data record, the SVM model was applied to segregate the bipolar from the non-bipolar values. The accuracy considered for the work is 83.1%. Here, the coverage area of ROC was

0.781, with a specificity of 91.7% and a sensitivity of 64.4%. A novel dual subspace classification algorithm utilizes resting-state functional connectivity (FC) by Chen *et al.* [1] to enhance identification accuracy. By learning ADHD and controlling subspaces, it compares projected energy on each subspace to predict labels. This framework, tested on the ADHD-200 dataset, achieves notable accuracy, outperforming other machine learning methods with approximately 90% success in cross-validation. The data from 103 participants, including 51 ADHD patients and 52 controls, were collected using a wrist-worn actigraphy device. Here, an ML model named random forest is applied with 10-fold cross-validation. The achievement is 72% accuracy.

The research conducted by Slobodin *et al.* [22] combined bootstrap methodology with retrospective factorial fitting to accomplish their training evaluation and cross-validation. Performance data from CPT were collected from 458 children aged 6 to 12 years. A total of 213 children received an ADHD diagnosis among the 458 participants studied, although the other 245 children did not receive an ADHD diagnosis. To evaluate ADD/ADHD, Hyperactivity/Impulsiveness, and Attention, the MOXO-CPT version used auditory and visual distractions. To differentiate between two categories of children- the first category is of developing stage children, and the other category is those with ADHD- the study's design included age, gender, DoW, and ToD as control variables. The model used for prediction was 87% accurate, 89% sensitive, and 84% specific. In 2021, Hicks and colleagues presented HYPERAKTIV, a publicly available dataset that includes health, activity, and heart rate information from 51 individuals with ADHD and 52 control subjects, along with attributes such as age, sex, mental state, and neuropsychological test outcomes [7]. The dataset aims to establish a benchmark for future ADHD research, offering baseline experiments with traditional machine learning models to predict ADHD from activity data. The analysis by Maniruzzaman *et al.* [15] involved data extraction from 45,779 children within the National Survey of Children's Health (NSCH) 2018–2019, aged 3–17 years, until researchers identified 5,218 children with ADHD, who represented 11.4% of the total, while the remaining population consisted of healthy children. This research had two primary aims: determining the main risk factors for ADHD in children while building a machine learning (ML) classification system. Propagation forest-based algorithms delivered 85.5% classification accuracy and presented 84.4% sensitivity combined with 86.4% specificity to classify ADHD children from their non-ADHD peers. The stop signal task acquired the EEG signals from both 24 participants with ADHD and 78 participants without ADHD.

Table 16.1 Description of datasets and models related to the classification of ADHD.

Paper (Year)	Data source	Classification technique	Accuracy (%)	Sensitivity (%)	Precision (%)	F1 score (%)	AUC score
Faedda *et al.*, [5]	Found 155 children and ADHD plus depression=44 and bipolar = 48 Controls = 42	SVM	83.1	64.4	91.7	_	0.781
Chen *et al.*, [1]	776 resting-state fMRI, 491 - Non ADHD285 - Children and adults having ADHD aged 7 to 21 years	SVM	88.1	_	_	_	_
Slobodin *et al.*, [22]	Research data evaluated the CPT skills of 458 children in the age range of years 6 to 12, which included 213 children with ADHD and 245 typically developing children.	Random forest	87	89	84	_	_
Hicks *et al.*, [7]	Patients with ADHD=103 and Normal =52	Random Forest	72	_	_	_	_

(*Continued*)

Table 16.1 Description of datasets and models related to the classification of ADHD. (*Continued*)

Paper (Year)	Data source	Classification technique	Accuracy (%)	Sensitivity (%)	Precision (%)	F1 score (%)	AUC score
Maniruzzaman *et al.*, [15]	45,779 children were born between the ages of three and seventeen. There were around 5218 children who were diagnosed with attention-deficit/ hyperactivity disorder (ADHD), whereas the remaining youngsters were healthy.	Random forest	85.5	84.4	86.4	–	–
Nam Trinh *et al.*, [23]	52 adults -ADHD and 98 - Non-ADHD	SVM KNN RF	–	–	–	–	0.523 0.534 0.541
Chauhan and Choi, [2]	ADHD infected EEGs of 61 children and 60 healthy EEGs.	Stacked classifier	92	93	91	–	–

The random forest ROC-AUC scores for both the resting state EEG and the stop signal task EEG are 0.541 and 0.575, respectively [23]. The research investigated ADHD diagnosis with EEG data through the acquisition of 121 child recordings, consisting of 60 healthy controls and 61 children diagnosed with ADHD. The stacked classifier used ten different classifiers, including random forest and multilayer perceptron (MLP), as well as k-nearest neighbors and extra trees classifier and XGBoost and support vector machines and Logistic Regression and AdaBoost and classification and regression trees to obtain combined outputs, and gradient boosting machines. The MLP acted as the meta-classifier. The stacked classifier outperformed the individual models, achieving an impressive accuracy of 92%, with a precision of 91% and sensitivity of 93%, indicating its superior ability to correctly identify ADHD-positive cases [2, 16, 17, 27].

Although there has been considerable advancement in classifying ADHD through EEG data (Table 16.1), many research gaps still exist and need further exploration. For this study model development, a random forest, AdaBoost, XGBoost, support vector machine, and K-nearest neighbor classifiers have been selected, which helps mitigate the issue of overfitting, commonly associated with single decision trees. This research employed a dataset of 121 individuals (61 with ADHD and 60 without), totaling 50,000 samples, which were randomly selected from 1048576 samples with greater variability. The objective was to ensure a more balanced and representative inclusion of both ADHD and healthy individuals, addressing potential limitations in participant diversity and sample distribution seen in earlier research. This method seeks to enhance the applicability and strength of the results by integrating a broader range of data. The dataset selection, as outlined in Section 3.1, was guided by these considerations.

16.3 Methodology

The study implemented contemporary machine learning methods in building a novel EEG data-driven technology for ADHD recognition. A machine learning algorithm enables the classification of ADHD and healthy controls (HC) through the system depicted in Figure 16.1. The construction of models occurred using XGBoost and support vector machine, K-nearest neighbor algorithms, random forest, and AdaBoost classifier [28–30]. Details of each step of the approach are provided, emphasizing the techniques employed to achieve reliable feature representation and high classification accuracy.

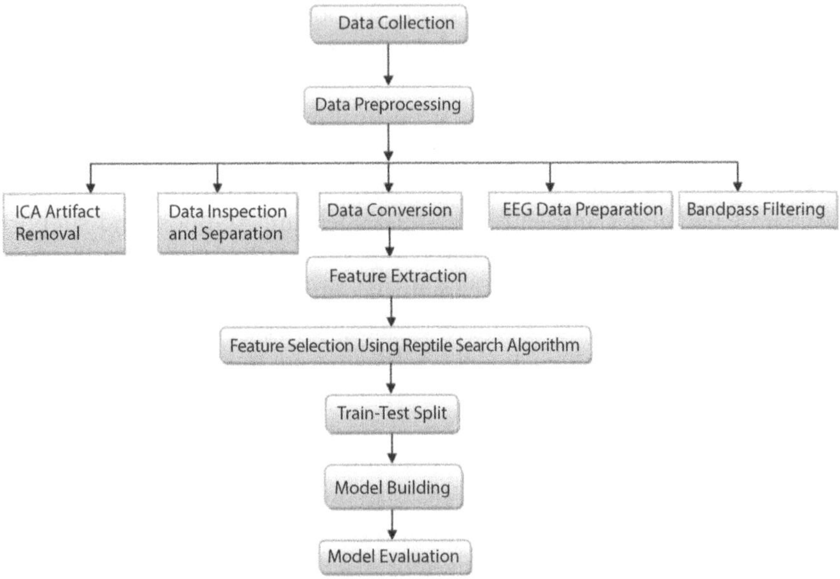

Figure 16.1 Pipeline for EEG signal classification.

16.3.1 Data Collection

Data from Kaggle, available through the IEEE database, was used. The study included a count of 121 entities, with ADHD diagnosed being 61, and the remaining 60 classified as not having ADHD. Electrical signals were sampled at 128 Hz from 19 channels using the 10–20 method. These channels have specific electrode placements: Fz, Cz, Pz, C3, T3, C4, T4, Fp1, Fp2, F3, F4, F7, F8, P3, P4, T5, T6, O1, O2 [8]. Alim *et al.* [32] measured EEG signals using electrodes A1 and A2 on the earlobes. These pre-processing approaches, which include noise reduction and artifact removal, ensure that feature extraction and category development use the highest-quality data.

16.3.2 Data Pre-Processing

This phase focuses on purifying and removing artifacts from EEG signals to facilitate data analysis. The subsequent actions guarantee that the pre-processing done within this investigation is observed.

- **Data Inspection and Separation**

Class distribution was verified by analyzing the dataset's normal and ADHD feature categories. While each class's data was retrieved and analyzed, its labels were saved in separate files.

- **EEG Data Preparation**

An MNE info object was produced using the MNE library to obtain channel information along with the sampling rate. The EEG data was displayed, therefore, according to the standard 10-20 system montage method.

- **Data Conversion**

The EEG data in Data Frame format from the normal and ADHD groups necessitated translation to NumPy arrays before the required modifications. The arrays were rearranged before conversion into MNE RawArray objects by transforming channels into rows and samples into columns.

- **Bandpass Filtering**

The bandpass filter operated within a frequency spectrum between 5 and 50 Hz. The filter evaluation required PSD plots to be generated before and after filtering.

- **ICA (Independent Component Analysis)**

ICA was employed to detect and remove artifacts from EEG data. The data cleaning process required the identification, followed by the elimination of artifacts in ICA components. The processed data visualizations let us verify that we eliminated all artifacts from the data successfully.

16.3.3 Feature Extraction Using Autoencoder

The preprocessing phase of EEG data makes way for autoencoders to extract multidimensional features and simultaneously detect complicated signal patterns. The procedure creates latent variables that successfully describe the foundational data structure by detecting high-level patterns and advanced signal-level interactions. Researchers evaluated PSD along with spectral entropy from frequency-domain aspects, mean and variance, and skewness from time-domain variables. An autoencoder developed a unified characteristic set that consisted of acceptable signal shapes combined with appropriate spectral and time-based features through the integration of time-area and frequency-domain functionalities. Complex functions processed by the autoencoder accomplished this.

16.3.3.1 Autoencoder

Generative methods known as automatic encoders teach an artificial neural network (ANN) to re-create its input data without human intervention.

An autoencoder features a symmetrical structure and consists of two primary components (as depicted in Figure 16.2(a) and Figure 16.2(b): the encoder, which processes input data to generate a low-dimensional representation capturing its key characteristics; and a decoder that uses the encoder's training to recreate the input using those features. The encoder part transforms into a powerful automated feature extractor when the unsupervised pretraining is finished. It may be supervised and fine-tuned to get the target estimate once it has an acceptable output layer.

It is possible to obtain features that may be even more efficient in handling the specific target estimation situation by fine-tuning, which involves adjusting the encoder settings. To carry out this process, the encoder block is extended with an extra layer. The encoder's successor layer might be a classification or regression one, depending on the situation at hand.

Encoder: It is included in an autoencoder for EEG feature extraction to reduce the dimensionality of the input data. When working with spatiotemporal data, the encoder may consist of convolutional layers or more completely coupled layers. The complexity of the data and the size of the input characteristics determine how many layers are needed.

Bottleneck Layer: A latent space representation is generated by 32 neurons in the bottleneck layer. This approach improves classifier performance by lowering dimensions. By sending the classifier only the most important traits and eliminating input variances, this is achieved. The network used the MSE function as the training loss to eliminate signal inconsistencies between input data and desired outputs. Because of its simplicity and effectiveness in evaluating reconstruction correctness by penalizing notable disparities, Mean Squared Error (MSE) was chosen. Other loss functions, such as Huber loss and Mean Absolute Error (MAE), were assessed but were determined to be insufficient because of their reduced sensitivity to important errors, which are essential for reconstructing EEG signals [26].

Decoder: Reconstructing the original input is accomplished by the decoder through the utilization of the latent representation. This part

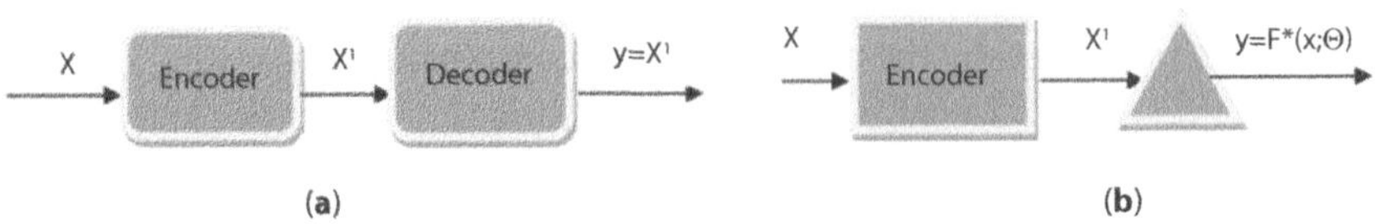

Figure 16.2 Autoencoder: (a) autoencoder's structure and (b) encoder employed in the final estimation.

restores the dimensionality to its initial state by replicating the encoder in reverse.

16.3.4 Reptile Search Algorithm

The research into reptile behavior during development and hunting, and social activities led to the creation of the reptile search algorithm, which operates as a swarm-based metaheuristic algorithm [15]. The algorithm known as reptile search has been developed, according to the team. By dividing the entire number of repetitions into four pieces, the RSA approach completes the shift from the surrounding to the hunting search phases.

16.3.4.1 Initialization

The following equation is used to generate a random collection of possible initial solutions in the first phase of the reptile search algorithm, as shown in Equation (16.1):

$$x_{jk} = \text{rand} \times (U_b - L_b) + L_b \qquad k-1,2\ldots\ n \qquad (16.1)$$

where x_{jk}= initialization matrix, j = 1,2....P. In the initialized matrix. The P value defines row quantity, which corresponds to population dimensions, and the variable n specifies column number that reflects problem dimensions. The program variables L_b, U_b, and rand represent the lower bound limit and upper bound limit alongside randomly generated values. The RSA is divided into two phases. The first phase is exploration, and the second phase is exploitation. Both phases are further categorized into two sub-phases based on certain conditions. Therefore, the RSA can be divided into four total parts.

16.3.4.2 Encircling Phase (Exploration)

During the encirclement phase, the primary operations take place in densely populated regions. The key locomotion strategies in this stage include elevated walking and low crawling, both of which are inspired by crocodilian movement patterns. These motions assist in identifying a broader search area, but they fail to aid in hunting prey, as shown in the equations (16.2) and (16.3).

$$x_{jk}(\tau+1) = Best_k(\tau) \times \left(-\mu_{(jk)}(\tau)\right) \times \beta - \left(R_{(jk)}(\tau) \times rand\right), \quad T \leq \frac{T}{4} \tag{16.2}$$

$$x_{jk}(\tau+1) = Best_k(\tau) \times x_{(r_1,k)} \times ES(\tau) \times rand, \quad \tau \leq 2\frac{T}{4} \text{ and } \tau > \frac{T}{4} \tag{16.3}$$

Under the formula provided, $Best(\tau)$ represents the best optimal solution discovered at the kth position of search. The random number symbolized by the rand functions within the context of τ, while T provides the maximum permissible number of iterations. At position k for solution j, the hunting operator maintains its worth level as defined by (j,k). The solution for calculating value is displayed through this mathematical format: (j, k) as shown in the equations (16.4) and (16.5):

$$\mu_{(j,k)} = Best_k(\tau) \times P_{(j,k)} \tag{16.4}$$

$$R_{(j,k)} = \frac{Best(\tau) - P_{(r_2,k)}}{Best_k(\tau) + \in} \tag{16.5}$$

The random number exists between values 1 and N, yet $r1$ shows its actual numerical value. The range of all available solutions is represented by the letter N in this scenario. The symbol i1 identifies the random point found in the hundredth solution. Random numbers within the N range are designated by the symbol ϵ, while small-value quantities are marked as f2. The probability-based ratio functions as the Evolutionary Sense (Evolutionary Sense). We will provide you with a mathematical example of evolutionary sense as shown below in the equation (16.6):

$$ES(\tau) = 2 \times r_3 \times \left(1 - \frac{1}{T}\right) \tag{16.6}$$

16.3.5 Reptile Search Algorithm-Based Feature Selection

After functions were extracted, the next step was to select the degree of function. The Reptile Seek method was utilized to identify the most significant features from an extensive set of features. Reptile, a meta-learning strategy, boosts feature selection by training the model on various feature subsets, thus enhancing its effectiveness. The most essential features were preserved after applying this repetitive method, which was overall seen as an enhancement in the model's effectiveness and precision. These chosen features were subsequently utilized to develop the final classification model.

16.3.6 Model Building

16.3.6.1 Random Forest

Random forest is among the most commonly utilized algorithms for supervised classification. A dataset is selected, and decision trees are created based on those subsets. This algorithm operates on the concept of bagging (Bootstrap Aggregating), where new datasets are selected at each iteration, and a decision tree is built for each subset of data. The algorithm splits the datasets into several smaller parts and builds a decision tree for each subset. In the prediction stage, the model uses each decision tree to make predictions, and the outcome is decided by a majority vote. As an ensemble classifier, random forest helps in resolving the overfitting issue that frequently plagues individual decision trees.

It outperforms individual decision trees in terms of prediction accuracy by averaging the output from several decision trees. The random forest classifier's work is shown in Figure 16.3.

16.3.6.2 AdaBoost

The principle of the AdaBoost classifier works on combining weak classifiers to create a strong classifier. The terms strong and weak refer to the classifier's accuracy in making predictions. In essence, AdaBoost enhances weak classification algorithms, transforming them into strong classifiers. It generates multiple decision trees sequentially, with each subsequent model concentrating on the data points that were misclassified by the previous model. This approach guarantees that the subsequent model is specifically trained on the more challenging instances to classify, thereby enhancing the classifier's overall effectiveness. Figure 16.4 illustrates the complete working of the AdaBoost classifier.

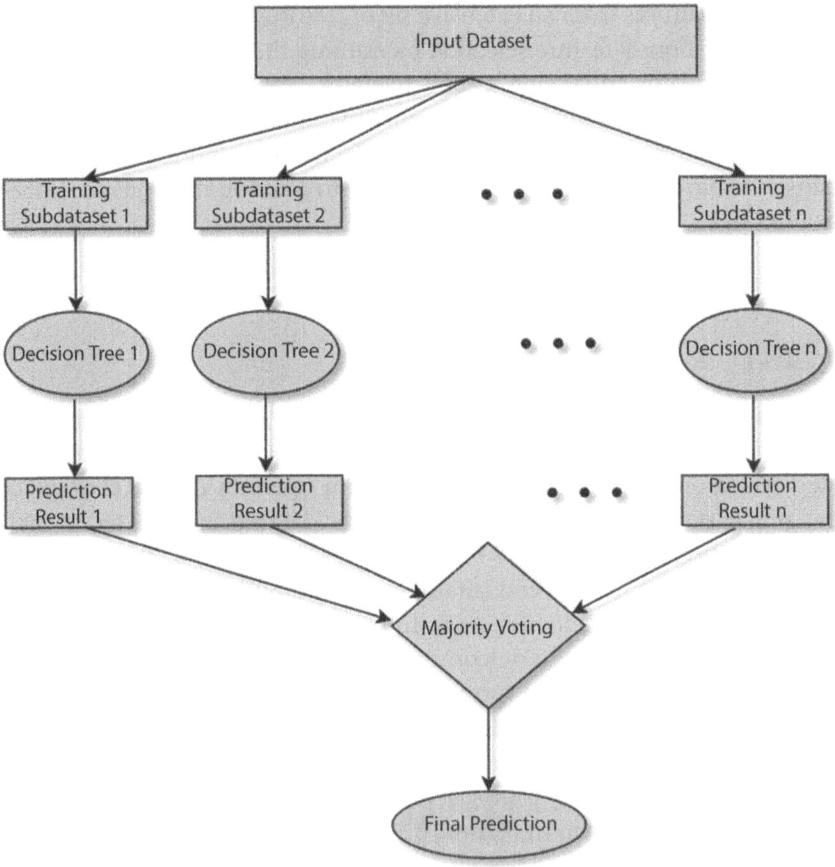

Figure 16.3 Working of the random forest classifier.

16.3.6.3 Support Vector Machine

It is a category of versatile supervised learning methods capable of performing both classification and regression analyses. This algorithm is based on creating an ideal decision boundary that divides an n-dimensional feature space into separate categories (Figure 16.5). The data points were classified by the boundary known as the hyperplane. To identify the ideal hyperplane, the support vectors act as crucial data points that define the margin separating the classes. The support vectors are essential for increasing the margin between classes, which in turn improves the proposed model for generalization.

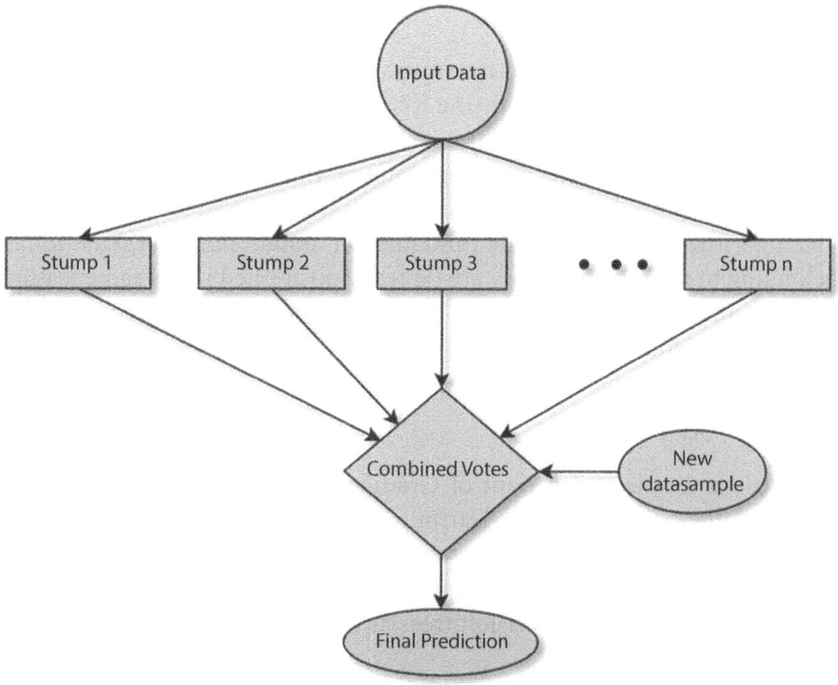

Figure 16.4 Working on the AdaBoost classifier.

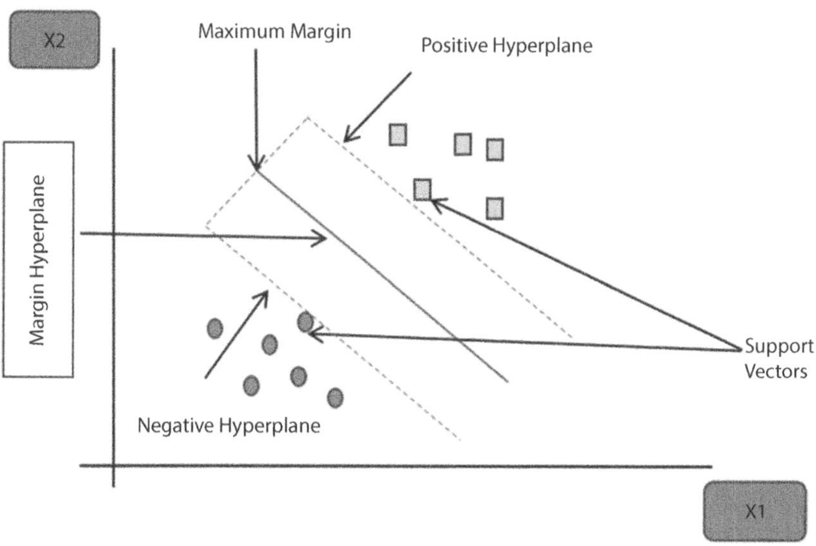

Figure 16.5 Working of the support vector machine.

16.3.6.4 K-Nearest Neighbor

It operates as a non-parametric supervised learning method that finds common usage within the field. The KNN algorithm uses proximity examination to identify where a data point should be categorized or predicted to exist. Within machine learning applications, this procedure functions for classifying and predicting new data. But it is mainly used for classification. The algorithm operates on the fundamental assumption that data points belonging to the same category are typically positioned in the same feature space in proximity to each other. Figure 16.6 shows the working of the K-nearest neighbor.

16.3.6.5 XGBoost

XGBoost is a powerful variant of Gradient Boosting and is classified as an ensemble-based machine-learning approach. Ensemble learning is enhanced by predicting performance with the integration of various weak models, so that a robust model can be created. The algorithm works on the principle of utilizing decision trees as base learners, which are trained

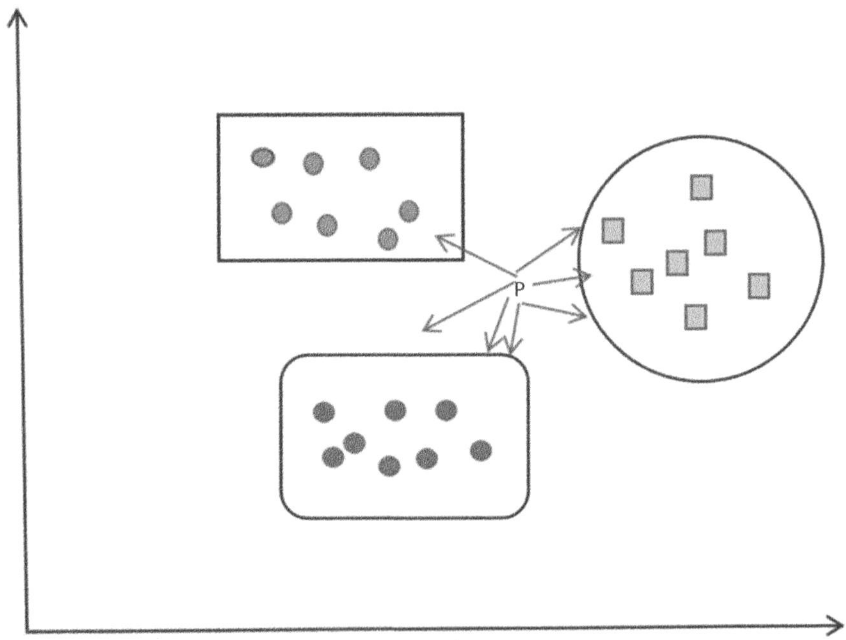

Figure 16.6 Working of K-nearest neighbor.

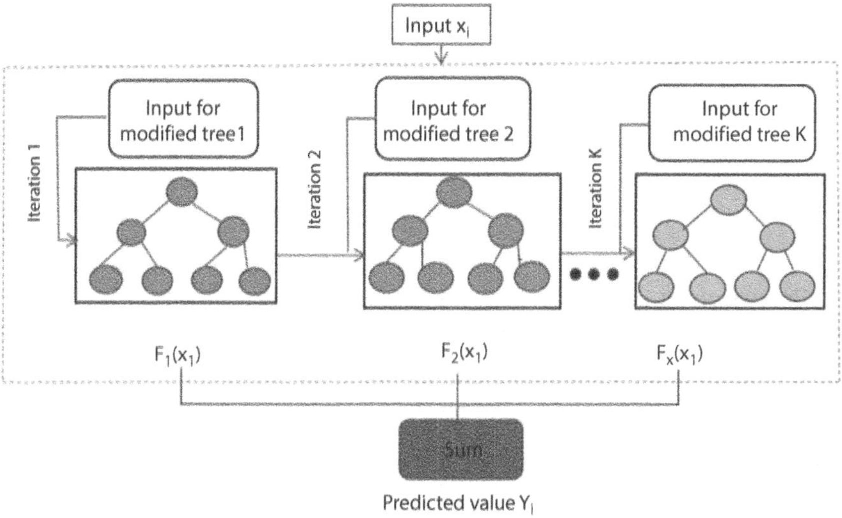

Figure 16.7 Working on XGBoost classifier.

sequentially to refine the performance of the model. Each new tree is designed to fix the error of the preceding one, a process known as *boosting*. One of XGBoost's key advantages is its built-in parallel processing capability, enabling efficient training on large datasets. Additionally, it provides a wide range of customization choices, allowing users to fine-tune model parameters for optimal performance based on the specific problem at hand. Figure 16.7 shows how the XGBoost classifier works.

16.3.7 Model Evaluation

The "version evaluation" method assesses whether a developed model can be applied to new data to determine its generalizability. Key metrics for classification performance include Correct Classification Rate, Positive Predictive Value (PPV), True Positive Rate (TPR), F-measure, True Negative Rate (TNR), and False Negative Rate (FNR). Cross-validation enhances reliability by repeatedly assessing estimates and providing rich insights, such as through confusion matrices. Thorough evaluation is crucial for both model improvement and successful deployment.

16.3.8 Performance Metrics

Accuracy: It means the correct predictions from all the possible predictions. It can be calculated using the formula given below in equation (16.7):

$$\text{Accuracy} = \frac{\text{TP} + \text{TN}}{\text{TP} + \text{TN} + \text{FP} + \text{FP}} \tag{16.7}$$

Precision: In contrast to this ratio, we have 1−Precision1, which indicates the percentage of false negatives. Additionally, the inverse of Precision gives Recall as shown in the equation (16.8).

$$\text{Precision} = \frac{\text{TP}}{\text{TP} + \text{FP}} \tag{16.8}$$

Recall: It is calculated by dividing the number of true positive predictions by the total count of actual positive cases, as shown in the equation (16.9).

$$\text{Recall} = \frac{\text{TP}}{\text{TP} + \text{FN}} \tag{16.9}$$

F1 Score: The F1 score serves as a performance measure for a classification model by integrating precision and recall into one comprehensive score, as shown in the equation (16.10).

$$\text{F1} = \frac{2{*}\text{Precision}{*}\text{Recall}}{\text{Precision}{+}\text{Recall}} \tag{16.10}$$

AUC Calculation: The ROC curve reflects the TPR/FPR relationship through different thresholds and enables the calculation of the AUC value. The model demonstrates outstanding performance when its area under the curve AUC comes close to 1. The higher AUC values typically indicate that the model is more effective at differentiating between various classes. We can calculate the AUC score using the equation below (16.11):

$$\text{AUC} = 0.5 * (\text{TPR} + \text{TNR}) \tag{16.11}$$

Table 16.2 Comparison of specificity and selectivity on different models.

	Specificity	**Sensitivity**
AdaBoost	0.89	0.89
Random forest	0.92	0.92
K-nearest neighbor	0.58	0.79
Support vector machine	0.62	0.83
XGBoost	0.67	0.78

Specificity: It determines the percentage of true negative instances that are correctly identified as negative. Specificity is determined by applying the following formula (Eq. 16.12):

$$\text{Specificity} = \text{TN} / (\text{TN} + \text{FP}) \tag{16.12}$$

Sensitivity: It determines the percentage of true positive instances that are accurately identified as positive. Sensitivity is determined using the following formula (Eq. 16.13):

$$\text{Sensitivity} = \text{TP} / (\text{TP} + \text{FN}) \tag{16.13}$$

Table 16.2 presents the negative predictive capabilities of all models. The proposed model demonstrates high sensitivity. It shows that it can perform detection on several relevant cases, making it particularly valuable for applications that prioritize identifying true positives, compared to the other models. Conversely, the proposed random forest model exhibits high selectivity, effectively filtering out irrelevant or negative instances, and it reduces false positives, thereby offering a precision advantage over other models.

16.4 Results and Discussion

16.4.1 Results

A detailed description of ADHD detection through EEG data accompanies this report, as well as the investigation results. This study includes random forest, AdaBoost, XGBoost, support vector machine, and K-nearest neighbor as the five machine learning models with their specific names. The auto-encoder performs feature extraction to achieve high model performance before the Reptile search Algorithm uses available features to select the best ones. Among the metrics used to evaluate machine learning model performance stand Accuracy, precision, recall, and F1 score. This method demonstrates its success through Figures 16.8 to 16.12, showing the improvement in ADHD diagnosis using EEG data analysis.

It is clear from the above confusion matrices, as shown in Figure 16.9, that the proposed random forest performs very well in terms of classification accuracy. The matrices distinguish between two classes: 0 (children without ADHD) and 1 (children with ADHD). Out of 10,000 samples, there were fewer misclassifications as a result of this model's accurate classification of 4,606 cases as class 1 (True Positives) and 4,630 genuine negatives as class 0 (True Negatives). In particular, 386 class 0 False Positives and 378 class 1 False Negatives were misclassified as class 0 and class 1, respectively. In comparison, as shown in Figure 16.8, AdaBoost identified 4,445 actual positives and 4,533 genuine negatives, but it also produced a large number of misclassification errors, including 520 false positives and 502 false negatives. Another model, as shown in Figure 16.12, XGBoost identified 3983 actual positives and 3299 genuine negatives; it also produced larger misclassification errors, including 1620 false positives and

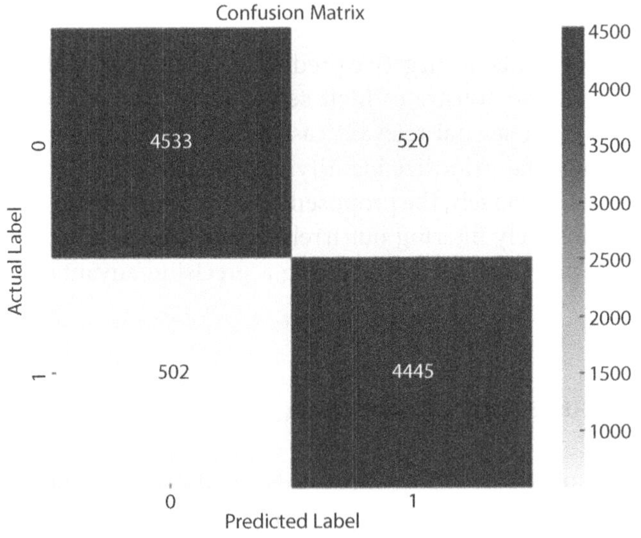

Figure 16.8 Error matrix of the AdaBoost model.

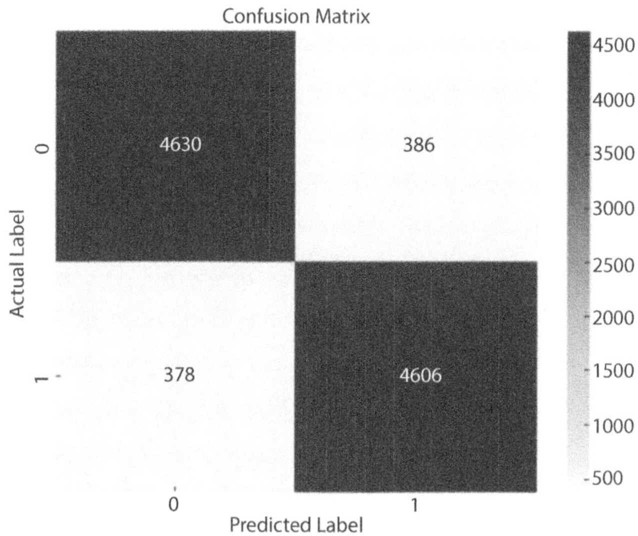

Figure 16.9 Error matrix of the random forest classifier.

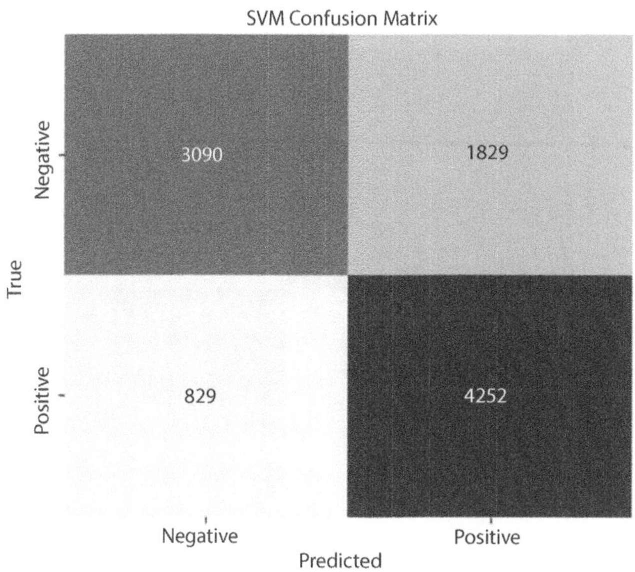

Figure 16.10 Error matrix of the support vector machine.

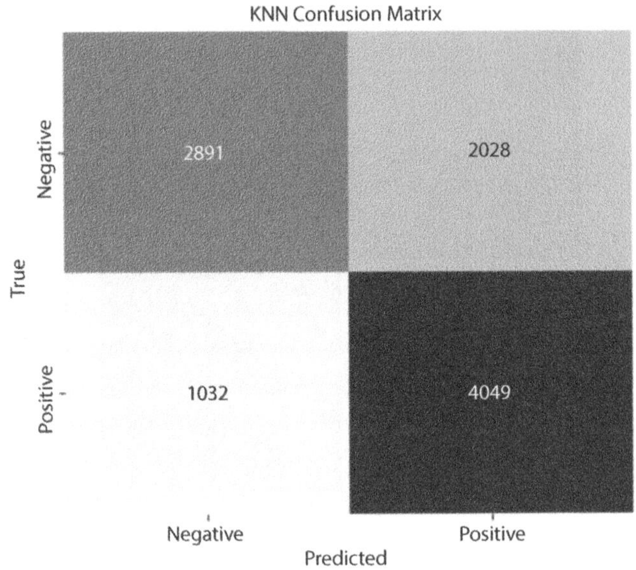

Figure 16.11 Error matrix of the K-nearest neighbor.

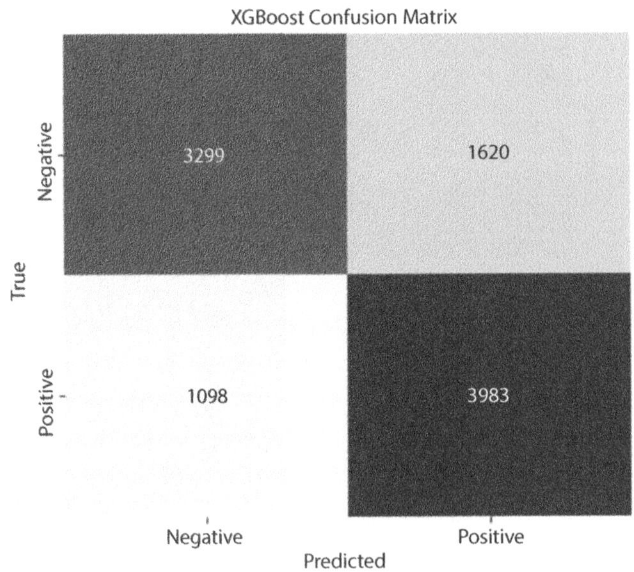

Figure 16.12 Error matrix of the XGBoost classifier.

1098 false negatives. In Figure 16.10, support vector machine identified 4,252 actual positives and 3090 genuine negatives, which also produced a large number of misclassification errors, including 1829 false positives and 829 false negatives, coming to Figure 16.11, K-nearest neighbor identified 4,049 actual positives and 2891 genuine negatives, this also shown a large number of misclassification errors, including 2028 false positives and 1032 false negatives This suggests that XGBoost is effective at distinguishing between kids with and without ADHD because it outperforms other models and has fewer misclassifications.

The results show that random forest has the best accuracy with fewer misclassifications. However, there are some notable increases in the rate of misclassifications using other models like AdaBoost, XGBoost, SVM, and K-NN, which may indicate a real deterioration in the model's performance. The five matrices show varying model performance, with the random forest model best performing and the others showing high misclassification rates, highlighting the need for improving the accuracy. Examining both the total accuracy and the misclassification rates would allow one to determine whether these performance variations are statistically significant. The performance differences between the two models are probably statistically significant because of the disparities in true positives, true negatives, false positives, and false negatives. The classification error for all the models is shown in Table 16.3.

$$\text{Misclassification rate} = (\text{FP} + \text{FN})/(\text{TP} + \text{TN} + \text{FP} + \text{FN}) \tag{16.14}$$

Table 16.3 Model-wise misclassification percentage.

Approach	Incorrect positive	Incorrect negative	Classification error
AdaBoost	520	502	10.2%
Random forest	386	378	7.6%
K-nearest neighbor	1032	2028	30.60%
Support vector machine	829	1829	26.58%
XGBoost	1098	1620	27.18%

The ROC_AUC curve for SVM, RF, XGBoost, K-nearest neighbor, and AdaBoost classifiers is shown in Figures 16.13 to 16.17, respectively.

From the above ROC_AUC curves as shown in Figure 16.16, it is evident that the proposed random forest model mechanism performs well in distinguishing between the true and false values, and therefore, it beats the other models in identifying ADHD in children. The random forest model's ROC AUC score of 0.93 demonstrates a splendid ability to distinguish

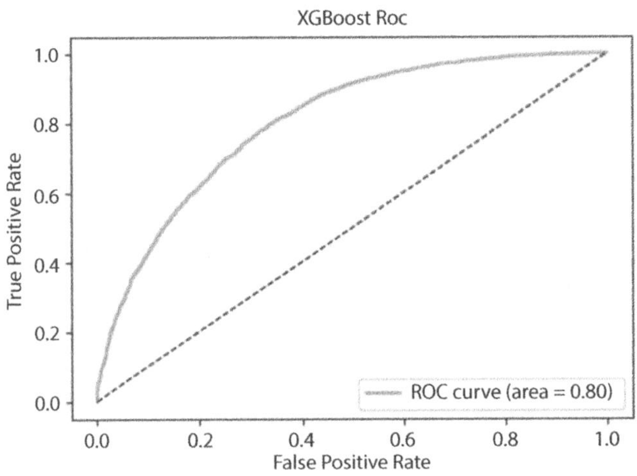

Figure 16.13 ROC_AUC plot of XGBoost classifier model.

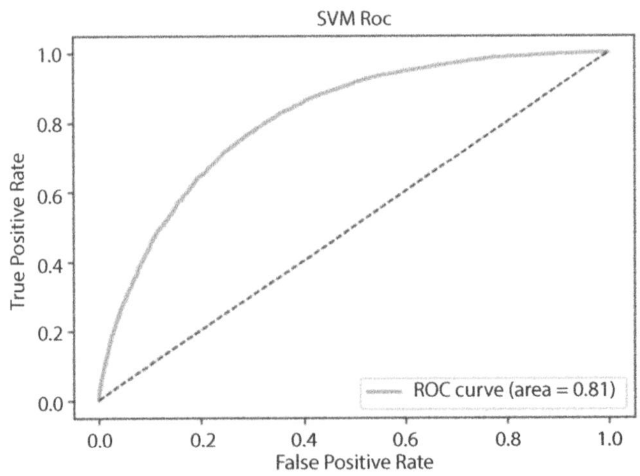

Figure 16.14 ROC_AUC plot for SVM model.

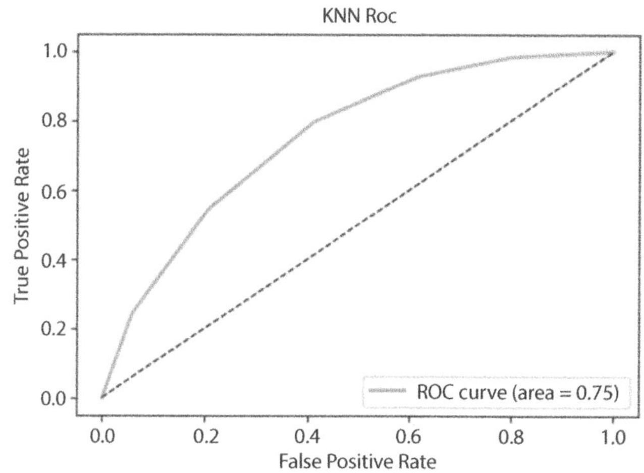

Figure 16.15 K-nearest neighbor model's ROC_AUC plot.

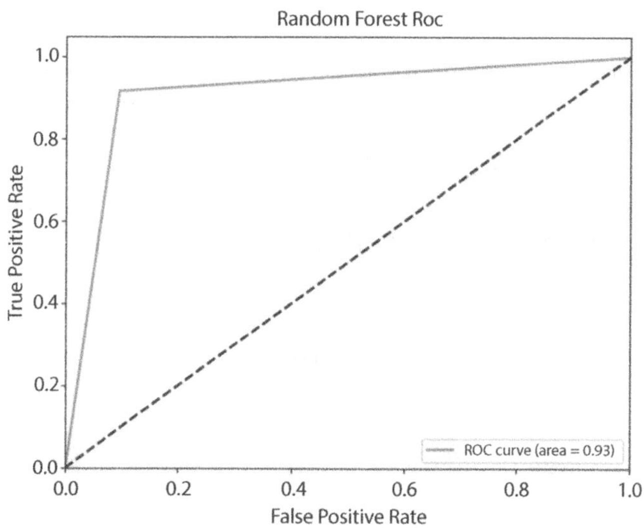

Figure 16.16 Random forest model's ROC_AUC plot.

between children with and without ADHD, demonstrating its excessive sensitivity and specificity. On the other hand, XGBoost, AdaBoost, support vector machine, and K-nearest neighbor received an ROC AUC of 0.80, 0.87, 0.81, and 0.75, as shown in Figure 16.13, Figure 16.17, Figure 16.14, and Figure 16.15, respectively. Random forest's better ROC_AUC score

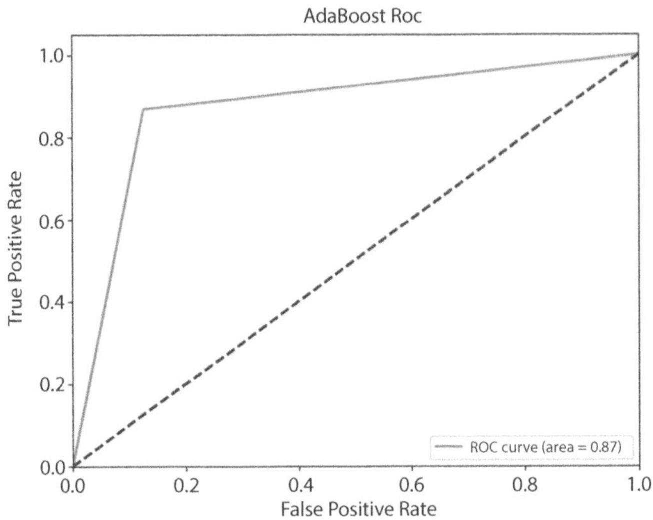

Figure 16.17 AdaBoost model's ROC_AUC plot.

validates its better standard overall performance, proving its resilience and dependability in growing accurate classifications when compared to other models.

According to the bar charts shown in various Figures numbered as Figures 16.18, 16.19, 16.20, and 16.21, the random forest beats other models in the categorization of ADHD in kids. With a score of F1 of 0.92,

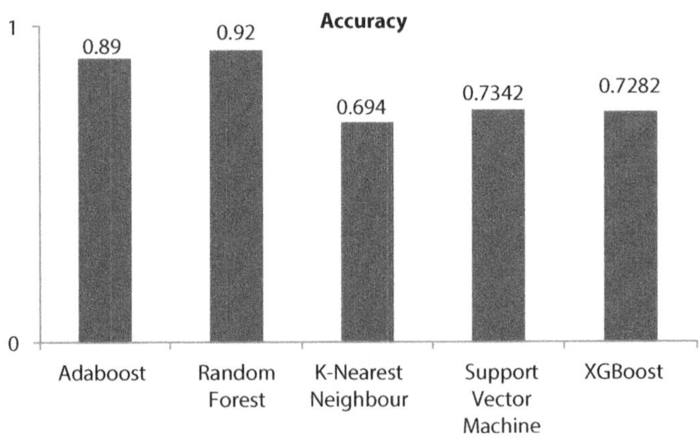

Figure 16.18 Accuracy of AdaBoost, random forest, K-nearest neighbor, support vector machine, and XGBoost classifiers.

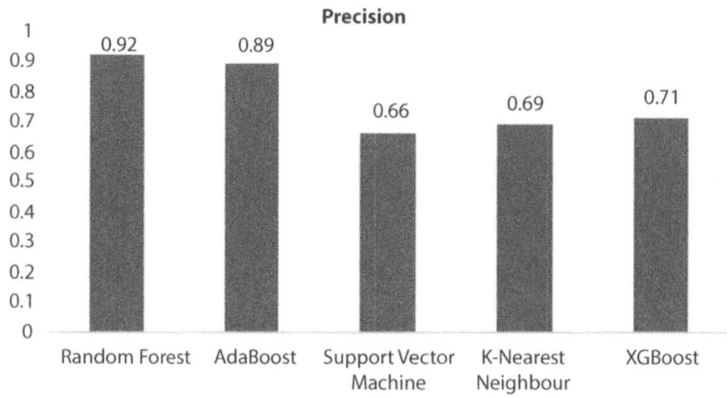

Figure 16.19 Precision of AdaBoost, random forest, K-nearest neighbor, support vector machine, and XGBoost classifiers.

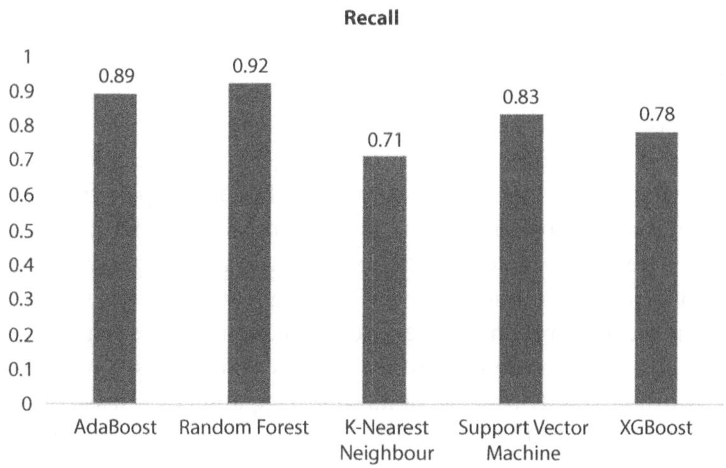

Figure 16.20 Recall of AdaBoost, random forest, K-nearest neighbor, support vector machine, and XGBoost classifiers.

a recall of 0.92, and a precision of 0.92, this model achieves a top-notch accuracy of 0.92, demonstrating an enhanced capacity to accurately classify ADHD sufferers while decreasing the range of false positives and negatives. XGBoost, AdaBoost, support vector machine, and K-nearest neighbor, on the other hand, showcase a decrease in overall performance measures, with lower accuracy, precision, recall, and F1 score. This comparison demonstrates the random forest's capability to collect complex styles and boost class accuracy, making it the most reliable of the fashions studied.

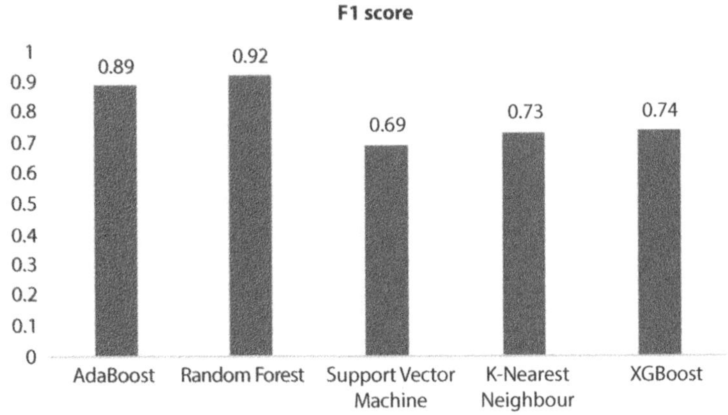

Figure 16.21 F1 score of AdaBoost, random forest, K-nearest neighbor, support vector machine, and XGBoost classifiers.

16.4.2 Discussion

The proposed random forest model successfully identifies ADHD through the analysis of EEG data. Although other models performed adequately, their lower scores across various metrics suggest that the algorithm is less effective when detecting subtle patterns in EEG data. Apart from this, the confusion matrix proposed in this study demonstrates that random forest is better at reducing misclassifications but also at effectively recognizing real negatives and genuine positives. In therapeutic settings, where misinterpretation can sometimes have dire consequences, this degree of accuracy is crucial. The random forest model was observed as a preferable tool for diagnosing ADHD because of its robust capability to classify both true positive and true negative instances accurately. In conclusion, random forest performs better than the current ADHD-style approach when compared to other models. In this case, the near-perfect AUC value achieved by the random forest model suggests that it consistently makes accurate predictions, both in identifying ADHD-positive individuals and correctly excluding those without ADHD. This high level of accuracy is further reflected in the model's sensitivity and specificity. By combining multiple decision trees and leveraging their collective insights, random forests are inherently adept at capturing complex patterns in data, which explains their superior ability to detect even subtle differences in EEG signals. The improvement in handling datasets with many variables, such as EEG features, enhances its robustness, making it a valuable asset for real-world applications in ADHD diagnosis. The evaluation indicates that the random forest model delivers better performance than ADHD-type approaches against other models for classification. The therapy of attention-deficit/hyperactivity disorder (ADHD) stands to gain through enhanced diagnostic precision, as well as personalized therapeutic programs and improved clinical outcomes through its implementation.

16.5 Conclusion

This study utilizes electroencephalogram (EEG) data and ML algorithms for enhancing the reliability as well as accuracy of ADHD diagnosis in both children and adults. The key findings of this study are as follows:

- Results demonstrate superior performance by random forest, which exceeded AdaBoost, XGBoost, SVM, and K-NN models while assessing accuracy together with precision and recall, and F1 score. The random forest model demonstrated superior performance over other models because of its successful outcomes, as proven by assessment results.
- Additionally, the model has a 0.93 ROC AUC score, which indicates that it can distinguish ADHD from non-ADHD cases. It has excellent sensitivity, specificity, and a low misclassification rate. This tool's excellent discrimination allows accurate and rapid ADHD diagnosis.
- Moreover, the integration of the Reptile searching algorithm for doing feature selection and autoencoder-based feature extraction contributed to improved model performance by effectively reducing noise and enhancing relevant data representation.
- The study confirms that EEG-based classification, when combined with advanced machine learning techniques, can effectively capture subtle patterns associated with ADHD, making it a viable approach for diagnosis.
- Given its high accuracy and ability to minimize diagnostic errors, the proposed model holds promise for real-world medical applications. It can serve as an early detection tool for ADHD and guide professionals in the healthcare sector to make more timely and precise treatments.

AI disclosure statement: The author acknowledges the use of AI-based tools for minor language editing or grammatical correction. However, all intellectual contributions, analyses, and conclusions presented in this chapter are entirely the author's own.

References

1. Chen, Y., Tang, Y., Wang, C., Liu, X., Zhao, L., Wang, Z., ADHD classification by dual subspace learning using resting-state functional connectivity. *Artif. Intell. Med.*, 103, 101786, 2020, doi: https://doi.org/10.1016/j.artmed.2019.101786.
2. Chauhan, N. and Choi, B.J., A Machine Learning Approach to ADHD Diagnosis Using Mutual Information and Stacked Classifiers. *Int. J. Fuzzy Log. Intell. Syst.*, 24, 1, 10–8, 2024, doi: https://doi.org/10.5391/IJFIS.2024.24.1.10.
3. Danielson, M.L., Bitsko, R.H., Ghandour, R.M., Holbrook, J.R., Kogan, M.D., Blumberg, S.J., Prevalence of parent-reported ADHD diagnosis and associated treatment among US children and adolescents, 2016. *J. Clin. Child Adolesc. Psychol.*, 47, 2, 199–212, 2018, doi: https://doi.org/10.1080/15374416.2017.1417860.
4. Drechsler, R., Brem, S., Brandeis, D., Grünblatt, E., Berger, G., Walitza, S., ADHD: Current concepts and treatments in children and adolescents. *Neuropediatrics*, 51, 5, 315–35, 2020, doi: https://doi.org/10.1055/s-0040-1710050.
5. Faedda, G.L., Ohashi, K., Hernandez, M., McGreenery, C.E., Grant, M.C., Baroni, A., *et al.*, Actigraph measures discriminate pediatric bipolar disorder from attention-deficit/hyperactivity disorder and typically developing controls. *J. Child Psychol. Psychiatry*, 57, 6, 706–16, 2016, doi: https://doi.org/10.1111/jcpp.12487.
6. Goodman, D.W., Lisdexamfetamine dimesylate (vyvanse), a prodrug stimulant for attention-deficit/hyperactivity disorder. *Pharm. Ther.*, 35, 5, 273, 2010, doi: https://pmc.ncbi.nlm.nih.gov/articles/PMC2873712/.
7. Hicks, S.A., Stautland, A., Fasmer, O.B., Førland, W., Hammer, H.L., Halvorsen, P., *et al.*, Hyperaktiv: An activity dataset from patients with attention-deficit/hyperactivity disorder (ADHD), in: *Proceedings of the 12th ACM Multimedia Systems Conference*, 2021 Jun, pp. 314–9, 2021, doi: https://doi.org/10.1145/3458305.3463362.
8. Jhala, K., ADHD Dataset balanced (1). https://www.kaggle.com/datasets/krupabajhala/adhd-new, 2024.
9. Arora, C. and Sandhu, R., Adoption of Quantum NLP for Improved Healthcare System. *International Conference on Computation of Artificial Intelligence & Machine Learning*, Springer Nature Switzerland, Cham, pp. 51–59, 2024.

10. Kessler, R.C., Adler, L.A., Berglund, P., Green, J.G., McLaughlin, K.A., Fayyad, J., *et al.*, The effects of temporally secondary co-morbid mental disorders on the associations of DSM-IV ADHD with adverse outcomes in the US National Comorbidity Survey Replication Adolescent Supplement (NCS-A). *Psychol. Med.*, 44, 8, 1779–92, 2014, doi: https://doi.org/10.1017/S0033291713002419.
11. Gupta, P. and Sandhu, R., A review on the role of deep learning for brain tumor detection and classification, in: *2024 4th International Conference on Technological Advancements in Computational Sciences (ICTACS)*, IEEE, pp. 1051–1055, 2024.
12. Kooij, S.J., Bejerot, S., Blackwell, A., Caci, H., Casas-Brugué, M., Carpentier, P.J., *et al.*, European consensus statement on diagnosis and treatment of adult ADHD: The European Network Adult ADHD. *BMC Psychiatry*, 10, 1–24, 2010, doi: https://doi.org/10.1186/1471-244X-10-67.
13. Lubar, J.F., Discourse on the development of EEG diagnostics and biofeedback for attention-deficit/hyperactivity disorders. *Biofeedback Self Regul.*, 16, 3, 201–25, 1991, doi: https://doi.org/10.1007/BF01000016.
14. Mazaheri, A., Coffey-Corina, S., Mangun, G.R., Bekker, E.M., Berry, A.S., Corbett, B.A., Functional disconnection of frontal cortex and visual cortex in attention-deficit/hyperactivity disorder. *Biol. Psychiatry*, 67, 7, 617–23, 2010, doi: https://doi.org/10.1016/j.biopsych.2009.11.022.
15. Maniruzzaman, M., Shin, J., Hasan, M.A.M., Predicting children with ADHD using behavioral activity: a machine learning analysis. *Appl. Sci.*, 12, 5, 2737, 2022, doi: https://doi.org/10.3390/app12052737.
16. Sandhu, R., Kumar, P., Bhasin, C., Fatima, N., Pal, A., Resnet-34 Model for Human Activity Recognition on Smartphone Sensor Data. *Int. J. Intell. Syst. Appl. Eng.*, 11, 9s, 644–652, 2023.
17. Faiz, M., Sandhu, R., Akbar, M., Shaikh, A., Bhasin, C., Fatima, N., Machine Learning Techniques in Wireless Sensor Networks: Algorithms, Strategies, and Applications. *Int. J. Intell. Syst. Appl. Eng.*, 11, 9s, 685–694, 2023.
18. Nasrabadi, A.M., Allahverdy, A., Samavati, M., Mohammadi, M.R., EEG data for ADHD / Control children, IEEE Dataport, 2020, doi: https://doi.org/10.21227/rzfh-zn36.
19. Pulini, A.A., Kerr, W.T., Loo, S.K., Lenartowicz, A., Classification accuracy of neuroimaging biomarkers in attention-deficit/hyperactivity disorder: effects of sample size and circular analysis. *Biol. Psychiatry Cogn. Neurosci. Neuroimaging*, 4, 2, 108–20, 2019, doi: https://doi.org/10.1016/j.bpsc.2018.08.004.
20. Rubia, K., Cubillo, A., Smith, A.B., Woolley, J., Heyman, I., Brammer, M.J., Disorder-specific dysfunction in right inferior prefrontal cortex during two inhibition tasks in boys with attention-deficit hyperactivity disorder compared to boys with obsessive-compulsive disorder. *Hum. Brain Mapp.*, 31, 2, 287–99, 2010, doi: https://doi.org/10.1002/hbm.20864.

21. Rubia, K., Halari, R., Smith, A.B., Mohammad, M., Scott, S., Brammer, M.J., Shared and disorder-specific prefrontal abnormalities in boys with pure attention-deficit/hyperactivity disorder compared to boys with pure CD during interference inhibition and attention allocation. *J. Child Psychol. Psychiatry*, 50, 6, 669–78, 2009, doi: https://doi.org/10.1111/j.1469-7610.2008.02022.x.
22. Slobodin, O., Yahav, I., Berger, I., A machine-based prediction model of ADHD using CPT data. *Front. Hum. Neurosci.*, 14, 560021, 2020, doi: https://doi.org/10.3389/fnhum.2020.560021.
23. Trinh, N., Whelan, R., Ward, T., Derosiere, G., Task-Related and Resting-State EEG Classification of Adult Patients with ADHD Using Machine Learning, in: *2023 IEEE 19th International Conference on Body Sensor Networks (BSN)*, 2023 Oct, pp. 1–4, 2023, doi: https://doi.org/10.1109/BSN57960.2023.10218831.
24. Van den Heuvel, M.P. and Sporns, O., Network hubs in the human brain. *Trends Cogn. Sci.*, 17, 12, 683–96, 2013, doi: https://doi.org/10.1016/j.tics.2013.09.012.
25. Yin, W., Li, T., Mucha, P.J., Cohen, J.R., Zhu, H., Zhu, Z., *et al.*, Altered neural flexibility in children with attention-deficit/hyperactivity disorder. *Mol. Psychiatry*, 27, 11, 4673–9, 2022, doi: https://doi.org/10.1038/s41380-022-01666-9.
26. Meng, Q., Catchpoole, D., Skillicom, D., Kennedy, P.J., Relational autoencoder for feature extraction, in: *Proceedings of the 2017 International Joint Conference on Neural Networks (IJCNN)*, Anchorage, AK, USA, 14–19 May 2017, pp. 364–371.
27. Soewu, T., Kaur, H., Sandhu, R., Soni, A., Ghai, D., Dhir, K., Tripathi, S.L., Machine learning and deep learning for cancer diagnosis, in: *Rehabilitation Robotics and Healthcare Devices*, pp. 83–129, Academic Press, Elsevier, San Diego, USA, 2025.
28. Ghai, D., Tripathi, S.L., Saxena, S., Chanda, M., Alazab, M. (Eds.), *Machine learning algorithms for signal and image processing*, John Wiley & Sons, Hoboken, New Jersey, USA, 2022.
29. Ghai, D., Saxena, S., Dhingra, G., Tripathi, S.L., A comprehensive review on performance-based comparative analysis, categorization, classification and mapping of text extraction system techniques for images. *Multimedia Tools Appl.*, 84, 5, 2327–2484, 2025.
30. Sandhu, R., Ghai, D., Tripathi, S.L., Kaur, R., Rawal, K., Dhir, K., Machine learning for cognitive treatment planning in patients with neurodisorder and trauma injuries, in: *Computational Intelligence and Deep Learning Methods for Neuro-rehabilitation Applications*, pp. 165–193, Academic Press, London, United Kingdom, 2024.
31. Rubia, K., Hyde, Z., Halari, R., Giampietro, V., Smith, A., Effects of age and sex on developmental neural networks of visual–spatial attention allocation. *Neuroimage*, 51, 2, 817–827, 2010.
32. Alim, A., Imtiaz, M.H., Automatic identification of children with ADHD from EEG brain waves, *Signals*, 4, 1, 193–205, 2023.

Index

Also of Interest

Check out these other related titles from Scrivener Publishing

Emotional Intelligence and Human-Machine Interaction in Advanced Hardware Systems, Edited by Chandra Singh and Rathishchandra R. Gatti, ISBN: 9781394384808. Unlock the future of human-machine collaboration with this essential guide to designing, optimizing, and deploying the next generation of emotionally intelligent hardware systems built for the Industry 5.0 landscape.

Retrieval Augmented Generation for Natural Language Processing, Edited by Sachin Minocha, Malathy Sathyamoorthy, Rajesh Kumar Dhanaraj, and Mayank Kumar Goyal, ISBN: 9781394336098. Master the cutting-edge technology bridging the gap between massive AI capabilities and precise corporate reality with this essential guide, to overcoming LLM limitations and deploying secure, domain-specific Retrieval-Augmented Generation solutions across real-world industries.

Emotional Intelligence-Driven Engineering, Edited by Abhishek Kumar, Suman Lata Tripathi, Inung Wijayanto, and Sugondo Hadiyoso, ISBN: 9781394389865. In a digital age where technical expertise is no longer enough, this book provides the essential tools to integrate empathy, psychology, and neuroscience into your design process for a deeper human-technology connection.

Content Delivery Networks Using Artificial Intelligence and Internet of Things: Revolutionizing Content Delivery, Edited by Tanusree Chatterjee, Rajib Banerjee, and Souvik Ganguli, ISBN: 9781394347155. Stay ahead of the curve by learning how to transform static CDNs into intelligent, AI-powered networks that deliver content faster, more securely, and with pinpoint personalization.

Distributed Algorithms and Protocols for the Metaverse: A Comprehensive Guide, Edited by Abhishek Kumar, Sashi Tarun, Anita Sardana, Abhineet Anand, ISBN: 9781394392605. Master the construction of robust distributed systems with this technical roadmap, providing the large-scale algorithms and synchronization protocols needed to power a seamless, low-latency metaverse.

Secure Blockchain and Quantum Technologies for 6G-Enabled IoT, Edited by T. Perarsi, M. Karthiga, S. Sountharrajan, E. Suganya, and Balamurugan Balusamy, ISBN: 9781394310678. Future-proof your hyper-connected infrastructure against the looming quantum threat bwith this guide to mastering blockchain-driven security frameworks and quantum-resistant architectures essential for safeguarding data integrity in the 6G-powered era.

Attacks and Defenses in Explainable Artificial Intelligence, Edited by Aml Dattatraya Vibhute, Rajesh Kumar Dhanaraj, Malathy Sathyamoorthy, and Paramasivam A. ISBN: 9781394305582. Bridge the critical gap between AI transparency and security with this essential guide to the systematic defense frameworks and ethical strategies needed to protect explainable AI (XAI) systems from sophisticated adversarial attacks.

Generative Artificial Intelligence for Next-Generation Security Paradigms, Edited by Santosh Kumar Srivastava, Durgesh Srivastava, Manoj Kumar Mahto, Ben Othman Soufiane, and Praveen Kantha, ISBN: 9781394305643. Fortify your digital defenses with this essential book, which provides a roadmap for moving beyond the limitations of traditional encryption by leveraging generative AI algorithms to proactively anticipate, detect, and mitigate the next generation of cyber threats in real-time.

Security and Privacy in 6G Communication Technology, Edited by Parita Jain, Puneet Kumar Aggarwal, Mandeep Singh, Sushil Kumar Singh, and Amit Singhal, ISBN: 9781394311002. Future-proof your knowledge and expertise in telecommunications with this essential guide, which provides a comprehensive analysis of the critical security and privacy challenges in the transition to 6G communication.

Development of 6G Networks and Technology, Edited by Suman Lata Tripathi, Mufti Mahmood, C. Narmadha, and S. Albert Alexander, ISBN: 9781394230655. *Development of 6G Networks and Technology* provides an in-depth exploration of the potential impact of 6G networks on various industries, including healthcare, agriculture, transport, and national security, making it an essential resource for researchers, scholars, and students working in the field of wireless networks and high-speed data processing systems.

Quantum Machine Learning for 6G Networks, Edited by Pallavi Sapkale, Shilpa Mehta and S. Balamurugan, ISBN: 9781394238088.

Virtual Reality and Augmented Reality with 6G Communication, Edited by B. Sundaravadivazhagan, N. Gnanasankaran, C. Pethuru Raj, and A. Saleem Raja, ISBN: 9781394336050. Stay ahead of the technological curve with this essential book, which provides a comprehensive guide to the transformative convergence of Virtual Reality (VR), Augmented Reality (AR), and 6G communication.

Integrated Devices for Artificial Intelligence and VLSI: VLSI Design, Simulation and Applications, Edited by Balwinder Raj, Suman Lata Tripathi, Tarun Chaudhary, K. Srinivasa Rao, and Mandeep Singh, ISBN: 9781394204359. With its in-depth exploration of the close connection between microelectronics, AI, and VLSI technology, this book offers valuable insights into the cutting-edge techniques and tools used in VLSI design automation, making it an essential resource for anyone seeking to stay ahead in the rapidly evolving field of VLSI design.

Decentralized Systems and Distributed Computing, Edited by Sandhya Avasthi, Suman Lata Tripathi, Namrata Dhanda, and Satya Bhushan Verma, ISBN: 978139420436. This book provides a comprehensive exploration of next-generation internet, distributed systems, and distributed computing, offering valuable insights into their impact on society and the future of technology.

Electric Vehicle Design: Design, Simulation and Applications, Edited by Krishan Arora, Suman Lata Tripathi, and Himashu Sharma, ISBN: 9781394204373. This book will serve as a definitive guide to conceptual and practical knowledge about the design of hybrid electrical vehicles (HEV), battery electrical vehicles (BEV), fuel cell electrical vehicles (FCEV), plug-in hybrid electrical vehicles (PHEV), and efficient EV charging techniques with advanced tools and methodologies for students, engineers, and academics alike.

Industrial Control Systems, Edited by Vipin Chandra Pal, Suman Lata Tripathi, and Souvik Ganguli, ISBN: 9781119829256. This volume serves as a comprehensive guide in the journey of industrial control systems with a multidisciplinary approach to the key engineering problems in the 21st century.

Modern Automotive Electrical Systems: Theory and Applications, Edited by Pedram Asef, Sanjeevikumar Padmanaban, and Andrew Lapthorn, ISBN: 1119801047. Presenting the concepts and advances of modern automotive electrical systems, this volume, written and edited by a global team of experts, also goes into the practical applications for the engineer, student, and other industry professionals.

Nanodevices for Integrated Circuit Design, Edited by Suman Lata Tripathi, Abhishek Kumar, K. Srinivasa Rao, and Prasantha R. Mudimela, ISBN: 9781394185788. Written and edited by a team of experts in the field, this important new volume broadly covers the design of nano-devices and their integrated applications in digital and analog integrated circuits (IC) design.

Explainable Machine Learning Models and Architectures: Real-Time System Implementation, Edited by Suman Lata Tripathi and Mufti Mahmud, ISBN: 9781394185849. This cutting-edge new volume covers the hardware architecture implementation, the software implementation approach, and the efficient hardware of machine learning applications.

Machine Learning Techniques for VLSI Chip Design, Edited by Abhishek Kumar, Suman Lata Tripathi, and K. Srinivasa Rao, ISBN: 9781119910398. This cutting-edge new volume covers the hardware architecture implementation, the software implementation approach, and the efficient hardware of machine learning applications with FPGA or CMOS circuits, and many other aspects and applications of machine learning techniques for VLSI chip design.

Intelligent Green Technologies for Smart Cities, Edited by Suman Lata Tripathi, Souvik Ganguli, Abhishek Kumar, and Tengiz Magradze, ISBN: 9781119816065.

Presenting the concepts and fundamentals of smart cities and developing "green" technologies, this volume, written and edited by a global team of experts, also goes into the practical applications that can be utilized across multiple disciplines and industries, for both the engineer and the student.

Design and Development of Efficient Energy Systems, edited by Suman Lata Tripathi, Dushyant Kumar Singh, Sanjeevikumar Padmanaban, and P. Raja, ISBN: 9781119761631. Covering the concepts and fundamentals of efficient energy systems, this volume, written and edited by a global team of experts, also goes into the practical applications that can be utilized across multiple industries, for both the engineer and the student.

Electrical and Electronic Devices, Circuits, and Materials: Technical Challenges and Solutions, edited by Suman Lata Tripathi, Parvej Ahmad Alvi, and Umashankar Subramaniam, ISBN: 9781119750369. Covering every aspect of the design and improvement needed for solid-state electronic devices and circuit and their reliability issues, this new volume also includes overall system design for all kinds of analog and digital applications and developments in power systems.

Printed and bound by CPI Group (UK) Ltd, Croydon, CR0 4YY
17/09/2026
14964282-0005